4.50

first
person
singular

D1565031

CT
104
M7.9
copy1

NORMANDALE COMMUNITY COLLEGE
9700 FRANCE AVENUE SOUTH
BLOOMINGTON, MINNESOTA 55431

DISCARDED

first person singular

Edited by
CHARLES MUSCATINE
University of California,
Berkeley

and
MARLENE GRIFFITH
Laney College

NORMANDALE COMMUNITY COLLEGE
9700 FRANCE AVENUE SOUTH
BLOOMINGTON, MINNESOTA 55431

Alfred A. Knopf
New York

First Edition

987654321

Copyright © 1973 by Alfred A. Knopf, Inc.

All rights reserved under International and Pan-American Copyright Conventions. No
part of this book may be reproduced in any form or by any means, electronic or
mechanical, including photocopying, without permission in writing from the publisher.
All inquiries should be addressed to Alfred A. Knopf, Inc., 201 East 50th Street, New
York, N.Y. 10022. Published in the United States by Alfred A. Knopf, Inc., New
York, and simultaneously in Canada by Random House of Canada Limited, Toronto.
Distributed by Random House, Inc., New York.

Library of Congress Cataloging in Publication Data

Muscatine, Charles, comp.
First person singular.

1. Autobiographies. I. Griffith, Marlene,
comp. II. Title
CT104.M79   920   72-12574
ISBN 0-394-31755-6

Manufactured in the United States of America

Since this page cannot legibly accommodate all the copyright notices, the pages
following constitute an extension of the copyright page.

Permissions Acknowledgments

PETER ABELARD, from *The Story of Abelard's Adversities.* Reprinted by permission of The Pontifical Institute of Mediaeval Studies.

ABIGAIL ADAMS, from *Letters of Mrs. Adams,* 2 vols., edited by Charles Francis Adams. Courtesy of Little, Brown and Company.

JAMES AGEE, "A Letter to Father Flye" from *Letters of James Agee to Father Flye.* Copyright 1962 by James Harold Flye and The James Agee Trust. Reprinted by permission of Houghton Mifflin Company.

MAYA ANGELOU, "Stamps, Arkansas" from *I Know Why the Caged Bird Sings.* Copyright © 1969 by Maya Angelou. Reprinted by permission of Random House, Inc.

JOAN BAEZ, "My Father" and "Morning Devils" from *Daybreak* by Joan Baez. Copyright © 1966, 1968 by Joan Baez. Reprinted by permission of the publisher, The Dial Press.

JAMES BLAKE, "Letters to Nelson Algren & Gertrude Abercrombie" from *The Joint* by James Blake. Copyright © 1970, 1971 by James Blake. Reprinted by permission of Doubleday & Company, Inc.

JAMES BOSWELL, from *Boswell's London Journal, 1762–1763* edited by Frederick A. Pottle. Copyright 1950 by Yale University. Published by McGraw-Hill Book Company. Reprinted by permission.

WILLIAM BYRD, from *The Secret Diary of William Byrd of Westover, 1709–1712* edited by Louis B. Wright and Marion Tinling. Published by permission of Louis B. Wright and Marion Tinling.

ALBERT CAMUS, from *The Notebooks (1935–1942),* Vol. I, translated by Philip Thody. Copyright © 1963 by Hamish Hamilton Ltd., and Alfred A. Knopf, Inc. Reprinted by permission of Alfred A. Knopf, Inc.

GIROLAMO CARDANO, from *The Book of My Life (De Vita Propria Liber)* translated by Jean Stoner. Copyright, 1930, by E. P. Dutton & Co., Inc. Reprinted by permission of E. P. Dutton & Co., Inc.

CARLOS CASTANEDA, "Finding the Spot" from *The Teachings of Don Juan: A Yaqui Way of Knowledge* by Carlos Castaneda. Originally published by the University of California Press. Reprinted by permission of The Regents of the University of California.

HOANG CHAU, "The Refugee Hamlet" from *Between Two Fires, The Unheard Voices of Vietnam* edited by Ly Qui Chung. Copyright © 1970 by Praeger Publishers, Inc. Reprinted by permission of Praeger Publishers, Inc.

MISS CRESS, "Letter to William Carlos Williams, signed C" from *Paterson,* Book II by William Carlos Williams. Copyright 1948 by William Carlos Williams. Reprinted by permission of New Directions Publishing Corporation.

SIMONE DE BEAUVOIR, from *The Prime of Life (La Force De L'Age)* translated by Peter Green. © Editions Gallimard 1960. Reprinted by permission of Editions Gallimard and Weidenfeld (Publishers) Ltd.

CAROLINA MARIA DE JESUS, from *Child of the Dark: The Diary of Carolina Maria de Jesus* translated by David St. Clair. Copyright, ©, 1962 by E. P. Dutton & Co., Inc., and Souvenir Press, Ltd. Published by E. P. Dutton & Co., Inc., and used with their permission.

ISAK DINESEN, "A Fugitive Rests on the Farm" from *Out of Africa* by Isak Dinesen. Copyright 1937, renewed 1965 by Rungstedlundfonden. Reprinted by permission of Random House, Inc.

ANNE FRANK, from *Anne Frank: The Diary of a Young Girl.* Copyright 1952 by Otto H. Frank. Reprinted by permission of Doubleday & Company, Inc.

GEORGE JACKSON from *Soledad Brother: The Prison Letters of George Jackson.* Copyright © 1970 by World Entertainers Limited. Published by Coward, McCann, & Geoghagen and Bantam Books, Inc. All rights reserved. Reprinted by permission of Bantam Books, Inc.

JACK KEROUAC, "Belief & Technique for Modern Prose" from the *Evergreen Review,* 2, 8 (Spring 1959), 7. Copyright © 1959 by Jack Kerouac. "Paris" from *Lonesome Traveler* published by McGraw-Hill Book Company. Copyright © 1960 by Jack Kerouac. Reprinted by permission of The Sterling Lord Agency.

D. H. LAWRENCE, from *Collected Letters of D. H. Lawrence* edited by Harry T. Moore. Copyright 1932 by The Estate of D. H. Lawrence, 1934 by Frieda Lawrence, 1933, 1948, 1953, 1954 and each year © 1956–1962 by Angelo Ravagli and C. M. Weekley, Executors of The Estate of Frieda Lawrence Ravagli. All rights reserved. Reprinted by permission of The Viking Press, Inc., the late Mrs. Frieda Lawrence, and Laurence Pollinger Limited.

FRIEDA LAWRENCE, "We Meet" and "Going Away Together" from *Not I But the Wind* by Frieda Lawrence. Copyright 1934 by Frieda Lawrence. Reprinted by permission of Curtis Brown, Ltd.

MARY MCCARTHY, "Names" from *Memories of a Catholic Girlhood* by Mary McCarthy. © 1957 by Mary McCarthy. Reprinted by permission of Harcourt Brace Jovanovich, Inc.

THOMAS MERTON, "First Mass" from *The Seven Storey Mountain* by Thomas Merton. Copyright, 1948, by Harcourt Brace Jovanovich, Inc. Reprinted by permission of Harcourt Brace Jovanovich, Inc.

JOHN STUART MILL, "A Crisis in My Mental History" from *The Autobiography of John Stuart Mill.* Reprinted by permission of Columbia University Press.

VLADIMIR NABOKOV, from *Speak, Memory.* Published by G. P. Putnam's Sons, 1966. Reprinted by permission of the author.

ANAÏS NIN, from *The Diary of Anaïs Nin,* Vol. 1. © 1966 by Anaïs Nin. Reprinted by permission of Harcourt Brace Jovanovich, Inc.

GEORGE ORWELL, "Such, Such Were the Joys" from *Such, Such Were the Joys* by George Orwell. Copyright, 1945, 1952, 1953, by Sonia Brownell Orwell. Reprinted by permission of Harcourt Brace Jovanovich, Inc., Mrs. Sonia Brownell Orwell, and Secker & Warburg.

DAVID PARKS, from *G. I. Diary.* Copyright © 1968 by David M. Parks. Reprinted by permission of Harper & Row, Publishers, Inc.

RAINER MARIA RILKE, from *Letters to a Young Poet* translated by M. D. Herter Norton. Copyright 1934 by W. W. Norton & Company, Inc. Renewed 1962 by M. D. Herter Norton. Revised edition Copyright 1954 by W. W. Norton & Company, Inc. Reprinted by permission of W. W. Norton & Company, Inc., St. John's College, Oxford, and The Hogarth Press.

KATIE ROWE, "Slavery Days" from *Lay My Burden Down* edited by Benjamin A. Botkin. Reprinted by permission of The University of Chicago Press.

ST. AUGUSTINE, from *The Confessions of St. Augustine* translated by F. J. Sheed. Copyright 1943 Sheed & Ward, Inc., New York. Reprinted by permission.

HANNAH SENESH, "Aged Nineteen" from *Hannah Senesh, Her Life and Diary.* Copyright © 1971 by Nigel Marsh. Reprinted by permission of Schocken Books, Inc.

PHILIP DORMER STANHOPE, 4TH EARL OF CHESTERFIELD, "Three Letters to His Son" from *The Letters of Philip Dormer Stanhope* edited by Bonamy Dobrée. Reprinted by permission of Eyre & Spottiswoode, Publishers, Ltd.

LINCOLN STEFFENS, "I Go to College" and "I Become a Student" from *The Autobiography of Lincoln Steffens.* Copyright, 1931, by Harcourt Brace Jovanovich, Inc.; copyright, 1959, by Peter Steffens. Reprinted by permission of Harcourt Brace Jovanovich, Inc.

GERTRUDE STEIN, "Gertrude Stein Before She Came to Paris" and "Gertrude Stein in Paris" from *The Autobiography of Alice B. Toklas.* Copyright 1933, renewed 1961 by Alice B. Toklas. Reprinted by permission of Random House, Inc.

PIRI THOMAS, "Hey, Barrio—I'm Home" from *Down These Mean Streets* by Piri Thomas. Copyright © 1967 by Piri Thomas. Reprinted by permission of Alfred A. Knopf, Inc.

HENRY D. THOREAU, from *The Making of Walden.* © 1957 University of Chicago Press. Reprinted by permission of The University of Chicago Press.

JAMES THURBER, "The Car We Had to Push" from *My Life and Hard Times* by James Thurber. Copr. © 1933, 1961 by James Thurber. Originally appeared in *The New Yorker.* Reprinted by permission.

LEONARD WOOLF, from *Sowing: An Autobiography of the Years 1880 to 1904.* © 1960 by Leonard Woolf. Reprinted by permission of Harcourt Brace Jovanovich, Inc., the Author's Literary Estate, and The Hogarth Press.

DOROTHY WORDSWORTH, from *Journals of D. Wordsworth,* Vol. 1, edited by E. De Selincourt. Reprinted by permission of Macmillan, London and Basingstoke.

WILLIAM WORDSWORTH, "I Wandered Lonely as a Cloud," "The Cock is Crowing," and "Sonnet Composed Upon Westminster Bridge" from *Journals of Dorothy Wordsworth* edited by Helen Darbishire. Reprinted by permission of Oxford University Press.

THANKS

to Robert J. Griffin, Myrna Harrison, Everett de P. Lightbody, Jr., Jeffrey Muscatine, and Paul Portuges, for advice and suggestions; to Nona Fienberg and Sandra Hudson, for research assistance; to Sue Dannenbaum and Robert J. Griffin, for editorial assistance; to Jim Smith, for encouragement; and to June Fischbein, for being the best editor imaginable.

C.M.
M.G.

Contents

Introduction

First Person Singular is a collection of diary and journal entries, letters, and autobiographical pieces, intended for the beginning college writer. It is designed particularly in answer to those students whose challenge to the course in writing is "Why write?" and "What have *I* got to write about?" These students have taught us that the desire to write must precede concern for form and correctness, that good writing will come from students who want to write, who have something to say. For them we have collected these "first person" pieces—writing about and from one's own feelings and experiences—to illustrate the value of writing for self-expression, self-discovery, and communication between people.

The integrity and directness of these writings should give the student writer confidence in his own natural language—often forceful, vivid, clear—and make him feel that it is a legitimate language, that to be eloquent you do not have to be academic. The personal quality of the writings can show that there is a subject which he knows best, on which he is the world-wide authority—his own experience—and that there can be perennially absorbing interest in sharing this experience with others, or even with one's other selves. We hope that he will be led to feel that it would be natural and congenial to begin as a writer by trying the various first-person genres for himself.

This collection provides aid in this beginning by showing the great variety of ways in which other people have written in these genres. It runs the whole range from the diary written from day to day about events then occurring (William Byrd, Dorothy Wordsworth, David Parks), to the piece of recollection over a span of many years (George Orwell, Thomas Merton, Maya Angelou). In styles it ranges from the spontaneous, unvarnished speech of Katie Rowe and Carolina Maria de Jesus to the high literary polish of Vladimir Nabokov and Lord Chesterfield. Some writings are intended for no audience but the writer himself (Jonathan Edwards, Byrd, Anne Frank); others for an audience of a single intimate acquaintance (Dorothy Wordsworth, James Agee, D. H. Lawrence), or of a single more distant acquaintance (James Blake, Rainer Maria Rilke); others for a smallish audience (St. Teresa, Abigail Adams), and yet others for a larger one (St. Augustine, Mary McCarthy, Simone de Beauvoir).

These selections show that writing about oneself is also a matter of choosing a perspective. Shall it be of external facts (Byrd, Girolamo Cardano) or internal feelings (St. Teresa, Edwards)? Or some blend of the two? It may remain engrossed in the subjective concerns of the moment (Jack Kerouac, Edwards, Lawrence in the letters to Frieda), or move by reflection and analysis outward toward broader generalization

(Orwell, Isak Dinesen, John Stuart Mill). It may be set down spon-
taneously, in fragments (Kerouac, Albert Camus, Henry David
Thoreau's *Journal*), or be worked and reworked into a literary whole
(James Boswell, Thoreau's *Walden*). Here and there we have provided
material that shows how different the same events will appear from
different points of view (Parks, Hoang Chau), or as described in different
genres (the Lawrences, the Wordsworths), or in different successive
versions (Thoreau). Each of the variants of form and style is a
possibility for the student writer, who may finally develop a blend
uniquely his own.

The selections offer help of another sort in their showing so directly
and candidly how other people feel and have felt. Many of the pieces
deal with moments in the lives of the writers when they were of an age
that college students know firsthand. Many describe crises and doubts in
those lives similar to the crises and doubts that many students undergo.
The idea is not to present these writings as models of feeling, but to
show that feelings and experiences can be written about.

The writings, then, are meant to be read as expressions of human
voices, and we have tried hard to find voices that have color, sincerity,
edge—voices that we hope will lure the reader into finding a voice of his
own. We have excluded many famous pieces as being too bland, too
canned, or too literary. But we have not hesitated to include a genuine
voice speaking a genuine language even when that language is outside
the boundaries of standard usage or deals with a subject not convention-
ally regarded as polite. One cannot learn honesty and directness, we feel,
from writers who are less than honest and direct themselves. (The
passage from Abelard's *Story of My Calamities,* included mainly for its
rare historical interest, is the only one that we feel may not be
absolutely genuine.)

Finally, we hope that this collection will make for good reading,
thought, and discussion on a subject to which even the most diffident
student will have something to contribute: human nature. "What kind
of a person is speaking?" is a question that is generated by every
selection, and each one raises its own specific questions of value and
judgment, and its own ideas. In this way the readings may be used as the
occasion for expository writing as well. For what we hope finally for the
reader is that having found a voice and a language, he will then look
outward to the concerns of the larger world with new confidence in his
ability to express himself and with new trust in the validity of his
honest judgments.

A Note on the Apparatus

The selections in the book are arranged roughly in reverse chronological order of the events described. Omissions are indicated by four dots (. . . .) when made by us, by three dots(. . .) when they occur in the text used. Each selection has a headnote containing the necessary biographical and bibliographical information, and some suggestion as to which features we find initially the most interesting.

In the back of the book there is the usual author and title index, plus two special indexes. One is a Rhetorical and Topical Index, which, in addition to rhetorical entries, tells where in the book the reader can find examples or discussions of each of a large number of topics—topics that might well come up in class discussion or provide an occasion for writing.

The Counter Index is organized by selection, in alphabetical order of authors' names. Under each entry is listed the date of the action discussed in the selection (for historical perspective), the author's age at the time of the action, and all the rhetorical and topical items under which the selection is listed in the Rhetorical and Topical Index.

With the two special indexes, the reader is given immediate access to all the items in the book, rhetorical or topical, relevant to any of the pieces.

first
person
singular

Jack Kerouac

Jack Kerouac (1922-1969) grew up in Lowell, Massachusetts, where, he writes, he "had a beautiful childhood . . . of roamed fields and riverbanks day and night, wrote little novels in my room, first novel written at age 11, also kept extensive diaries. . . ." In 1940 he entered Columbia University where he made the football team, flunked chemistry, and got an A in English. He left college after a year to join the navy. Discharged because his personality was considered abnormal, he served briefly in the merchant marine, briefly reentered Columbia, met poet Allen Ginsberg and novelist William Burroughs, then spent six or seven years leading the life of "an adventurer, a lonesome traveller" all over the United States and Mexico.

His first published novel, *The Town and the City* (1950), was formal, conventional, and a commercial failure. Then he discovered "spontaneous prose." He wrote the best-selling novel *On the Road* (1957) in three weeks, typing on rolls of art paper pasted together to form a continuous sheet. *The Subterraneans* (1958), he said, took but three nights. Kerouac's novels are highly autobiographical. *On the Road* tells of the adventures of Kerouac, Allen Ginsberg, an early hippie named Neal Cassady, and their friends both on the road and at various stops across the United States. *The Dharma Bums* (1958) describes Kerouac, Ginsberg, the poet Gary Snyder, and others in the western mountains and into Zen Buddhism. Works such as these established Kerouac as the father and spokesman of the so-called "beat" generation, which preceded the "hippie" movement. Kerouac's feelings and life style did not evolve with the latter movement, however, and his later years and many more novels show an increasing sense of loneliness and bitterness.

Although Kerouac never achieved wide critical acclaim in his lifetime—his writing was often parodied—he may well have had an important influence on recent American prose style, opening it up in the direction of freedom, directness, and spontaneity. The editors of the present volume cannot recommend Kerouac's style in its wildest flights for everyone's imitation; but for beginning college writers we can recommend the freedom, directness, and spontaneity prescribed in his "Belief & Technique for Modern Prose," a one-page article that appeared in *The Evergreen Review* for Spring 1959. "Paris" is part of "Big Trip to Europe," an account of a trip taken in 1957 and published in *Lonesome Traveller* (1960) along with other essays on Kerouac's favorite theme. He calls the volume "a mishmash of life as lived by an independent educated penniless rake going anywhere." The selection by no means is as unconventional in style as some of his other writings, but it well represents his taste for a simple narrative sequence and for description in zestful catalogues full of concrete detail. The reader might try to catch the flavor of a place he knows in a similar way.

Belief & Technique for Modern Prose

List of Essentials

1. Scribbled secret notebooks, and wild typewritten pages, for yr own joy
2. Submissive to everything, open, listening
3. Try never get drunk outside yr own house
4. Be in love with yr life
5. Something that you feel will find its own form
6. Be crazy dumbsaint of the mind
7. Blow as deep as you want to blow
8. Write what you want bottomless from bottom of the mind
9. The unspeakable visions of the individual
10. No time for poetry but exactly what is
11. Visionary tics shivering in the chest
12. In tranced fixation dreaming upon object before you
13. Remove literary, grammatical and syntactical inhibition
14. Like Proust be an old teahead of time
15. Telling the true story of the world in interior monolog
16. The jewel center of interest is the eye within the eye
17. Write in recollection and amazement for yourself
18. Work from pithy middle eye out, swimming in language sea
19. Accept loss forever
20. Believe in the holy contour of life
21. Struggle to sketch the flow that already exists intact in mind
22. Dont think of words when you stop but to see picture better
23. Keep track of every day the date emblazoned in yr morning
24. No fear or shame in the dignity of yr experience, language & knowledge
25. Write for the world to read and see yr exact pictures of it
26. Bookmovie is the movie in words, the visual American form
27. In Praise of Character in the Bleak inhuman Loneliness
28. Composing wild, undisciplined, pure, coming in from under, crazier the better
29. You're a Genius all the time
30. Writer-Director of Earthly movies Sponsored & Angeled in Heaven

Paris, from *Big Trip to Europe*

Ah but in the morning, the suburbs of Paris, the dawn spreading over the moody Seine (like a little canal), the boats on the river, the outer industrial smokes of the city, then the Gare de Lyon and when I stepped out on Boulevàrd Diderot I thought seeing one glimpse of long boulevards leading every direction with great eight-story ornate apartments with monarchial façades, "Yes, they made themselves a *city!"*——Then crossing Boulevard Diderot to have coffee, good *espresso* coffee and *croissants* in a big city place full of workingmen, and through the glass I could see women in full long dresses rushing to work on motorbikes, and men with silly crash helmets *(La Sporting France),* taxis, broad old cobblestoned streets, and that nameless city smell of coffee, antiseptics and wine.

Walking, thence, in a cold brisk-red morning, over the Austerlitz Bridge, past the Zoo on the Quai St.-Bernard where one little old deer stood in the morning dew, then past the Sorbonne, and my first sight of Notre Dame strange as a lost dream.——And when I saw a big rimed woman statue on Boulevard St.-Germain I remembered my dream that I was once a French schoolboy in Paris.——I stopped at a café, ordered Cinzano, and realized the racket of going-to-work was the same here as in Houston or in Boston and no better——but I felt a vast promise, endless streets, streets, girls, places, meanings, and I could understand why Americans stayed here, some for lifetimes.——And the first man in Paris I had looked at in the Gare de Lyon was a dignified Negro in a Homburg.

What endless human types passed my café table: old French ladies, Malay girls, schoolboys, blond boys going to college, tall young brunettes headed for the law classes, hippy pimply secretaries, bereted goggled clerks, bereted scarved carriers of milk bottles, dikes in long blue laboratory coats, frowning older students striding in trench coats like in Boston, seedy little cops (in blue caps) fishing through their pockets, cute pony-tailed blondes in high heels with zip notebooks, goggled bicyclists with motors attached to the rear of their cycles, bespectacled Homburgs walking around reading *Le Parisien* and breathing mist, bushyheaded mulattoes with long cigarettes in their mouths, old ladies carrying milk cans and shopping bags, rummy W. C. Fieldses spitting in the gutter and with hands-a-pockets going to their shops for another day, a young Chinese-looking French girl of twelve with separated teeth almost in tears (frowning, and with a bruise on her shin, schoolbooks in hand, cute and serious like Negro girls in Greenwich Village), porkpie executive running and catching his bus sensationally and vanishing with it, mustachioed long-haired Italian youths coming in the bar for their morning shot of wine, huge bumbling bankers of the Bourse in expensive suits fishing for newspaper pennies in their palms (bumping into women at the bus stop), serious thinkers with pipes and packages, a lovely redhead with dark glasses trotting pip pip on her heels to the bus, and a waitress slopping mop water in the gutter.——

Ravishing brunettes with tight-fitting skirts. Schoolgirlies with long boyish bobs plirping lips over books and memorizing lessons fidgetly (waiting to meet young Marcel Proust in the park after school), lovely young girls of seventeen walking with low-heeled sure strides in long red coats to downtown Paris.——An apparent East Indian, whistling, leading a dog on a leash.——Serious young lovers, boy arming girl's shoulder.——Statue of Danton pointing nowhere, Paris hepcat in dark glasses faintly mustached waiting there.——Little suited boy in black beret, with well-off father going to morning joys.

The next day I strolled down Boulevard St.-Germain in a spring wind, turned in at the church of St.-Thomas-d'Aquin and saw a huge gloomy painting on the wall showing a warrior, fallen off his horse, being stabbed in the heart by an enemy, at whom he looked directly with sad understanding Gallic eyes and one hand outheld as if to say, "It's my life" (it had that Delacroix horror). I meditated on this painting in the bright colorful Champs-Élysées and watched the multitudes go by. Glum I walked past a movie house advertising *War and Peace,* where two Russian-sabered sable-caped grenadiers chatted amiably and in French come-on with two American women tourists.

Long walks down the boulevards with a flask of cognac.——Each night a different room, each day four hours to find a room, on foot with full pack.——In the skid-row sections of Paris numerous frowsy dames said *"complet"* coldly when I asked for unheated cockroach rooms in the gray Paris gloom.——I walked and hurried angrily bumping people along the Seine.——In little cafés I had compensatory steaks and wine, chewing slowly.

Noon, a café near Les Halles, onion soup, *pâté de maison* and bread, for a quarter.——Afternoon, the girls in fur coats along Boulevard St.-Denis, perfumed.——*"Monsieur?"*

"Sure. . ."

Finally I found a room I could keep for all of three days, a dismal dirty cold hovel hotel run by two Turkish pimps but the kindest fellows I'd met yet in Paris. Here, window open to dreary rains of April, I slept my best sleeps and gathered strength for daily twenty-mile hikes around the Queen of Cities.

But the next day I was suddenly unaccountably happy as I sat in the park in front of Trinité Church near Gare St.-Lazare among children and then went inside and saw a mother praying with a devotion that startled her son.——A moment later I saw a tiny mother with a barelegged little son already as tall as she.

I walked around, it started to sleet on Pigalle, suddenly the sun broke out on Rochechouart and I discovered Montmartre.——Now I knew where I would live if I ever came back to Paris.——Carousels for children, marvelous markets, *hors d'oeuvres* stalls, wine-barrel stores, cafés at the foot of the magnificent white Sacré-Coeur basilica, lines of women and children waiting for hot German crullers, new Norman cider inside.——Beautiful girls coming home from parochial school.——A place to get married and raise a family, narrow happy streets full of children carrying long loaves of bread.——For a quarter I bought a huge chunk of Gruyère cheese from a stall, then a huge chunk of jellied meat delicious as crime, then in a bar a quiet glass of port, and then I went to see the church high on the cliff looking down on the rain-wet roofs of Paris.——

La Basilique du Sacré-Coeur de Jésus is beauteous, maybe in its way one of the most beautiful of all churches (if you have a rococo soul as I have): blood-red crosses in the stained-glass windows with a westerly sun sending golden shafts against opposite bizarre Byzantine blues representing other sacristies——regular blood baths in the blue sea——and all the poor sad plaques commemorating the building of the church after the sack by Bismarck.

Down the hill in the rain, I went to a magnificent restaurant on Rue de Clignancourt and had that unbeatable French pureed soup and a whole meal with a basket of French bread and my wine and the thin-stemmed glasses I had dreamed about.——Looking across the restaurant at the shy thighs of a newlywed girl having her big honeymoon supper with her young farmer husband, neither of them saying anything.——Fifty years of this they'd do now in some provincial kitchen or dining room.——The sun breaking through again, and with full belly I wandered among the shooting galleries and carousels of Montmartre and I saw a young mother hugging her little girlie with a doll, bouncing her and laughing and hugging her because they had had so much fun on the hobbyhorse and I saw Dostoevski's divine love in her eyes (and above on the hill over Montmarte, He held out His arms).

Feeling wonderful now, I strolled about and cashed a traveler's check at the Gare du Nord and walked all the way, gay and fine, down Boulevard de Magenta to the huge Place de la Republique and on down, cutting sometimes into side streets.——Night now, down Boulevard du Temple and Avenue Voltaire (peeking into windows of obscure Breton restaurants) to Boulevard Beaumarchais where I thought I'd see the gloomy Bastille prison but I didn't even know it was torn down in 1789 and asked a guy, *"Ou est la vieille prison de la Revolution?"* and he laughed and told me there were a few remnant stones in the subway station.——Then down in the subway: amazing clean artistic ads, imagine an ad for wine in America showing a naked ten-year-old girl with a party hat coiled around a bottle of wine.——And the amazing map that lights up and shows your route in colored buttons when you press the destination button.——Imagine the New York I.R.T. And the clean trains, a bum on a bench in clean surrealistic atmosphere (not to be compared with the 14th Street stop on the Canarsie line).

Paris paddywagons flew by singing *dee* da, *dee* da.——

The next day I strolled examining bookstores and went into the Benjamin Franklin Library, the site of the old Cafe Voltaire (facing the Comedie Francaise) where everybody from Voltaire to Gauguin to Scott Fitzgerald drank and now the scene of prim American librarians with no expression.——Then I strolled to the Pantheon and had delicious pea soup and a small steak in a fine crowded restaurant full of students and vegetarian law professors.——Then I sat in a little park in Place Paul-Painleve and dreamily watched a curving row of beautiful rosy tulips rigid and swaying fat shaggy sparrows, beautiful short-haired *mademoiselles* strolling by. It's not that French girls are beautiful, it's their cute mouths and the sweet way they talk French (their mouths pout rosily), the way they've perfected the short haircut and the way they amble slowly when they walk, with great sophistication, and of course their chic way of dressing and undressing.

Paris, a stab in the heart finally.

Joan Baez

Joan Baez was born in 1941, one of the three daughters of physicist Albert V. Baez. She began playing rock 'n' roll guitar in high school in Palo Alto, California, when she was fourteen. She became interested in folk music in 1958 when her father took her to Tulla's Coffee Grinder, a Boston coffee house where amateur folksingers performed. The same year, after attending Boston University's Fine Arts School of Drama for one month, she began performing in Boston and Cambridge as an amateur. A paying job in Chicago resulted in an invitation to sing at the 1959 Newport Folk Festival. Since 1960, when her first album brought her widespread recognition, she has recorded a dozen albums and toured the United States and Europe in concert.

Since the early years of her career, Joan Baez has worked in various ways to influence U.S. foreign policy, particularly in Vietnam. According to her mother, "her desire for human brotherhood in one world far surpasses her enjoyment of folk singing, and for that reason she felt progress for herself was made when she was dubbed lately a 'folksinging pacifist' rather than a 'pacifist folksinger.' " In 1965 she founded the Institute for the Study of Nonviolence. The film *Carry It On* (1969) records her struggle against the war in Vietnam, framed by the arrest of her then husband, David Harris, for resisting the draft. Her firm belief that "it's not what you sing really, but what you do" is reflected in her autobiography, *Daybreak* (1968), in which she emphasizes the development of her personality and ideals, rather than her singing. The following passages are taken from the early part of the book.

Miss Baez describes herself as an unwilling reader of books, and a stranger to the dictionary. She has had little formal education past high school, and she is hardly a professional writer. Yet her book makes interesting reading. The present passage shows why. The account of her father can be examined for the plainness of its language, and for its candor and realism—the writer's willingness to face herself and her relationships honestly yet with tact and with respect. The second passage, a vivid encapsulation of high-school experiences, illustrates in addition her capacity to accept her own imaginative life and to deal directly with her feelings.

My Father

My father is short, honest, dark, and very handsome. He's good, he's a good man. He was born in Mexico, and brought up in Brooklyn. His father was a Mexican who left the Catholic church to become a Methodist minister. My father worked hard in school. He loved God and the church and his parents. At one time in his life he was going to be a minister, but the hypocrisy of the church bothered him and he became a scientist instead. He has a vision of how science can play the major role in saving the world. This vision puts a light into his eyes. He is a compulsive worker, and I know that he will never stop his work long enough to have a look at some of the things in his life which are blind and tragic. But it's not my business to print. About me and my father I don't know. I keep thinking of how hard it was for him to say anything nice about me to my face. Maybe he favored me and felt guilty about it, but he couldn't sày anything nice. A lot of times I thought he would break my heart. Once he complimented me for something I was wearing. "You ought to wear that kind of thing more often," he said, and I looked into the mirror and I was wearing a black dress which I hated. I was fourteen then and I remember thinking, "Hah. I remind him of his mother in this thing."

My father is the saint of the family. You work at something until you exhaust yourself, so that you can be good at it, and with it you try to improve the lot of the sad ones, the hungry ones, the sick ones. You raise your children trying to teach them decency and respect for human life. Once when I was about thirteen he asked me if I would accept a large sum of money for the death of a man who was going to die anyway. I didn't quite understand. If I was off the hook, and just standing by, and then the man was killed by someone else, why shouldn't I take a couple of million? I told him sure, I'd take the money, and he laughed his head off. "That's immoral," he said. I didn't know what immoral meant, but I knew something was definitely wrong taking money for a man's life.

Once in my life I spent a month alone with my father. In 1950, when he was assigned to a project in Baghdad, Iraq, for UNESCO, my sisters got jaundice, and couldn't leave the States. My father left on schedule, for a month of briefing in Paris before going to Baghdad. I had jaundice too, but I didn't tell anyone. I wanted very badly to go to Paris. So despite bad pains in my stomach and black urine which I flushed in a hurry so he wouldn't see, and a general yellow hue which was creeping over my skin, and sometimes seemed to be tinting everything I looked at, I took full advantage of that time with my old man in Gay Paree. We bicycled everywhere, and bought long fresh bread and cheese and milk. We sat in outdoor cafés and had tea, and while he was busy at UNESCO house, I would run the elevators and visit secretaries and draw pictures of everyone and go off to feed pigeons in the park. Neither of us spoke French, but we faked it. One night in a restaurant, we couldn't understand anything on the dessert menu, so my father took a gamble and said, *"Ça, s'il vous plaît,"* pointing to the word *"Confiture,"* and they brought him a dish of strawberry jam, which he ate.

Once the family was together in Baghdad, I developed a terrible fear that my father was going to die. The fact is he almost killed himself tampering with the stupid brick oven which had to be lit in order to get hot bath water. He was "experimenting" with it—trying to˙ determine how fast he could get the fire going by increasing the flow of kerosene into the oven. It exploded in his face, setting his clothes on fire and giving him third degree burns on his hands and face. He covered his eyes instinctively, or he would probably have been blinded, but his eyelashes and eyebrows were burned off anyway. Pauline passed out after telling Mother that "Popsy is on fire," and Mother wrapped him up in a sheet and called the English hospital for an ambulance. While we waited for the ambulance, my father tapped his feet in rhythm on the kitchen tiles, and cleared his throat every four or five seconds. He smelled terrible, and except for Mother, we just stood there. I was probably praying. Mother took me to the hospital to see him once, and I felt bad because I got dizzy when I saw his hands. They had big pussy blisters on them, and his face looked like a Rice Krispie, and I wanted to make him feel better, but I also wanted to go stick my head out the window and get some fresh air. When he came home from the hospital he was bandaged so that all you could see were his eyes and his ears. He held classes for his students at home. He is a brilliant teacher, and they loved him. I know they loved him, because the room smelled so awful from burnt flesh and Middle East medication that I felt sick every time I passed his door. And they came every day to learn and to see him.

My father teaches physics. He is a Ph.D. in physics, and we all wish he'd had just one boy who wasn't so opposed to school, to degrees, to formal education of any kind. One child to show some interest when he does physics experiments at the dinner table. But then it must be partly because we felt obligated to be student-types that we have all rebelled so completely. I can barely read. That is to say, I would rather do a thousand things before sitting down to read.

He used to tell us we should read the dictionary. He said it was fun and very educational. I've never gotten into it.

When we lived in Clarence Center, New York (it was a town of eight hundred people, and as far as they knew, we were niggers; Mother says that someone yelled out the window to me, "Hey, nigger!" and I said, "You ought to see me in the summertime!"), my father had a job working in Buffalo. It was some kind of armaments work. I just knew that it was secret, or part of it was secret, and that we began to get new things like a vacuum cleaner, a refrigerator, a fancy coffee pot, and one day my father came home with a little Crosley car. We were so excited about it that we drove it all over the front lawn, around the trees and through the piles of leaves. He was driving, Mother was in the front seat, and we three kids were in the back. The neighbors knew we were odd to begin with, but this confirmed it. Mother was embarrassed and she kept clutching my father's arm and saying, "Oh, Abo!" but he would take a quick corner around a tree and we'd all scream with laughter and Mother gave up and had hysterics.

Then something started my father going to Quaker meetings. We all had to go. It meant we had to sit and squelch giggles for about twenty minutes, and then go off with some kind old lady who planted each of us a bean in a tin can, and told us it was a miracle that it would push its little head up above the damp earth and grow into a plant. We knew it was a miracle, and we knew she was kind, but we made terrible fun of her the entire time and felt guilty about it afterwards.

While we were in the side room with the kind old lady, watching our beans perform miracles, my father was in the grown-up room, the room where they observe silence for a whole hour, and he was having a fight with his conscience. It took him less than a year of those confrontations with himself in that once a week silence to realize that he would have to give up either the silences or his job. Next thing I knew we were packing up and moving across the country. My father had taken a job as a professor of physics at the University of Redlands for about one-half the pay, and one-tenth the prestige—against the advice of everyone he knew except my mother. Since leaving Buffalo in 1947, he's never accepted a job that had anything to do with armaments, offense, defense, or whatever they prefer to call it. Last night I had a dream about him. I dreamed he was sitting next to himself in a theater. One of him was as he is now, and the other was the man of thirty years ago. I kept trying to get him to look at himself and say hello. Both faces smiled very understandingly, but neither would turn to greet the other.

I don't think he's ever understood me very well. He's never understood my compulsiveness, my brashness, my neuroses, my fears, my antinationalism (though he's changing on that), my sex habits, my loose way of handling money. I think often I startle him, and many times I please him. Sometimes I have put him through hell, like when I decided to live with Michael when I was twenty. "You mean you're going to . . . *live* with him?" "Yes," I said, and my father took a sleeping bag and went to the beach for two days, because Michael was staying in the house. Years later he sent me an article by Bertrand Russell, whom he respects very much, underlining the part which said that if young people could have a chance at "experimental marriages" while they were in college, they might know more about what it's all about before they actually got married. My father wrote that it always amazed him how I came to conclusions intuitively which took him years to realize.

At one time, my father couldn't stand to have a bottle of wine in the house. Whenever my aunt on my mother's side came to visit us in Cambridge, Mother would buy a bottle of wine, and she and my aunt would have a glass of wine before dinner. Sometimes my sisters and I took a glass, too, though I think Pauline was the only one who ever actually drank it down. One time, after my aunt had left, Father called a pow-wow, and we all gathered in the kitchen. Father's forehead was crumpled and overcast. He cleared his throat about a hundred times and made some vague opening statements about this generation and how we were still kids, and how he didn't really know how to deal with the problem at hand. Mother finally asked him what he was talking about, and he said, "Well, if any of my kids turns out to be an alcoholic, I'll know where it started. Right here in my own home." We looked at Mother to feel out the appropriate reaction, and she tried to be serious but couldn't be so we got into a half-humorous argument with Father. I told him he was lucky because none of us was at all interested in booze, and most of our friends got crocked every weekend, if not more often, and he said where were our standards, that his father would have had to leave home if he'd ever so much as tasted alcohol. It was all so entirely ridiculous that we ladies had to check ourselves to keep from making too much fun, or his feelings would be hurt, and he would get really angry. A few years later, my mother and father moved to Paris, and he learned to drink, and I think even to enjoy, wine with dinner. Knowing the way I am, it's amazing that my father's puritanism about liquor did not set me up nicely for dipsomania, but for some reason, I have a total dislike for alcohol. And for cigarettes. And for the more recent fads: I don't smoke marijuana, or, needless to say, use any other drugs. I get high as a cloud on one sleeping pill, if that's what it means to get high, and it's not a whole lot different from what I feel like on a fall day in New England, or listening to the Faure Requiem, or dancing to soul music or singing in a Mississippi church.

About him and money. I guess he had to be conscious of budgets and things while he was bringing us up. I remember hearing the word "budget" all the time, and seeing Mother take dollar bills out of separate pockets in a little brown envelope which folded like an accordion. I never understood why, if there was five dollars in "food" she couldn't switch it over to "movies." I think sometimes she did. But my old man has plenty of money now. He's worked compulsively ever since I can remember. Now that he has a certain amount of wealth, I think he likes it, even though he may not be able, really, to accept it. He buys tons of life insurance. And things like encyclopedias and science journals. I remember the first time I really made any money: I came home to Cambridge from Chicago, where I'd had my first and only job singing in a nightclub. I had made four hundred dollars in two weeks, and I carried it all home in cash—mostly twenties. I walked in the front door and put down my suitcase, ripped the four hundred out of my purse and threw it into the air and yelled, "Up for grabs!" as it fluttered around me to the living room floor. I probably gave everyone some, because I remember feeling bad for having all of it, and I didn't realize until much later that the incident upset him—perhaps only because I could earn four hundred dollars in two weeks, without having had to study for it. But I don't know. Just before I made that money singing, I had the only legitimate job I've ever had outside of singing (which I've always felt was cheating). I taught people how to drive Vespa motor scooters, and took them for their license when they'd learned. My father let me use his old beat-up Vespa to get to work, though I know he liked using it himself. I was paid a dollar and a quarter an hour for the most hair-raising job on the payroll, and eventually I quit because, a) I was going crazy from people who had no sense of balance, and b) I was offered the job singing in the nightclub. But I saved enough money from dragging people into the store to buy motor scooters and making 20 percent on the sale, to buy a new scooter, one with mirrors and four speeds and rubber footmats and a book carrier, and I drove it home, dizzy with delight, and presented it to my father as a gift. I recall a strange, stilted response when I told him it was for him. There was some wisecrack about money. Mother told me later that she went into the bathroom and cried, but I think I was so pleased about my gift that I wasn't really put off. I had never thought that it might hurt my father's pride to receive something from his child which was, by our standards, expensive. He must have been pleased too, though, because he drove it all the time. Sometimes I think he has a double reaction to everything I do.

The major part of my childhood was spent in fighting off terror of things which don't exist, and I don't think my father ever understood that kind of fear. The overriding and most terrifying bogeyman of my life, which has been with me since my earliest memories, and remains faithfully with me though now it seldom puts me out of commission, has been a fear of vomiting. It has used up and wasted and blackened many hours of my life. But my father never had a notion of what I was talking about when I cried and shook and said, "You know . . . It's that thing again . . ." While I was in junior high school and even high school, I was still going to my parents' bedroom, sometimes five nights a week, and climbing in their bed, all hot and cold and shaking, pleading for Mother to say the key sentences which would begin to send the fear away. Always I felt dreadfully ill. Always I wanted to hear only one thing: "You won't be sick." Always I kept my food down, though the nausea was so extreme that anyone in his right mind would have stuck his finger down his throat and been done with it. My father would follow Mother and me to the bathroom in the middle of the night, and as I sat on the toilet clutching their hands, he would pat my head and say things to Mother like, "Did she eat something funny?" or, "S'pose she's got a little bug?" and Mother would shake her head and signal him that he was saying the wrong thing again. Once, as I was crawling into bed crying, and Mother was moving over to give me room, mumbling to me that everything would be all right, my father half woke up and said to Mother in a soft voice which had shades of annoyance, "What's the matter with her? Is it her stomach?" I think I said, "No, it's my head," and the degree to which my anger rose equaled the degree to which the nausea sank. One time my mother was out of the house, and I had a bad attack of whatever you would call that terror, and I had no one to call but my father. I was crying, and I told him what to say. "Just tell me I won't throw up. You know I won't, so just tell me I don't have to."

"What's so bad about throwing up?" he asked. Those perfectly reasonable words threw me into a fresh panic and I let go of his arm and covered my ears and sobbed and said, "No, no, don't say that, you can't say that . . ."

"Look," he said, "right now there must be a hundred sick Arabs throwing up this very minute. It's nothing. You just, blughh, and it's over, and then you feel great . . ." That was advice I was in no way ready to hear, and I simply hated him for it. He has to admit now that the doctors I've seen over the past ten years have been a great help to me. But his general feeling is that psychiatry is for the rich, and one could rise above time-consuming phobias (which, I'm convinced, are as foreign to him as the joy of physics is to me) and carry on in a healthy manner if one only had enough to do. In a sense I agree with him. Part of the fact that my fears play a minor role in my life now is that I have so many passions and commitments that terror is replaced and pushed aside. But no one can force constructive activity upon a child who is, above all things, paralyzed with fear. The network of short circuits and crossed wires that forced my father and me to play in such a way upon each other's weaknesses was, and probably still is, more entangled than either of us would like to admit. We have reduced the entire situation, which is more than partially solved, to his accepting the fact that psychiatry has helped me, and my accepting his jokes about psychiatry; and neither of us ever gives the other so much as a peek at what has gone on between us for the last twenty-six years, and what goes on still. Perhaps it's easier this way.

Lately my father has told me, off and on, that he is 100 percent behind me in the things I do. I think that's hard for him to say, for lots of reasons, one being the reason I mentioned earlier—that he has trouble telling me nice things about myself or what I do. Another is that he hasn't always gone along with my radical ideas of nonviolence and antinationalism, or my feelings that formal education is meaningless at best, and that universities are baby-sitting operations. Even though he was peace-marching long before I was, when I swung, I swung all the way, and left my father looking and acting, in my opinion, fairly moderate. But he has changed very much in the last five years, and I know that when my mother and Mimi and I went to jail for doing Civil Disobedience at the Army induction center, he had no doubts that we were doing the right thing, and he took over the Institute for Non-Violence for the weekend seminars. I think that all the while he was working with UNESCO in Paris, traveling around the world, trying to help find ways of teaching science in underdeveloped countries, he was more concerned than he admitted to himself about two problems: One was how he could teach people the wonders of science and at the same time keep them from simply trying to ape the powerful nations of the world and race to discover new scientific ways to destroy themselves and each other. The temptation for power is so great, and unfortunately, what power has always meant is one's ability and efficiency to murder one's neighbor. The other problem that haunted my father had to do with UNESCO itself: It was filled with power-hungry and money-hungry individuals, and he never wanted to admit it. My mother told me of a time when they were at a dinner party of UNESCO science division men and their wives. Some of the men were loosening up on wine and my father was talking about his difficulties in South America. His colleagues were not really interested in his successes or failures in teaching science to Brazilians, and that fact became more and more apparent. Finally, one of them said something to the effect of, "Aw c'mon, Baez, you don't really give a damn about science teaching methods, do you?" My mother was completely floored by this, and she said, "That's what we're here for," and asked the man why *he* was with UNESCO. He had a publishing job, the man said, and it hadn't really paid much: UNESCO paid a hell of a lot more, plus you got to travel, so he had gone to work for UNESCO and ended up in Paris. Not a bad deal all the way around. He went on kidding my father, who was struck dumb; and Mother did something she doesn't do unless she's in a state of shock or fury—she gave something resembling a speech. "My husband was an idealist when he came to work for UNESCO. He's a pacifist. He's concerned about the fact that people are starving to death and he thought the best way he could help out would be through UNESCO, to spread the uses of science to people who need it. Maybe we're just crazy, but I never imagined anyone came to work here for any other reason."

While he was with UNESCO, he seemed to lose his sense of humor. When I would visit them in Paris, sometimes it seemed that all I ever heard him say was, "I have this deadline . . . You know I just have to keep to this schedule . . ." He was trying to finish a book, which took him eight years to write. A basic text in physics. I seriously thought he would not ever complete that book, that it was like an eternally incomplete project he had to have to keep himself worn out. And I thought he was afraid to get it printed. But it was published while he was still in Paris. It's beautiful. The introduction is preceded by a picture of a huge rock suspended over the ocean. The picture makes you want to sit down heavily on the floor, or throw a paperweight out the window and watch it hit the sidewalk. There are little bits of human philosophy preceding each chapter, over eight hundred pictures, and the book is dedicated to "my wife, Joan, and my three daughters, Pauline, Joanie, and Mimi." And on page 274 there is a drawing which illustrates how an image is projected onto a television screen, and the image being projected is of a familiar-looking girl with long black hair, who stands holding a guitar.

In my estimation, my old man got his sense of humor back when he left Paris, and returned to the States. Toward the end of a course he was teaching at Harvard, a crash summer course, based on his book, he gave what he later described to me as the "demonstration of the century." He told the class that he was going to give an example of jet propulsion. He had a little red wagon brought in, and then he took the fire extinguisher off the wall and sat down in. the wagon and jet propelled himself in circles around the front of the room, explaining, at the top of his voice, exactly what was happening technically. The students stood on their chairs and gave him an ovation, and it was all so overwhelming that he repeated the experiment. He shouted halfway through it for someone to open the door, and shot himself out into the hall, and disappeared. When he came back the bell had rung and the class was still there, cheering.

Right now, in 1967, my mother has planted my father and herself in a beautiful place in Carmel Valley, about one mile from my house, and not far from Pauline. A while after they began to be settled, I asked him if he could give himself permission to enjoy the luxury of his new home, his swimming pool, the endless beauty of the hills around. He tried to avoid my question by making a joke, but I said I was serious. We were sitting on the floor on a nice carpet, and he smoothed his hands over it as he leaned back against the wall. He looked very brown and Mexican in that moment, and I watched his profile against the valley hills as he struggled with himself. He said something about other people in the world, and about hunger. Then he looked up and gave me a smile of such a combination of things. "Yes, honey," he said, "I think I can enjoy it . . . if I keep myself busy enough . . ."

Morning Devils

Some of the past creeps up on me: cold metal green lockers, and the girls' gym volleyball court, the cold nurse's room and the ice-cold nurse, and the warm safety of the school cot and blanket.

Tenth grade and I am still fighting my sunless morning devils. Ice forms in my bones and something vile erupts in my stomach. The kids' faces become animated familiarity and the noise is unbearable. I'm freezing. If I stop walking, I'll feel how dizzy I am. Please. Get out of my way. You don't understand. No books. No binders. No questions, no quizzes, no tiptoeing around the library, because I am on a different planet, and not a single one of you understands. I want to go home. I'll go to the nurse's room.

"Got your period, dear?"

"I have to lie down."

"Are you ill?"

"I'll be all right after a while. If I can lie down."

"Do you have a fever?"

"No. It's just something that happened to me. If I can sleep it will probably go away."

"Well, gosh . . . I don't think that sounds like much of a reason to be out of class . . ."

She changes her mind when she looks at me. I'm shaking all over like a skinny kid who's been in a pool until his mouth has turned purple and he can't hold his Coke without spilling. She gives me a bed and a blanket. I'll keep my legs moving, my hands rubbing together in some pattern, and my mind is racing in spirals around the center of fright. Each time I reach the narrowing bottom of the spiral something almost automatically throws me back to the rim like a pinball, and then, as if by gravitational force, I begin the downward whirl again. There are other girls in the room. That's a help. Their voices drone. My hands are warming up. I scrunch down and warm my feet with my hands. The shaking has stopped. I'll listen to the girls for a while.

They are two society girls. They set it up the day before to have phony cramps and skip a test they know they will both flunk and go to the nurse's room to jabber about someone they both hate. They talk in animated whispers.

My God, they are cruel.

I am no threat to them.

How nice it would be to be a threat. If I were the one they were concerned about, all the flaws they were whispering about would be mine and would mean nothing to me. Their silly gossip would just be part of the game that would make me their equal. Their pretty, painted, eggshell equal. And when I came into the nurse's room they would have shushed and started fingering their Saint Christophers. Then, with big "Hi's" they would have called me over, and drummed up fake secrets that included me. And I would have been their pal and we'd have talked about someone else until the bell rang.

The room is cold, but I am warm under the school blanket. There is an unformed thought in my head. Without my being aware of it, someone has placed a portrait of calm just in front of the spiral, and the spiral is fading into the distance, as though I were driving away from a ghastly carnival. I turn my head on the pillow and move my hand up to my face, following up a sudden desire to inspect my nails. I look at my hands. I know my hands are beautiful. They are very special. At dusk, when the dimming sky compliments everything and makes it either glow, or fade and look dreamlike, I watch my hands. The nails and the webbed part at the base of my fingers jump out at me like platinum on brown velvet, and I know that these are the hands of an Indian princess. Sometimes I put a gold ring on the longest toe of my foot, and it glows against the dusty ground. My hair is soft and black and it shines blue when it is just washed.

I glance over at the girls. I feel unworried, and I smile at them. They smile back in a funny way, and as I turn away I wonder if I didn't count to them when I smiled like that. I wonder if I like them. I wonder if they like me . . .

But the portrait of calm has moved in on me, and the blessed drowsiness has slowed my thoughts into daydreams, and the daydreams are floating me off into dreams . . . I will sleep away all the sunless ghouls and tiring fears . . . I will float when the two girls recover from their cramps and get nurse's slips back to class. I will sleep an anxious sleep during the bell-clanging racket of class change, when the nurse might come in and wake me up . . . but she has forgotten, or remembered that she never knows what to say to me, so today I can stay. I will sleep an exhausted sleep. I will dream a multitude of happy summers, and wake up in harmony with the noon of day, ready for the sun.

David Parks

David Parks was born on March 4, 1944, in Minneapolis, Minnesota. He attended the Storm King School and Ricker College in Houlton, Maine, and when he was twenty-one he enlisted in the army. His father, Gordon Parks, himself a writer and photographer, suggested that he keep a written and photographic record of his experiences, which he did. *G I Diary* is the result. "This book," writes Parks, "is based on a diary I kept through my army service" and with the help of his father he then expanded and polished it for publication. It begins on the day of his induction in 1965 and continues through basic training, Vietnam combat, to his return home.

Since a diary records daily thoughts, feelings, and responses as well as daily events, it often reveals the many changes that happen within a person. In the passages printed below, do Parks' feelings toward the army, his buddies, the enemy, himself, stay the same? What are those feelings? Are they generally simple, or are they sometimes mixed, and how do we know? Miss Hoang Chau's narrative, following, tells of her experiences in Vietnam at roughly the same time and place that Parks describes; the two provide an opportunity to compare the poignantly different perspectives of two decent people in the same terrible situation.

from *GI Diary*

December 7, 1965

Riley is broken up into four camp sites, each about five miles apart: Main Post, Custer Hill, Forsyth and Funston. We're at Custer Hill.

There are men here from all over the country. Many of them are from the South. So far everything is cool. Our company commander is a Negro, Lt. Baker. Reminds me of Dad, quiet and dark, with the ability to pinpoint defects in a minute. He's a big brute of a man with bulging muscles. Only a fool would tangle with him.

Our day starts at 4 A.M. We dress quickly and get outside for reveille in our shirtsleeves. Our teeth chatter from the cold, and I can't wait until they raise the flag and fire the gun salute. Why we don't put on hats and coats is a puzzle. Still trying to toughen us up, I suppose. We'll either turn to leather or die of pneumonia. We eat in our own barracks, which are one hell of a lot better than those at Dix. Everything is clean and orderly here. The dining hall reminds me of the cafeteria back at school. The food isn't bad either, but they give us less than five minutes to eat it.

The rest of the morning it's weapons classes, M-14 rifles. I was actually afraid to pick mine up at first. I've never handled a real gun before. And I don't like the idea now, knowing what it's supposed to do to a person. I don't know. I just can't imagine myself killing anyone with it. I keep dropping the damned thing, and Crouch eats me out each time. He was really pissed off today. "You clumsy idiot," he hollered at me. "You're here to learn to kill! And this is what you will kill with! You better learn that fast or the VC will blow your ass to hell! Drop it in combat and you're dead! You get that?"

"Got it, *sir*."

"Fifteen push-ups with your weapon on the back of your hands. Get going!" I did the fifteen in record time while he stood in front of me. All I could see were those razor-sharp creases in his pants and those shiny boots. Ten minutes later I dropped that damned gun again. Thank God it landed on the toe of my boot and Crouch didn't notice. He'd be shocked to hear it, but I respect him as an instructor. He's got all the answers. But he does keep his foot up my backside.

These drill instructors drive you nuts. They go around hollering the same thing every day. "Don't think! The army thinks for you! Stand straight! Keep quiet! Try and look like human beings, idiots! Shape up there, boy! Spit out that gum!" All day long they give it to you. Hour after hour they're bugging us, how to salute, how to present ourselves to an officer, how to say "sir," how to obey orders—how to become robots. They're right. No need to think.

December 8, 1965

Drill—drill—drill. March—march—march. I've had it. Got to be a good soldier if I want to get home for Christmas. Drew KP duty for tomorrow. More pots and pans. Crouch is beginning to make it tough for several of us souls.

Very few Negroes here and only a few of them non-coms. I'm wondering how some of the Southern white boys will take orders from them. There are lots of them from Georgia, Alabama and Mississippi. They never speak to me. I tried breaking the ice with one the other day. I asked him how he liked the army. He just gave me an evil look and turned away. It got to be a game with me. I asked another one the same question on the PT course this morning. "That's my business," he said. I've decided they're not worth being curious about.

We've got nice new barracks here, built about two years ago. Each floor has two large rooms divided into cubicles that accommodate two people. I'm on the third floor with a good view of the Kansas plains out my window. My roommate is a white kid from Missouri. Nice but strange. No liquor, no smoking, no women. He's very shy and soft-spoken and reads the Bible every night. Somehow I feel he's not cut out for army life, but who is? He's absent-minded, so he catches hell all the time. I feel sorry for him. But who knows, he's liable to make a damn good soldier when combat time comes around.

January 8, 1966

The fellows in my platoon are becoming nicer guys. It's about time, over five weeks now. Maybe it's because they are making a team of us, getting us to realize we will have to depend upon one another in combat. A white guy from New York, who hadn't known Negroes before, said he feels we are no different from his own people. He feels that a lot of the other white guys are beginning to feel the same way. Big deal.

The commanding officer thinks our platoon is the best in the company. He said last night that if he had our company for six months more, he would take us into battle. I guess we really proved ourselves on that march. Crouch thinks differently. He always does when it comes to us. He's a real prickhead. He's from New York and thinks he knows how most of us from there shape up. Some fellows say he was a failure on the outside. He's a pain in the ass, a mean bastard, and getting meaner every day.

My roommate seemed better today. Got two letters from home. He read each one of them several times, then stuck them in his Bible. He's as quiet as a tombstone. I don't know why, but I feel sorry for him.

Training is moving fast now. Lots of studying and class after class. They work us harder than the average college student. But there's a reason. We are learning how to kill, while the college student is learning how to live. Damn, this place is getting me down. Suddenly everything seems so distorted. Home doesn't seem real any more.

March 10, 1966

Strange, I'm beginning to have more self-confidence. Maybe it's because I resent the army thinking for me. I don't like being pushed around. Never had such bad feelings against white guys before either. But then I've never met white guys like these before. They don't let you forget that you're colored and that they're white for one minute. I've never thought so much about color before, even at school when I was the only soul. The question of color never comes up at home. Everyone is treated the same. I'd like to take one of these cats home with me and let him get an eyeful. Ever since I was a kid our backyard has looked like the

United Nations. Well, I'll see what these fair-skinned brothers do when we're under fire. Maybe those live bullets will change their attitudes a little.

[*Vietnam*]
April 4, 1967

Just found out our company is being deadlined for a couple of days. It comes as no surprise. We rode through some towns with five dead VCs tied to our tracks. This, I suppose, was revenge for our guys who were killed and castrated yesterday. The Vietnamese people were horrified. And you couldn't blame them. It was a bad scene, those bloody corpses turning gray from the heat and paddy mud. Then some of the guys have been mutilating the VC bodies like they claim Charlie does. I've seen Sergeant Young wearing a pair of dried-out VC ears around his neck on a string. I've heard others were cutting off privates. I've never seen this, thank God.

"Higher-up" has ordered our company out of this area. It seems the villagers complained about our company's looting and burning their homes. They are right to a great extent. The dead bodies on the tracks didn't help us any. It's back down to our battalion at Camp Bravo.

Since we are under investigation, the company morale is at its lowest. We'd rather be out looking for Charlie than sitting here in base camp. Most of the guys resent what a few others have done to us. But we are part of the company. Until this is over it's pull guard, drink beer and share one another's fruit. A lot of the guys are working over their tracks as if they were their cars, adding guns, painting cartoons on the side. One track even has rubber skirts for a mudguard. Lots of time for letter writing and washing up. Wouldn't be bad if we didn't have this cloud hanging over us.

Just heard that my old infantry unit lost 80 percent of their men so far. Wonder about Cha Cha and Ashworth.

Also heard that my new platoon leader, a lieutenant from North Carolina, is up for an Article 15 for making an old woman crawl through the mud with his gun pointed at her head. He's got to be sick if it's true. Sounds like the guy. He loves to chalk up kills. Emory says he got mad at the old woman because she wouldn't give info on the VC.

April 5, 1967

A general from headquarters came in by chopper at morning chow today and gave Capt. Thomas hell in front of us all. The general said we were "a pack of thieves and untrained dogs," and that if Thomas didn't exercise more control over us he would be missing a bar. It was real funny seeing the old man standing tall, saying, "Yes, sir. No, sir. You're right, sir." I got a solid kick out of that. I didn't show it though. He's going to have to write me out my recommendation for school. What the hell, he'll eat somebody out just to even things. Davey boy intends to stay clear.

April 6, 1967

Greenfield got it today. It was our first day on Operation Hammer, a search-and-destroy deal. We had two photographers along, one from CBS and one from NBC. It was quiet and we were rumbling along beside a wood line that separated us from a shallow river. Greenfield was sitting to my left just behind the driver. Suddenly two shots whined over our heads. We scrambled over the top of the track and jumped down into the hatch, leaving just our heads exposed. I called the mortar platoon leader and reported that we were receiving sniper fire. But as usual there were choppers overhead and so the mortars were held. The artillery was pounding away from the rear, and we let go with our 50- and 60-cals. I heard Thomas order a cease-fire over the earphones, and the guns stopped. Then the snipers opened up again. There was a cracking sound to my left. I turned just in time to see blood gushing through a hole in Greenfield's helmet. He'd been hit and his head disappeared beneath the top of the track. I jumped down beside him, but Lt. Wyeth was already reaching for a bandage to try and stop the bleeding. When Greenfield started choking on his own blood, Wyeth stuck his fingers between his teeth so the blood could run out of his mouth. "Hold on, Greenfield. Hold on. You're gonna make it." His head was moving. Our guns were blasting the wood line again. I called Thomas for a chopper to take Greenfield out, and he said one was already on the way to pick up a Third Platoon leader who'd been hit.

A medic from another track jumped in to give first aid. He tried to open a morphine can with a key and it broke off. "Oh, shit!" He tried to pull the top of the can off with his bare hand and cut himself. "Shit! Shit! Shit!" Now *his* blood was all over the place.

Sachs, looking sick, said, "He's dead, man, he's dead!"

The choppers came in, firing at the wood line. Our guns were going full blast. We carried Greenfield to a chopper and the medic got in with him. I knew that was the last of Greenfield. No one could survive a wound like that. Another good Joe gone.

I jumped back on the track and Wyeth ordered us to sweep toward the wood line. The photographers wanted to get off, but we couldn't stop then. We rammed through to the river. The NBC guy had called a chopper to take their team out, but the CBS man wanted to come in with us. The chopper came in, but the VC opened up on it. On top of that they hit a booby trap. Now the VC were really pouring it on. Bullets were flying everywhere. I think two NBC men were wounded.

The observation plane came in on my frequency and reported about fifty Charlies running out of the wood line five hundred meters to the east. They were in a rice paddy heading for the river. Wyeth ordered us to dismount and pursue: "Keep firing and moving."

As we hit the water, we flushed out about fifteen Charlies hiding in the reeds. We shot them up like fish in a barrel—and I got my third kill.

Well, that's the way it went. What a hell of a way to start a mission. Poor Greenfield. Just a few more inches to the left and it would have been me. Maybe tomorrow will be my day. Who knows? Only yesterday he was talking about the girl back home he wanted to marry. He was a simple guy. He wanted to be a carpenter.

I'm dog-tired tonight, and depressed. We'll be out on this operation at least another two weeks. When will it end?

August 16, 1967
Manila

Called Dad in the States tonight. We talked for about half an hour. It all seemed unreal. It's hard to believe that I will be seeing my family again. I'm one lucky bastard. So many won't make it. It's incredible when you think of all the hell back there in Nam, the mud, blood and death. It's difficult also to realize that you have taken a human life, even though it belonged to an enemy. But back there it's either him or you. And you always want it to be him. The funny thing is that I never really got to hate Charlie, simply because I seldom saw him before he was dead. It was what he did to Greenfield, Gurney, Harris and the others that I hated.

Met a lovely Filipino girl. Name is Fely and we are going out on the town every night. It's all wonderful, but I am anxious to get back to Nam and put in my check-out time. Then home.

September 9, 1967

I take off for home day after tomorrow. Yowie!

Just got back from Bravo. The guys were out on the wood line patrolling, so I didn't see them. Several guys got it while I was on R and R. Don't know exactly who they are. Did see Passmore, who is being transferred to headquarters company. I never liked that guy, but when he walked me to the chopper that was taking me out, I couldn't help feeling some kinship with him. We've been through a lot together. I wished him the best and meant it. He said he hoped he'd see me on the other side and didn't mean it. I could do without that anyway.

The chopper ride back to Zulu is probably the last one I take in Nam. Looking down over the rice paddies I knew so well made me wonder if I had a right to be there. When I came into the army I had no questions, but I am leaving with some. Back in basic they told us over and over again that these people needed help, that they were poor and don't know how to solve their own problems, that we promised them our help, and that we couldn't go back on them. Well, there were times when it seemed we were doing them more harm than good.

I never felt that I was fighting for any particular cause. I fought to stay alive, and I killed to keep from being killed. Now that it's all over there is a funny feeling running through my stomach, when I think of what could have happened to me. When you're in the middle of the fighting, you become strong and do things you didn't think possible. You only think about it afterward. It's hard for me to believe I'm all here and in one piece. Somebody up there is with me after all.

Hoang Chau

This story, written by a forty-two-year-old schoolteacher living in Kien Hoa province, south of Saigon, won first prize in a public writing contest organized by the Saigon newspaper *Tieng Noi Dan Toc (The People's Voice)* in 1969. The contest attracted stories and personal narratives by teachers, students, and soldiers from all over South Vietnam.

Ly Qui Chung, editor of the sponsoring newspaper, felt that the publication in English of some of the stories would give voice to the great majority of Vietnamese who live between the opposing armies, but who support neither side. As an appeal to "the conscience of humanity, " nine stories from the newspaper contest were published in *Between Two Fires* (1970), from which we reprint "The Refugee Hamlet."

All the published stories emphasize personal experiences rather than political opinion. This attitude was popular with neither side in the war. After receiving her prize in Saigon, Hoang Chau was severely reproached by representatives of the Viet Cong for writing about the suffering accompanying the war. The South Vietnamese government, in turn, closed down the *Tieng Noi Dan Toc* a few days after the contest, accusing the newspaper of "promoting neutrality."

In "The Refugee Hamlet," Miss Chau describes her visit to a former pupil, an eighteen-year-old girl who lost her leg when a shell exploded as she was gathering firewood and coconuts. Much of the essay consists of factual reporting, and it thus raises the question of how a writer can best convey suffering and horror, usually exploited by sentimental appeals that demand a greater response than the subject merits. Miss Chau's reportage is low key, and she rarely tells us directly what to feel or think. She manages instead to bring the reader into her experience and thus creates a strong emotional impact. To understand how this comes about, note how she decribes the area "across from the garbage dump," the people, the young children with "heads full of scabies," and—perhaps most importantly—how she lets her people talk, in their own voices, from their own experiences. Castaneda's report of his beginning apprenticeship with don Juan also relies on detailed description and dialogue to convey strong feeling in a low key and may provide a helpful comparison for style. David Parks, whose diary entries precede this essay, served in the U.S. Army in Vietnam at the same time and place that Miss Chau describes. Their two accounts should be read together.

The Refugee Hamlet

I visited the "refugee hamlet" one morning. It was called that because all the families living there were refugees who had left their own villages to come to that place to form a small hamlet.

It was only nine o'clock in the morning, but the southern March sun was already scorching. The road topped with crushed stone leading to the hamlet ran along a river. On the river bank in the direction where the sun sets, rows of *tram bau* trees with burned leaves still stood with their skinny branches. Some coconut trees without tops stood out, lonely in the ruins of an area that had received at least one bombing or shelling every day.

A little further away, where the river curved around a big promontory, an old temple was still burning, with clouds of smoke slowly rising into the sky.

On the near side of the river the current had eaten into the road. The Public Works Service had dumped three hundred truckloads of garbage to protect the side of the road. Despite the effort, the water had continued to carve the road away, and now it looked like a piece of cardboard nibbled by rats. Finally, another road was built more than one hundred meters further in, and the strip of nibbled cardboard had become the world of several hundred refugees.

In addition to the giant heap of garbage dumped by the Public Works Service, there were now halved coconut shells gnawed by rats, rotten palm stems fished out of the water and spread under the sun to dry, tin cans, rags, leaves, dung, and so on. In short, the road had become a place where the people of the hamlet threw their discarded things. Some wandering pigs nosed about the garbage. Not a dog was to be seen, not even a skinny one. At this difficult period, rice was used only to feed human beings. Moreover, the refugees possessed nothing that was worth keeping a dog to guard.

The water of the season's first rain, which had begun the previous day, lay in pools. The heat became intense, and an undescribable odor assailed the nostrils.

On the other side of the road, across from the garbage dump, two untidy rows of houses stood on low ground. I call them houses, but in fact they were just huts a little bigger than chicken coops.

I entered the third house. Two pot-bellied children, half naked, played in front of the house, and, seeing a stranger, one of them called out "Grandma, there is someone here."

A long fit of coughing answered the child. Then, from the kitchen door, appeared an elderly woman leaning on a bamboo cane. She shaded her eyes with her hand and looked at me.

"Oh, Miss Nam! It is a very long time since I've seen you."

"I have learned that Miss Hien met with an accident so I came over to inquire about her condition," I replied.

The old woman took a corner of her dress to wipe her blurred eyes. "She is hospitalized. Please sit down. I'm sorry I have no other chair."

I looked around the house: an old plank bed, a small bamboo bed, the entrance of a deep and dark underground shelter with some chickens scratching in front of it throwing dirt in all directions.

The old woman chased the chickens away with her stick and continued: "A few days ago Hien went over there"—she pointed to the other side of the river by the ruined temple—"to gather firewood and coconuts. While she was working on the river bank a shell exploded. She was seriously hit by shell fragments. Fortunately, someone was nearby and took her to the hospital. I am told that her leg has been amputated."

"Who has been taking care of her?"

The old woman wiped her eyes again. "Ngoan, that twelve-year-old girl. I have been very ill, so I couldn't go. Hau has to stay home. From time to time she goes over there to find something that we can exchange for rice. If only their parents were still alive!"

The old woman did not weep, but her voice was strangled. I looked at the small table in the corner. On it were a can used as an incense burner, three small bowls, and two tiny portraits. Neither of the people in the portraits was over forty.

The old woman kept silent for a while, as if remembering something, and then went on:

"A couple of years ago all the villagers left. I left behind my house and my orchard to come here. Hai, the father of these children, stayed behind to pick coconuts for the landowners who had left the village and gone to town. At that time making a living was still easy, so Hien and Hau were able to go to private schools. They were over the age limit, so they could not study at public schools.

"Then their father was killed one day by a stray bullet. Their mother had to rear the six children. She went back over there every day. Sometimes she would bring back a boatload of firewood, sometimes coconuts to exchange for rice to live on."

I interrupted her: "I recall she met with some kind of mishap."

"True. On that day she had been helping Mrs. Muoi to transport coconuts. Everybody had already got into the boats to come back, but something, I don't know what, made her look back and she spotted a stem of ripe bananas on the other side of a shallow ditch. She probably remembered that on that very morning her son Men and her daughter De had said they would love so much to eat boiled bananas again"—the old woman glanced at the two children playing in the sand before the door—"so she quickly went across the ditch.

"The moment she touched the banana tree with her knife a hand grenade set as a booby trap at the foot of the tree blew up. A long while later, those who were already in their boats got up courage to retrieve her body. They saw that she was lying face down on a board—er, what do you call it, Miss Nam?

"A death-warning signboard."

"Yes, the death-warning signboard. Because it had fallen down under the long grass, and so she did not see it. I was told that she could utter only two words, 'Oh, God.' "

At that moment, a boy who looked about ten years of age came in, a satchel in his hand. He greeted me politely. De and Men rushed in.

"Lunch, Grandma. Brother Doan has already come home from school," they called.

"All right. Your sister Hau has already prepared your meal and put it on the bamboo bed. All three of you take bowls and chopsticks and have your lunch."

The boy whom the two children called Brother Doan lifted a basket with a misshapen rim. Underneath there were a large bowl of rice, a small bowl of cucumber, and salted fish mixed with some pieces of red pepper. Some blowflies from the garbage dump, attracted by the salted fish, began swarming around the bowl. Doan swatted at the flies and told his kid brother and sister, "Try to economize. Sister Hau has told me to spare some for dinner."

The two kids said nothing. They picked up the salted cucumber with their chopsticks and chewed it with relish. Quickly, half the bowlful of rice disappeared. The flies, after clustering on the bowl, alighted on the children's heads, which were full of scabies, and stuck themselves to their lips. When I was about to stand up to take leave, I heard some noise coming from a boat at the landing place. The old woman looked happy. "Hau has come home," she said. "Please stay a little longer."

Three or four years ago, Hau had been my pupil. Seeing her again, I realized she was quite different, with big, round eyes, full cheeks, and tanned skin. Hau had the healthy beauty of a girl who had reached puberty. She greeted me with a smile, displaying white teeth as regular as kernels of corn.

I asked her, "Don't you go to school today?"

A look of sadness flickered over her face. "I have left school."

Apparently afraid I would not understand, she explained: "Since Sister Hien was hospitalized, I had to replace her to go back to our garden and also take care of my kid brother and sister. Before, when my mother died, Sister Hien had to quit her studies while she was in fifth grade, just like me."

I looked across the river at the group of burned trees, the coconut trees without tops, the burning, ruined temple. A big bird flew up suddenly uttering its grave, sad call. I suddenly asked Hau a foolish question: "Aren't you afraid of going back there?"

She was busy tying up the boat to one of the few remaining clumps of reeds at the garbage dump, and she replied indifferently, "Yes, I am. But I am careful. When I hear a plane or helicopter coming, I run as fast as I can to a shelter or down to the river. I have to keep going back over there because there is nothing else."

Then she added sourly: "I have to risk my life in exchange for those things."

I glanced at the boat, and I saw ten coconuts, a stem of bananas, some bundles of firewood. Yes, she had told the truth. Those things were what sustained her grandmother and the children. They were the sustenance also of the other families in the hamlet. They had all risked the loss of an arm, a leg, sometimes their lives, to exchange a boatful of firewood or a dozen coconuts. They had resigned themselves to live miserably in these fetid huts on the muddy ground so that they could be within sight of their home village across the river.

A piece of land, a grave, a house shattered by bombs or shells, the call of the *bim bip* bird when the tide was flowing—these things were precious to them.

They lived here for the present, but when they died they would be buried over there with their ancestors. Every two or three days they rowed their boats across the river to cultivate their old gardens, even though booby traps lay hidden there with death-warning signs. Some went over never to return. But they did not mind. Many of them were still ready to continue their course. They died in order to keep life going on in this vicious circle for a decade.

Seeing that I was lost in thought, Hau started the conversation again. "You look thinner than before."

I smiled. "You are right. Others have told me so."

"You must eat nutritious foods and not work too hard so you can keep up your health."

When Hau was still my pupil, I used to tell her and the other school children the same thing. Now she repeated it easily, as if she were reciting her lesson. I did not know how to explain to Hau. Eat nutritious foods? For years I had not been able to buy a chicken or a dozen oranges. It was easy to understand for those who had a meager salary like mine. Not work too hard? Sixty pupils as naughty as little devils, two roofs of iron sheets as hot as a furnace, long compositions, hard mathematics to be explained until I was hoarse. . .

What else? Sleepless nights because of the guns firing, because of the barking AR15's or AK47's. Always my loneliness, the pity for the destiny of human beings.

Hau carried the firewood bundle by bundle into the small house. The sun was burning hot. The rotten garbage gave out a putrid smell. I watched Hau moving quickly, her black jacket soaked with sweat sticking to her skin. The breast of the sixteen-year-old was full. Her round legs were partly visible under the trousers rolled up to her knees.

I suddenly thought of Hien's leg. Was it true?

An eighteen-year-old girl who also had round black eyes, full rosy cheeks. . .

And in the days to come she would have to limp on crutches, with one leg of her trousers fluttering at each step. Tears welled up and stung my eyes. I thought about going and seeing Hien. I took leave of the old woman and Hau. As I left, I glanced back at the tiny house.

A three-wheeled Lambretta arrived. I waved and it stopped for me a minute, then puttered on again. In the dry rice fields the soil was cracked hard. Abandoned gardens had been overgrown with grass, and the stumps of coconut trees stood out of the grass. One or two houses by themselves falling little by little into ruin. A watchtower high on the approach of a bridge with a soldier sitting behind a firing port and looking around vaguely. All these sights passed quickly before the bouncing Lambretta.

I suddenly felt very sad and more lonely than ever. War! The war would go on and on—until when?

Three o'clock in the afternoon at Kien Hoa Hospital. Still with the scorching southern sun of March. The shade thrown by the old tamarind trees barely covered the long rows of houses.

Ward Six was here! I looked into each door: white beds, white bedclothes, white bandages—all mourning white! On this bed, a patient was breathing with an artificial apparatus. On that, a patient was receiving a blood transfusion. On still another, a child whose body was covered with bandages lay, only the eyes visible.

Bottles of serum with bottoms up let fluid run down drop by drop. Fans stirred incessantly, and almost all the patients were half naked. I looked around for Hien.

There she was. She lay motionless with a thin blanket covering her from her belly down. Only one foot stuck out.

"Hien!"

"Teacher!"

Only two greeting words. Both of us had tears in our eyes. But after only a short time Hien managed to smile.

"How did you know I was here, Teacher?"

"I went to see your grandmother this morning," I said.

I sat at the edge of her bed and fell silent again. What I wanted to find out about her health, about her accident, I had found out from Hau that morning. I thought it would be superfluous to ask her about those things again. It might open the wounds in Hien's soul.

As if guessing my thoughts, Hien tried to be talkative. She looked at the oranges I had bought for her.

"Oh, in this hot weather I like your oranges very much." She smacked her lips, then continued:

"At this season oranges must be very expensive. Those are worth ten liters of rice."

I kept her warm hand in mine. "Don't worry. This is the orange season!"

She looked vaguely out the window, then spoke normally as if to herself.

"You know, when I came to after the operation, I wanted only to die. But I could not. I still had my grandmother, my brothers and sisters. Now the thought of death has ceased to obsess me."

I gazed silently at the untidy hair covering her shoulders. Hien continued:

"Some friends of mine have blamed me for not looking for a job in town, for clinging to the garden until the accident happened. They didn't know that I had applied for a job at several places and waited in vain. At one place I was told that employment was restricted to children or wives of dead soldiers, at another I was told that the deadline for applications was past. Still others told me that my level of education was too low. Meanwhile, I saw a lot of people whose education level was lower than mine and whose fathers and brothers had not been killed in battle at all being accepted. I could have gotten a job like them if I had been willing to agree to one condition. . ."

She said no more, but I knew what the condition was. I answered with a cliché.

"You don't have a job, but you have your honor still."

She gave a rather bitter smile. "Yes, I still have my honor, but only one leg." She fell silent for awhile, then smacked her lips and continued:

"Now, even if I wanted to work as a servant I could not."

All of a sudden I asked her the one question that had been on my mind all morning: "And how about Hau? Will she . . .?"

Hien guessed what I wanted to ask her through my hesitation. She said: "When I get out of hospital, I'm sure that I can do household chores like a whole person. Then Hau will not have to go back to our garden any more."

She mumbled: "Hau is a sixteen-year-old and a sixth-grade student. She can work as a baby-sitter, a housewasher or, at worst, as a bar girl, whatever occupation she chooses. But I will certainly not let her share the fate of my mother and myself."

"A bar girl or whatever occupation she chooses." The words stuck hard in my mind. I saw whirling images: Hien on crutches, Hau at a snack bar. Was this the solution for girls in wartime?

I shook my head. "No, it is impossible."

At that moment, a hospital attendant pushed a stretcher past us. The eyes of the girl lying on the stretcher were closed tight, a string of saliva dripped from the corner of her mouth. A woman, probably her mother, followed behind, sobbing. Some curious people nearby asked her: "What happened to her. She looks quite healthy."

The woman replied in a low voice: "She has committed suicide."

"How terrible! What was the cause of her unhappiness?"

"Nothing important. Yesterday some American troops came and set up camp near our house. She went over to make friends with them and ask for food. I scolded her a bit for this. But her father grew very angry with her and made a mountain out of a molehill. He beat her, so she committed suicide. I never thought it would come to that."

Some ill-thinking people whispered to each other: "Maybe she did have intimate relations with the Americans so her father was right to give her a beating."

Hien said: "She is tired of living and wants to die. If only she could give me her leg!"

Hien's joke was slightly malicious, but I could not blame her. She was still young. Her constant suffering had changed her character.

The time had gone quickly. It was already six o'clock. I rose and took Hien's hand.

"Don't think of silly things any more," I said. "Be calm. I promise you I will look for a decent job for Hau. Now I must leave."

Just then a plane swooped low over the hospital. Then, a short while later, deafening explosions rattled the window panes.

"Stay here a little longer and you will see," Hien said.

"No. The morning before last the Hue Lien Restaurant was bombed. Yesterday afternoon my hamlet was mortared. Seven people were killed and over twenty others wounded. I have seen too much. I don't want to see more. Moreover, my lungs have just been healed. Let me sleep tonight."

"So, you must go. Thank you for coming, Teacher."

Hien rolled over on to her side. A teardrop fell on her pillow. I turned and went out in a hurry, as if I were a fugitive.

Outside, it was evening. The lights in the town were on. Sleek Honda motor bikes moved swiftly past. Flaps of dresses fluttered. The ice cream parlors were noisy with music.

I bent my head and walked. A day had passed. How many more days like this would come? Before me was the night, the night with many-colored snack-bar signs and darkness in poor alleyways.

Carlos Castaneda

Carlos Castaneda was born in 1931 in São Paulo, Brazil. He studied anthropology at UCLA (B.A. 1962; M.A. 1964) and has taught at the University of California at Irvine. In 1968 a revised version of his master's thesis was published as *The Teachings of Don Juan, A Yaqui Way of Knowledge*. Part I is Castaneda's journal of his experiences as an apprentice to Juan Matus, a Yaqui Indian *brujo*, or sorcerer, living in Northwestern Mexico.

Castaneda says he recorded the conversations as they occurred, but wrote the description of each experience several days later, when he could treat it calmly and objectively. He also says he wanted "to describe the emotional impact as completely as possible." Calm and objective descriptions may seem an unusual way of reaching emotional impact, but the passage printed below shows that it can be done. Always faithful to the facts of the experience and always reporting in great detail only what he knows, Castaneda describes seemingly silly actions that take on something like mystical significance. He manages to portray himself objectively, as don Juan must have seen him, as well as subjectively, recording his own mixed feelings, from embarrassment to fear. The reader should examine how Castaneda mingles direct and indirect dialogue, factual description and narrative, and then try to report an experience of his own in a similar way.

Don Juan had nothing but contempt for the untutored use of drugs. The purpose of his teaching was to give his student access to the understanding and power of a "man of knowledge," partly through learning new techniques of perception, and partly through contact with forces called allies and protectors, reached through the ritualized use of peyote, jimson weed, and hallucinogenic mushrooms. Central to don Juan's teaching was the idea that drug-induced states are "states of non-ordinary reality," that is, not hallucinations or distortions of reality, but other, valid forms of reality. In Castaneda's analysis, every part of don Juan's teaching fitted into "a system of logical thought from which don Juan drew meaningful inferences for his day-to-day life, a vastly complex system of beliefs in which inquiry was an experience leading to exultation."

Castaneda's apprenticeship was rigorous and frequently terrifying: he felt compelled to abandon it in 1965. Three years later he revisited don Juan to show him a copy of the book recording his teachings, and the master-student relationship was reestablished. *A Separate Reality, Further Conversations with Don Juan* (1971) is Castaneda's record of his continued apprenticeship, interrupted for the second time in 1970. A final volume, *Journey to Ixtlan, the Lessons of Don Juan,* appeared in 1972.

Finding the Spot,
from *The Teachings of Don Juan*

My notes on my first session with don Juan are dated June 23, 1961. That was the occasion when the teachings began. I had seen him several times previously in the capacity of an observer only. At every opportunity I had asked him to teach me about peyote. He ignored my request every time, but he never completely dismissed the subject, and I interpreted his hesitancy as a possibility that he might be inclined to talk about his knowledge with more coaxing.

In this particular session he made it obvious to me that he might consider my request provided I possessed clarity of mind and purpose in reference to what I had asked him. It was impossible for me to fulfill such a condition, for I had asked him to teach me about peyote only as a means of establishing a link of communication with him. I thought his familiarity with the subject might predispose him to be more open and willing to talk, thus allowing me an entrance into his knowledge on the properties of plants. He had interpreted my request literally, however, and was concerned about my purpose in wishing to learn about peyote.

Friday, June 23, 1961

"Would you teach me about peyote, don Juan?"

"Why would you like to undertake such learning?"

"I really would like to know about it. Is not just to want to know a good reason?"

"No! You must search in your heart and find out why a young man like you wants to undertake such a task of learning."

"Why did you learn about it yourself, don Juan?"

"Why do you ask that?"

"Maybe we both have the same reasons."

"I doubt that. I am an Indian. We don't have the same paths."

"The only reason I have is that I *want* to learn about it, just to know. But I assure you, don Juan, my intentions are not bad."

"I believe you. I've smoked you."

"I beg your pardon!"

"It doesn't matter now. I know your intentions."

"Do you mean you saw through me?"

"You could put it that way."

"Will you teach me, then?"

"No!"

"Is it because I'm not an Indian?"

"No. It is because you don't know your heart. What is important is that you know exactly why you want to involve yourself. Learning about 'Mescalito' is a most serious act. If you were an Indian your desire alone would be sufficient. Very few Indians have such a desire."

Sunday, June 25, 1961

I stayed with don Juan all afternoon on Friday. I was going to leave about 7 P.M. We were sitting on the porch in front of his house and I decided to ask him once more about the teaching. It was almost a routine question and I expected him to refuse again. I asked him if there was a way in which he could accept just my desire to learn, as if I were an Indian. He took a long time to answer. I was compelled to stay because he seemed to be trying to decide something.

Finally he told me that there was a way, and proceeded to delineate a problem. He pointed out that I was very tired sitting on the floor, and that the proper thing to do was to find a "spot" (*sitio*) on the floor where I could sit without fatigue. I had been sitting with my knees up against my chest and my arms locked around my calves. When he said I was tired, I realized that my back ached and that I was quite exhausted.

I waited for him to explain what he meant by a "spot," but he made no overt attempt to elucidate the point. I thought that perhaps he meant that I should change positions, so I got up and sat closer to him. He protested my movement and clearly emphasized that a spot meant a place where a man could feel naturally happy and strong. He patted the place where he sat and said it was his own spot, adding that he had posed a riddle I had to solve by myself without any further deliberation.

What he had posed as a problem to be solved was certainly a riddle. I had no idea how to begin or even what he had in mind. Several times I asked for a clue, or at least a hint, as to how to proceed in locating a point where I felt happy and strong. I insisted and argued that I had no idea what he really meant because I couldn't conceive the problem. He suggested I walk around the porch until I found the spot.

I got up and began to pace the floor. I felt silly and sat down in front of him.

He became very annoyed with me and accused me of not listening, saying that perhaps I did not want to learn. After a while he calmed down and explained to me that not every place was good to sit or be on, and that within the confines of the porch there was one spot that was unique, a spot where I could be at my very best. It was my task to distinguish it from all the other places. The general pattern was that I had to "feel" all the possible spots that were accessible until I could determine without a doubt which was the right one.

I argued that although the porch was not too large (12 X 8 feet), the number of possible spots was overwhelming, and it would take me a very long time to check all of them, and that since he had not specified the size of the spot, the possibilities might be infinite. My arguments were futile. He got up and very sternly warned me that it might take me days to figure it out, but that if I did not solve the problem, I might as well leave because he would have nothing to say to me. He emphasized that he knew where my spot was, and that therefore I could not lie to him; he said this was the only way he could accept my desire to learn about Mescalito as a valid reason. He added that nothing in his world was a gift, that whatever there was to learn had to be learned the hard way.

He went around the house to the chaparral to urinate. He returned directly into his house through the back.

I thought the assignment to find the alleged spot of happiness was his own way of dismissing me, but I got up and started to pace back and forth. The sky was clear. I could see everything on and near the porch. I must have paced for an hour or more, but nothing happened to reveal the location of the spot. I got tired of walking and sat down; after a few minutes I sat somewhere else, and then at another place, until I had covered the whole floor in a semisystematic fashion. I deliberately tried to "feel" differences between places, but I lacked the criteria for differentiation. I felt I was wasting my time, but I stayed. My rationalization was that I had come a long way just to see don Juan, and I really had nothing else to do.

I lay down on my back and put my hands under my head like a pillow. Then I rolled over and lay on my stomach for a while. I repeated this rolling process over the entire floor. For the first time I thought I had stumbled upon a vague criterion. I felt warmer when I lay on my back.

I rolled again, this time in the opposite direction, and again covered the length of the floor, lying face down on all the places where I had lain face up during my first rolling tour. I experienced the same warm and cold sensations, depending on my position, but there was no difference between spots.

Then an idea occurred to me which I thought to be brilliant: don Juan's spot! I sat there, and then lay, face down at first, and later on my back, but the place was just like all the others. I stood up. I had had enough. I wanted to say good-bye to don Juan, but I was embarrassed to wake him up. I looked at my watch. It was two o'clock in the morning! I had been rolling for six hours.

At that moment don Juan came out and went around the house to the chaparral. He came back and stood at the door. I felt utterly dejected, and I wanted to say something nasty to him and leave. But I realized that it was not his fault; that it was my own choice to go through all that nonsense. I told him I had failed; I had been rolling on his floor like an idiot all night and still couldn't make any sense of his riddle.

He laughed and said that it did not surprise him because I had not proceeded correctly. I had not been using my eyes. That was true, yet I was very sure he had said to feel the difference. I brought that point up, but he argued that one can feel with the eyes, when the eyes are not looking right into things. As far as I was concerned, he said, I had no other means to solve this problem but to use all I had—my eyes.

He went inside. I was certain that he had been watching me. I thought there was no other way for him to know that I had not been using my eyes.

I began to roll again, because that was the most comfortable procedure. This time, however, I rested my chin on my hands and looked at every detail.

After an interval the darkness around me changed. When I focused on the point directly in front of me, the whole peripheral area of my field of vision became brilliantly colored with a homogeneous greenish yellow. The effect was startling. I kept my eyes fixed on the point in front of me and began to crawl sideways on my stomach, one foot at a time.

Suddenly, at a point near the middle of the floor, I became aware of another change in hue. At a place to my right, still in the periphery of my field of vision, the greenish yellow became intensely purple. I concentrated my attention on it. The purple faded into a pale, but still brilliant, color which remained steady for the time I kept my attention on it.

I marked the place with my jacket, and called don Juan. He came out to the porch. I was truly excited; I had actually seen the change in hues. He seemed unimpressed, but told me to sit on the spot and report to him what kind of feeling I had.

I sat down and then lay on my back. He stood by me and asked me repeatedly how I felt; but I did not feel anything different. For about fifteen minutes I tried to feel or to see a difference, while don Juan stood by me patiently. I felt disgusted. I had a metallic taste in my mouth. Suddenly I had developed a headache. I was about to get sick. The thought of my nonsensical endeavors irritated me to a point of fury. I got up.

Don Juan must have noticed my profound frustration. He did not laugh, but very seriously stated that I had to be inflexible with myself if I wanted to learn. Only two choices were open to me, he said: either to quit and go home, in which case I would never learn, or to solve the riddle.

He went inside again. I wanted to leave immediately, but I was too tired to drive; besides, perceiving the hues had been so startling that I was sure it was a criterion of some sort, and perhaps there were other changes to be detected. Anyway, it was too late to leave. So I sat down, stretched my legs back, and began all over again.

During this round I moved rapidly through each place, passing don Juan's spot, to the end of the floor, and then turned around to cover the outer edge. When I reached the center, I realized that another change in coloration was taking place, again on the edge of my field of vision. The uniform chartreuse I was seeing all over the area turned, at one spot to my right, into a sharp verdigris. It remained for a moment and then abruptly metamorphosed into another steady hue, different from the other one I had detected earlier. I took off one of my shoes and marked the point, and kept on rolling until I had covered the floor in all possible directions. No other change of coloration took place.

I came back to the point marked with my shoe, and examined it. It was located five to six feet away from the spot marked by my jacket, in a southeasterly direction. There was a large rock next to it. I lay down there for quite some time trying to find clues, looking at every detail, but I did not feel anything different.

I decided to try the other spot. I quickly pivoted on my knees and was about to lie down on my jacket when I felt an unusual apprehension. It was more like a physical sensation of something actually pushing on my stomach. I jumped up and retreated in one movement. The hair on my neck pricked up. My legs had arched slightly, my trunk was bent forward, and my arms stuck out in front of me rigidly with my fingers contracted like a claw. I took notice of my strange posture and my fright increased.

I walked back involuntarily and sat down on the rock next to my shoe. From the rock, I slumped to the floor. I tried to figure out what had happened to cause me such a fright. I thought it must have been the fatigue I was experiencing. It was nearly daytime. I felt silly and embarrassed. Yet I had no way to explain what had frightened me, nor had I figured out what don Juan wanted.

I decided to give it one last try. I got up and slowly approached the place marked by my jacket, and again I felt the same apprehension. This time I made a strong effort to control myself. I sat down, and then knelt in order to lie face down, but I could not lie in spite of my will. I put my hands on the floor in front of me. My breathing accelerated; my stomach was upset. I had a clear sensation of panic, and fought not to run away. I thought don Juan was perhaps watching me. Slowly I crawled back to the other spot and propped my back against the rock. I wanted to rest for a while to organize my thoughts, but I fell asleep.

I heard don Juan talking and laughing above my head. I woke up.

"You have found the spot." he said.

I did not understand him at first, but he assured me again that the place where I had fallen asleep was the spot in question. He again asked me how I felt lying there. I told him I really did not notice any difference.

He asked me to compare my feelings at that moment with what I had felt while lying on the other spot. For the first time it occurred to me that I could not possibly explain my apprehension of the preceding night. He urged me in a kind of challenging way to sit on the other spot. For some inexplicable reason I was actually afraid of the other place, and did not sit on it. He asserted that only a fool could fail to see the difference.

I asked him if each of the two spots had a special name. He said that the good one was called the *sitio* and the bad one the enemy; he said these two places were the key to a man's well-being, especially for a man who was pursuing knowledge. The sheer act of sitting on one's spot created superior strength; on the other hand, the enemy weakened a man and could even cause his death. He said I had replenished my energy, which I had spent lavishly the night before, by taking a nap on my spot.

He also said that the colors I had seen in association with each specific spot had the same overall effect either of giving strength or of curtailing it.

I asked him if there were other spots for me like the two I had found, and how I should go about finding them. He said that many places in the world would be comparable to those two, and that the best way to find them was by detecting their respective colors.

It was not clear to me whether or not I had solved the problem, and in fact I was not even convinced that there had been a problem; I could not avoid feeling that the whole experience was forced and arbitrary. I was certain that don Juan had watched me all night and then proceeded to humor me by saying that wherever I had fallen asleep *was* the place I was looking for. Yet I failed to see a logical reason for such an act, and when he challenged me to sit on the other spot I could not do it. There was a strange cleavage between my pragmatic experience of fearing the "other spot" and my rational deliberations about the total event.

Don Juan, on the other hand, was very sure I had succeeded, and, acting in accordance with my success, let me know he was going to teach me about peyote.

"You asked me to teach you about Mescalito," he said. "I wanted to find out if you had enough backbone to meet him face to face. Mescalito is not something to make fun of. You must have command over your resources. Now I know I can take your desire alone as a good reason to learn."

"You really are going to teach me about peyote?"

"I prefer to call him Mescalito. Do the same."

"When are you going to start?"

"It is not so simple as that. You must be ready first."

"I think I am ready."

"This is not a joke. You must wait until there is no doubt, and then you will meet him."

"Do I have to prepare myself?"

"No. You simply have to wait. You may give up the whole idea after a while. You get tired easily. Last night you were ready to quit as soon as it got difficult. Mescalito requires a very serious intent."

Carolina Maria de Jesus

Carolina Maria de Jesus was born in a small town in Brazil in 1913. Her mother, an illiterate farm worker, sent her to school, where she learned to read in three months. "It was a Wednesday," she remembers, "and when I left school I saw a paper with some writing on it. It was an announcement of the local movie house. 'Today. Pure Blood. Tom Mix.' I shouted happily—'I can read!—I can read!' " She attended school for only two years. As a young woman, she worked in a hospital, sang in a circus, and worked as a maid, until her first pregnancy made her unemployable. She moved to a *favela* or slum district in São Paulo, constructed her own shack from boards, cardboard, and tin cans, and bore her first child there in 1947. For a living she began collecting old paper and discarded metal to sell to junk yards. "On good days I would have twenty-five or thirty cents," she writes. "Some days I made nothing." Of her seven illegitimate children, only the oldest, João, a second son, and a daughter have survived.

During the years she lived in the favela, Carolina de Jesus wrote highly romantic stories and poems, "for when I was writing I was in a golden palace, with crystal windows and silver chandeliers. My dress was finest satin and diamonds sat shining in my black hair." She also kept a diary, written on the blank pages of notebooks she found in the trash. When newspaperman Audalio Dantas discovered her writing in 1958 and preferred her realistic diary to her fantasies, she protested, "I didn't write it for anyone to see. It is filled with ugly things and ugly people. Maybe after I die it will be published, but not now." Persuading her of its power, Dantas published excerpts from the diary in his newspaper and in the weekly magazine *O Cruzeiro*. Published in book form in 1960, the diary sold more copies than any other Brazilian book in history and led to housing reforms throughout the country. But it is more than a social document. Here is a voice of such distinctive quality that one might ask what exactly in the text conveys such a strong personality. The passage below is the beginning of the English translation, published in 1962 as *Child of the Dark*.

Since moving from the favela in 1960, Carolina de Jesus has published two books in Portuguese, *Proverbs* and *Many Phases of Hunger*.

from *The Diary*

July 15, 1955

The birthday of my daughter Vera Eunice. I wanted to buy a pair of shoes for her, but the price of food keeps us from realizing our desires. Actually we are slaves to the cost of living. I found a pair of shoes in the garbage, washed them, and patched them for her to wear.

I didn't have one cent to buy bread. So I washed three bottles and traded them to Arnaldo. He kept the bottles and gave me bread. Then I went to sell my paper. I received 65 cruzeiros. I spent 20 cruzeiros for meat. I got one kilo of ham and one kilo of sugar and spent six cruzeiros on cheese. And the money was gone.

I was ill all day. I thought I had a cold. At night my chest pained me. I started to cough. I decided not to go out at night to look for paper. I searched for my son João. He was at Felisberto de Carvalho Street near the market. A bus had knocked a boy into the sidewalk and a crowd gathered. João was in the middle of it all. I poked him a couple of times and within five minutes he was home.

I washed the children, put them to bed, then washed myself and went to bed. I waited until 11:00 for a certain someone. He didn't come. I took an aspirin and laid down again. When I awoke the sun was sliding in space. My daughter Vera Eunice said: "Go get some water, Mother!"

July 16

I got up and obeyed Vera Eunice. I went to get the water. I made coffee. I told the children that I didn't have any bread, that they would have to drink their coffee plain and eat meat with *farinha*. I was feeling ill and decided to cure myself. I stuck my finger down my throat twice, vomited, and knew I was under the evil eye. The upset feeling left and I went to Senhor Manuel, carrying some cans to sell. Everything that I find in the garbage I sell. He gave me 13 cruzeiros. I kept thinking that I had to buy bread, soap, and milk for Vera Eunice. The 13 cruzeiros wouldn't make it. I returned home, or rather to my shack, nervous and exhausted. I thought of the worrisome life that I led. Carrying paper, washing clothes for the children, staying in the street all day long. Yet I'm always lacking things, Vera doesn't have shoes and she doesn't like to go barefoot. For at least two years I've wanted to buy a meat grinder. And a sewing machine.

I came home and made lunch for the two boys. Rice, beans, and meat, and I'm going out to look for paper. I left the children, told them to play in the yard and not go into the street, because the terrible neighbors I have won't leave my children alone. I was feeling ill and wished I could lie down. But the poor don't rest nor are they permitted the pleasure of relaxation. I was nervous inside, cursing my luck. I collected two sacks full of paper. Afterward I went back and gathered up some scrap metal, some cans, and some kindling wood. As I walked I thought—when I return to the favela there is going to be something new. Maybe Dona Rosa or the insolent Angel Mary fought with my children. I found Vera Eunice sleeping and the boys playing in the street. I thought: it's 2:00. Maybe I'm going to get through this day without anything happening. João told me that the truck that gives out money was here to give out food. I took a sack and hurried out. It was the leader of the Spiritist Center at 103 Vergueiro Street. I got two kilos of rice, two of beans, and two kilos of macaroni. I was happy. The truck went away. The nervousness that I had inside left me. I took advantage of my calmness to read. I picked up a magazine and sat on the grass, letting the rays of the sun warm me as I read a story. I wrote a note and gave it to my boy João to take to Senhor Arnaldo to buy soap, two aspirins, and some bread. Then I put water on the stove to make coffee. Joao came back saying he had lost the aspirins. I went back with him to look. We didn't find them.

When I came home there was a crowd at my door. Children and women claiming José Carlos had thrown stones at their houses. They wanted me to punish him.

July 17 Sunday

A marvelous day. The sky was blue without one cloud. The sun was warm. I got out of bed at 6:30 and went to get water. I only had one piece of bread and three cruzeiros. I gave a small piece to each child and put the beans, that I got yesterday from the Spiritist Center, on the fire. Then I went to wash clothes. When I returned from the river the beans were cooked. The children asked for bread. I gave the three cruzeiros to João to go and buy some. Today it was Nair Mathias who started an argument with my children. Silvia and her husband have begun an open-air spectacle. He is hitting her and I'm disgusted because the children are present. They heard words of the lowest kind. Oh, if I could move from here to a more decent neighborhood!

I went to Dona Florela to ask for a piece of garlic. I went to Dona Analia and got exactly what I expected:

"I don't have any!"

I went to collect my clothes. Dona Aparecida asked me:

"Are you pregnant?"

"No, Senhora," I replied gently.

I cursed her under my breath. If I am pregnant it's not your business.

I can't stand these favela women, they want to know everything. Their tongues are like chicken feet. Scratching at everything. The rumor is circulating that I am pregnant! If I am, I don't know about it!

I went out at night to look for paper. When I was passing the São Paulo football stadium many people were coming out. All of them were white and only one black. And the black started to insult me:

"Are you looking for paper, auntie? Watch your step, auntie dear!"

I was ill and wanted to lie down, but I went on. I met several friends and stopped to talk to them. When I was going up Tiradentes Avenue I met some women. One of them asked me:

"Are your legs healed?"

After I was operated on, I got better, thanks to God. I could even dance at Carnival in my feather costume. Dr. José Torres Netto was who operated on me. A good doctor. And we spoke of politics. When a woman asked me what I thought of Carlos Lacerda, I replied truthfully:

"He is very intelligent, but he doesn't have an education. He is a slum politician. He likes intrigues, to agitate."

One woman said it was a pity, that the bullet that got the major didn't get Carlos Lacerda.

"But his day . . . it's coming," commented another.

Many people had gathered and I was the center of attention. I was embarrassed because I was looking for paper and dressed in rags. I didn't want to talk to anyone, because I had to collect paper. I needed the money. There was none in the house to buy bread. I worked until 11:30. When I returned home it was midnight. I warmed up some food, gave some to Vera Eunice, ate and laid down. When I awoke the rays of the sun were coming through the gaps of the shack.

July 18

I got up at 7. Happy and content. Weariness would be here soon enough. I went to the junk dealer and received 60 cruzeiros. I passed by Arnaldo, bought bread, milk, paid what I owed him, and still had enough to buy Vera some chocolate. I returned to a Hell. I opened the door and threw the children outside. Dona Rosa, as soon as she saw my boy José Carlos, started to fight with him. She didn't want the boy to come near her shack. She ran out with a stick to hit him. A woman of 48 years fighting with a child! At times, after I leave, she comes to my window and throws a filled chamber pot onto the children. When I return I find the pillows dirty and the children fetid. She hates me. She says that the handsome and distinguished men prefer me and that I make more money than she does.

Dona Cecilia appeared. She came to punish my children. I threw a right at her and she stepped back. I told her:

"There are women that say they know how to raise children, but some have children in jails listed as delinquents."

She went away. Then came that bitch Angel Mary. I said:

"I was fighting with the banknotes, now the small change is arriving. I don't go to anybody's door, and you people who come to my door only bore me. I never bother anyone's children or come to your shack shouting against your kids. And don't think that yours are saints; it's just that I tolerate them."

Dona Silvia came to complain about my children. That they were badly educated. I don't look for defects in children. Neither in mine nor in others. I know that a child is not born with sense. When I speak with a child I use pleasant words. What infuriates me is that the parents come to my door to disrupt my rare moments of inner tranquillity. But when they upset me, I write. I know how to dominate my impulses. I only had two years of schooling, but I got enough to form my character. The only thing that does not exist in the favela is friendship.

Then came the fishmonger Senhor Antonio Lira and he gave me some fish. I started preparing lunch. The women went away, leaving me in peace for today. They had put on their show. My door is actually a theater. All children throw stones, but my boys are the scapegoats. They gossip that I'm not married, but I'm happier than they are. They have husbands but they are forced to beg. They are supported by charity organizations.

My kids are not kept alive by the church's bread. I take on all kinds of work to keep them. And those women have to beg or even steal. At night when they are begging I peacefully sit in my shack listening to Viennese waltzes. While their husbands break the boards of the shack, I and my children sleep peacefully. I don't envy the married women of the favelas who lead lives like Indian slaves.

I never got married and I'm not unhappy. Those who wanted to marry me were mean and the conditions they imposed on me were horrible.

Take Maria José, better known as Zefa, who lives in shack number nine on "B" Street. She is an alcoholic and when she is pregnant she drinks to excess. The children are born and they die before they reach two months. She hates me because my children thrive and I have a radio. One day she asked to borrow my radio. I told her I wouldn't loan it, and as she didn't have any children, she could work and buy one. But it is well known that people who are given to the vice of drink never buy anything. Not even clothes. Drunks don't prosper. Sometimes she throws water on my children. She claims I never punish my kids. I'm not given to violence. José Carlos said:

"Don't be sad, Mama. Our Lady of Aparecida will help you, and when I grow up I'll buy a brick house for you."

I went to collect paper and stayed away from the house an hour. When I returned I saw several people at the river bank. There was a man unconscious from alcohol and the worthless men of the favela were cleaning out his pockets. They stole his money and tore up his documents. It is 5 p.m. Now Senhor Heitor turns on the light. And I, I have to wash the children so they can go to bed, for I have to go out. I need money to pay the light bill. That's the way it is here. Person doesn't use the lights but must pay for them. I left and went to collect paper. I walked fast because it was late. I met a woman complaining about her married life. I listened but said nothing. I tied up the sacks, put the tin cans that I found in another sack, and went home. When I arrived I turned on the radio to see what time it was. It was 11:55. I heated some food, read, undressed, and laid down. Sleep came soon.

Piri Thomas

Piri Thomas was born John Peter Thomas in 1928. He writes about his childhood and youth in East Harlem, the Barrio, in *Down These Mean Streets* (1967). His love for East Harlem and for his people mingles, throughout his autobiography, with his search for identity between the Puerto Rican and black worlds, his involvement in drug traffic, and his addiction to heroin. A series of robberies led to his conviction in 1950 on a charge of attempted robbery and felonious assault. In prison, he learned brick masonry and completed his high-school education. He served six years of a fifteen-year sentence, winning parole in 1956 at the age of twenty-eight. The passage which follows, from the end of *Down These Mean Streets,* begins at this point.

Thomas' language is striking; the reader may wish to examine how it reflects his particular culture and tensions. His remarks on four-letter words invite comparison with those of D. H. Lawrence (p. 172). Also worthy of notice is his use of the theme of imprisonment and release throughout this passage. Having been released from prison, he is still not free. In what prisons does he remain? What is meant by his imagined escape with Trina and what is learned by his actual meeting with her?

Since the time covered in his autobiography, Thomas has held creative writing seminars in East Harlem and elsewhere, trying to communicate to disadvantaged people "a sense of their being able to create beauty instead of ugliness and . . . . to develop their minds for a sense of harmony instead of disorder." His work with addicts and street gangs in his Barrio is shown in the award-winning Time-Life film *Petey and Johnny.*

Hey, Barrio—I'm Home

The big day came at last, November 28, the day I would find out what was shaking. Once again I made it to the courtroom. My aunt and her pastor were there, their heads bowed in prayer.

My name was called and I rose, and the judge's voice came down from behind the big desk in that big paneled room.

"Have you been promised anything for accepting a plea of robbery in the second degree?" he asked.

"No, sir," I replied.

"Have you anything to say before sentence is passed?"

My Legal Aid court-appointed lawyer said something about six years in prison and rehabilitation. Then the district attorney, who's supposed to sink your lemon for you, opened his mouth and he talked better for me than my lawyer, saying he was willing to go along with leniency, a suspended sentence and probation. This shook me up inside, but my face still stood *cara palo.*

The judge said, "Can you keep your nose clean?"

"Yes, sir, I can."

"Okay, I'm going to let you go on probation for three years. Do right. You can go now."

Just like that, it was over. I was free. I turned and walked out through the swinging doors, my aunt and her pastor right behind me. We had to stop at the probation officer's desk, where I was given a card and told to report every week. The P.O. asked me if I had a job. I said no; he said get one fast. If I needed help I could get it, but if I messed up I'd be in trouble and back again. He told me I would have to report to him and to my parole officer, and if I screwed up on one I'd automatically screw up on the other. He warned me to stay away from my "old associates" and not to fuck anybody who wasn't my wife and said I could go.

I walked to the last door, the one that led to the street. One push and I was out. I stood there blinking at the bright sun. "I'm out! I'm out!" I said. Inside, the dizziness of being free was like a night that changed into day; all the shadows became daylight sharp. My first urge was to break out running as fast as I could, but I held myself down; I played cool and collected.

"You can thank God for all He's done," my aunt's pastor said.

"Yeah, Reverend," I said. But the thought of God was like having an obligation, and I didn't want any obligations, not after six years of obligations. I wanted to feel the street, and smell it and hold it between the fingers of my heart. The roar of a nearby elevated train drowned out all thoughts of God. I smelled the street and the people and the cold November air that meant freedom. I was gonna stay free, whether I made it to another country or whether I made it the right way. My head spun from the thought of having to go back to jail.

The next morning I went downtown with my aunt to make my first report to my parole officer. There were a lot of ex-cons in the office making their initial reports. A few of us knew one another. But each of us acted as though the other was a stranger, for one of the bad scenes of parole violation is associating with ex-cons or known criminals.

My P.O. didn't waste any time. He looked at his watch and told me, "You're thirty minutes late."

I nodded in agreement.

"It's a good way to start off, eh?" He was pretty insistent, but I wasn't gonna get mad, no matter what. I made my face stay the same, relaxed and soft. "You got a job?" he finally asked me.

"No sir, not yet."

"Get one, fast."

"Yes sir."

He looked at my records, and after a long while he crossed his eyes at me and said, "If you do right, you're gonna stay out, otherwise you go back so fast it's gonna make your head spin."

I nodded.

"We're here to help you, and if you got any kind of problem we'll be glad to help you solve it."

I thanked him and he told me to report every Thursday. I stood up and he smiled for the first time, and I figured that all that crap he had blown on me was just to see if I would blow my top.

We left and took the Lexington Avenue subway back to Spanish Harlem. The rumbling and noise of the train made me nervous. I still wasn't used to city noise. The noise in prison is different; it's the sound of people who have a single frustration in common. But in the city, in Spanish Harlem, there is more of a choice of noise. I watched the walls of the tunnel whip by as the train lurched like a drunk along the rails. Finally, we pulled into the 110th Street station.

"Let's get off, *Tía*," I said.

"But it's only 110th Street, *hijo*. We go one more stop."

But I didn't wait. I jumped through the closing doors, and waved her on, shouting, "I'll see you at home." My God! it felt good to be able to leave when I wanted to. How many times at Comstock had I wanted to jump through the closing doors of my cell before they locked on me? And now I had jumped through some closing doors. It was such a little thing, but what a great feeling it produced. I ran up the subway steps to the street. The air felt great, and I ran over to my aunt's house and bounced up the stairs thinking about the job I hadda get for myself, my parole officer, and my probation officer.

The next day a rabbi and his brother-in-law gave me a job in their dress-and-shirt company as an all-around handyman and clean-up man. For $40 a week I ran errands, hung up dresses, put pins and tags on them, and delivered them.

I worked steadily and reported steadily and visited my aunt's church from time to time. I saw Pops and my brothers and sister on Long Island, but I lived with my aunt in stone-cool Harlem. It was great to be back in the street. A lot of my boys were either hollowed-out junkies or in prison, but a few of them were still making the scene, and after a few weeks I was making it with them. In the back of my mind, I was a little worried, but after all, I told myself, I had spent a lifetime in that fucking jail and I owed myself some ballin'.

The first rule I broke was the one about not fucking broads who weren't your wife. I shacked up with one of the homeliest broads I ever had seen, but she looked great after my long fast. Having broken one rule, I found it easier to break another, and soon I was drinking again. Then I started smoking pot. This went on for some weeks; then, one morning, after a wild, all-night pot party, I crept into *Tía*'s apartment and dug myself in the mirror. What I saw shook me up. My eyes were red from smoke and my face was strained from the effort of trying to be cool. I saw myself as I had been six years ago, hustling, whoring, and hating, heading toward the same long years and the hard bit. I didn't want to go that route; I didn't want to go dig that past scene again.

I pulled away from the mirror and sat on the edge of my bed. My head was still full of pot, and I felt scared. I couldn't stop trembling inside. I felt as though I had found a hole in my face and out of it were pouring all the different masks that my *cara-palo* face had fought so hard to keep hidden. I thought, *I ain't goin' back to what I was.* Then I asked myself, *You remember all that crap you went through? What you want to do, go on for the rest of your life with your ass hangin'? Man, don't forget, you only get what you take. You can make a couple of yards a week and be cool about it. Just by the by, hustle a piece of junk and you're in. You don't use no more, so keep on not using and you're in like a mother. You can make cool bread now; why knock yourself out working? You ain't gonna live forever.*

The thoughts pressed on my brain. I grabbed my face with both hands and squeezed hard, pushing it all out of shape; I pulled my lips out and my face down. The reefer kick was still on, and I could feel the smallness of the room and the neatness of its humble furniture and the smell of its credit, which $1.50 a week paid off. I pushed my way to the window, pulled the light cord and hid from myself in the friendly darkness. Easing the noise from the old-time window shade, I pushed up the window and squeezed my hand through the iron gate my aunt had put in to keep the crooks out. I breathed in the air; it was the same air that I had breathed as a kid. The garbage-filled backyards were the same. Man, everything was the same; only I had changed. I wasn't the grubby-faced Puerto Rican kid any more; I was a grubby-faced Puerto Rican man. I am an *hombre* that wants to be better. Man! I don't want to be nuttin'. I want to be somebody. I want to laugh clean. I want to smile for real, not because I have to . . .

I peered through the darkness. My lips wanted to form words; I wanted to tell somebody I wanted to be somebody. I heard the squeaking of old bed springs, the scrounging of alley cats in overturned garbage cans. I saw the stars up there in God's pad and the gray-white outline of clothes swinging on the black morning breeze, and I leaned hard against the gate that kept crooks out and me in and looked at my dark, long fingers wrapped tightly around the cold black metal. I felt like I was back at Comstock, looking out, hoping, dreaming, wanting. I felt like I wasn't real, that I was like a shadow on a dingy hallway wall next to scribbled graffiti: "Joe loves Lucy," "Baby was laid underneath these stairs, 1947," "The super is a rotten motherfucker," "Piri is a Coolie," "Wait for me, Trina"—*Trina didn't wait . . .*

I felt a wave of loneliness smack over me, almost like getting high. "Fuck it, fuck it," I said. The four-letter words sounded strange, dirty, like I shouldn't have been saying them. I said, "Motherfucker," and it sounded different, too. It didn't sound like long ago. It sounded not like a challenge thrown at the world but like a cry of helplessness. I pressed my eyes hard into the curve of my elbow. *I don't want to keep on being shit in a cesspool, squishing out through long pipes to hell knows where: I wanna be nice, all the way, for real . . .*

I remembered my aunt's church around the corner. *If God is right, so what if He's white?* I thought, *God, I wanna get out of this hole. Help me out. I promise if You help me climb out, I ain't gonna push the cover back on that cesspool. Let me out and I'll push my arm back down there and help some other guy get a break.*

The rest of my first year out drained away fast. I fought to keep from being swallowed up again by Harlem's hustles and rackets; I started to visit *Tía*'s church on 118th Street; I got a raise from the rabbi and encouragement from my probation officers. But there was something missing and I knew what it was: Trina. I couldn't get her out of my mind. I couldn't walk through familiar streets without thinking, *There's where we used to go,* or *There's where we used to eat.* I tried to push her away from my mind but I knew I'd have to see her again. Her husband had turned out no good; I heard from here and there what a hard life he was giving her. I wondered if she had changed.

One night I met her cousin Ava on the street. She was married now and had two children. We talked about old times and she invited me up to her mother's house. "We're having a little get-together and all the family will be there," she said.

"All?" I asked.

"Yeah, all," she repeated.

"When?"

"Tonight. It's about seven o'clock now—say about nine."

"Great. I may just drop on by."

"May?"

"Yeah," I replied, *"may,"* but I knew I'd be there.

I went home thinking all the way. I tried to lay out the scene I'd pass through at nine o'clock that night.

I'd walk up the stairs at number 129 cool, oh so cool, wearing my best vines. Ava would answer the door.

"Hi, Piri."

I'd smile. "Hi."

"Come on in."

I'd step in and dig the scene. Ava's brothers would be on the sofa, her mother would be in the easy chair and Georgie, Trina's husband, would be sitting on the other chair. Trina would be standing by the window looking outside, her face in profile, sad-looking but bravely beautiful.

I'd walk into the parlor and there would be a breather silence, like if God walked in on a bunch of sinners. Ava and her brothers would look at each other knowingly and expectantly. Ava's mom would sit still and quiet, and Georgie, that dirty rat, would turn pale and start shaking all over, smiling like a scared punk. I'd ignore him and look into Trina's eyes, and she'd whisper, "I've waited so long, Johnny Gringo, my Piri, I've waited so long."

I'd look, oh, so cool, so bad, so brave, and hold out my arms and say, "Come on, Marine Tiger, we're going home, baby. And bring your kid; it's my kid now."

Trina would melt into my arms and I'd bruise her lips and I'd crush her tight and we'd be like one Puerto Rican instead of two, and we'd turn and walk away toward the door. And Ava would shout, "Look out, Piri, he's gonna jump you!" and I'd feel the knife bite into my shoulder muscle, the pain going deep, and I'd hear screams from Trina's throat.

I'd lurch forward and with a great effort straighten up and face Georgie. His face would turn gray and splotchy with fear; he'd stand there paralyzed. I'd reach my arm behind me and grab the handle of the knife that is sticking in my back and, with a suave pull, squish it out of my back.

"Don't kill me, please," Georgie would beg.

I'd look at him with contempt, fling the bloody knife away and start walking slowly toward him. Georgie would back away, trap himself in a corner. I'd measure his face and crash my fist into it. He'd fight back weakly and I'd hit him with one fist and then another until he sagged slowly to the floor.

I'd feel blood in my mouth—the knife has punctured my lung; I may be dying—and I'd lean on Trina. She'd kiss me, and we'd walk out the door and . . .

"Hey, Piri, wanna go to a flick tonight?"

"No, I'm sorry, I got some place to go tonight."

"Oh, okay."

Back in reality, I walked down the cold street and ran up the long, dingy steps to my aunt's apartment. Twenty minutes later I was in the bath, getting ready for I didn't know what.

At nine o'clock I stood in front of the apartment in number 129 and knocked and waited. The door opened. It was Ava's mom. "Come in, *hijo,* come in," she said, hugging me.

I stepped into the apartment. There was no one on the couch, no one in the parlor. I saw a stranger sitting at the kitchen table. *Georgie,* I thought. Ava was just coming out of the john. She hugged me and I looked past her into the bedroom, where Trina was standing at the door looking at me. Georgie smiled and I was introduced to him. He smiled and offered me a drink.

"No, thank you," I said, and as a chair was offered to me, I added, "Mind if I sit in the parlor?" I sat on the chair that I imagined Georgie would have been sitting in and I looked at Trina. There was nothing to say, nothing to do. I just sat there and made small talk. *Trina, say something,* I thought, *anything.*

But Trina didn't say anything, and after what seemed like many days,

I heard myself saying, "Well, it's been nice visiting you all. I'm sorry, but I gotta go now, I, uh, got an appointment."

"Oh, I'm sorry you have to go, *hijo*," said Ava's mom.

"We'll see you again, won't we?" Ava asked.

"Yeah, sure," I said. I looked at Trina. She smiled something at me, and I walked out the door and down the stairs and out into the cold street, thinking, *What a blank that was. I should have known, nothing is run the same, nothing stays the same. You can't make yesterday come back today.*

George Jackson

George Jackson was born in 1941 in Chicago, where he attended a Catholic school until his family moved to Los Angeles. There he quickly had several brushes with the law. During his third arrest, for breaking into a furniture store, a police bullet grazed his elbow; he was committed to Paso Robles School for Boys from which he was paroled six months later. In September 1958 he was again arrested, for robbing a service station of $105, and served time until June 1960. In September of that year, five days before his nineteenth birthday, he was arrested for robbing a service station of $71.

The actual facts surrounding that case are unclear, as is much in George Jackson's relations with the law. He later said, in a letter, that he had agreed to confess to "spare the county court costs in return for a light county jail sentence." But when the time came for sentencing, he was given one year to life in the penitentiary and was in prison from that time on, frequently in solitary confinement, until he was killed at San Quentin eleven years later. While he was a prisoner at Soledad prison, a tense racial situation had led to the killing of three black prisoners. The following week, a white guard was killed, and George Jackson, together with John W. Cluchette and Fleeta Drumgo, was accused of the murder. The three became known as the Soledad brothers. On August 7, 1970, Jackson's younger brother Jonathan led a raid on the Marin County Courthouse designed to take hostages for later exchange to free the Soledad Brothers. He was killed in the raid, as were the judge and two other prisoners. Angela Davis, to whom the last letter is addressed, was accused and later acquitted of having been an accessory to the raid. Shortly after George Jackson's death in September 1971, the other Soledad brothers were acquitted.

Nothing about George Jackson's career or reputation is unambiguous. Some see him as a self-educated revolutionary, a dedicated leader and hero; to others he is a man who could not stay out of trouble, a confirmed outlaw and provocateur. His death is equally ambiguous. Some insist he was killed trying to escape, others that he was set up and murdered. The young lawyer, Stephen Bingham, who was the last outsider to see Jackson before the shooting, has disappeared and not been heard from since.

Soledad Brother, The Prison Letters of George Jackson was published shortly before his death. The letters reflect the changes—in his mind, his feelings, his tone— as his increase in self-awareness is paralleled by a focusing of his revolutionary fervor. We reprint seven of these letters below. The first is a response to the letter his father had written to prison officials about him in May 1961. The reader should ask himself what sort of man he thinks the author is and should examine carefully his own response to both the message and the tone. Do they push you in the same direction? Jackson's writing may be compared with that of Piri Thomas (p. 49) and James Blake (p. 66) for an interesting triangle of attitudes toward prison.

Seven Prison Letters

July, 1965

Dear Father,

I am perplexed and hard pressed in finding a solution or reason that will adequately explain why we are so eager to follow Charlie. Why we are so impressed with his apparent know-how. A glance at his history shows that it has been one long continuous war. At no time in European history has there been a period of peace and harmony. Every moment of his past has been spent in the breakdown of civilization by causing war, disruption, disease, and artificial famine. You send me a date from the moment he emerged from his cave-dwelling days and I'll tell you which of his tribes were at war, either on us or on themselves. The whole of the Western European's existence here in the U.S. has been the same one long war with different peoples. This is the only thing they understand, the only thing they respect—the only thing they can do with any dexterity. Do you accept this miscreant as the architect of the patterns that must guide your future life! If so, we must part company, and it is best we do so now, before the trouble begins. But please stop and think so that you can turn yourself around in time, so that the developments to come won't shock you so badly. I have not wasted my time these last three or four years. I speak with some authority and people are listening. People like me are going to be shaping your tomorrows. So just sit back, open your mind, and watch, since you can't marshall the fundamentals to help me.

Yes, my friend, I remember everything, the reason that Delora and I had to spend that summer and winter in Harrisburg is known and remembered by me. I remember the garbage right under the side and back of our place on Racine. Mama having to wash and wring clothes by hand, carrying Penny and Jon while some fat redheaded mama sat on her behind. I remember how strange people looked to me when I finally had to be sent to Skinner School. You never knew why I was almost killed the first day I went, but I do. I remember how the rent and clothes for us children kept you broke and ragged. All of us hungry, if not for food—for other things that make life bearable. After you and Mama settled down you had no recreational outlets whatever. And everyone on Warren Blvd. knows how you would beat me all the way home from our baseball games in the alley. Robert, can you see how absurd you sound to me when you speak on "the good life," or something about being a free adult? I know you have never been free. I know that few blacks over here have ever been free. The forms of slavery merely *changed* at the signing of the Emancipation Proclamation from chattel slavery to economic slavery. If you could see and talk to some of the blacks I meet in here you would immediately understand what I mean, and see that I'm right. They are all average, all with the same backgrounds, and in for the same thing, some form of food getting. About 70 to 80 percent of all crime in the U.S. is perpetrated by blacks, "the sole reason for this is that 98 percent of our number live below the poverty level in bitter and abject misery"! You must take off your rose-colored glasses and stop pretending. We have suffered an unmitigated wrong! How do you think I felt when I saw you come home each day a little more depressed than the day before? How do you think I felt when I looked in your face and saw the clouds forming, when I saw you look around and see your best efforts go for nothing—nothing. I can count the times on my hands that you managed to work up a smile.

George

July 15, 1967

My Friend,

I got your letter of June 5. I have it here before me. I told Les to cooperate with your efforts for me. I sure do need some of the benefits of togetherness now. As I explained I am in adjustment center here for an undefined amount of time.

Les speaks of me coming home with optimism, but I would benefit largely from a transfer. No one, among the officials that is, ever calls me out of my cell anymore to speak with me of my progress or my future. I'm just locked down and forgotten. Can a lawyer do anything about getting me a transfer? He would have to go through Sacramento. The justification for such action is obvious: I cannot adjust here, the officials have preconceived notions about my behavioral patterns and consequently look for the worst in me. The atmosphere here is aggressive, and I'm too far away from home. I cannot get regular visits and thus miss the beneficial influence of you and my parents.

My friend, my thinking has changed somewhat since I saw you last. That fellow who sent pictures of his Cadillac auto up here can explain some of the workings and progress of my thoughts. I hope he doesn't betray himself with that fast living I hear he is doing. Seems he has learned nothing from bitter experience!! I have trained away, pressed out forever the last of my Western habits. You remember I never got intoxicated or spent any money or time on trifles, but in the passing of these last couple of years, I have completely retrained myself and my thinking to the point now that I think and dream of one thing only, 24 hours of each day. I have no habits, no ego, no name, no face. I feel no love, no tenderness, for anyone who does not think as I do. There can be no ties of blood or kinship strong enough to move me from my course. I'll never, never trade my self-determination for a car, cheap mass-produced clothes, clapboard house, or a couple of nights a week at the go-go. Control over the circumstances that surround my existence is of the first importance to me. Without this control, or with control in someone else's hands, I am forever insecure, subject at all times to the whim and caprice of the man in control, and you and I know how whimsical some men can be. Well, Pop, I'll be going outside to court the seventh of August to testify for a friend. I'll get a glimpse of the world at large, if you can call San Rafael the world at large.

I hope you are doing well. I would have written before now but I was in isolation up until the eleventh of this month, as you know.

Do you have time to read? I'll suggest some books if so, next letter. Take care.

George

October 11, 1967

Dear Robert,

I received the letter with the money in it all right, thank you. I'm going pretty good here, no problems, no new ones anyway.

I went before a formal two-man review committee here recently. They gave me at least four more months to do here in the adjustment center. I guess we can call this improvement of a sort since I'm usually told nothing.

You say Jon is having trouble with math. And that you feel it's just a matter of his settling down to his work. I wondered when you mentioned this just what it was that is keeping him from his studies. How does he spend his time? Is there anyone there to help him with his studies? Of course, you are right that all he has to do is apply himself to his work. At this stage of the schooling structure, nothing is really difficult. Math is never difficult, since its laws are positive. All that needs to be done is take the necessary time and learn the formulas and principles. Of course, if too much time is spent in class on religious matters, the teacher is at fault, not the student. In fact if *any time* is spent on religious matters during the school hours the student is being cheated.

Take care of yourself.

George

October 17, 1967

Dear Robert,

The time slips away from me. I'm surrounded here by fools, degenerates, and phonies. I suffer a constant bombardment of nonsense from all sides.

There is no rest from it even at night. Twenty-four hours a day all my senses must endure the shock of this attack from the lunatic fringe. So I insert my earplugs, and bury myself in my thoughts and my work. The days, even the weeks lapse one into the other, endlessly into one another. Each day that comes and goes is exactly like the one that went before. If I am lax in my duties toward you, forgive me. I am living under strain.

I am sorry to hear about your friend. The same has happened to some of mine here. I think I know how you feel; however, I try to think of those things as releases.

How was my letter to Jon received? Mama may have torn it up. If Jon wants to go to the trouble of framing those parts that trouble him into a letter, I have a fair understanding of math.

No new problems here. Just waiting it out. Time is on my side. I'm twenty-six now, and I'll be twenty-six when I leave here. Be it 40 years from today.

Take care.

George

October 18, 1967

Dear Robert,

How is Penny and the little guy? I guess I miss them quite a bit. What a difference their presence makes here.

My language studies are coming along well. I guess if I don't get out before January—and it's not likely that I will—I'll go into Arabic next. With four languages plus English I'll be able to communicate with three-fourths of the people on earth. I am presently working on Spanish and Swahili. Spanish is spoken by most peoples from Mexico to Chile in what is the fastest-growing population area in the world. Swahili is spoken by all of eastern Africa. I may find communication with these peoples important in my work. All that remains is for me to learn Arabic and Chinese.

Perhaps I'll start on these two next year, I've done well with the Spanish.

I trust you are well. Don't work yourself too hard. You cannot get rich on wages. I have had no response from Jon to my last two letters. What's happening? Has he forgotten his brother; it has been a long time. He was just a baby when first I came here to the concentration camp. It's been seven years, one month now.

Take care of yourself.

George

April 11, 1968

Dear Robert,

M.L.K. organized his thoughts much in the same manner as you have organized yours. If you really knew and fully understood his platform you would never have expressed such sentiments as you did in your last letter. I am sure you are acquainted with the fact that he was opposed to violence and war; he was indeed a devout pacifist. It is very odd, almost unbelievable, that so violent and tumultuous a setting as this can still produce such men. He was out of place, out of season, too naive, too innocent, too cultured, too civil for these times. That is why his end was so predictable.

Violence in its various forms he opposed, but this does not mean that he was passive. He knew that nature allows no such imbalances to exist for long. He was perceptive enough to see that the men of color across the world were on the march and their example would soon influence those in the U.S. to also stand up and stop trembling. So he attempted to direct the emotions and the movement in general along lines that he thought best suited to our unique situation: nonviolent civil disobedience, political and economic in character. I was beginning to warm somewhat to him because of his new ideas concerning U.S. foreign wars against colored peoples. I am certain that he was sincere in his stated purpose to "feed the hungry, clothe the naked, comfort those in prisons, and trying to love somebody." I really never disliked him as a man. As a man I accorded him the respect that his sincerity deserved.

It is just as a leader of black thought that I disagreed with him. The concept of nonviolence is a false ideal. It presupposes the existence of compassion and a sense of justice on the part of one's adversary. When this adversary has everything to lose and nothing to gain by exercising justice and compassion, his reaction can only be negative.

The symbol of the male here in North America has always been the gun, the knife, the club. Violence is extolled at every exchange: the TV, the motion pictures, the best-seller lists. The newspapers that sell best are those that carry the boldest, bloodiest headlines and most sports coverage. To die for king and country is to die a hero.

The Kings, Wilkinses, and Youngs exhort us in King's words to "put away your knives, put away your arms and clothe yourselves in the breastplate of righteousness" and "turn the other cheek to prove our capacity to endure, to love." Well, that is good for them perhaps but I most certainly need both sides of my head.

George

May 28, 1970

Dear Angela,

I sincerely hope you understand this situation here with me, the overall thing I mean, you probably do. I don't want to be bash with you, the relative levels of our insecurity are too disparate for me to dwell on feelings, the warm, very personal, elemental thing. I can never express it in this form anyway, but I want you to know, and then we can get on with the work.

I have, like most people, a recurring dream. In this dream there is a great deal of abstract activity. Have you ever seen the pig they have named——General Something-or-other——. I don't know why my mind locked on him, but part of this dream is a still shot of my trying to fit a large steel boomerang into his mouth. It switches then to a scene where me and two other brothers, T.G. and a brother named H.B., are holding hands to form a large circle, in the ring. Inside the ring formed by the three of us is this guy. He's wearing top hat and tails—stars and stripes— beard and bushy eyebrows. The action part goes like this: Old Sam tries to break out of the circle; we stop him; after ten tries—we're wearing track shoes—he's ragged as an old mophead. It goes on that way, scenes running into each other, overlapping, all very pleasing—wish fulfill- ment?—very gratifying stuff; but the high point, the climax—well, a tall slim African woman, firelight, and the beautiful dance of death. This wonderful woman didn't become part of my dream until last year sometime. I never thought this kind of environment could produce one like her, but at the same time I knew that things never could be good with me without her.

But I promised not to be bash with you. It's crazy, all women, even the very phenomenal, want at least a promise of brighter days, brighter tomorrows. I have no tomorrows at all. The worst thing that could have ever happened to the woman in the dream was letting me touch her. I'll tell you the whole thing if we can ever find somewhere to relax. . . Until then I promise not to bore you. You probably hear these devotions all day, and with your incentive factors they're probably all sincere devotions. Let me heap mine on you (with these pitiful little strokes of the pen) for the last time (unless seized by ungovernable impulse) with a statement made at the risk of seeming immodest; but I am modest and I hope that it is righteous for me to feel that—no one, and much more meaningful no black, wherever the hurricane has washed up his broken body, no one at all, can love like I.

In our last communication I made a statement about women, and their part in revolutionary culture (people's war). It wasn't a clear statement. I meant to return to it but was diverted. I understand exactly what the woman's role should be. The very same as the man's. Intellectually, there is very little difference between male and female. The differences we see in bourgeois society are all conditioned and artificial.

I was leading up to the obvious fact that black women in this country are far more aggressive than black males. But this is qualified by the fact that their aggression has, until very recently, been within the system—that "get a diploma boy" stuff, or "earn you some money." Where it should have been the gun. Development of the ability for serious fighting and organized violence was surely not encouraged in the black female, but neither was it discouraged, as it was in the case of the black male.

Please don't dismiss this yet. Let me rush to remind you that we have already established that bourgeois society has relegated women in general to a very distinct level of existence, even the slave woman. I'm not about to say they loved you better. Love doesn't even enter this equation, but socially primitive bourgeois thinking and the sex mystique does. First, a woman wasn't considered dangerous. Second, the most important experience in the Amerikan white male's "coming into manhood" was entering the body of the black female. These two circumstances contributed to the longevity and the matriarchal status of black women greatly.

Add to all of this the fact that the black mother wanted to see her son survive in a grim and murderous white male society and the grotesque misshapen pieces come together.

I was saying that if the black mother wants her revenge she will have to stop teaching her sons to fear death. By default she dominates the black subculture, and her son must be the catalyst in any great changes that go down in this country. The head and the fist, no one else has as much to gain.

Power to the People.

George

James Blake

James Blake was born in Edinburgh, Scotland, in 1922. He came to the United States at the age of ten. After attending the University of Illinois and Northwestern, he worked for several years as a jazz pianist. Since 1951, when he was sentenced to eighteen months for petty larceny and breaking and entering, he has spent more than half his years in prison. "When I was IN I cried for OUT, when OUT I yearned for IN," he remembers. While serving four separate sentences during the 1950s and 1960s, Blake wrote a great many letters, "out of a need to communicate, mostly. And for diversion, a change of pace from the peaceful monotony of the joint I'd gone to so much trouble to bust into." One of his first correspondents was author Nelson Algren, whom he had met in a Chicago night club in 1948. Algren urged him to develop his talent for writing and sent him books and a typewriter. Blake first published a few prison letters in the French existentialist review *Les Temps Modernes,* through the interest of Simone de Beauvoir, who saw the letters at Algren's Chicago apartment. Since 1956 he has published short stories and prison letters in *The Paris Review* and *Esquire.*

The letters below are reprinted from Blake's collection, *The Joint* (1971). They were written to Nelson Algren and to Gertrude Abercrombie, a Chicago painter, in the weeks following his release from the Florida State Penitentiary at Raiford in 1956. Six months later he was reimprisoned for robbing a drugstore. Reflecting on the feelings which led to his fourth imprisonment in 1965, Blake concludes, "I realized I wanted to go back to the tribe, to my people, in the joint. And I said to myself, home is where, when you go there, they can't turn you away. Homesick, how about that? And homesick is where, when you go home, they make you sick."

Blake's letters are noteworthy for their combination of sensitivity and candor. The characterizations of Stony and of Dan, and the quick descriptions of places and of lesser characters, illustrate his capacity to look about him and tell what he sees precisely and economically, with a remarkable range of language. But of even greater interest is his account of himself. His tone has a quality of cool, often amused objectivity, even when he is describing events very stimulating (and often very unflattering) to himself. The homosexual episode with Dan will bear study in this regard. A few weeks later he wrote to Gertrude of this relationship: "What I feel is beyond shame or guilt, or even embarrassment. . . ." Blake candidly portrays himself as a very weak man; what, then, is the source of the strength that he nevertheless seems to salvage at the same time? His feelings on being released from prison—his bout with the problem of confinement and freedom—should be compared with Piri Thomas' (p. 49).

Letters to Nelson Algren
and Gertrude Abercrombie

Charleston, South Carolina
June 30, 1956

Dear Nelson:

Well, I left the Academy after a simple but moving graduation ceremony, with a big sawbuck courtesy the State of Florida, and literally hit the road. Impossible to describe the mixed emotions I had walking away from the penitentiary. For a considerable stretch, I could still see the Rock, where I had spent two and a half years. Could still see the big recreation field and the path around the edge of it where I had walked so many miles in confusion and anxiety. I could even recognize some of the convicts on the field. And I did not, for a fact, know whether I had been cast out of Heaven or Hell. I had left behind the young Sandy, in a grinding scene of farewell that left a knot in my gut.

But when I crossed the bridge over the river and the road took a sharp turn, I was in the world I had not been able to see from behind the fences. I took a deep breath and said to myself, ready or not, motherfuckers, here I come, and felt exhilaration on top of the apprehension.

The nearest town to the prison, Starke, is about five miles, and I guess I walked about half of it. Just dawdling along, looking at the fields, looking at the cows (feeling myself watched as I passed the few houses along the road). A pickup truck came along and gave me a lift into Starke. One of the guards at the prison, a decent sort, but there was some grisly conversation that gave me the feeling of being half In, half Out. From Starke, a bus to Jacksonville. I didn't pause there, it's a miserable town at best and on Sunday it's chilling, and I wanted to get on with it, so I took a city bus to the northern city limits.

I planned to go to Atlanta, and I expected to wait a long time for a ride, Sunday being a bad day. To my surprise, I waited only a little while at the side of the highway, when a bigass Chrysler stopped. I ran towards it and discovered, with a shaft of dismay, that the driver was a spade, very black and very rough looking. Not for nothing all that training in the Rock. I jumped in, with a "Thanks a lot, man."

I told him I was going to Atlanta, he said he was bound for Charleston, but would give me a lift as far as he could. It took me a couple of minutes to surmise this cat was getting blocked. When he told me to open the glove compartment and there was a big jug of Canadian Club, and beer in a cooler on the floor in back, I knew he was getting blocked in a very methodical fashion.

I had a couple of drinks and a beer, and started to get carefree, I hadn't had any real juice in over two years—man, I was *clean*. By the time we got to the turnoff for Atlanta, I had decided to go to Charleston with my buddy. What the hell, I had never *seen* Charleston.

After a bit, though, the paranoid caution I'd acquired in the Rock began to take over, and I started to worry about his driving, which was becoming fairly free-form. A pusher friend of mine in the joint had given me some 'bennies as a bon voyage gift (talk about pagan decency) and I started to ply him with an antidote to all that juice. It seemed only to intensify his anarchical mood.

He was called Stony, he told me, he had been to Jacksonville trying to get his wife to come back to him. He ran a shrimp boat out of Mount Pleasant, across the harbor from Charleston, and was on his way to acquiring another boat. Devoting himself to rising above his station had cost him his wife, and he was a bitter somber black man.

By this time, we were well into Georgia, and started hitting all the small Deep-South towns; somnolent at their brightest, on Sunday they were graveyards with traffic lights. We stopped in one for gas, Darien, I think it was, at a combination gas station and general store. The usual loafers and stooges were hanging around. Stony's manner as he ordered gas was peremptory (the air of a "smart nigger") and the air was full of knives.

We got away from that, though expecting them to call ahead and have the state troopers on our ass. It was odd, too, how the vibrations between Stony and me changed for quite a while after we pulled away from that pool of ugliness.

Somewhere along the road in the afternoon, we saw a truck, decorated with bunting, parked on the shoulder of the road. Stony slowed down, saw it was some kind of black picnic (it was a church outing) and he stopped. Instantly all kinds of black gals, high on beer, were sticking their heads in the window. ("Lookit that beautiful breed. Come outa there, boy!") I found myself surrounded by shrieking satirical black women, found myself dancing with one on a stretch of concrete from some abandoned building, while a radio brayed rhythm-and-blues.

When we finally got away from that, after an eternity of strain and embarrassment for me, Stony said drily, "You don't dig broads, do you?"

"I don't mind broads. I just don't like loud broads."

"Uh huh."

When we got to Charleston it was night, and raining like hell. Stony knew that I was just out of the joint, had no bread, and no place to go. Without a word he drove through Charleston onto the long high humpbacked bridge that crosses the Cooper and Ashley rivers to Mount Pleasant. It was pitch dark, and I could smell the fish and salt smell of the ocean. I followed him out on to a wharf, and we were on board his boat. I spent the night there with him. By the light of the oil lamp in that small fishy cabin, I felt a tenuous security—and a strong sense of brotherly love such as I had not known before.

In the morning we faced the facts—it was impossible for me to stay there. He drove me back to Charleston, and I spent the day missing the strength of Stony, and casing the town. There was no doubt in my mind I had to move fast and I looked for a joint to break into.

That night, prowling, I was picked up on suspicion (I didn't know that Charleston had two fuzz for every citizen) and taken to the station. They shook me down and found my discharge from the Florida joint. The sergeant was indignant.

"Just got out and trying to get back in, huh? Well, you ain't gonna do it, not here." He calls up a mission on Skid Row and tells somebody I'm coming over. They even gave me a ride.

And that's where I am now. An Irishman, the Reverend Ryan runs it, and he seems, I would say, intrigued by my case. Besides, I worked like a dog cleaning up the dormitory they got here, and I play piano for the phony services he holds every night for the winos and drifters. (It's a highly polished grand piano, in good shape, and when all the saints are away, I get to play it.)

I have moments of speculation, about my friends. Permitting me to be run through the grinder, once again. (Out of curiosity, to see what I'd look like, reconstituted?) I think you could say I'm a little different.

That bridge, incidentally, between confinement and freedom—it's a suspension bridge, and it hangs by a thread. Very difficult from the one that leads the other way. That is a triumph of engineering, solid as a rock. I seem to be on the other side of the bridge now, but I'll be goddammed if I know where I am.

Charleston, South Carolina
July 26, 1956

Dear Nelson:

Remember the song that "nothin' could be finah than to be in Carolinah"? Lies, all lies, the guy that wrote it lived in Far Rockaway. In fleeing from the Reverend Ryan and his counterfeit Christians, I've become entangled in a new set of Carolina complications. I got so depressed and fed up with the Rev and his Holy Bobble that I swung with the collection one night (a cool 83¢) and went out looking for trouble.

I figured I'd given the Rev more than 83¢ worth of happiness. Twofold happiness, in fact. When he first saw me, he thought he'd found the 13th Disciple. Later, when the true nature of the beast became apparent, he was able to say he had personally encountered the Anti-Christ. So it was kicks coming and going.

Anyway, I went looking for mischief, and found Dan Cooper. He owns a night club called the Magnolia Room, which is the haunt of the racier element in Charleston aristocracy. And when it comes to genealogy-conscious stuffed owls, Charleston can show the Beacon Hill interlopers a thing or two; everybody I meet descends from a Huguenot.

Dan is one of the Charleston pioneers; the Coopers were on hand to greet the Huguenots and sell them the acres of malarial marshland they settled on. Only Dan is a renegade; instead of living in genteel decline, and hocking the family ormolu, he gets rich running a saloon.

He's a combination of Old South punctilio and dockhand aggressiveness. Thirty-eight years old, stocky, muscled, rugged-ugly, with an unsettling charm that comes from a poetic, perverse, avidly curious mind. Disturbing because while his talk is compelling, fantastic, hypnotic, I can never be sure how much of it is mendacious and satirical.

Last night he transfixed me with a tale of shooting a kangaroo in Australia. He shot him (he said, with passionate sincerity) against his finer instincts. Which also forbid him to shoot deer and elephants. "You couldn't make me shoot an elephant," he declared, and eyed me accusingly as if I had tried. "An elephant is a gentle tender animal."

The kangaroo, shot squarely between the eyes, gave a prodigious leap of more than thirty feet, and died.

"Imagine, a death leap," he said. "But you couldn't make me shoot *another* kangaroo, not for a million dollars!" And he surveyed me challengingly, as if I had the money ready in my pocket.

What bothered me was that I knew he actually had spent considerable time in Australia, and that he was a crack marksman. He practices often on a pistol range he has out here. But I speculated that this yarn was simply a savagely contemptuous way of proving to himself that I was a gullible fool, or too cowardly to say I thought he was a liar. He and I have had this particular passage before, with variations. Then too, it's a peculiarly southern thing, they have perfected the fine art of lying with flair.

Anyway, when I drifted into the joint (with the price of one beer in my pocket) and auditioned, he hired me to play the piano. For the first week, during intermissions, I sat and drank with him, while he questioned me about myself. Did it so deftly, deviously, sympathetically, that I gave him more of the truth than I otherwise might have.

His drinking is a methodical, curiously joyless affair, leading to moods that veer from lyrical to sardonic to ugly. The next day, with the same cold precision and concentration, he lifts weights, rides a horse, shoots a pistol, swims, and shows me no trace of the night's dissipation. I drink only moderately now, and I don't join him in getting bagged. In a way I'm afraid to.

I had only worked a few nights at the club when Dan informed me that he didn't want me living at the Reverend Ryan's. Actually I'd been prowling a little on my own, and wanted to move into the Dock Street Theatre building (Charleston's bohemia; I met a couple of interesting types there). But he moved me out on the island with him.

It's about twenty miles out of Charleston, in the Sound, the open ocean nearby. These are the haunted brooding Carolina lowlands, the tidewater country where the stalwart pioneers displayed false shore lights in order to wreck and plunder ships. Our Murcan heritage. Dan pointed out another island, low on the horizon, which still has Civil War fortifications. The South will rise again.

I'd say this island is only some twenty-five acres, if that. Dan owns the whole tiny continent, the fief of his ancestors. There's a big house where Dan stays, beautiful, ghostly, decadent (sinking into the sand), and I live in an old slave hut "fixed up." There are never any callers, not so far, and we are the sole inhabitants, outside of the "Nigras." All day the stillness is massive, pervasive, dense, except for the pistol shots when he practices, and these trifling noises seem to drown immediately. The atmosphere seems to be waiting, waiting.

From my windows I can see for unbroken miles—miles of water and sky and lonely marshland. Nothing moves but the fishing birds, wheeling languidly in the air, and the palmettos, fanning themselves in the heat. Waiting, waiting.

I try to tell myself *toujours l'audace,* but I don't like at all what I feel. You should have sent me the bread, and by now I'd be safe with some Rush Street Mafia hoodlum in Chicago. I don't know about these southern aristocrats. There's an old Arabian proverb I just made up: "Lie down with the adder, get up sadder."

alors, Jim

Charleston, South Carolina
August 3, 1956

Dear Gertrude:

Because I'm thinking of you and wishing I could be with you in Chicago this morning, I'm making do with this. If it gets rather magenta, forgive, this exile is a much-tried pilgrim.

It is five a.m., the birds are stirring in the palms outside and from the windows I can see the first smoke-gray light of day, turning to silver the dark quiet waters of the sound.

The grizzly who owns this island departed about an hour ago, pleased with himself and his world, and I'm left vibrating and wishing myself far from him and this hostile geechee country.

His name is Dan, one of the Huguenots of Charleston, thirtyish, muscled, an arresting ugliness, befurred like the bear. Nor was it the physical charms that put me where I am. Rather it was the cunning, intelligence, deviousness and imagination of the scoundrel that arrested me. That and the need for bread to maneuver on this burning deck.

He owns the Magnolia, the joint where I play. It's a reproduction of a Carolina-style patio, common brick and wrought iron, deep leather booths, murky darkness, and I furnish the unobtrusive piano music. Aside from a discreet sign outside, there's no indication at all of a night club. Underplayed all the way, which results in SRO all the time, and the host's consistently inimical attitude towards customers merely charms them the more.

Wouldn't you think, from all this, as many gutters as I've been in, that I would gather there was a mind at work? Not that there was a hell of a lot of choice at first, I fell into the joint one night, a month or so out of jail, broke and on my ass, played the piano, was hired. Beautiful piano, sharp club, cordial reception from the aristocrats assembled. Terms were attractive, and I felt I'd finally landed, escaping disaster and the looming threat of return to jail. Somewhere over the rainbow bluebirds fly.

I wish now I'd never left the Rock in Florida, but this maniac didn't come on like a maniac at first.

I should have suspected something from the attitude of the rich rebels that haunt the joint, touched with awe, pathetically glad when he warms to cordiality and offers them a drink. Methodically, he plies everyone around him, occupying his booth like a throne at a levee, the wit and charm flows freely, and there is laughing it up while he sparkles.

Not till he drove me home the first night, sober in an instant, did I discover the wiliness, the savagery of his method. In their innocent faith and drunkenness his companions were but specimens for observation. With cold satisfaction he estimated in what way this or that friend was vulnerable and dispensable, how far from ruin and collapse. This engaging misanthrope was compiling for them a dossier of doom.

I was intrigued by such bland villainy, but chilled, and decided to keep as much distance as was compatible with keeping the job.

It took some skating. Being lonely and strange, I looked about for something interesting in a southern gent. They all seemed to adore my playing and were eager to be friends. I settled on a couple of actors from the Dock Street Theatre. The older one, improbably called Julian Ravenal, had a face ancient with weary satiety; his beautiful young companion a face of placid dreaming wickedness. There was not a doubt in my mind that we three could wind up in some piquant erotic arrangement, the winter seemed made, so hungry was I for just such raffish companions after a long starvation.

The three of us seated at the bar, Dan passed by, swept us casually with a glance, stopped, said to Julian, "I want to see you." Julian murmured, "I know what the son of a bitch will say." I never discovered what that was, but that night after work, Dan said, "If you're really in earnest about wanting to write, Charleston's not the place for you. I want you to see where I live."

He brought me out to the island that morning. It was still dark, the stars were on top of us, the Atlantic breeze murmured in the palms, the waters of the sound whispered liquidly. Naturally, I was enchanted.

He brought out the liquor and stayed to talk (in the small house he said I should "try"). Talked amiably, winningly, mostly of the arts, and without halting the flow of urbanity, complained of the heat and stripped to his shorts. (It may have been the record, "Alborado del Gracioso.") He kept the talk spinning, but the bronzed hairy maleness of him was making the air crackle around me, as difficult to inhale as noodle soup. And while the bastard was gauging his effect, my treacherous face was selling me out. Even while I reached frantically for a coherent reply to some damnable observation he'd made on Christopher Fry, I could read a small tinge of pity in the green eyes as they weighed the imminence of my collapse.

Oh well. I encountered some variations he must have picked up from a Bedouin camel-skinner in one of the murkier streets of Tangier. Even in the holocaust, it crossed my mind that he could not bear to be bested in anything and was satisfying himself that in this, too, I was a mere dabbler. It was an excursion into eroticism along roads I never saw on any map. The calm steady dispassionate degradation and debasement, sure, strong, relentless. When it was done—this silent, contemptuous and curiously onanistic performance—the first daylight was rising over the water. I had been coolly employed, crumpled and discarded like a Kleenex.

Sated, sure of one more egg in the basket, he paced the floor, outlining a program of reclamation and renovation. Regarding me with mixed distaste and pity, "Your hair is too long, too—musicianish." Twined spatulate fingers in it, nearly lifting my scalp. "Uglier than I am," he mused. "You're a find, a positive find." Then, "Cut your hair. At the Magnolia, you won't look hired. You should look like a performing amateur, like a guest sitting down to amuse your friends. Then your professional sound will come as an irritating surprise to your listeners."

He looked at me with distress. "And your clothes . . . well, tomorrow we'll cut your hair and get you some sunburn." On, and on.

He paused, only then aware of my anger and embarrassment, and measured it. I had a strength he knew nothing about: I was wishing I was back in jail. Sensing the hidden reserve, he retreated. "It's only sensible, Mr. Blake—" He brayed the long A as Charlestonians do, and drew a smile from me. "I won't have those moribund bastards sniping at you while you're working for me. I intend to see you succeed in the job, and while I'm behind you they won't dare anything but like you. And nobody but me understands what you're doing."

A formal bow. "I'll be over in the afternoon, if it won't disturb you at your writing. If you need anything, press the button, and one of the Nigras will come."

The Nigras. . . Thus I was appropriated, another weapon in his war with Charleston. When I awoke, it was to gunfire. He was killing the phantom enemy on the pistol range.

Numb with shock, catatonic with dread, I ventured timidly into the kitchen to make myself some coffee. There was brandy left in the bottle, I had a couple of Dexies, and I gulped it all against the fearful appearance.

When he showed it was in riding habit, looking as wide and high as Cyclops. He coolly recorded the degree of my confusion, but his manner was bantering, lightly paternal, there was no sign of the previous night's fever. "Jupiter and I had a good ride, I feel great." He looked closer at me. "Maybe you should eat something. I thought we'd go into town later."

Benevolent commands. The grand seigneur and the poverty-struck transient he has just remembered sheltering in the storm. A nuisance, but noblesse oblige.

Rattled, distrait, I scrambled to escape. "No need to hurry, I brought some trunks, thought we might swim a little first. It's good for a hangover."

So we swam and lay in the sun while he talked quietly, putting the unaccountable waif at ease. Showed me the big house. "My brother left some clothes here. He's about like you. Try them on, those trousers of yours sag in the ass. Is that what they gave you when you left the pen? A shame."

I stand for inspection. He appears to have forgotten me. "Oh yea, much better. By the way. Did you register as an ex-convict when you came into Charleston? State law, six months and a fine. I can probably arrange something. The cops in this town are venal as hell. I wouldn't worry about it."

I look at him. The velvet threat.

So here I am—trapped, beset, lonely, bored, frightened and confused. I don't know anybody except momentarily. We live alone on the island with only the jigs, all starry-eyed for Mistah Dan. "Pappy wuhk for Mistah Dan's daddy. He a caution, Mistah Dan, yuk, yuk, yuk."

But you know something? When I play piano, he listens. And he understands. *Que voulez-vous?*

Later, Jim

Miss Cress

William Carlos Williams (1883-1963) was both a medical doctor and one of America's most original, influential, and productive poets. The present selection is from his longest and most ambitious poem, *Paterson.* Book I of *Paterson* was published in 1946, the fifth book appeared in 1958 when Williams was seventy-five, and parts of a sixth book were written in his last years. Intending *Paterson* to encompass all modern life, Williams recalls that he wanted "to find an image large enough to embody the whole knowable world about me." Thus he interweaves his poetry with excerpts from local historical records, scientific texts, criticism, and letters from friends and patients. The letter reprinted below is taken from the end of Book II. Shorter sections of other letters from the same woman, known to us only as Miss Cress, appear throughout the first two books. Miss Cress, a poet who felt rejected in her attempts to communicate professionally and personally with him, embodies Williams' conviction that women are distanced, divorced, and silenced in modern American society. He has edited her letters slightly to remove details of her personal history, so that her frustration and inability to fulfill herself or to communicate as she wishes may speak for women in general. The anger and indignation of Miss Cress give voice to these women, as she speaks to Paterson of "my failure with you" and of the "serious psychological injury" which has left her "maimed," "misunderstood and misjudged."

In this particular letter, Miss Cress touches on many ideas that bear a closer look, often related to her identity as a woman and as a writer: "those very ideas and feelings which make one a writer with some kind of new vision, are often the *very same ones* which, in living itself, make one clumsy, awkward, absurd, ungrateful . . ." (p. 76); "women in general—will never be content with their lot until the light seeps down to them, not from one of their own, but from the eyes of changed male attitudes toward them . . ." (p. 77); "A completely down and out person with months of stripped bare hardship behind him needs all kinds of things to even get himself in shape for looking for a respectable, important white-collar job" (p. 78). But these ideas seem to spurt out, like the crests of waves of feelings that have been bottled up and are now released by the act of writing. Do Miss Cress' feelings lead her to protest too much? Letters, especially letters like this, provide a good outlet, a good relief from pressure, but they can do more. In the process of writing, sometimes the writer himself discovers thoughts and feelings that he didn't know he had when he started. Feelings and ideas rarely are as separate as we think, or, to put it differently, the separation is often an artificial one. In this letter the feeling changes ("I am too unhappy and lonely to be angry," p. 80), and the reader should ask himself if the ideas do too.

Finally, any strong letter creates interest in the writer and also suggests some particular kind of character in the recipient. What kind of person is writing and what is the implied character of the recipient?

A Letter to
William Carlos Williams

My attitude toward woman's wretched position in society and my ideas about all the changes necessary there, were interesting to you, weren't they, in so far as they made for *literature?* That my particular emotional orientation, in wrenching myself free from patterned standardized feminine feelings, enabled me to do some passably good work with *poetry*—all that was fine, wasn't it—something for you to sit up and take notice of! And you saw in one of my first letters to you (the one you had wanted to make use of, then, in the Introduction to your Paterson) an indication that my thoughts were to be taken seriously, because that too could be turned by you into literature, as something disconnected from life.

But when my actual personal life crept in, stamped all over with the *very same* attitudes and sensibilities and preoccupations that you found quite admirable as *literature*—that was an entirely different matter, wasn't it? No longer admirable, but, on the contrary, deplorable, annoying, stupid, or in some other way unpardonable; because those very ideas and feelings which make one a writer with some kind of new vision, are often the *very same ones* which, in living itself, make one clumsy, awkward, absurd, ungrateful, confidential where most people are reticent, and reticent where one should be confidential, and which cause one, all too often, to step on the toes of other people's sensitive egos as a result of one's stumbling earnestness or honesty carried too far. And that they *are* the very same ones—that's important, something to be remembered at all times, especially by writers like yourself who are so sheltered from life in the raw by the glass-walled conditions of their own safe lives.

Only my writing (when I write) is myself: only that is the real me in any essential way. Not because I bring to literature and to life two different inconsistent sets of values, as you do. No, *I* don't do that; and I feel that when anyone does do it, literature is turned into just so much intellectual excrement fit for the same stinking hole as any other kind.

But in writing (as in all forms of creative art) one derives one's unity of being and one's freedom to be one's self, from one's relationship to those particular externals (language, clay, paints, et cetera) over which one has complete control and the shaping of which lies entirely in one's own power; whereas in living, one's shaping of the externals involved there (of one's friendships, the structure of society, et cetera) is no longer entirely within one's own power but requires the cooperation and the understanding and the humanity of others in order to bring out what is best and most real in one's self.

That's why all that fine talk of yours about woman's need to "sail free in her own element" as a *poet,* becomes nothing but empty rhetoric in the light of your behavior towards me. No woman will ever be able to do that, completely, until she is able *first* to "sail free in her own element" in living itself—which means in her relationships with men even before she can do so in her relationships with other women. The members of any underprivileged class distrust and hate the "outsider" who is *one of them,* and women therefore—women in general—will never be content with their lot until the light seeps down to them, not from one of their own, but from the eyes of changed male attitudes toward them—so that in the meantime, the problems and the awareness of a woman like myself are looked upon even more unsympathetically by other women than by men.

And that, my dear doctor, is another reason why I needed of you a very different kind of friendship from the one you offered me.

I still don't know of course the specific thing that caused the cooling of your friendliness toward me. But I do know that if you were going to bother with me *at all,* there were only two things for you to have considered: (1) that I was, as I still am, a woman dying of loneliness—yes, really dying of it almost in the same way that people die slowly of cancer or consumption or any other such disease (and with all my efficiency in the practical world continually undermined by that loneliness); and (2) that I needed desperately, and still do, some ways and means of leading a *writer's* life, either by securing some sort of writer's job (or any other job having to do with my cultural interests) or else through some kind of literary journalism such as the book reviews—because only in work and jobs of that kind, can I turn into assets what are liabilities for me in jobs of a different kind.

Those were the two problems of mine that you continually and almost deliberately placed in the background of your attempts to help me. And yet they were, and remain, much greater than whether or not I get my poetry published. I didn't need the *publication* of my poetry with your name lent to it, in order to go on writing poetry, half as much as I needed your friendship in other ways (the very ways you ignored) in order to write it. I couldn't, for that reason, have brought the kind of responsiveness and appreciation that you expected of me (not with any real honesty) to the kind of help from you which I needed so much less than the kind you withheld.

Your whole relationship with me amounted to pretty much the same thing as your trying to come to the aid of a patient suffering from pneumonia by handing her a box of aspirin or Grove's cold pills and a glass of hot lemonade. I couldn't tell you that outright. And how were you, a man of letters, to have realized it when the imagination, so quick to assert itself most powerfully in the creation of a piece of literature, seems to have no power at all in enabling writers in your circumstances to fully understand the maladjustment and impotencies of a woman in my position?

When you wrote to me up in W. about that possible censor job, it seemed a very simple matter to you, didn't it, for me to make all the necessary inquiries about the job, arrange for the necessary interviews, start work (if I was hired) with all the necessary living conditions for holding down such a job, and thus find my life all straightened out in its practical aspects, at least—as if by magic?

But it's never so simple as that to get on one's feet even in the most ordinary practical ways, for anyone on *my* side of the railway tracks— which isn't your side, nor the side of your great admirer, Miss Fleming, nor even the side of those well cared for people like S. T. and S. S. who've spent most of their lives with some Clara or some Jeanne to look after them even when they themselves have been flat broke.

A completely down and out person with months of stripped, bare hardship behind him needs all kinds of things to even get himself in shape for looking for a respectable, important white-collar job. And then he needs ample funds for eating and sleeping and keeping up appearances (especially the latter) while going around for various interviews involved. And even if and when a job of that kind is obtained, he still needs the eating and the sleeping and the carfares and the keeping up of appearances and what not, waiting for his first pay check and even perhaps for the second pay check since the first one might have to go almost entirely for back rent or something else of that sort.

And all that takes a hell of a lot of money (especially for a woman)—a lot more than ten dollars or twenty five dollars. Or else it takes the kind of very close friends at whose apartment one is quite welcome to stay for a month or two, and whose typewriter one can use in getting off some of the required letters asking for interviews, and whose electric iron one can use in keeping one's clothes pressed, et cetera—the kind of close friends that I don't have and never have had, for reasons which you know.

Naturally, I couldn't turn to *you,* a stranger, for any such practical help on so large a scale; and it was stupid of me to have minimized the extent of help I needed when I asked you for that first money-order that got stolen and later for the second twenty five dollars—stupid because it was misleading. But the different kind of help I asked for, *finally* (and which you placed in the background) would have been an adequate substitute, because I could have carried out *those* plans which I mentioned to you in the late fall (the book reviews, supplemented by almost any kind of part-time job, and later some articles, and maybe a month at Yaddo this summer) *without* what it takes to get on one's feet in other very different ways. And the, eventually, the very fact that my name had appeared here and there in the book review sections of a few publications (I'd prefer not to *use* poetry that way) would have enabled me to obtain certain kinds of jobs (such as an O. W. I. job for instance) without all that red tape which affects only obscure, unknown people.

The anger and the indignation which I feel towards you now has served to pierce through the rough ice of that congealment which my creative faculties began to suffer from as a result of that last note from you. I find myself thinking and feeling in terms of poetry again. But over and against that is the fact that I'm even more lacking in anchorage of any kind than when I first got to know you. My loneliness is a million fathoms deeper, and my physical energies even more seriously sapped by it; and my economic situation is naturally worse, with living costs so terribly high now, and with my contact with your friend Miss X having come off so badly.

However, she may have had another reason for paying no attention to that note of mine—perhaps the reason of having found out that your friendliness toward me had cooled—which would have made a difference to her, I suppose, since she is such a great "admirer" of yours. But I don't know. That I'm in the dark about, too; and when I went up to the "Times" last week, to try, on my own, to get some of their fiction reviews (the "Times" publishes so many of those), nothing came of that either. And it's *writing* that I want to do—not operating a machine or a lathe, because with literature more and more tied up with the social problems and social progress (for me, in my way of thinking) any contribution I might be able to make to the wellfare of humanity (in war-time or peace-time) would have to be as a writer, and not as a factory worker.

When I was very young, ridiculously young (of school-girl age) for a critical role, with my mind not at all developed and all my ideas in a state of first-week embryonic formlessness, I was able to obtain book-reviews from any number of magazines without any difficulty—and *all* of them books by writers of accepted importance (such as Cummings, Babette Deutsch, H. D.) whereas now when my ideas have matured, and when I really have something to say, I can get no work of that kind at all. And why is that? It's because in all those intervening years, I have been forced, as a woman not content with woman's position in the world, to do a lot of pioneer *living* which writers of your sex and with your particular social background do not have thrust upon them, and which the members of my own sex frown upon (for reasons I've already referred to)—so that at the very moment when I wanted to return to writing from living (with my ideas clarified and enriched by living) there I was (and still am)—because of that living—completely in exile socially.

I glossed over and treated very lightly (in my first conversation with you) those literary activities of my early girlhood, because the work in itself was not much better than that which any talented college freshman or precocious prep-school senior contributes to her school paper. But, after all, that work, instead of appearing in a school paper where it belonged, was taken so seriously by editors of the acceptably important literary publications of that time, that I was able to average as much as $15 a week, very easily, from it. And I go into that now and stress it here; because you can better imagine, in the light of that, just how I feel in realizing that on the basis of just a few superficials (such as possessing a lot of appealingly youthful sex-appeal and getting in with the right set) I was able to maintain my personal identity as a writer in my relationship to the world, whereas now I am cut off from doing so because it was necessary for me in my living, to strip myself of those superficials.

You've never had to live, Dr. P—not in any of the by-ways and dark underground passages where life so often has to be tested. The very circumstances of your birth and social background provided you with an escape from life in the raw; and you confuse that protection from life with an *inability* to live—and are thus able to regard literature as nothing more than a desperate last extremity resulting from that illusionary inability to live. (I've been looking at some of your autobiographical works, as this indicates.)

But living (unsafe living, I mean) isn't something one just sits back and decides about. It happens to one, in a small way, like measles; or in a big way, like a leaking boat or an earthquake. Or else it doesn't happen. And when it does, then one must bring, as I must, one's life to literature; and when it doesn't then one brings to life (as you do) purely literary sympathies and understandings, the insights and humanity of words on paper *only*—and also, alas, the ego of the literary man which most likely played an important part in the change of your attitude toward me. That literary man's ego wanted to help me in such a way, I think, that my own achievements might serve as a flower in his buttonhole, if that kind of help had been enough to make me bloom.

But I have no blossoms to bring to any man in the way of either love *or* friendship. That's one of the reasons why I didn't want that introduction to my poems. And I'm not wanting to be nasty or sarcastic in the last lines of this letter. On the contrary a feeling of profound sadness has replaced now the anger and the indignation with which I started to write all this. I wanted your friendship more than I ever wanted anything else (yes, *more*, and I've wanted other things badly) I wanted it desperately, not because I have a single thing with which to adorn any man's pride—but just because I haven't.

Yes, the anger which I imagined myself to feel on all the previous pages, was false. I am too unhappy and too lonely to be angry; and if some of the things to which I have called your attention here should cause any change of heart in you regarding me, that would be just about the only thing I can conceive of as occurring in my life right now.

La votre

C.

P. S. That I'm back here at 21 Pine Street causes me to add that that mystery as to who forged the "Cress" on that money order and also took one of Brown's checks (though his was *not* cashed, and therefore replaced later) never did get cleared up. And the janitor who was here at the time, is dead now. I don't think it was he took any of the money. But still I was rather glad that the post-office didn't follow it through because just in case Bob did have anything to do with it, he would have gotten into serious trouble—which I shouldn't have welcomed, because he was one of those miserably underpaid negroes and an awfully decent human being in lots of ways. But now I wish it *had* been followed through *after* he died (which was over two months ago) because the crooks may have been those low vile upstate farm people whose year-round exploitation of down and out farm help ought to be brought to light in some fashion, and because if they *did* steal the money order and were arrested for it, that in itself would have brought to the attention of the proper authorities all their other illegal activities as well: And yet that kind of justice doesn't interest me greatly. What's at the root of this or that crime or antisocial act, both psychologically and environ- mentally, always interests me more. But as I make that last statement, I'm reminded of how much I'd like to do a lot of things with *people* in some prose—some stories, maybe a novel. I can't tell you how much I want the living which I need in order to write. And I simply can't achieve them entirely alone. I don't even possess a typewriter now, nor have even a rented one—and I can't think properly except on a typewriter. I can do poetry (though only the first draft) in long-hand, and letters. But for any prose writing, other than letters, I can't do any work without a typewriter. But that of course is the least of my problems—the typewriter; at least the easiest to do something about.

C.

Dr. P.:

This is the simplest, most outright letter I've ever written to you; and you ought to read it all the way through, and carefully, because it's about you, as a writer, and about the ideas regarding women that you expressed in your article on A. N., and because in regard to myself, it contains certain information which I did not think it necessary to give you before, and which I do think now you ought to have. And if my anger in the beginning makes you too angry to go on from there—well, that anger of mine isn't there in the last part, now as I attach this post- script.

C.

And if you don't feel like reading it even for those reasons, will you then do so, *please,* merely out of fairness to me—much time and much thought and much unhappiness having gone into those pages.

Anne Frank

Anne Frank was born in 1929 in Germany. In 1933, her father, Otto Frank, moved his family to the Netherlands to escape the anti-Jewish decrees of the Nazi government, and Anne attended a Montessori school in Amsterdam from 1934 until just after the German invasion of the Netherlands in 1940. Forbidden to continue in a non-Jewish school, she and her older sister Margot then entered the Jewish Secondary School in 1941. In July 1942, to avoid internment in concentration camps, the Franks moved to a hidden apartment in the upper floors of Otto Frank's office building. They were soon joined by Mr. and Mrs. Van Daan and their son Peter, and later by Mr. Dussel, a dentist. The eight of them were kept alive by food and books smuggled in by the office workers in the building.

Three weeks before going into hiding, Anne Frank had received a diary for her thirteenth birthday. "I want to bring out all kinds of things that lie buried deep in my heart," she wrote in an early entry. "I don't want to set down a series of bald facts in a diary like most people do, but I want this diary itself to be my friend, and I shall call my friend Kitty." The entries often read like letters; they tell much of the fugitive's way of life, but even more of a young girl's feelings and thoughts as she passes puberty and begins to grow into womanhood. Anne kept her diary for just over two years, until the hidden apartment was discovered by the Nazi police in 1945. Of the eight inhabitants of the secret rooms, only Otto Frank survived. Mrs. Frank died at Auschwitz, Anne and Margot at Bergen-Belsen in 1945. The diary was first published in 1947 in Dutch and has since been translated into thirty-seven languages.

During the years in hiding, Anne Frank had hopes of becoming a journalist or a writer. A notebook of her short stories and the beginnings of a novel survive. Realizing that "there's a lot in my diary that speaks," she exclaims, "I want to go on living even after my death! And therefore I am grateful to God for giving me this gift, this possibility of developing myself and of writing, of expressing all that is in me." Isolated from any real friends during these years of change, she made the imaginary Kitty a receiver of confidences, a safe outlet for strong feelings, a mirror to self. In the first entry printed below, she reports responding to a previous entry by asking, "Anne, is it really you who mentioned hate? Oh, Anne, how could you!" She then reflects that "these violent outbursts on paper were only giving vent to anger which in a normal life could have been worked off by stamping my feet a couple of times in a locked room, or calling Mummy names behind her back," concluding that "it is better for hard words to be on paper than that Mummy should carry them in her heart." As she well knew, her life was not normal at this time. The passage below was written after seventeen months in hiding and this unusual and extreme situation poignantly reveals what a diary can become to its writer: a way of distancing, or talking out, perhaps of coming to terms with the world around and within.

from *The Diary of a Young Girl*

Sunday, 2 January, 1944

Dear Kitty,

This morning when I had nothing to do I turned over some of the pages of my diary and several times I came across letters dealing with the subject "Mummy" in such a hotheaded way that I was quite shocked, and asked myself: "Anne, is it really you who mentioned hate? Oh, Anne, how could you!" I remained sitting with the open page in my hand, and thought about it and how it came about that I should have been so brimful of rage and really so filled with such a thing as hate that I had to confide it all in you. I have been trying to understand the Anne of a year ago and to excuse her, because my conscience isn't clear as long as I leave you with these accusations, without being able to explain, on looking back, how it happened.

I suffer now—and suffered then—from moods which kept my head under water (so to speak) and only allowed me to see the things subjectively without enabling me to consider quietly the words of the other side, and to answer them as the words of one whom I, with my hotheaded temperament, had offended or made unhappy.

I hid myself within myself, I only considered myself and quietly wrote down all my joys, sorrows, and contempt in my diary. This diary is of great value to me, because it has become a book of memoirs in many places, but on a good many pages I could certainly put "past and done with."

I used to be furious with Mummy, and still am sometimes. It's true that she doesn't understand me, but I don't understand her either. She did love me very much and she was tender, but as she landed in so many unpleasant situations through me, and was nervous and irritable because of other worries and difficulties, it is certainly understandable that she snapped at me.

I took it much too seriously, was offended, and was rude and aggravating to Mummy, which, in turn, made her unhappy. So it was really a matter of unpleasantness and misery rebounding all the time. It wasn't nice for either of us, but it is passing.

I just didn't want to see all this, and pitied myself very much; but that, too, is understandable. Those violent outbursts on paper were only giving vent to anger which in a normal life could have been worked off by stamping my feet a couple of times in a locked room, or calling Mummy names behind her back.

The period when I caused Mummy to shed tears is over. I have grown wiser and Mummy's nerves are not so much on edge. I usually keep my mouth shut if I get annoyed, and so does she, so we appear to get on much better together. I can't really love Mummy in a dependent childlike way—I just don't have that feeling.

I soothe my conscience now with the thought that it is better for hard words to be on paper than that Mummy should carry them in her heart.

Yours, Anne

Wednesday, 5 January, 1944

Dear Kitty,

I have two things to confess to you today, which will take a long time. But I must tell someone and you are the best one to tell, as I know that, come what may, you always keep a secret.

The first is about Mummy. You know that I've grumbled a lot about Mummy, yet still tried to be nice to her again. Now it is suddenly clear to me what she lacks. Mummy herself has told us that she looked upon us more as her friends than her daughters. Now that is all very fine, but still, a friend can't take a mother's place. I need my mother as an example which I can follow, I want to be able to respect her. I have the feeling that Margot thinks differently about these things and would never be able to understand what I've just told you. And Daddy avoids all arguments about Mummy.

I imagine a mother as a woman who, in the first place, shows great tact, especially towards her children when they reach our age, and who does not laugh at me if I cry about something—not pain, but other things—like "Mums" does.

One thing, which perhaps may seem rather fatuous, I have never forgiven her. It was on a day that I had to go to the dentist. Mummy and Margot were going to come with me, and agreed that I should take my bicycle. When we had finished at the dentist, and were outside again, Margot and Mummy told me that they were going into the town to look at something or buy something—I don't remember exactly what. I wanted to go, too, but was not allowed to, as I had my bicycle with me. Tears of rage sprang into my eyes, and Mummy and Margot began laughing at me. Then I became so furious that I stuck my tongue out at them in the street just as an old woman happened to pass by, who looked very shocked! I rode home on my bicycle, and I know I cried for a long time.

It is queer that the wound that Mummy made then still burns, when I think of how angry I was that afternoon.

The second is something that is very difficult to tell you, because it is about myself.

Yesterday I read an article about blushing by Sis Heyster. This article might have been addressed to me personally. Although I don't blush very easily, the other things in it certainly all fit me. She writes roughly something like this—that a girl in the years of puberty becomes quiet within and begins to think about the wonders that are happening to her body.

I experience that, too, and that is why I get the feeling lately of being embarrassed about Margot, Mummy, and Daddy. Funnily enough, Margot, who is much more shy than I am, isn't at all embarrassed.

I think what is happening to me is so wonderful, and not only what can be seen on my body, but all that is taking place inside. I never discuss myself or any of these things with anybody; that is why I have to talk to myself about them.

Each time I have a period—and that has only been three times—I have the feeling that in spite of all the pain, unpleasantness, and nastiness, I have a sweet secret, and that is why, although it is nothing but a nuisance to me in a way, I always long for the time that I shall feel that secret within me again.

Sis Heyster also writes that girls of this age don't feel quite certain of themselves, and discover that they themselves are individuals with ideas, thoughts, and habits. After I came here, when I was just fourteen, I began to think about myself sooner than most girls, and to know that I am a "person." Sometimes, when I lie in bed at night, I have a terrible desire to feel my breasts and to listen to the quiet rhythmic beat of my heart.

I already had these kinds of feelings subconsciously before I came here, because I remember that once when I slept with a girl friend I had a strong desire to kiss her, and that I did do so. I could not help being terribly inquisitive over her body, for she had always kept it hidden from me. I asked her whether, as a proof of our friendship, we should feel one another's breasts, but she refused. I go into ecstasies every time I see the naked figure of a woman, such as Venus, for example. It strikes me as so wonderful and exquisite that I have difficulty in stopping the tears rolling down my cheeks.

If only I had a girl friend!

Yours, Anne

Thursday, 6 January, 1944

Dear Kitty,

My longing to talk to someone became so intense that somehow or other I took it into my head to choose Peter.

Sometimes if I've been upstairs into Peter's room during the day, it always struck me as very snug, but because Peter is so retiring and would never turn anyone out who became a nuisance, I never dared stay long, because I was afraid he might think me a bore. I tried to think of an excuse to stay in his room and get him talking, without it being too noticeable, and my chance came yesterday. Peter has a mania for crossword puzzles at the moment and hardly does anything else. I helped him with them and we soon sat opposite each other at his little table, he on the chair and me on the divan.

It gave me a queer feeling each time I looked into his deep blue eyes, and he sat there with that mysterious laugh playing round his lips. I was able to read his inward thoughts. I could see on his face that look of helplessness and uncertainty as to how to behave, and, at the same time, a trace of his sense of manhood. I noticed his shy manner and it made me feel very gentle; I couldn't refrain from meeting those dark eyes again and again, and with my whole heart I almost beseeched him: oh, tell me, what is going on inside you, oh, can't you look beyond this ridiculous chatter?

But the evening passed and nothing happened, except that I told him about blushing—naturally not what I have written, but just so that he would become more sure of himself as he grew older.

When I lay in bed and thought over the whole situation, I found it far from encouraging, and the idea that I should beg for Peter's patronage was simply repellent. One can do a lot to satisfy one's longings, which certainly sticks out in my case, for I have made up my mind to go and sit with Peter more often and to get him talking somehow or other.

Whatever you do, don't think I'm in love with Peter—not a bit of it! If the Van Daans had had a daughter instead of a son, I should have tried to make friends with her too.

I woke at about five to seven this morning and knew at once, quite positively, what I had dreamed. I sat on a chair and opposite me sat Peter . . . Wessel. We were looking together at a book of drawings by Mary Bos. The dream was so vivid that I can still partly remember the drawings. But that was not all—the dream went on. Suddenly Peter's eyes met mine and I looked into those fine, velvet brown eyes for a long time. Then Peter said very softly, "If I had only known, I would have come to you long before!" I turned around brusquely because the emotion was too much for me. And after that I felt a soft, and oh, such a cool kind cheek against mine and it felt so good, so good. . .

I awoke at this point, while I could still feel his cheek against mine and felt his brown eyes looking deep into my heart, so deep, that there he read how much I had loved him and how much I still love him. Tears sprang into my eyes once more, and I was very sad that I had lost him again, but at the same time glad because it made me feel quite certain that Peter was still the chosen one.

It is strange that I should often see such vivid images in my dreams here. First I saw Grandma so clearly one night that I could even distinguish her thick, soft, wrinkled velvety skin. Then Granny appeared as a guardian angel; then followed Lies, who seems to be a symbol to me of the sufferings of all my girl friends and all Jews. When I pray for her, I pray for all Jews and all those in need. And now Peter, my darling Peter—never before have I had such a clear picture of him in my mind. I don't need a photo of him, I can see him before my eyes, and oh, so well!

Yours, Anne

Friday, 7 January, 1944

Dear Kitty,

What a silly ass I am! I am quite forgetting that I have never told you the history of myself and all my boy friends.

When I was quite small—I was even still at a kindergarten—I became attached to Karel Samson. He had lost his father, and he and his mother lived with an aunt. One of Karel's cousins, Robby, was a slender, good-looking dark boy, who aroused more admiration than the little, humorous fellow, Karel. But looks did not count with me and I was very fond of Karel for years.

We used to be together a lot for quite a long time, but for the rest, my love was unreturned.

Then Peter crossed my path, and in my childish way I really fell in love. He liked me very much, too, and we were inseparable for one whole summer. I can still remember us walking hand in hand through the streets together, he in a white cotton suit and me in a short summer dress. At the end of the summer holidays he went into the first form of the high school and I into the sixth form of the lower school. He used to meet me from school and, vice versa, I would meet him. Peter was a very good-looking boy, tall, handsome, and slim, with an earnest, calm, intelligent face. He had dark hair, and wonderful brown eyes, ruddy cheeks, and a pointed nose. I was mad about his laugh, above all, when he looked so mischievous and naughty!

I went to the country for the holidays; when I returned, Peter had in the meantime moved, and a much older boy lived in the same house. He apparently drew Peter's attention to the fact that I was a childish little imp, and Peter gave me up. I adored him so that I didn't want to face the truth. I tried to hold on to him until it dawned on me that if I went on running after him I should soon get the name of being boy-mad. The years passed. Peter went around with girls of his own age and didn't even think of saying "Hello" to me any more; but I couldn't forget him.

I went to the Jewish Secondary School. Lots of boys in our class were keen on me—I thought it was fun, felt honored, but was otherwise quite untouched. Then later on, Harry was mad about me, but, as I've already told you, I never fell in love again.

There is a saying "Time heals all wounds," and so it was with me. I imagined that I had forgotten Peter and that I didn't like him a bit any more. The memory of him, however, lived so strongly in my subconscious mind that I admitted to myself sometimes I was jealous of the other girls, and that was why I didn't like him any more. This morning I knew that nothing has changed; on the contrary, as I grew older and more mature my love grew with me. I can quite understand now that Peter thought me childish, and yet it still hurt that he had so completely forgotten me. His face was shown so clearly to me, and now I know that no one else could remain with me like he does.

I am completely upset by the dream. When Daddy kissed me this morning, I could have cried out: "Oh, if only you were Peter!" I think of him all the time and I keep repeating to myself the whole day, "Oh, Petel, darling, darling Petel . . . !"

Who can help me now? I must live on and pray to God that He will let Peter cross my path when I come out of here, and that when he reads the love in my eyes he will say, "Oh, Anne, if I had only known, I would have come to you long before!"

I saw my face in the mirror and it looks quite different. My eyes look so clear and deep, my cheeks are pink—which they haven't been for weeks—my mouth is much softer; I look as if I am happy, and yet there is something so sad in my expression and my smile slips away from my lips as soon as it has come. I'm not happy, because I might know that Peter's thoughts are not with me, and yet I still feel his wonderful eyes upon me and his cool soft cheek against mine.

Oh, Petel, Petel, how will I ever free myself of your image? Wouldn't any other in your place be a miserable substitute? I love you, and with such great love that it can't grow in my heart any more but has to leap out into the open and suddenly manifest itself in such a devastating way!

A week ago, even yesterday, if anyone had asked me, "Which of your friends do you consider would be the most suitable to marry?" I would have answered, "I don't know"; but now I would cry, "Petel, because I love him with all my heart and soul. I give myself completely!" But one thing, he may touch my face, but no more.

Once, when we spoke about sex, Daddy told me that I couldn't possibly understand the longing yet; I always knew that I did understand it and now I understand it fully. Nothing is so beloved to me now as he, my Petel.

Yours, Anne

Wednesday, 12 January, 1944

Dear Kitty,

Elli has been back a fortnight. Miep and Henk were away from their work for two days—they both had tummy upsets.

I have a craze for dancing and ballet at the moment, and practice dance steps every evening diligently. I have made a supermodern dance frock from a light blue petticoat edged with lace belonging to Mansa. A ribbon is threaded through round the top and ties in a bow in the center, and a pink corded ribbon completes the creation. I tried in vain to convert my gym shoes into real ballet shoes. My stiff limbs are well on the way to becoming supple again like they used to be. One terrific exercise is to sit on the floor, hold a heel in each hand, and then lift both legs up in the air. I have to have a cushion under me, otherwise my poor little behind has a rough time.

Everyone here is reading the book *Cloudless Morn*. Mummy thought it exceptionally good; there are a lot of youth problems in it. I thought to myself rather ironically: "Take a bit more trouble with your own young people first!"

I believe Mummy thinks there could be no better relationship between parents and their children, and that no one could take a greater interest in their children's lives than she. But quite definitely she only looks at Margot, who I don't think ever had such problems and thoughts as I do. Still, I wouldn't dream of pointing out to Mummy that, in the case of her daughters, it isn't at all as she imagines, because she would be utterly amazed and wouldn't know how to change anyway; I want to save her the unhappiness it would cause her, especially as I know that for me everything would remain the same anyway.

Mummy certainly feels that Margot loves her much more than I do, but she thinks that this just goes in phases! Margot has grown so sweet; she seems quite different from what she used to be, isn't nearly so catty these days and is becoming a real friend. Nor does she any longer regard me as a little kid who counts for nothing.

I have an odd way of sometimes, as it were, being able to see myself through someone else's eyes. Then I view the affairs of a certain "Anne" at my ease, and browse through the pages of her life as if she were a stranger. Before we came here, when I didn't think about things as much as I do now, I used at times to have the feeling that I didn't belong to Mansa, Pim, and Margot, and that I would always be a bit of an outsider. Sometimes I used to pretend I was an orphan, until I reproached and punished myself, telling myself it was all my own fault that I played this self-pitying role, when I was really so fortunate. Then came the time that I used to force myself to be friendly. Every morning, as soon as someone came downstairs I hoped that it would be Mummy who would say good morning to me; I greeted her warmly, because I really longed for her to look lovingly at me. Then she made some remark or other that seemed unfriendly, and I would go off to school again feeling thoroughly disheartened. On the way home I would make excuses for her because she had so many worries, arrive home very cheerful, chatter nineteen to the dozen, until I began repeating myself, and left the room wearing a pensive expression, my satchel under my arm. Sometimes I decided to remain cross, but when I came home from school I always had so much news that my resolutions were gone with the wind and Mummy, whatever she might be doing, had to lend me an ear to all my adventures. Then the time came once more when I didn't listen for footsteps on the staircase any longer, and at night my pillow was wet with tears.

Everything grew much worse at that point; *enfin,* you know all about it.

Now God has sent me a helper—Peter . . . I just clasp my pendant, kiss it, and think to myself, "What do I care about the lot of them! Peter belongs to me and no one knows anything about it." This way I can get over all the snubs I receive. Who would ever think that so much can go on in the soul of a young girl?

Yours, Anne

Hannah Senesh

Hannah Senesh was born in Hungary in 1921, the only daughter of a middle-class Jewish family. Her father, a successful playwright and writer, died when she was six. She attended a Jewish school until she was ten, then a Protestant school that had just begun to admit Jews and Catholics; there she had her first taste of injustice when her election as officer in the school's literary society was reversed because of her religion. She began keeping a diary when she was thirteen and often recorded her desire to become a teacher or a writer.

Becoming a Zionist at seventeen was a turning point in her life. She writes in her diary, "I am immeasurably happy that I've found this ideal, that I now feel firm ground under my feet, and can see a definite goal toward which it is really worth striving . . . . one needs to feel that one's life has meaning, that one is needed in this world." Zionism led her to learn Hebrew, and then to apply to Nahalal Girls' Farm, an agricultural school in Palestine. She emigrated to Palestine just after the outbreak of World War II. The passage below from her diary covers the summer of 1940 and most of her second year in agricultural school.

Hannah Senesh was eighteen when she came to Palestine and her years there were rich and full; they were also years of questioning, of trying to find her own mission in life. Some of her doubts for the future are recorded in the entries below. "I wonder," she asks, "is this way I've chosen the right one?" There is added resonance in her awareness that her adopted country is going through similar stages of adolescence and that the world she knows is as much in transition as she feels herself to be.

Some of her doubts came to an end when, in 1943, she joined a special group of Palestine soldiers training within the British Armed Forces to become resistance fighters and to organize Jewish emigration from occupied countries. Remembering her departure for Palestine four years earlier, she writes in her diary, "Now again I sense the excitement of something important and vital ahead, the feeling of inevitablity connected with a decisive and urgent step." Then she adds, "Concerning the circumstances of my enlistment, and my feelings in connection with it, and with all that led up to it, I don't want to write. I want to believe that what I've done, and will do, are right. Time will tell the rest." Her unit parachuted into Yugoslavia in March 1944. She was captured by the Nazis and executed a few months later in Budapest. She has since become a national heroine of Israel.

In the following passage, Hannah Senesh seems almost bombarded with new experiences and new ideas that demand attention and absorption: everything from a two-week vacation to her thoughts on religion and politics, from Alex "who asked me to marry him" to her sense of loneliness and vague stirrings of what is to come. Her diary makes a noteworthy contrast to that of Anne Frank (preceding), who was isolated from people, confined in space, and thus deprived of the constant stimulation from the outside that characterizes these entries.

Aged Nineteen, from *The Diary*

In the Land
July 5–26, 1940

Aged nineteen

How shall I begin? I have seen and felt so much during these past days. At the moment we're in a eucalyptus grove near Kfar Gil'adi. Miryam is carving her name on a tree, and I'm trying to record everything before a car comes along to take us further.

Early Saturday morning I climbed the hills facing Kfar Gil'adi. Wonderful scenery. And in the brilliance of the beautiful morning I understood why Moses received the Torah on a mountain top. Only on the mountains is it possible to receive orders from above, when one sees how small is man yet feels secure in the nearness of God. From there one's horizons broaden in every respect, and the order of things becomes more understandable. In the mountains one can believe—and must believe. In the mountains one involuntarily hears the query: *'Whom shall I send?'* And the answer, *'Send me to serve the beautiful and the good!'* Will I succeed? Will I be able to fulfil God's command?

In the morning we went on an excursion with several members of the kibbutz. We rode up to Metulla in a kibbutz truck, and from there, along beautiful paths, to Tannur. We returned around noon, and immediately got a ride as far as Dan.

What else can I say about Kfar Gil'adi? It's a large, pleasant, orderly, well-developed kibbutz. Among its members I particularly want to remember Gershon, a kind, charming man. We got to know him on the road, and he took particular care of us. A real pioneer, a man of goodwill; I was delighted to meet him.

Another spot we visited was Dan. It's a little settlement, an island in the heart of a luxuriant region. Its members, mostly Transylvanian immigrants, received us warmly. One of them took particularly devoted care of us. He guided us to Tel-El-Kadi, the source of the River Dan. It's an enchanting spring, next to it a primitive Arab mill. I must note how well, in general, the inhabitants of Dan get on with their Arab neighbours, and even with the Syrians who live across the border. Of course they can't depend entirely upon their goodwill, but the friendly relationship adds to their feeling of security.

We spent a night at Dan, and set out the next morning to tour the countryside. Sasa, Dafna, Sh'ar Yashuv—new settlements whose situations are still difficult. The soil is good, water is abundant, but the land must be cleared of stones, and from a political point of view, carefully guarded. However, should their development remain unhampered by events, they can look forward to a happy future. They have all the requirements to develop into fertile agricultural settlements.

We also visited some of the girls who have graduated from the school at Nahalal. All of them are getting along well, and judging by this we concluded that the school has really prepared them properly, and given them a sound foundation.

The following day we waited at the roadside until evening, and nearly gave up. Towards nightfall we lost patience and agreed to wait only another fifteen minutes, though we certainly did not feel like returning to Kfar Gil'adi. Even Tel-Hai, which lay ahead, is more a symbol than a good place to spend the night. But finally a car came along. If Mother had seen me standing in the middle of the road, hitch-hiking! In fact, if she could have seen me at any time throughout the trip I wonder what she would have said!

We reached Hulata that very evening. It's a young collective with a charming group in a wonderful setting. Excellent opportunities to swim and row. It's superfluous to add that I enjoyed myself enormously.

We rowed on to the mouth of the Jordan, the place where it flows into Lake Huleh. The region is tropical, with papyrus reeds, water lilies, flamingoes, and the placid green waters reflect the surrounding beauty. Later we went rowing with two of the fishermen (twenty men from the collective are fishermen). One of them, Moshe, was 'mine,' the other Miryam's. I saw he liked me, and I liked him a little too. He is really an attractive young man, strong, handsome, simple, likeable.

That evening we went out with the entire fishing fleet to watch them at work. It was a moonlit night. The lake was absolutely calm, and the night still. We could hear only the soft and monotonous splashing of the oars. The muscular bodies of the fishermen swayed left and right in the course of their work. They are familiar with the marshes, with the places where the fish teem, thus cast their nets with assurance. We returned to the collective at 10:30; the nets were left in the marshes until early morning.

When we reached home Moshe visited us for a while. He said he loved me, wanted to kiss me, but I wouldn't let him. He suggested we keep in touch but I said that although I had enjoyed the day we spent together, I saw no point in corresponding since we had so little in common, and in all honesty I was not that interested in him. I wanted to part with a handshake but he kissed my hand.

I thought about him after he left and realized I had actually been rather foolish, and even apprehensive. What harm would there have been in a kiss? Yet I could not. . . I suppose it's ridiculous that I'm still 'waiting for the right one. . . '

We went on early next morning, and reached Safed, the ancient city high in the hills. The scenery is beautiful, the types of people fascinating. We wandered about the town for hours, just looking. Then we turned back to Rosh Pina, and from there continued on to Ginosar, where we spent the night. It's a settlement of young people who are struggling against great odds, and are having considerable difficulty with the soil. We didn't have time to see much of the kibbutz because we left early in the morning so as to reach Afikim before noon.

If only I could describe it all: Lake Kinneret, the Yarmuk River, the Jordan, the old and new kibbutzim, the delightful people we met everywhere, the beautiful excursions we arranged to place around Afikim, Ya'akov who 'sort of' fell in love with me, the beautiful vineyards, the ride to Yarmuk on horseback, the soft nights sitting on the grass, talking, discussing life. It was all beautiful and I could fill an entire notebook describing everything, particularly the way a kibbutz is run, managed. In short, it was all wonderful, absolutely wonderful.

We spent about five days there, then finally left the Jordan Valley by train for the Emek. We saw Bet-Alfa, Tel Amal, Ein-Harod in the distance, and before we knew it our journey ended. I spent the last day of my holiday with the Farkas family at moshav* Merhavya. They were very friendly and hospitable, and the warm family atmosphere was most welcome after so many days of communal life in the various kibbutzim, and I was happy to have the opportunity of comparing the two different ways of life.

Beyond a doubt the kibbutz, economically speaking, is far more rational, and from the point of view of working conditions, simpler; and life, lived on a communal basis, is easier on the kibbutz. But from a spiritual point of view village life has its positive advantages. Certainly it's very obvious that not everyone is suited to life on a kibbutz. I suppose in a matter of years a middle-of-the-road way will be found, which may successfully combine the advantages of both.

The entire holiday was glorious. I was so strongly aware of the beauty of youth in everything I did and saw: in song, in laughter, in boundless energy, in my overwhelming desire to see and absorb everything, to enjoy all the wonders of the Land, to glory in it. And certainly there was endless opportunity to sample every phase of life in the Land, to see all its wonders. This holiday strengthened my faith in the country, in myself, and in our common future. For two weeks I forgot that there is a war raging, that it is so close to us. Haifa has been bombed twice, and on the second occasion there were a good many victims. Here, in Nahalal, life continues as before. At night, blackout; and when Haifa is bombed we hurry to our shelter.

My work consists of field work and housework. Four hours indoors, four hours outdoors.

The books I'm reading: Rachel's poems, which are beautiful. And Kautsky on socialism. This last is a fundamental explanation of Marx's *Das Kapital*. I wasn't acquainted with these works, but now I must familiarize myself with them as well.

---

*A moshav is an agricultural village whose inhabitants possess individual homes and smallholdings but cooperate in the purchase of equipment, the marketing of produce, etc.

Nahalal
September 6, 1940

It's been two years since I last saw my brother, except for the few days spent in Lyon, and I'm so afraid that by the time we meet again we'll be like strangers. The title of a book keeps ringing in my ears: *The Burnt-out Soul* by Lajos Zilahy. It's about two people who are separated for a long time, grow apart, and when they finally meet have nothing to talk about, no mutual interests, and stare at each other like strangers. Two years . . . and how many more? I'm still hopeful. I want to continue being hopeful.

October 11, 1940
Yom Kippur Eve

I want to record a poem I've attempted in Hebrew.

In the fires of war, in the flame, in the flare,
In the eye-blinding, searing glare
My little lantern I carry high
To search, to search for true Man.

In the glare, the light of my lantern burns dim,
In the fire-glow my eye cannot see;
How to look, to see, to discover, to know
When he stands there facing me?

Set a sign, O Lord, set a sign on his brow
That in heat, fire and burning I may
Know the pure, the eternal spark
Of what I seek: true Man.

November 2, 1940

I dream and plan as if there was nothing happening in the world, as if there was no war, no destruction, as if thousands upon thousands were not being killed daily; as if Germany, England, Italy, and Greece were not destroying each other. Only in our little country—which is also in danger and may yet find itself in the centre of hostilities—is there an illusion of peace and quiet. And I'm sitting here, thinking of the future. And what do I think about my personal future?

One of my most beautiful plans is to be a poultry farming instructor, to travel from one farm to another, to visit settlements, to advise and to assist, to organize, to introduce record-keeping, to develop this branch of the economy. In the evenings I would conduct brief seminars for kibbutz members, teach them the important facts of the trade. And at the same time I would get to know the people, their way of life, and would be able to travel about the country.

My other plan is to instruct (seems I only want to teach) children in some sort of school. Perhaps in the institute at Shfeya, or in a regional agricultural school. The old dream is to combine agricultural work with child guidance and teaching.

My third plan—a plan I consider only rarely—has nothing to do with agriculture or children, but with writing. (As I write this the *Unfinished Symphony* is being played on the radio downstairs.) I want to write books, or plays, or I don't know what. Sometimes I think I have talent, and that it's sinful to waste or neglect it. Sometimes I think that if I really do have talent I'll eventually write without worrying about it, that if I feel the need of self-expression, the urge to write, I'll write. The important thing is to have a command of the language. I've made considerable progress during this first year in the Land, but I must do better.

And I've yet another plan. I'd like to live on a kibbutz. This can, however, be in conjunction with the other plans. I'm quite sure I would fit in, if only the possibility of working at something that really interested me existed.

When I visited Merhavya during my holiday, I was able to imagine myself finding purpose and satisfaction in a moshav, but this way of life seems to me to be the least satisfactory. Generally speaking, it's difficult to discover what suits me best since I take easily to all conditions, environments, kinds of work.

I don't think I've written anything about my daily life. I haven't even mentioned my work in the chicken house, which I really like very much. Nor have I said anything about the Bible Society, nor about the end of term celebration. Yesterday was both Pnina's and Miryam's birthday, which I didn't mention either. Nor about my relationship with them, nor my feelings about the school, nor about my visit to the Vadash family in Kfar Baruch. They're really very nice people.

I haven't mentioned my horseback riding, one of my greatest pleasures and one in which, unfortunately, I can indulge only rarely. But that's all right . . . I don't mind leaving all these things out of my diary, but it's impossible for me not to write about a book I recently read. It's called *Jeremiah,* and was written by Kastein. This book made a tremendous impression on me. Considering the present situation of world Jewry, it is extremely timely. He penetrates and analyzes the basic questions of the Jewish religion through his characterization of the Prophet Jeremiah. It is impossible not to be impressed. It was doubly interesting to me since it gave expression to my own interpretation of religion.

Before I was familiar with the point of view of the prophets, and what, in general, the Jewish religion was about, I instinctively objected to empty religious forms, and searched for its true content and morality as expressed in deeds. Needless to say, I only searched but did not always find. Yet at least I tried. I was never able to pray in the usual manner, by rote, and even now neither can nor want to. But the dialogue man holds with his Creator, and about which the prophet preaches, is what I, too, have found. I see the sincere, inner link, even if it comes through struggle within myself, and through some doubt. But I cannot fit into a conventional mould which is, in part, dead, and which in part crystallizes thoughts which are so foreign to me. The book touched my heart because of its sharp expression of all this. In many respects I had the same feeling about Buber's book.

November 27, 1940

A ship filled with illegal immigrants reached the coast. The British would not allow them to disembark, for 'strategic reasons', and for fear there might be spies among them. The ship sank. Part of the passengers drowned, part were saved and taken to Atlit. I brood over this and ask, What is right? From a humane point of view there is no question, no doubt. One must cry out, Let them land! Haven't they endured enough, suffered enough? Do you want to send them far away until the end of the war? They came home; they want to rest; who has the right to prevent them from doing so? But from the point of view of the country . . . really, who knows? They come from German-occupied countries. Perhaps there are elements among them likely to endanger the peace of the Land, particularly at a time when the front is drawing closer.

We argued about these matters among ourselves today. I tried to take the side of the British, but didn't believe in my own argument. Perhaps this is born of our fear of objectively seeing our insoluble dilemma—a tiny country between two formidable adversaries: one the representative of anti-Semitism, the other author of the White Paper. Needless to say, we have but one road: to side with Britain against Germany. The British are taking advantage of our situation. We stand here powerless, awaiting events. We can do nothing else; we're forbidden to take action, though there is certainly a difference between passivity and inactivity.

They're putting out the lights. I don't have time to explain now. That's the way life goes on here. I don't have time to clarify these burning problems even to myself, to get any deep knowledge of the issues involved, and to reach a conclusion. I feel superficial and wanting, lacking in the years normally devoted to contemplation and dedication. I'm afraid those years will never come, not because of my age, but because of circumstances.

December 14, 1940

A ship of refugees sailed for New Zealand. The demonstrations and protests didn't help. The entire Jewish community unanimously demanded that they be allowed to remain in the Land. But the ship sailed during the night, stealthily leaving the coast and Haifa. What is there to add? What can we feel as human beings, as a people? And the question arises, 'How much longer?'

Today is the Sabbath. An empty Sabbath which offers only a part of the day's significance: a day of rest, but not a holiday, not a day of festivity. I read a bit of *The Mother* by Shalom Asch, and an article in a trade journal. There is an emptiness about me; I've no interest in reading any more. I would like to go riding, or to meet people. Perhaps this is a strange parallel, but it stems from the same source: I'd like to break out of my physical bounds, to fly across the fields and feel the wind in my face as I once did during a storm on my way back from the village. Running in the wind I want to cast off everyday shackles, to use words I don't use every day, to meet people I don't meet day after day.

January 2, 1941

I was ill for a few days. I had jaundice. I'm not yet completely recovered. But what worries me most is that I again have those stabbing pains in my heart. I'm terrified by the thought that there may be something wrong. I'm not only afraid of dying young (I really do love life) but also that this may prevent me from following my chosen path and from choosing the work I like best. I haven't spoken to the doctor yet; I postpone doing so from day to day. I want to reassure myself that it amounts to nothing at all. This is what is known as 'ostrich diplomacy.'

February 25, 1941

It's time I wrote about Alex. Even though it's more 'his' affair than something we share. Several things happened last month which I didn't write about, not only because I was busy working at the incubator, but also because I find it difficult to write about matters that aren't entirely clear to me, or about which I am undecided.

I've known Alex for about a year, but only recently have our meetings become more frequent. There is no question at all but that he is extremely fond of me, and that he is serious about me. But what I'm not sure about are my feelings towards him. He is honest, decent, good, and loves me. But I'm convinced we aren't suited. Our educational background, our interests, perspectives are too different. I could probably live a pleasant, simple life with him, but one which would not satisfy or fulfil me.

He recently told me he loves me, and asked me to marry him. I told him that although I respect and like him, I don't feel as he does. Nonetheless, I couldn't say this with absolute certainty, and the matter was left unresolved. He comes to see me as usual, but I asked him to wait a while before demanding a definite answer.

Why this hesitation? If I feel so certain the relationship ought to be discontinued, why continue it? Perhaps because I feel a certain responsibility towards him, and towards myself as well. I want to be as sure as possible before making a decision one way or the other.

But what about myself? This question raises many problems concerning my future, problems not too clear to me, and therefore difficult to solve. I think living on a kibbutz is likely to be an interesting experience for a year or two. But I can't see myself living out my entire life on a kibbutz. On the one hand I feel bound to some form of public service, yet everyone must have personal freedom, quiet, an opportunity for individual initiative and development.

Of course I am fully aware of the advantages of a working life, and of the opportunities it offers. I constantly have new ideas concerning my work, 'invent' things that are reasonably good and make the work easier. I'm now working on a plan connected with the automatic brooder, which is really keeping me busy. I have an idea (though still don't know whether it's feasible) which entails introducing coloured chalk, or some other colouring agent into the chicken, which would then mark every egg. Each hen would have its special marking. This sounds a bit strange and comical, but I don't think the idea is impossible, and want to pursue it further.

However, I think poultry farming, and agriculture in general, are relatively well organized here, or at least eventually will be without any help from me! The agrarian economy is based on a firm foundation, and is in good hands. The general problem here is organizational. Political, educational, and social conditions are very disorganized, though these are exactly the areas in which our future and our fate are determined. I wonder whether I wasn't really meant to lend a helping hand in government? I've noticed at times that I have the ability to influence people, to comfort and reassure them, or to inspire them. Have I the right to waste this facility, hide it, ignore it, and to think about the automatic brooder instead? I don't know whether it's a blessing or a curse that everything I become involved with stimulates my interest so that I instantly begin thinking of ways of repairing, renovating, improving, developing whatever I come in contact with, be it the filling of sacks with potatoes, or the problems of mankind.

I'm not afraid of overestimating myself, and I'm not bragging about my positive qualities. It's not to my credit that I have been given these attributes; I didn't do anything to merit them. They're talents I was born with, probably inherited. The joy is in the knowledge I was granted them, and I think it's my duty to utilize them. I wonder, will I be able to take advantage of them? I wonder, is this way I've chosen the right one? Whatever my future, I won't regret these two years for an instant. Wherever I am, these two years will make it possible for me to understand everything, everyone better: the working man, and all kinds of crafts and trades. These two years will bind me to the Hebrew village, both in deed and spirit.

I started to write about Alex, and seem to have gone far afield. But perhaps therein lies the answer. The problem I now face is whether to marry a man 'just like that', to disrupt my plans, give up my independence. Naturally, it's difficult not to be impressed and flattered by the love of a man of character, a man you respect and esteem. But this is still not love, and thus there is really no reason to continue.

April 12, 1941

Why am I so lonely? Not long ago I strolled through the moshav one evening. It was a fabulous, starry night. Small lights glittered in the lanes, and in the middle of the wide road. Sounds of music, songs, conversation, and laughter came from all around; and far, far in the distance I heard the barking of dogs. The houses seemed so distant; only the stars were near.

Suddenly I was gripped by fear. Where is life leading me? Will I always go on alone in the night, looking at the sparkling stars, thinking they are close? Will I be unable to hear the songs . . . the songs and the laughter around me? Will I fail to turn off the lonely road in order to enter the little houses? What must I choose? The weak lights, filtering through the chinks in the houses, or the distant light of the stars? Worst of all, when I'm among the stars I long for the small lights, and when I find my way into one of the little houses my soul yearns for the heavenly bodies. I'm filled with discontent, hesitancy, insecurity, anxiety, lack of confidence.

Sometimes I feel I am an emissary who has been entrusted with a mission. What this mission is—is not clear to me. (After all, everyone has a mission in life.) I feel I have a duty towards others, as if I were obligated to them. At times this appears to be all sheer nonsense, and I wonder why all this individual effort . . . and why particularly me?

Maya Angelou

Maya Angelou was born Marguerite Johnson in 1929. In early childhood she and her brother Bailey were sent to live with their maternal grandmother, called Momma, in the rural community of Stamps, Arkansas. Her autobiography *I Know Why the Caged Bird Sings* (1970), from which we print the second and fourth chapters, recalls the strength and goodness of her family and community, as well as the painful sense of awkwardness and inferiority which pursued her through adolescence.

After the turbulent childhood described in her autobiography, Maya Angelou studied dance in San Francisco and became a successful night club singer during the 1950s. She toured Europe and Africa with the State Department's *Porgy and Bess*. In New York, she starred in *Cabaret for Freedom* and Jean Genet's *The Blacks*. During 1960 and 1961 she was the northern coordinator for the Southern Christian Leadership Conference. After working as a journalist and university lecturer in Cairo and Ghana, she wrote and produced a television series on African traditions in American society. A book of her poetry, *Just Give Me a Cool Drink of Water 'fore I Diiie,* was published in 1970. While living in New York, she participated in the Harlem Writers' Guild and in women's liberation activities. Speaking in part of her childhood battles with prejudice and circumstance, she writes, "The fact that the adult American Negro female emerges a formidable character is often met with amazement, distaste and even belligerence. It is seldom accepted as an inevitable outcome of the struggle won by survivors and deserves respect if not enthusiastic acceptance."

To evoke the texture of one's own childhood with all its particular quality is not easy. Too often facts remain stripped of the feel, of the child's own special perception. Maya Angelou is particularly successful in recalling the child in her, remembering people and events, smells and sounds, the way they must have seemed then. Note, for example, the dialogue and the many evocative facts that characterize Bailey and her relationship with him. Her adult voice never overshadows the child she evokes. Also noteworthy are her characterization of Uncle Willie and the last passage, in which one memory leads to the next so that the sensuous description of a sausage-making finally leads her to the distinction between people and "whitefolks." Both of these techniques are worth imitating. For another accurate recollection of childhood, see Orwell (p. 176).

Stamps, Arkansas, from
I Know Why the Caged Bird Sings

When Bailey was six and I a year younger, we used to rattle off the times tables with the speed I was later to see Chinese children in San Francisco employ on their abacuses. Our summer-gray pot-bellied stove bloomed rosy red during winter, and became a severe disciplinarian threat if we were so foolish as to indulge in making mistakes.

Uncle Willie used to sit, like a giant black Z (he had been crippled as a child), and hear us testify to the Lafayette County Training Schools' abilities. His face pulled down on the left side, as if a pulley had been attached to his lower teeth, and his left hand was only a mite bigger than Bailey's, but on the second mistake or on the third hesitation his big overgrown right hand would catch one of us behind the collar, and in the same moment would thrust the culprit toward the dull red heater, which throbbed like a devil's toothache. We were never burned, although once I might have been when I was so terrified I tried to jump onto the stove to remove the possibility of its remaining a threat. Like most children, I thought if I could face the worst danger voluntarily, and *triumph*, I would forever have power over it. But in my case of sacrificial effort I was thwarted. Uncle Willie held tight to my dress and I only got close enough to smell the clean dry scent of hot iron. We learned the times tables without understanding their grand principle, simply because we had the capacity and no alternative.

The tragedy of lameness seems so unfair to children that they are embarrassed in its presence. And they, most recently off nature's mold, sense that they have only narrowly missed being another of her jokes. In relief at the narrow escape, they vent their emotions in impatience and criticism of the unlucky cripple.

Momma related times without end, and without any show of emotion, how Uncle Willie had been dropped when he was three years old by a woman who was minding him. She seemed to hold no rancor against the baby-sitter, nor for her just God who allowed the accident. She felt it necessary to explain over and over again to those who knew the story by heart that he wasn't "born that way."

In our society, where two-legged, two-armed strong Black men were able at best to eke out only the necessities of life, Uncle Willie, with his starched shirts, shined shoes and shelves full of food, was the whipping boy and butt of jokes of the underemployed and underpaid. Fate not only disabled him but laid a double-tiered barrier in his path. He was also proud and sensitive. Therefore he couldn't pretend that he wasn't crippled, nor could he deceive himself that people were not repelled by his defect.

Only once in all the years of trying not to watch him, I saw him pretend to himself and others that he wasn't lame.

Coming home from school one day, I saw a dark car in our front yard. I rushed in to find a strange man and woman (Uncle Willie said later they were schoolteachers from Little Rock) drinking Dr. Pepper in the cool of the Store. I sensed a wrongness around me, like an alarm clock that had gone off without being set.

I knew it couldn't be the strangers. Not frequently, but often enough, travelers pulled off the main road to buy tobacco or soft drinks in the only Negro store in Stamps. When I looked at Uncle Willie, I knew what was pulling my mind's coattails. He was standing erect behind the counter, not leaning forward or resting on the small shelf that had been built for him. Erect. His eyes seemed to hold me with a mixture of threats and appeal.

I dutifully greeted the strangers and roamed my eyes around for his walking stick. It was nowhere to be seen. He said, "Uh . . . this this . . . this . . . uh, my niece. She's . . . uh . . . just come from school." Then to the couple—"You know . . . how, uh, children are . . . th-th-these days . . . they play all d-d-day at school and c-c-can't wait to get home and pl-play some more."

The people smiled, very friendly.

He added, "Go on out and pl-play, Sister."

The lady laughed in a soft Arkansas voice and said, "Well, you know, Mr. Johnson, they say, you're only a child once. Have you children of your own?"

Uncle Willie looked at me with an impatience I hadn't seen in his face even when he took thirty minutes to loop the laces over his high-topped shoes. "I . . . I thought I told you to go . . . go outside and play."

Before I left I saw him lean back on the shelves of Garret Snuff, Prince Albert and Spark Plug chewing tobacco.

"No, ma'am . . . no ch-children and no wife." He tried a laugh. "I have an old m-m-mother and my brother's t-two children to l-look after."

I didn't mind his using us to make himself look good. In fact, I would have pretended to be his daughter if he wanted me to. Not only did I not feel any loyalty to my own father, I figured that if I had been Uncle Willie's child I would have received much better treatment.

The couple left after a few minutes, and from the back of the house I watched the red car scare chickens, raise dust and disappear toward Magnolia.

Uncle Willie was making his way down the long shadowed aisle between the shelves and the counter—hand over hand, like a man climbing out of a dream. I stayed quiet and watched him lurch from one side, bumping to the other, until he reached the coal-oil tank. He put his hand behind that dark recess and took his cane in the strong fist and shifted his weight on the wooden support. He thought he had pulled it off.

I'll never know why it was important to him that the couple (he said later that he'd never seen them before) would take a picture of a whole Mr. Johnson back to Little Rock.

He must have tired of being crippled, as prisoners tire of penitentiary bars and the guilty tire of blame. The high-topped shoes and the cane, his uncontrollable muscles and thick tongue, and the looks he suffered of either contempt or pity had simply worn him out, and for one afternoon, one part of an afternoon, he wanted no part of them.

I understood and felt closer to him at that moment than ever before or since.

During these years in Stamps, I met and fell in love with William Shakespeare. He was my first white love. Although I enjoyed and respected Kipling, Poe, Butler, Thackeray and Henley, I saved my young and loyal passion for Paul Lawrence Dunbar, Langston Hughes, James Weldon Johnson and W.E.B. Du Bois' "Litany at Atlanta." But it was Shakespeare who said, "When in disgrace with fortune and men's eyes." It was a state with which I felt myself most familiar. I pacified myself about his whiteness by saying that after all he had been dead so long it couldn't matter to anyone any more.

Bailey and I decided to memorize a scene from *The Merchant of Venice,* but we realized that Momma would question us about the author and that we'd have to tell her that Shakespeare was white, and it wouldn't matter to her whether he was dead or not. So we chose "The Creation" by James Weldon Johnson instead.

What sets one Southern town apart from another, or from a Northern town or hamlet, or city high-rise? The answer must be the experience shared between the unknowing majority (it) and the knowing minority (you). All of childhood's unanswered questions must finally be passed back to the town and answered there. Heroes and bogey men, values and dislikes, are first encountered and labeled in that early environment. In later years they change faces, places and maybe races, tactics, intensities and goals, but beneath those penetrable masks they wear forever the stocking-capped faces of childhood.

Mr. McElroy, who lived in the big rambling house next to the Store, was very tall and broad, and although the years had eaten away the flesh from his shoulders, they had not, at the time of my knowing him, gotten to his high stomach, or his hands or feet.

He was the only Negro I knew, except for the school principal and the visiting teachers, who wore matching pants and jackets. When I learned that men's clothes were sold like that and called suits, I remember thinking that somebody had been very bright, for it made men look less manly, less threatening and a little more like women.

Mr. McElroy never laughed, and seldom smiled, and to his credit was the fact that he liked to talk to Uncle Willie. He never went to church, which Bailey and I thought also proved he was a very courageous person. How great it would be to grow up like that, to be able to stare religion down, especially living next door to a woman like Momma.

I watched him with the excitement of expecting him to do anything at any time. I never tired of this, or became disappointed or disenchanted with him, although from the perch of age, I see him now as a very simple and uninteresting man who sold patent medicine and tonics to the less sophisticated people in towns (villages) surrounding the metropolis of Stamps.

There seemed to be an understanding between Mr. McElroy and Grandmother. This was obvious to us because he never chased us off his land. In summer's late sunshine I often sat under the chinaberry tree in his yard, surrounded by the bitter aroma of its fruit and lulled by the drone of flies that fed on the berries. He sat in a slotted swing on his porch, rocking in his brown three-piece, his wide Panama nodding in time with the whir of insects.

One greeting a day was all that could be expected from Mr. McElroy. After his "Good morning, child," or "Good afternoon, child," he never said a word, even if I met him again on the road in front of his house or down by the well, or ran into him behind the house escaping in a game of hide-and-seek.

He remained a mystery in my childhood. A man who owned his land and the big many-windowed house with a porch that clung to its sides all around the house. An independent Black man. A near anachronism in Stamps.

Bailey was the greatest person in my world. And the fact that he was my brother, my only brother, and I had no sisters to share him with, was such good fortune that it made me want to live a Christian life just to show God that I was grateful. Where I was big, elbowy and grating, he was small, graceful and smooth. When I was described by our playmates as being shit color, he was lauded for his velvet-black skin. His hair fell down in black curls, and my head was covered with black steel wool. And yet he loved me.

When our elders said unkind things about my features (my family was handsome to a point of pain for me), Bailey would wink at me from across the room, and I knew that it was a matter of time before he would take revenge. He would allow the old ladies to finish wondering how on earth I came about, then he would ask, in a voice like cooling bacon grease, "Oh Mizeriz Coleman, how is your son? I saw him the other day, and he looked sick enough to die."

Aghast, the ladies would ask, "Die? From what? He ain't sick."

And in a voice oilier than the one before, he'd answer with a straight face, "From the Uglies."

I would hold my laugh, bite my tongue, grit my teeth and very seriously erase even the touch of a smile from my face. Later, behind the house by the black-walnut tree, we'd laugh and laugh and howl.

Bailey could count on very few punishments for his consistently outrageous behavior, for he was the pride of the Henderson/Johnson family.

His movements, as he was later to describe those of an acquaintance, were activated with oiled precision. He was also able to find more hours in the day than I thought existed. He finished chores, homework, read more books than I and played the group games on the side of the hill with the best of them. He could even pray out loud in church, and was apt at stealing pickles from the barrel that sat under the fruit counter and Uncle Willie's nose.

Once when the Store was full of lunchtime customers, he dipped the strainer, which we also used to sift weevils from meal and flour, into the barrel and fished for two fat pickles. He caught them and hooked the strainer onto the side of the barrel where they dripped until he was ready for them. When the last school bell rang, he picked the nearly dry pickles out of the strainer, jammed them into his pockets and threw the strainer behind the oranges. We ran out of the Store. It was summer and his pants were short, so the pickle juice made clean streams down his ashy legs, and he jumped with his pockets full of loot and his eyes laughing a "How about that?" He smelled like a vinegar barrel or a sour angel.

After our early chores were done, while Uncle Willie or Momma minded the Store, we were free to play the children's games as long as we stayed within yelling distance. Playing hide-and-seek, his voice was easily identified, singing, "Last night, night before, twenty-four robbers at my door. Who all is hid? Ask me to let them in, hit 'em in the head with a rolling pin. Who all is hid?" In follow the leader, naturally he was the one who created the most daring and interesting things to do. And when he was on the tail of the pop the whip, he would twirl off the end like a top, spinning, falling, laughing, finally stopping just before my heart beat its last, and then he was back in the game, still laughing.

Of all the needs (there are none imaginary) a lonely child has, the one that must be satisfied, if there is going to be hope and a hope of wholeness, is the unshaking need for an unshakable God. My pretty Black brother was my Kingdom Come.

In Stamps the custom was to can everything that could possibly be preserved. During the killing season, after the first frost, all neighbors helped each other to slaughter hogs and even the quiet, big-eyed cows if they had stopped giving milk.

The missionary ladies of the Christian Methodist Episcopal Church helped Momma prepare the pork for sausage. They squeezed their fat arms elbow deep in the ground meat, mixed it with gray nose-opening sage, pepper and salt, and made tasty little samples for all obedient children who brought wood for the slick black stove. The men chopped off the larger pieces of meat and laid them in the smokehouse to begin the curing process. They opened the knuckle of the hams with their deadly-looking knives, took out a certain round harmless bone ("it could make the meat go bad") and rubbed salt, coarse brown salt that looked like fine gravel, into the flesh, and the blood popped to the surface.

Throughout the year, until the next frost, we took our meals from the smokehouse, the little garden that lay cousin-close to the Store and from the shelves of canned foods. There were choices on the shelves that could set a hungry child's mouth to watering. Green beans, snapped always the right length, collards, cabbage, juicy red tomato preserves that came into their own on steaming buttered biscuits, and sausage, beets, berries and every fruit grown in Arkansas.

But at least twice yearly Momma would feel that as children we should have fresh meat included in our diets. We were then given money—pennies, nickels, and dimes entrusted to Bailey—and sent to town to buy liver. Since the whites had refrigerators, their butchers bought the meat from commercial slaughterhouses in Texarkana and sold it to the wealthy even in the peak of summer.

Crossing the Black area of Stamps which in childhood's narrow measure seemed a whole world, we were obliged by custom to stop and speak to every person we met, and Bailey felt constrained to spend a few minutes playing with each friend. There was a joy in going to town with money in our pockets (Bailey's pockets were as good as my own) and time on our hands. But the pleasure fled when we reached the white part of town. After we left Mr. Willie Williams' Do Drop Inn, the last stop before whitefolksville, we had to cross the pond and adventure the railroad tracks. We were explorers walking without weapons into man-eating animals' territory.

In Stamps the segregation was so complete that most Black children didn't really, absolutely know what whites looked like. Other than that they were different, to be dreaded, and in that dread was included the hostility of the powerless against the powerful, the poor against the rich, the worker against the worked for and the ragged against the well dressed.

I remember never believing that whites were really real.

Many women who worked in their kitchens traded at our Store, and when they carried their finished laundry back to town they often set the big baskets down on our front porch to pull a singular piece from the starched collection and show either how graceful was their ironing hand or how rich and opulent was the property of their employers.

I looked at the items that weren't on display. I knew, for instance, that white men wore shorts, as Uncle Willie did, and that they had an opening for taking out their "things" and peeing, and that white women's breasts weren't built into their dresses, as some people said, because I saw their brassieres in the baskets. But I couldn't force myself to think of them as people. People were Mrs. LaGrone, Mrs. Hendricks, Momma, Reverend Sneed, Lillie B, and Louise and Rex. Whitefolks couldn't be people because their feet were too small, their skin too white and see-throughy, and they didn't walk on the balls of their feet the way people did—they walked on their heels like horses.

People were those who lived on my side of town. I didn't like them all, or, in fact, any of them very much, but they were people. These others, the strange pale creatures that lived in their alien unlife, weren't considered folks. They were whitefolks.

James Agee

James Rufus Agee was born in Tennessee in 1909. His father died when he was six; four years later, his mother enrolled him in St. Andrew's, an Episcopal school where he met Father James Flye, who became a second father to him and a close friend. He later attended Phillips Exeter Academy and then entered Harvard in 1928. The letter we print below was written while he was a student there.

Agee wrote stories, poems, and journalism as an undergraduate, and he became a professional writer after graduation. As a journalist, his articles for *Fortune* and his cover stories for *Time* on the death of President Roosevelt and the bombing of Hiroshima were model examples of news coverage; and his film column for the *Nation* is now recognized as the first significant film criticism in America. Nevertheless, he must have felt a certain subversion of his full talent in magazine work; he wrote to Father Flye just after joining the staff of *Time* in 1939, "I am thirty and have missed irretrievably all the trains I should have caught."

His first published book was *Permit Me Voyage* (1934), a collection of early poems; *Let Us Now Praise Famous Men* (1941) is the one that comes closest to his ambition of "inventing a sort of amphibious style—prose that would run into poetry when the occasion demanded" with words that *"must* be alive." The book is a lengthy exploration of tenant farmers' lives, originally undertaken with photographer Walker Evans for a series of *Fortune* articles. Agee himself called it "an effort in human actuality, in which the reader is no less centrally involved than the authors and those of whom they tell."

In 1945 he wrote to Father Flye that he was beginning a novel "about my first six years, ending the day of my father's burial," finally published in 1957, posthumously and incomplete, as *A Death in the Family;* it received the Pulitzer Prize for that year. Moving from film criticism to script writing in the late 1940s, Agee worked on several movies, among them *The African Queen.* He tried his hand at so many facets of writing, so successfully, that he made of his professional life what he had said he had always wanted to do with words: "cover the whole range of events." His work was never widely acclaimed during his lifetime, but it has grown in reputation since his death in 1955. Much of his serious work for periodicals has been published in *The Collected Short Prose of James Agee* (1968), *The Collected Poems of James Agee* (1968), and *Agee on Film: Reviews and Comments* (1958). The letter we print, following, suggests his many talents during the time just before, or perhaps just as, "writing" emerged as his primary commitment. College age readers should compare his stage of resolution with that of Hannah Senesh (p. 94) and then chart their own position in relation to the two.

A Letter to Father Flye

[*Cambridge, Mass.*]
November 19th, 1930

Dear Father Flye:

Last summer, and more this fall, I've thought of you often, and wished I could see you, and intended to write you. Until now I haven't even begun and lost a letter to you—as I did several times last spring. I'd like to make this a long letter, and a good one; but as is usual these days I feel fairly tongue-tied the minute I have a sheet of paper before me. If I could see you for any decent length of time, I'd without effort say what here I can't write. But I haven't seen you or even written you in a very long time—and would like if possible to give some sort of account of myself in the interim. That's a difficult job for me, and I don't know just how to go about it.

I suppose the two chief things that have happened to me, and that after a fashion include the others, have to do with what I want to do with my life, and with the nasty process of growing up, or developing, or whatever it may best be called.

So far as I can tell, I definitely want to write—probably poetry in the main. At any rate, nothing else holds me in the same way. As you know, I had two other interests just as strong a few years ago—music and directing movies of my own authorship. These have slowly been killed off, partly by brute and voluntary force on my part, chiefly by the overcrowding of my wish to write. Each of them occasionally flares up; last spring I was all but ready to quit college and bum to California and trust to luck for the rest. And more often, I feel I'd give anything to have forgotten everything but music, because I want so to compose. I really think I could have done it—possibly better than writing. I suppose a native inertia has as much to do with my keeping on with writing instead, as has an instinct (which I over-credit) for knowing that writing is my one even moderate talent.

Up to 6 or 8 months ago, I took this with only sporadic seriousness. But as I read more and wrote somewhat more carefully, it took hold of me more. Last spring I finished a fairly longish poem that finally finished the business. For one thing, I worked harder on it than ever before. And, when it was finished, various people thought it was very good, and encouraged me a good deal. I don't know what I think of the poem itself—but I'm from now on committed to writing with a horrible definiteness.

In fact it amounts to a rather unhealthy obsession. I'm thinking about it every waking minute, in one way or another; and my head is spinning and often—as now—dull with the continuous overwork. The sad part of it—but necessary—is that, most of the time, I'm absorbed in no tangible subject that can be thought through and put aside. The thing I'm trying hardest to do is, to decide what I want to write, and in exactly what way. After a fashion, I know, but it will take a lot more time before I'm able to do it. The great trouble is, I'm terribly anxious to do as well as I possibly can. It sounds conceited; whether it is or not: I'd do anything on earth to become a really great writer. That's as sincere a thing as I've ever said. Do you see, though, where it leads me? In the first place I have no faith to speak of in my native ability to become more than a very minor writer. My intellectual pelvic girdle simply is not Milton-ically wide. So, I have, pretty much, to keep same on a stretcher, or more properly a rack, day and night. I've got to make my mind as broad and deep and rich as possible, as quick and fluent as possible; abnormally sympathetic and yet perfectly balanced. At the same time, I've got to strengthen those segments of my talent which are naturally weak; and must work out for myself a way of expressing what I want to write. You see, I should like to parallel, foolish as it sounds, what Shakespeare did. That is, in general—to write primarily about people—giving their emotions and dramas the expression that, because of its beauty and power, will be most likely to last. But—worse than that: I'd like, in a sense, to combine what Chekhov did with what Shakespeare did—that is, to move from the dim, rather eventless beauty of C. to huge geometric plots such as Lear. And to make this transition without its seeming ridiculous. And to do the whole so that it flows naturally, and yet, so that the whole—words, emotion, characters, situation, etc.—has a discernible symmetry and a very definite *musical* quality—inaccurately speaking—I want to *write symphonies*. That is, characters introduced quietly (as are themes in a symphony, say) will recur in new lights, with new verbal orchestration, will work into counterpoint and get a sort of monstrous grinding beauty—and so on. By now you probably see what I mean at least as well as I do.

Well—this can't be done to best advantage in a novel. Prose holds you down from the possibility of such music. And put into poetic drama, it would certainly be stillborn or worse; besides, much of what I want to get can't well be expressed in dialogue. It's got to be narrative poetry, but of a sort that so far as I know has never been tried. In the sort I've read, the medium is too stiff to allow you to get exactly a finely shaded atmosphere, for instance—in brief, to get the effects that *can* be got in a short story or novel. I've thought of inventing a sort of amphibious style—prose that would run into poetry when the occasion demanded poetic expression. That may be the solution; but I don't entirely like the idea. What I want to do is, to devise a poetic diction that will cover the whole range of events as perfectly and evenly as skin covers every organ, vital as well as trivial, of the human body. And this style can't, of course, be incongruous, no matter what I'm writing about. For instance,

I'm quite determined to include comedy in it—of a sort that would demand realistic slangy dialogue and description.

That leads to another thing—the use of words in general. I'm very anxious not to fall into archaism or "literary" diction. I want my vocabulary to have a very large range, but the words *must* be alive.

Well, that's one thing that keeps me busy: you can see what it leads to. For instance, what sort of characters to use? I want them to be of the present day—at least superficially. Well, present-day characters are obviously good for novels, but not so obviously material for high poetry. Further, just how shall they speak? At the climaxes they certainly can't speak realistically: and in the calmer stretches it would be just as silly for them to speak idealized blank verse.

Life is too short to try to go further into details about this. But it's part of what serves to keep me busy; and unhappy. The whole thing still seems just within the bounds of possible achievement; but highly improbable. There are too many other things crowding in to ruin it: the whole course of everyday life. And yet, of course, it's absolutely necessary for me to live as easily and calmly and fully as I can; and to be and feel human rather than coldblooded about the whole thing. It's only too easy, I find, to be "Human." I care as much as I ever did about other people's feelings, and worry much more when I hurt them. Of course I should be and am thankful for this, but it certainly helps complicate matters. For one thing, with most of my best friends, I feel rather dumb. I don't like to be unhappy or introspective to any noticeable extent in their presence; the result is that I'm pretty dull. Also, most of them are graduated or otherwise removed from the neighborhood, so that I'm pretty awfully lonely a good deal of the time. I'm too preoccupied with the whole business sketched in above to give my courses constant or thorough attention; I don't do much actual work; yet I feel exhausted most of the time. There are a few ways of relaxing, to a certain extent; I like to walk—especially at night; but frequently am too tired. I love to listen to music; but that involves being parasitic around music stores, or cutting classes to get rush seat at Friday symphony. At times, I like to play the piano. Just now, I'm cracked about it, having got a lovely thing by Cesar Franck: Prelude, Eugue and Variation. I played it for three hours tonight. I've been to half-a-dozen movies, one play, and three concerts. Once a week or so Franklin Miner comes in from the suburbs and we take a walk and eat together. I see a young tutor named Ted Spencer when I can . . .

I've got to stop, and get to bed soon. This isn't as full a letter as I'd like to have written, but I'm deadly tired. I hope you'll write soon—and I shall, too. Will you tell me about any further plans for your school? And about yourself and Mrs. Flye? I wish I could see you both again. Are you by any chance coming north this Christmas? Maybe I could see you then. I hope you are.

Much love to you both,

Rufus.

Thomas Merton

Thomas Merton was born in France in 1915. He attended school in France and England, and in 1933 entered Cambridge, where he remembers "breaking my neck trying to get everything out of life that you can get out of it when you are 18. [And] I ran with a pack of hearties who wore multicolored scarves around their necks and would have barked all night. . . ." He refers to these years as his "mental Pompeii," filled with frenetic, empty activity.

Merton then crossed the ocean to attend Columbia University, where he received his B.A. and M.A. degrees; he also taught English, reviewed books, joined a Young Communist Group, and worked in a Harlem settlement house. It was during this time that he attended his first Mass, described below. In 1938 he converted to Roman Catholicism and in 1941 became a Trappist (Cistercian) Monk. He made solemn vows in 1947 and was ordained a priest in 1949.

The vows of a Trappist Monk include the vow of silence, but Merton's taste for solitude was so deep that he became a hermit even in his own monastery, the Abbey of Gethsemani in Kentucky; he lived in a cabin in the woods, where he chopped his own wood, and received no visitors. He walked to the monastery only to say Mass and eat his one meal. Yet he continued to study and write. He was an accomplished poet and essayist, as well as a translator and editor. Merton himself felt and said that he had "written too much and published too much." He was dismayed that his early work was sometimes labeled "inspirational" or "spiritual," but he continued to stand behind his "strong criticism of prevailing trends toward global war, totalism, racism, spiritual inertia and crass materialism," and of the "volatile idealism" that is quick to shift ground when the game gets rough. Among his more than thirty volumes are *Selected Poems* (1959), *Gandhi on Non-Violence* (1965), *Conjectures of a Guilty Bystander* (1966), and *Zen and the Birds of Appetite* (1968).

Merton's autobiography, *The Seven Storey Mountain* (1948), tells of his early years of contradiction and confusion with their implied hunger for community and communion, and his gradual awakening to grace. From it, we reprint the passage below. Though he wrote it ten years later, Merton nevertheless recaptures the feeling of hesitation, even fear, of his first serious entry into a church. The reader should look closely at the language where he describes how he felt the day he made up his mind to go to Mass and at the details with which he now remembers that day. The nature of Merton's relationship to God and grace can be compared to that of Jonathan Edwards (p. 288), St. Teresa (p. 309), and St. Augustine (p. 326). His sense of anxious anticipation, of approaching a momentous turning point, of finding his way, can also be compared to that of Hannah Senesh (p. 94) and of James Agee (p. 112).

First Mass,
from *The Seven Storey Mountain*

. . . . By the time I was ready to begin the actual writing of my thesis, that is, around the beginning of September 1938, the groundwork of conversion was more or less complete. And how easily and sweetly it had all been done, with all the external graces that had been arranged, along my path, by the kind Providence of God! It had taken little more than a year and a half, counting from the time I read Gilson's *The Spirit of Medieval Philosophy* to bring me up from an "atheist"—as I considered myself—to one who accepted all the full range and possibilities of religious experience right up to the highest degree of glory.

I not only accepted all this, intellectually, but now I began to desire it. And not only did I begin to desire it, but I began to do so efficaciously: I began to want to take the necessary means to achieve this union, this peace. I began to desire to dedicate my life to God, to His service. The notion was still vague and obscure, and it was ludicrously impractical in the sense that I was already dreaming of mystical union when I did not even keep the simplest rudiments of the moral law. But nevertheless I was convinced of the reality of the goal, and confident that it could be achieved: and whatever element of presumption was in this confidence I am sure God excused, in His mercy, because of my stupidity and helplessness, and because I was really beginning to be ready to do whatever I thought He wanted me to do to bring me to Him.

But, oh, how blind and weak and sick I was, although I thought I saw where I was going, and half understood the way! How deluded we sometimes are by the clear notions we get out of books. They make us think that we really understand things of which we have no practical knowledge at all. I remember how learnedly and enthusiastically I could talk for hours about mysticism and the experimental knowledge of God, and all the while I was stoking the fires of the argument with Scotch and soda.

That was the way it turned out that Labor Day, for instance. I went to Philadelphia with Joe Roberts, who had a room in the same house as I, and who had been through all the battles on the Fourth Floor of John Jay for the past four years. He had graduated and was working on some trade magazine about women's hats. All one night we sat, with a friend of his, in a big dark roadhouse outside of Philadelphia, arguing and arguing about mysticism, and smoking more and more cigarettes and gradually getting drunk. Eventually, filled with enthusiasm for the purity of heart which begets the vision of God, I went on with them into the city, after the closing of the bars, to a big speak-easy where we completed the work of getting plastered.

My internal contradictions were resolving themselves out, indeed, but still only on the plane of theory, not of practice: not for lack of good-will, but because I was still so completely chained and fettered by my sins and my attachments.

I think that if there is one truth that people need to learn, in the world, especially today, it is this: the intellect is only theoretically independent of desire and appetite in ordinary, actual practice. It is constantly being blinded and perverted by the ends and aims of passion, and the evidence it presents to us with such a show of impartiality and objectivity is fraught with interest and propaganda. We have become marvelous at self-delusion; all the more so, because we have gone to such trouble to convince ourselves of our own absolute infallibility. The desire of the flesh—and by that I mean not only sinful desires, but even the ordinary, normal appetites for comfort and ease and human respect, are fruitful sources of every kind of error and misjudgement, and because we have these yearnings in us, our intellects (which, if they operated all alone in a vacuum, would indeed register with pure impartiality what they saw) present to us everything distorted and accommodated to the norms of our desire.

And therefore, even when we are acting with the best of intentions, and imagine that we are doing great good, we may be actually doing tremendous material harm and contradicting all our good intentions. There are ways that seem to men to be good, the end whereof is in the depths of hell.

The only answer to the problem is grace, grace, docility to grace. I was still in the precarious position of being my own guide and my own interpreter of grace. It is a wonder I ever got to the harbor at all!

Sometime in August, I finally answered an impulsion that had been working on me for a long time. Every Sunday, I had been going out on Long Island to spend the day with the same girl who had brought me back in such a hurry from Lax's town Olean. But every week, as Sunday came around, I was filled with a growing desire to stay in the city and go to some kind of a church.

At first, I had vaguely thought I might try to find some Quakers, and go and sit with them. There still remained in me something of the favorable notion about Quakers that I had picked up as a child, and which the reading of William Penn had not been able to overcome.

But, naturally enough, with the work I was doing in the library, a stronger drive began to assert itself, and I was drawn much more imperatively to the Catholic Church. Finally the urge became so strong that I could not resist it. I called up my girl and told her that I was not coming out that week-end, and made up my mind to go to Mass for the first time in my life.

The first time in my life! That was true. I had lived for several years on the continent, I had been to Rome, I had been in and out of a thousand Catholic cathedrals and churches, and yet I had never heard

Mass. If anything had ever been going on in the churches I visited, I had always fled, in wild Protestant panic.

I will not easily forget how I felt that day. First, there was this sweet, strong, gentle, clean urge in me which said: "Go to Mass! Go to Mass!" It was something quite new and strange, this voice that seemed to prompt me, this firm, growing interior conviction of what I needed to do. It had a suavity, a simplicity about it that I could not easily account for. And when I gave in to it, it did not exult over me, and trample me down in its raging haste to land on its prey, but it carried me forward serenely and with purposeful direction.

That does not mean that my emotions yielded to it altogether quietly. I was really still a little afraid to go to a Catholic church of set purpose, with all the other people, and dispose myself in a pew, and lay myself open to the mysterious perils of that strange and powerful thing they called their "Mass."

God made it a very beautiful Sunday. And since it was the first time I had ever really spent a sober Sunday in New York, I was surprised at the clean, quiet atmosphere of the empty streets uptown. The sun was blazing bright. At the end of the street, as I came out the front door, I could see a burst of green, and the blue river and the hills of Jersey on the other side.

Broadway was empty. A solitary trolley came speeding down in front of Barnard College and past the School of Journalism. Then, from the high, grey, expensive tower of the Rockefeller Church, huge bells began to boom. It served very well for the eleven o'clock Mass at the little brick Church of Corpus Christi, hidden behind Teachers College on 121st Street.

How bright the little building seemed. Indeed, it was quite new. The sun shone on the clean bricks. People were going in the wide open door, into the cool darkness and, all at once, all the churches of Italy and France came back to me. The richness and fulness of the atmosphere of Catholicism that I had not been able to avoid apprehending and loving as a child, came back to me with a rush: but now I was to enter into it fully for the first time. So far, I had known nothing but the outward surface.

It was a gay, clean church, with big plain windows and white columns and pilasters and a well-lighted, simple sanctuary. Its style was a trifle eclectic, but much less perverted with incongruities than the average Catholic church in America. It had a kind of a seventeenth-century, oratorian character about it, though with a sort of American colonial tinge of simplicity. The blend was effective and original: but although all this affected me, without my thinking about it, the thing that impressed me most was that the place was full, absolutely full. It was full not only of old ladies and broken-down gentlemen with one foot in the grave, but of men and women and children young and old—especially young: people of all classes, and all ranks on a solid foundation of workingmen and -women and their families.

I found a place that I hoped would be obscure, over on one side, in the back, and went to it without genuflecting, and knelt down. As I knelt, the first thing I noticed was a young girl, very pretty too, perhaps fifteen or sixteen, kneeling straight up and praying quite seriously. I was very much impressed to see that someone who was young and beautiful could with such simplicity make prayer the real and serious and principal reason for going to church. She was clearly kneeling that way because she meant it, not in order to show off, and she was praying with an absorption which, though not the deep recollection of a saint, was serious enough to show that she was not thinking at all about the other people who were there.

What a revelation it was, to discover so many ordinary people in a place together, more conscious of God than of one another: not there to show off their hats or their clothes, but to pray, or at least to fulfil a religious obligation, not a human one. For even those who might have been there for no better motive than that they were obliged to be, were at least free from any of the self-conscious and human constraint which is never absent from a Protestant church where people are definitely gathered together as people, as neighbors, and always have at least half an eye for one another, if not all of both eyes.

Since it was summer time, the eleven o'clock Mass was a Low Mass: but I had not come expecting to hear music. Before I knew it, the priest was in the sanctuary with the two altar boys, and was busy at the altar with something or other which I could not see very well, but the people were praying by themselves, and I was engrossed and absorbed in the thing as a whole: the business at the altar and the presence of the people. And still I had not got rid of my fear. Seeing the late-comers hastily genuflecting before entering the pew, I realised my omission, and got the idea that people had spotted me for a pagan and were just waiting for me to miss a few more genuflections before throwing me out or, at least, giving me looks of reproof.

Soon we all stood up. I did not know what it was for. The priest was at the other end of the altar, and, as I afterwards learned, he was reading the Gospel. And then the next thing I knew there was someone in the pulpit.

It was a young priest, perhaps not much over thirty-three or -four years old. His face was rather ascetic and thin, and its asceticism was heightened with a note of intellectuality by his horn-rimmed glasses, although he was only one of the assistants, and he did not consider himself an intellectual, nor did anyone else apparently consider him so. But anyway, that was the impression he made on me: and his sermon, which was simple enough, did not belie it.

It was not long: but to me it was very interesting to hear this young man quietly telling the people in language that was plain, yet tinged with scholastic terminology, about a point in Catholic Doctrine. How clear and solid the doctrine was: for behind those words you felt the full force not only of Scripture but of centuries of a unified and continuous and consistent tradition. And above all, it was a vital tradition: there was nothing studied or antique about it. These words, this terminology, this doctrine, and these convictions fell from the lips of the young priest as something that were most intimately part of his own life. What was more, I sensed that the people were familiar with it all, and that it was also, in due proportion, part of their life also: it was just as much integrated into their spiritual organism as the air they breathed or the food they ate worked in to their blood and flesh.

What was he saying? That Christ was the Son of God. That, in Him, the Second Person of the Holy Trinity, God, had assumed a Human Nature, a Human Body and Soul, and had taken Flesh and dwelt amongst us, full of grace and truth: and that this Man, Whom men called the Christ, was God. He was both Man and God: two Natures hypostatically united in one Person or suppositum, one individual Who was a Divine Person, having assumed to Himself a Human Nature. And His works were the works of God: His acts were the acts of God. He loved us: God, and walked among us: God, and died for us on the Cross, God of God, Light of Light, True God of True God.

Jesus Christ was not simply a man, a good man, a great man, the greatest prophet, a wonderful healer, a saint: He was something that made all such trivial words pale into irrelevance. He was God. But nevertheless He was not merely a spirit without a true body, God hiding under a visionary body: He was also truly a Man, born of the Flesh of the Most Pure Virgin, formed of her Flesh by the Holy Spirit. And what He did, in that Flesh, on earth, He did not only as Man but as God. He loved us as God, He suffered and died for us, God.

And how did we know? Because it was revealed to us in the Scriptures and confirmed by the teaching of the Church and of the powerful unanimity of Catholic Tradition from the First Apostles, from the first Popes and the early Fathers, on down through the Doctors of the Church and the great scholastics, to our own day. *De Fide Divina.* If you believed it, you would receive light to grasp it, to understand it in some measure. If you did not believe it, you would never understand: it would never be anything but scandal or folly.

And no one can believe these things merely by wanting to, of his own volition. Unless he receive grace, an actual light and impulsion of the mind and will from God, he cannot even make an act of living faith. It is God Who gives us faith, and no one cometh to Christ unless the Father draweth him.

I wonder what would have happened in my life if I had been given this grace in the days when I had almost discovered the Divinity of Christ in the ancient mosaics of the churches of Rome. What scores of self-murdering and Christ-murdering sins would have been avoided—all the filth I had plastered upon His image in my soul during those last five years that I had been scourging and crucifying God within me?

It is easy to say, after it all, that God had probably foreseen my infidelities and had never given me the grace in those days because He saw how I would waste and despise it: and perhaps that rejection would have been my ruin. For there is no doubt that one of the reasons why grace is not given to souls is because they have so hardened their wills in greed and cruelty and selfishness that their refusal of it would only harden them more. . . But now I had been beaten into the semblance of some kind of humility by misery and confusion and perplexity and secret, interior fear, and my ploughed soul was better ground for the reception of good seed.

The sermon was what I most needed to hear that day. When the Mass of the Catechumens was over, I, who was not even a catechumen, but only a blind and deaf and dumb pagan as weak and dirty as anything that ever came out of the darkness of Imperial Rome or Corinth or Ephesus, was not able to understand anything else.

It all became completely mysterious when the attention was refocussed on the altar. When the silence grew more and more profound, and little bells began to ring, I got scared again and, finally, genuflecting hastily on my left knee, I hurried out of the church in the middle of the most important part of the Mass. But it was just as well. In a way, I suppose I was responding to a kind of liturgical instinct that told me I did not belong there for the celebration of the Mysteries as such. I had no idea what took place in them: but the fact was that Christ, God, would be visibly present on the altar in the Sacred Species. And although He was there, yes, for love of me: yet He was there in His power and His might, and what was I? What was on my soul? What was I in His sight?

It was liturgically fitting that I should kick myself out at the end of the Mass of the Catechumens, when the ordained *ostiarii* should have been there to do it. Anyway, it was done.

Now I walked leisurely down Broadway in the sun, and my eyes looked about me at a new world. I could not understand what it was that had happened to make me so happy, why I was so much at peace, so content with life for I was not yet used to the clean savor that comes with an actual grace—indeed, there was no impossibility in a person's hearing and believing such a sermon and being justified, that is, receiving sanctifying grace in his soul as a habit, and beginning, from that moment, to live the divine and supernatural life for good and all. But that is something I will not speculate about.

All I know is that I walked in a new world. Even the ugly buildings of Columbia were transfigured in it, and everywhere was peace in these streets designed for violence and noise. Sitting outside the gloomy little Childs restaurant at 111th Street, behind the dirty, boxed bushes, and eating breakfast, was like sitting in the Elysian Fields.

Albert Camus

Born in 1913 in the French colony of Algeria, Albert Camus grew up fatherless in the slums of Algiers. He won a scholarship to secondary school at the age of ten and entered the University of Algiers in 1932, supporting himself with a variety of part-time jobs. After a severe attack of tuberculosis prevented him from taking the government examination which would have led to a teaching career, Camus gradually decided to become a writer. In 1935, while he was still at the University, he began keeping notebooks of ideas and sketches for books, scraps of conversation, and impressions of people and places; he continued keeping them until his death in 1960. A typed and slightly edited copy that Camus made in 1954 furnished the text for *Carnets* (1962), a French edition of the early notebooks, translated by Philip Thody in 1963 as *Notebooks 1935-1942*. From this translation we reprint selections from 1936 and 1937.

The events of these years of Camus' life—working for the Communist party, founding and directing the *Théâtre du travail (Workers' Theater)*, graduating from the University of Algiers, writing literary criticism for the newspaper *Alger-Républicain*—are seldom alluded to in the notebooks. Instead, they record a general concern with ethical values, expressed in ideas and drafts for two novels, *La Mort heureuse (A Happy Death)*, posthumously published in 1971, and *L'Etranger (The Stranger)*, 1942. Both explore themes of suicide, death, the absurdity of life, and the beauty and affirmative power in nature. Ideas for two books of essays involving the same themes, *L'Envers et l'endroit (The Wrong Side and the Right Side)*, 1937, and *Noces (Nuptials)*, 1938, are also developed in the notebooks and may be found in the excerpts below.

During World War II, Camus worked as a journalist in Algiers and Paris, becoming, by the war's end, an editor of *Combat*, one of the leading voices of the French Resistance. In the years after the war, he developed his ideas about the nature of modern life in the novels *La Peste (The Plague)*, 1947, and *La Chute (The Fall)*, 1956, in short stories, and in essays such as those in *Le Mythe de Sisyphe (The Myth of Sisyphus)*, 1942, and *L'Homme revolté (The Revolt)*, 1951. He received the Nobel Prize for Literature in 1957.

The *Notebook* is selective and seems mainly to include experiences, themes, and ideas that Camus thought he might later find useful in his writings. Not originally intended for publication, it has much of the spontaneity and fragmentariness of a personal diary—in this case an intellectual and literary diary such as writers often keep. It may be studied for the quality of the writer's mind, the nature of his feelings, and the kind of person he was. It may also be profitably imitated. Its open form makes it easy to use as a storehouse of impressions and ideas for later writing-up, for safekeeping, or just for the pleasure of getting things off one's mind by getting them down on paper.

from *The Notebooks*

M——Every day he used to put the gun on the table. When he had finished work, he would put his papers in order, put his head close to the revolver, place his forehead against it, roll his temples on it, cooling his hot, feverish cheeks against the cool metal. Then, for a long time, he would let his fingers wander along the trigger, playing with the safety catch, until the world grew silent about him, and, already half asleep, his whole being huddled down into the one sensation of this cold and salty metal from which could spring death.

As soon as one does not kill oneself, one must keep silent about life. And, as he woke up, his mouth filled with an already bitter saliva, he licked the barrel, poking his tongue into it, and with a death rattle of infinite happiness said again and again in wonder and astonishment: "My joy is priceless."

M–PART II

The successive catastrophes—his courage—life made up of these misfortunes. He settles down into the painful cloth from which his life is woven, builds up his days around his loneliness, his return home in the evening, his suspicion and disgust. People think he is tough and stoical. Really, things seem to be going quite well. One day, an insignificant incident: one of his friends speaks to him in an offhand manner. He goes home. Kills himself.

I seem to be gradually emerging.
The gentle and restrained friendship of women.

The social question is now settled, and I have found my balance again. In a fortnight's time, I shall decide where I am. Think of my book all the time. From Sunday onwards, immediately start to organize my work.

I must start to build again after this long period of anguish and despair. Finally the sun and my panting body. Keep silent—and have confidence in myself.

April

The first hot days of the year. Stifling. All the animals are lying on their side. At dusk, the air above the town takes on a strange quality. Noises rise and are lost in the air like balloons. Trees and men stand motionless. On the terrace of their houses, the Arab women gossip while waiting for evening to fall. The smell of coffee being roasted also rises in the air. An hour of tenderness and despair, with nothing to embrace, nothing at whose feet to throw oneself, overcome with gratitude.

The heat on the quays—it crushes you with its enormous weight and takes away your breath. The thick and heavy smell of tar rasping in your throat. Annihilation and the taste of death. It is this which is the real climate of tragedy and not, as people usually consider, the night.

Senses and the world—a mingling of desires. And in this body which I keep close to my own, I hold this strange joy which comes down from sky to sea.

Sun and death. The docker with a broken leg. The drops of blood, falling one by one on the hot stones of the quay, sizzle and shrivel up. In the café, he tells me the story of his life. The others have gone. Six glasses stand on the table. He lived alone, in a small house in the suburbs, going home only in the evening to do the cooking. A dog, a tom and a female cat, six kittens, which the cat cannot feed. They die one by one. Every evening, a stiff dead body and filth. Two smells: death and urine mingling together. On the last evening (he stretches his arms across the table, wider and wider apart, slowly and gently pushing the glasses toward the edge) the last kitten died. But the mother had eaten half of it—half a cat left, as you might say. And still all the filth. The wind howling around the house. A piano, in the far distance. He sat in the middle of these ruins and wretchedness. And the whole meaning of the world had suddenly surged up into his mouth. (One by one, the glasses fall from the table, as he stretches his arms wider and wider apart.) He stayed there for a long time, shaking with a vast, wordless anger, his hands in the urine and the thought that he had got to get his dinner ready.

All the glasses are broken. And he smiles. "O.K.," he says to the owner, "I'll pay for everything."

The docker's broken leg. In a corner, a young man laughs silently to himself.

"It's nothing. What hurt most were general ideas." Running after the truck, speed, dust, and din. The wild rhythm of windlasses and machines, the masts dancing on the horizon, the hulls of the vessels lurching from side to side. On the truck: bouncing over the uneven cobbles of the quay. And in the white, chalky dust, in the sun and blood, against the immense and fantastic background of the port, two young men being carried swiftly away, breathless with laughter as if overcome with dizziness.

May

One must not cut oneself off from the world. No one who lives in the sunlight makes a failure of his life. My whole effort, whatever the situation, misfortune or disillusion, must be to make contact again. But even within this sadness I feel a great leap of joy and a great desire to love simply at the sight of a hill against the evening sky.

Contacts with truth, with nature first of all, and then with the art of those who have understood and with my own art if I am capable of it. Otherwise, the sea, sunshine and delight, with the moist lips of desire, will simply lie there in front of me.

Smiling despair. No solution, but constantly exercising an authority over myself that I know is useless. The essential thing is not to lose oneself, and not to lose that part of oneself that lies sleeping in the world.

May

All contacts—does this mean the Cult of the Self? No.

The Cult of the Self presupposes either optimism or a dilettante's attitude toward life. Both nonsense. Do not select a life, but make the one you have stretch out.

Attention: for Kierkegaard, the origin of our suffering lies in comparisons.

Commit yourself completely. Then, show equal strength in accepting both yes and no.

May

These early evenings in Algiers when the women are so beautiful.

May

That life is the strongest force—true. But the starting point of all kinds of cowardice. We must make a point of thinking the opposite.

And now they start to bellow: I am immoral.

They must be translated as meaning: I need to give myself an ethic. Admit it then, you fool. I do too.

Another way of looking at it: you must be simple, truthful, not go in for literary declamations—accept and commit yourself. But we do nothing else.

If you are convinced of your despair, you must either act as if you did hope after all—or kill yourself. Suffering gives no rights.

An intellectual? Yes. And never deny it. An intellectual is someone whose mind watches itself. I like this, because I am happy to be both halves, the watcher and the watched. "Can they be brought together?" This is a practical question. We must get down to it. "I despise intelligence" really means: "I cannot bear my doubts."

I prefer to keep my eyes open.

April 1937

Strange: inability to be alone, inability not to be alone. One accepts both. Both profit.

The most dangerous temptation: to be like nothing at all.

Kasbah: there always comes a moment when you draw away from yourself. A small charcoal fire crackling in the middle of a dark and slimy alleyway.

Madness—beautiful setting for a magnificent morning—the sun. The sky and bones. Music. A finger at the window.

The need to be right—the sign of a vulgar mind.

Story—the man who refuses to justify himself. Other people prefer their idea of him. He dies, alone in his awareness of what he really is—Vanity of this consolation.

May

Mistake of a psychology which concentrates on details. Men who are seeking and analyzing themselves. To know oneself, one should assert oneself. Psychology is action, not thinking about oneself. We continue to shape our personality all our life. If we knew ourselves perfectly, we should die.

(1) The wondrous poetry that precedes love.
(2) The man who makes a failure of everything, even his death.
(3) In our youth, we attach ourselves more easily to a landscape than to a man.
It is because landscapes allow themselves to be interpreted.

May

Projected preface for *L'Envers et l'Endroit.*

In their present state, most of these essays will appear rather formless. This does not spring from a convenient disregard for form, but simply from an insufficient maturity. Those readers who take these pages for what they are, that is to say *essays* in the full sense of the word, can be asked only to follow the general development of the ideas they express. They will then perhaps feel, between the first page and the last, a secret movement which gives them unity. I would be tempted to say that this movement justifies their existence, if I did not look upon all attempts at justification as useless, and if I did not know that people always prefer their own idea of what a man is like to what he really is.

To write is to become disinterested. There is a certain renunciation in art. Rewrite—the effort always brings some profit, whatever this may be. Those who do not succeed fail because they are lazy.

July

In the case of voluntary self-denial, one can go without food for six weeks. (Water is sufficient.) When famine deprives us of food, ten days at the most.
Reservoir of real energy.

Breathing habits of the Tibetan yogis. What we should do is apply our methods of scientific study to experiences of this scale. Have "revelations" in which we do not believe. *What I like to do:* remain lucid in ecstasy.

Women in the street. The warm beast of desire that lies curled up in our loins and stretches itself with a fierce gentleness.

August

On the way to Paris: this fever beating in my temples. The strange and sudden withdrawal from the world and from men. The struggle with one's body. Sitting in the wind, emptied and hollowed out inside, I spent all my time thinking of K. Mansfield, about that long, painful, and tender story of a struggle against illness. What awaits me in the Alps is, together with loneliness and the idea that I shall be there to look after myself, the *awareness* of my illness.

To keep going to the end means not only resisting but also relaxing. I need to be aware of myself, in so far as this is also an awareness of something that goes beyond me as an individual. I sometimes need to write things which I cannot completely control but which therefore prove that what is in me is stronger than I am.

August

Tenderness and emotion of Paris. The cats, the children, the free and easy attitude of the people. The gray colors, the sky, a great show of stones and water.

August 1937

Every day he went off into the mountains and came back speechless, his hair full of grass, and his body covered with the scratches of a whole day's rambling. And each time it was the same conquest without seduction. He was gradually wearing down the resistance of this hostile country, managing to make himself like the round, white clouds behind the solitary pine tree standing out on the crest of a hill, like the fields of pinkish willow herb, rowan trees, and bellflowers. He was becoming part of this fragrant, rocky world. When he reached the distant summit and saw the immense countryside stretching out before him, he felt not the calm peace of love but a kind of inner pact which he was signing with this alien nature, a truce concluded between two hard and savage faces, the intimacy of enemies rather than the ease of friendship.

Gentleness of Savoy.

August 1937

A man who had sought life where most people find it (marriage, work, etc.) and who suddenly notices, while reading a fashion catalogue, how foreign he has been to his own life (life as it is seen in fashion catalogues).

Part I—His life until then.

Part II—Life as a game.

Part III—The rejection of compromise and the discovery of truth in nature.

August 1937

Last chapter? Paris–Marseilles. The descent toward the Mediterranean.

And he went into the water, washing off the dark and contorted images left there by the world. Suddenly, the rhythm of his muscles brought back to life the smell of his own skin. Perhaps never before had he been so aware of the harmony between himself and the world, of the rhythm linking his movements with the daily course of the sun. Now, when the night was overflowing with stars, his gestures stood out against the sky's immense and silent face. By moving his arm, he can sketch out the space between this bright star and its flickering, intermittent neighbor, carrying with him sheaves of stars and trails of clouds. So that the waters of the sky foam with the movement of his arm, while the town lies around him like a cloak of glittering shells.

Two characters. Suicide of one of them?

Anaïs Nin

Anaïs Nin was born in Paris in 1903, the daughter of Spanish pianist and composer Joaquin Nin. When she was eleven, her father deserted the family, and they moved abruptly to New York. During this difficult year, she began keeping a journal, which she has continued to keep with great faithfulness, at first in French and later in English, throughout her life. Since leaving school at fifteen, she has worked as an artist's model, studied Spanish dance, practiced psychoanalysis, taught creative writing, and written ten subjective novels based on her life experience.

Anaïs Nin's diary amounted to 126 handwritten volumes when it was being edited for publication in 1965. *The Diary of Anaïs Nin,* the four published volumes of excerpts, includes only the years from 1931 to 1947. The passage we print here begins the first volume of the published diary, which covers the years from 1931, as her first book *D.H. Lawrence: An Unprofessional Study,* was being published, to 1934, just before her departure from Paris to New York.

The passage is full of concrete detail—the house, the green iron gate, the memory of toys on a bed, alchemists' bottles—but somehow these *things* are surrounded by auras of feeling and suggested significance and seem almost dreamlike. In order to understand how this effect is achieved, one might begin by examining the passage's strong appeal to the senses, especially in the description of the house; the linking of the external thing and the internal state (the gate, the bottles); and, with Osborn, the weaving together of the visible ("the stains and wrinkles on his suit") with the judgments and metaphors ("He acts like a man on a trapeze . . .").

Although the passage reads almost like stream-of-consciousness, a closer examination reveals unifying themes (ordinary life vs. high moments, living vs. hibernating). According to Henry Miller, the diary was begun not as a secret record but "as something to be read by someone else." Perhaps the author's awareness that she was writing the passage *for* someone helps account for its coherence. The student who is asked to write with full honesty, but also to show his work to others, may find himself in a similar situation and may wish to identify for himself the differences between writing for others and writing for oneself.

from *The Diary*

[*Winter, 1931–1932*]

Louveciennes resembles the village where Madame Bovary lived and died. It is old, untouched and unchanged by modern life. It is built on a hill overlooking the Seine. On clear nights one can see Paris. It has an old church dominating a group of small houses, cobblestone streets, and several large properties, manor houses, a castle on the outskirts of the village. One of the properties belonged to Madame du Barry. During the revolution her lover was guillotined and his head thrown over the ivy-covered wall into her garden. This is now the property of Coty.

There is a forest all around in which the Kings of France once hunted. There is a very fat and very old miser who owns most of the property of Louveciennes. He is one of Balzac's misers. He questions every expense, every repair, and always ends by letting his houses deteriorate with rust, rain, weeds, leaks, cold.

Behind the windows of the village houses old women sit watching people passing by. The street runs down unevenly towards the Seine. By the Seine there is a tavern and a restaurant. On Sundays people come from Paris and have lunch and take the rowboats down the Seine as Maupassant loved to do.

The dogs bark at night. The garden smells of honeysuckle in the summer, of wet leaves in the winter. One hears the whistle of the small train from and to Paris. It is a train which looks ancient, as if it were still carrying the personages of Proust's novels to dine in the country.

My house is two hundred years old. It has walls a yard thick, a big garden, a very large green iron gate for cars, flanked by a small green gate for people. The big garden is in the back of the house. In the front there is a gravel driveway, and a pool which is now filled with dirt and planted with ivy. The fountain emerges like the headstone of a tomb. The bell people pull sounds like a giant cowbell. It shakes and echoes a long time after it has been pulled. When it rings, the Spanish maid, Emilia, swings open the large gate and the cars drive up the gravel path, making a crackling sound.

There are eleven windows showing between the wooden trellis covered with ivy. One shutter in the middle was put there for symmetry only, but I often dream about this mysterious room which does not exist behind the closed shutter.

Behind the house lies a vast wild tangled garden. I never liked formal gardens. At the very back is a wooded section with a small brook, a small bridge, overrun with ivy and moss and ferns.

The day begins always with the sound of gravel crushed by the car.

The shutters are pushed open by Emilia, and the day admitted.

With the first crushing of the gravel under wheels comes the barking of the police dog, Banquo, and the carillon of the church bells.

When I look at the large green iron gate from my window it takes on the air of a prison gate. An unjust feeling, since I know I can leave the place whenever I want to, and since I know that human beings place upon an object, or a person, this responsibility of being the obstacle when the obstacle lies always within one's self.

In spite of this knowledge I often stand at the window staring at the large closed iron gate, as if hoping to obtain from this contemplation a reflection of my inner obstacles to a full, open life.

No amount of oil can subdue its rheumatic creaks, for it takes a historical pride in its two-hundred-year-old rust.

But the little gate, with its overhanging ivy like disordered hair over a running child's forehead, has a sleepy and sly air, an air of being always half open.

I chose the house for many reasons.

Because it seemed to have sprouted out of the earth like a tree, so deeply grooved it was within the old garden. It had no cellar and the rooms rested right on the ground. Below the rug, I felt, was the earth. I could take root here, feel at one with the house and garden, take nourishment from them like the plants.

The first thing I did was to have the basin and fountain unearthed and restored. Then it seemed to me that the house came alive. The fountain was gay ahd sprightly.

I had a sense of preparation for a love to come. Like the extension of canopies, the unrolling of ceremonial carpets, as if I must first create a marvelous world in which to house it, in which to receive adequately this guest of honor.

It is in this mood of preparation that I pass through the house, painting a wall through which stains of humidity show, hanging a lamp where it will throw Balinese shadow plays, draping a bed, placing logs in the fireplace.

Every room is painted a different color. As if there were one room for every separate mood: lacquer red for vehemence, pale turquoise for reveries, peach color for gentleness, green for repose, grey for work at the typewriter.

Ordinary life does not interest me. I seek only the high moments. I am in accord with the surrealists, searching for the marvelous.

I want to be a writer who reminds others that these moments exist; I want to prove that there is infinite space, infinite meaning, infinite dimension.

But I am not always in what I call a state of grace. I have days of illuminations and fevers. I have days when the music in my head stops. Then I mend socks, prune trees, can fruits, polish furniture. But while I am doing this I feel I am not living.

Unlike Madame Bovary, I am not going to take poison. I am not sure that being a writer will help me escape from Louveciennes. I have finished my book *D. H. Lawrence: An Unprofessional Study.* I wrote it in sixteen days. I had to go to Paris to present it to Edward Titus for publication. It will not be published and out by tomorrow, which is what a writer would like when the book is hot out of the oven, when it is alive within one's self. He gave it to his assistant to revise.

As soon as I go to Paris too often, my mother looks disapprovingly out of her window, and does not wave good-bye. She looks, at times, like the old women who raise their curtains to stare at me when I take Banquo for a walk. My brother Joaquin plays the piano continuously, as if he would melt the walls of the house.

I take walks along the railroad tracks on bad days. But as I have never been able to read a timetable, I never walk here at the right time and I get tired before the train comes to deliver me from the difficulties of living, and I walk back home. Does this fascination for a possible accident come from the traumatic time when I missed such a death as a child? We had a servant in Neuilly (when I was two years old, and my brother Thorvald just born). My father must have seduced her and then forgotten her. Anyway, she sought revenge. She took my brother and me on an outing and left the carriage, and me beside it, in the middle of the railroad track. But the signal gateman saw us, and as he had seven children of his own, he took a chance on his own life and rushed out in time to kick the carriage out of the way and carry me off in his arms. The event remained in our memory. I still remember the beds covered with toys for the seven children of the man who saved our lives.

Richard Osborn is a lawyer. He had to be consulted on the copyrights of my D. H. Lawrence book. He is trying to be both a Bohemian and a lawyer for a big firm. He likes to leave his office with money in his pocket and go to Montparnasse. He pays for everyone's dinner and drinks. When he is drunk he talks about the novel he is going to write. He gets very little sleep and often arrives at his office the next morning with stains and wrinkles on his suit. As if to detract attention from such details, he talks more volubly and brilliantly than ever, giving his listeners no time to interrupt or respond, so that everyone is saying, "Richard is losing his clients. He cannot stop talking." He acts like a man on a trapeze who must not look down at the public. If he looks below he will fall. He will fall somewhere between his lawyer's office and Montparnasse. No one will know where to look for him for he hides his two faces from all. There are times when he is still asleep in some unknown hotel with an unknown woman when he should be at his office, and other times when he is working late at his office, while his friends are waiting for him at the Café du Dôme.

He has two recurrent monologues. One is patterned after a trial for plagiarism. It seems that a great many people have copied his novels, his plays, and his ideas. He is preparing a long brief to sue them. "They" always steal his briefcase. One of the novels stolen from him is now published, and one of his plays is being acted on Broadway. That is why he does not show his present novel to me or to anyone.

His other monologue concerns his friend Henry Miller. Henry Miller is writing a book one thousand pages long which has everything in it that is left out of other novels. He has now taken refuge in Richard's hotel room. "Every morning when I leave he is still asleep. I leave ten francs on the table, and when I return there is another batch of writing done."

A few days ago he brought me an article by Henry Miller on Buñuel's film *L'Âge d'Or*. It was as potent as a bomb. It reminded me of D. H. Lawrence's "I am a human bomb."

There is in this piece of writing a primitive, savage quality. By contrast with the writers I have been reading, it seems like a jungle. Only a short article, but the words are slung like hatchets, explode with hatred, and it was like hearing wild drums in the midst of the Tuileries gardens.

You live like this, sheltered, in a delicate world, and you believe you are living. Then you read a book (*Lady Chatterley,* for instance), or you take a trip, or you talk with Richard, and you discover that you are not living, that you are hibernating. The symptoms of hibernating are easily detectable: first, restlessness. The second symptom (when hibernating becomes dangerous and might degenerate into death): absence of pleasure. That is all. It appears like an innocuous illness. Monotony, boredom, death. Millions live like this (or die like this) without knowing it. They work in offices. They drive a car. They picnic with their families. They raise children. And then some shock treatment takes place, a person, a book, a song, and it awakens them and saves them from death.

Some never awaken. They are like the people who go to sleep in the snow and never awaken. But I am not in danger because my home, my garden, my beautiful life do not lull me. I am aware of being in a beautiful prison, from which I can only escape by writing. So I have written a book about D. H. Lawrence out of gratitude, because it was he who awakened me. I took it to Richard and he prepared the contracts, and then he talked about his friend Henry Miller. He had shown my manuscript to Henry Miller and Miller had said, "I have never read such strong truths told with such delicacy."

"I would like to bring him to dinner," said Richard. And I said yes.

So delicacy and violence are about to meet and challenge each other.

The image this brings to my mind is an alchemist workshop. Beautiful crystal bottles communicating with each other by a system of fragile crystal canals. These transparent bottles show nothing but jeweled, colored liquids or clouded water or smoke, giving to the external eye an abstract aesthetic pleasure. The consciousness of danger, fatal mixtures, is known only to the chemist.

I feel like a well-appointed laboratory of the soul—myself, my home, my life—in which none of the vitally fecund or destructive, explosive experiments has yet begun. I like the shape of the bottles, the colors of the chemicals. I collect bottles, and the more they look like alchemist bottles the more I like them for their eloquent forms.

Simone de Beauvoir

Simone de Beauvoir was born in Paris in 1908, the daughter of a conservative, middle-class French family. Always a passionately dedicated student, she was educated at a Catholic girls' school and at the Sorbonne, where she received her degree in philosophy in 1929. She has written extensively on her development through childhood and adulthood, both in novels and in autobiographical works such as the trilogy *Mémoires d'une jeune fille rangée (Memoirs of a Dutiful Daughter,* 1958, *La Force de l'âge (The Prime of Life),* 1960, and *La Force des choses (The Force of Circumstance),* 1962. She presents her girlhood as a continuing struggle to free herself from the expectations and values of her family, in order to make her own choices based on her own character. As a small child, she remembers, "I felt I was not only the prey of grown-up wills, but also of their consciences, which sometimes played the role of a kindly mirror in which I was unwillingly and unrecognizably reflected." Moving from Catholicism to atheism, she decided in early adolescence to become a writer, feeling that "by writing a work based on my own experience I would recreate myself and justify my existence." From her adolescence on she sought with great vigor and optimism to replace conventionality with "a whole way of life which I would build up with my own hands."

The central figure of Simone's childhood, outside of her family, was her friend Zaza, to whom she was tremendously devoted. The first volume of her autobiography closes as Zaza dies, never successfully breaking away from her background to find personal freedom.

Simone de Beauvoir's young adulthood was as profoundly influenced by her first encounters with Jean-Paul Sartre and his friends, whom she met as fellow-students at the Sorbonne. "It was the first time in my life that I had felt intellectually inferior to anyone else," she remembers, adding that "after so many years of arrogant solitude, it was something serious to discover that I wasn't the One and Only, but one among many, by no means first, and suddenly uncertain of my true capacity." She and Sartre soon felt a profound personal and philosophical bond which has permanently united their lives and work. With Sartre, she has edited *Les Temps modernes* since 1945. In addition to her works of fiction, philosophy, and autobiography, she has produced in *Le Deuxième sexe (The Second Sex),* 1949, and *La Vieillesse (The Coming of Age),* 1970, monumental studies of the social position of women and of the aged, uniting rigorous factual analysis with personal sensitivity and concern. Her novel *The Mandarins* was awarded the Prix Goncourt in 1954.

After receiving her degree, Simone de Beauvoir set herself up at the age of twenty-one in a one-room fifth-floor apartment in Paris to begin her career as a writer. She was very pleased at the outset with her unaccustomed freedom, but she soon encountered psychological difficulties, described in the passage below from *The Prime of Life*. The passage records the first stirrings of her consciousness of the special plight of being a woman in a traditional society and of the embarrassing urging of human sexuality. Her record of her moods of doubt and humiliation may be compared with that of James Agee (p. 112) at a similar age. Many a reader will sympathize with her report "I had no idea what to write *about*" and find in the passage itself his own solution to the problem. As Mlle. de Beauvoir says in her preface to *The Prime of Life:* "It may be that such an inquiry concerns no one but myself. Not so; if any individual—a Pepys or a Rousseau, an exceptional or a run-of-the-mill character—reveals himself honestly, everyone, more or less, becomes involved. It is impossible for him to shed light on his own life without at some point illuminating the lives of others."

from *The Prime of Life*

At the age of nineteen, despite my ignorance and incompetence, I had genuinely wanted to write: I felt myself an exile, whose one remedy against solitude lay in self-expression. But now I no longer experienced this urge at all. In one way or another, every book is an appeal for help: but to whom, at this point, should I appeal—and for what help? I had all I could want. My emotions, my joys and pleasures, all constantly dragged me forward into the future with overwhelming intensity. Faced with such a press of people and events, I lacked the distance which lends perspective to one's judgments and enables one to discuss them. I could not bring myself to give up anything, and hence I was incapable of making my choice; the result was that I sank into a delectable but chaotic stew. As far as my past life was concerned, I did, it is true, feel a reaction against it: I had had more than enough of that phase. But it neither stirred me to nostalgia, which might have made me want to revive it, nor did it fire the kind of grudging resentment that drives one to a settling of old scores. I felt mere indifference, for which silence seemed the only appropriate expression.

Meanwhile, remembering my previous resolutions—not that Sartre would ever let me forget them—I decided to start work on a novel. I sat down on one of my orange-covered chairs, breathed in the fumes of the kerosene stove, and stared, with a perplexed eye, at the blank sheet of paper in front of me: I had no idea what to write *about.* Any literary work involves a portrayal of the world; I found the world's crude immediacy stupefying, and saw nothing in it; therefore I had no viewpoint of it to present. My only way out of this difficulty was by copying the imagery that other writers had employed for the task: without admitting it to myself, I was indulging in pastiche, an always regrettable habit. But why did I make things worse by choosing *Le Grand Meaulnes* and *Dusty Answer* as my models? I had loved these books. I wanted literature to get away from common humanity, and they delighted me by opening up a magic world for my benefit. Jacques and Herbaud had encouraged my taste for sublimation of this sort, since they themselves both went in for it with some enthusiasm. Sartre, on the other hand, found all faking or illusion repellent; yet this did not stop his daily myth-making activities for our joint amusement, and in his own writings fable and legend still played a considerable part. At all events, he had, without success, advised me to be honest in my work: the only kind of honesty open to me at this point would have been silence.

So I set about manufacturing a story that, I hoped, would borrow a little of Alain Fournier's and Rosamond Lehmann's magic. There was an old château with a big park, where a young girl lived with her gloomy, taciturn father. One day, out on a walk, she passed three handsome, carefree young creatures who were staying in a nearby manor house for the holidays. She reminded herself that she was eighteen years old, and a sudden urge came upon her to go where she pleased and to see something of the world. She managed to get away to Paris, where she met a girl resembling Stépha, and an older woman rather like Madame Lemaire. She was to have had all sorts of most poetic adventures, but just what they were I never found out, since I gave up at the third chapter. I became vaguely aware that the magic wasn't working in my case, though this didn't prevent me from chasing it stubbornly, and for a long time. I still kept a touch of original "Delly" about me, which was very noticeable in the first drafts of my novels.

My work lacked all real conviction. Sometimes I felt I was doing a school assignment, sometimes that I had lapsed into parody. But in any case there was no hurry. I was happy, and for the time being that was enough. Yet after a while I found it *wasn't* enough. I had hoped for something very different from myself. I no longer kept a private diary, but I still scribbled things down in a notebook from time to time: "I cannot reconcile myself to living if there is no purpose in my life," I wrote, in the spring of 1930, and a little later, in June: "I have lost my pride—and that means I have lost everything." I had sometimes lived at odds with my environment, but never with myself; during those eighteen months I learned that one's real and imagined desires may be very different—and learned, too, something of the malaise which such uncertainty can engender. Though I still enthusiastically ran after all the good things of this world, I was beginning to think that they kept me from my real vocation: I was well on the road to self-betrayal and self-destruction. I regarded this conflict—at least, there were moments when I did—as a tragedy; but looking back I fancy there was very little to worry about. In those days I could always make something out of nothing at the drop of a hat.

What, you may ask, did I reproach myself with? In the first place, there was the overeasy tenor of my life. To begin with, I had reveled in this, but very shortly it began to disgust me. The scholar in me began to revolt against such feckless truancy. My random reading was for amusement only, and led me nowhere. I did no work apart from my writing, and that I undertook without any deep conviction, because Sartre was adamant that I should. Many young people of both sexes who have the courage and ambition to battle through a tough academic course experience this kind of disappointment afterward. The struggle itself, the mastery of a subject, the daily rivalry—these bring satisfaction of a special kind, for which there is no substitute. The more passive pleasures of idleness seem dull by comparison, and time spent on other things, however dazzling, is time unjustifiably wasted.

Besides, I had not yet recovered from the blow which my first encounter with Sartre's *petits camarades* had inflicted upon me. In order to recover my self-esteem to any extent I should have had to *do* something, and do it well; I chose to be idle. My indolence confirmed my conviction that I was a mediocre sort of person. I was, beyond any doubt, abdicating. Perhaps it is hard for anyone to learn the art of peaceful coexistence with somebody else: certainly I had never been capable of it. Either I reigned supreme or sank into the abyss. During my subjugation by Zaza I plumbed the black depths of humility; now the same story was repeated, except that I fell from a greater height, and my self-confidence had been more rudely shaken. In both cases I preserved my peace of mind: so fascinated was I by the other person that I forgot myself, so much so indeed that no part of me remained to register the statement: *I am nothing.* Yet this voice did raise itself fitfully; and then I realized that I had ceased to exist on my own account, and was now a mere parasite. When I quarreled with Herbaud he accused me of having betrayed that concept of individualism which had previously won me his esteem; and I had to admit he was right. What caused me much greater pain was the fact that Sartre himself felt anxious about me. "You used to be full of little ideas, Beaver," he said, in an astonished voice. He also told me to watch out that I didn't become a female introvert. There was, indeed, no danger of my turning into a mere housewife, but he compared me to those heroines of Meredith's who after a long battle for their independence ended up quite content to be some man's helpmeet. I was furious with myself for disappointing him in this way. My previous distrust of happiness had, after all, been justified. However attractive it might appear, it dragged me into every kind of compromise. When I first met Sartre I felt I had everything, that in his company I could not fail to fulfill myself completely. Now I reflected that to adapt one's outlook to another person's salvation is the surest and quickest way of losing him.

But why, when all is said and done, should I have felt such qualms of remorse? I was certainly not a militant feminist: I had no theories concerning the rights and duties of women. Just as previously I had refused to be labeled "a child," so now I did not think of myself as "a woman": I was *me.* It was in this particular that I felt myself at fault.

The notion of salvation had lingered on in my mind after belief in God had vanished, and my chief conviction was that each individual was responsible for securing his own. The difficulty nagging at me was not so much a social as a moral, almost a religious, contradiction in terms. To accept a secondary status in life, that of a merely ancillary being, would have been to degrade my own humanity; and my entire past rose up in protest against such a step. Obviously, the only reason for the problem presenting itself to me in these terms was because I happened to be a woman. But it was qua individual that I attempted to resolve it. The idea of feminism or the sex war made no sense whatever to me.

My resentment would have been less acute if I had not at the same time been forced to endure another, and more agonizing, humiliation, which stemmed not from my external relationship but rather from a private and intimate lack of harmony within myself. I had surrendered my virginity with glad abandon: when heart, head, and body are all in unison, there is high delight to be had from the physical expression of that oneness. At first I had experienced nothing but pleasure, which matched my natural optimism and was balm to my pride. But very soon circumstances forced me into awareness of something which I had uneasily foreseen when I was twenty: simple physical desire. I knew nothing of such an appetite: I had never in my life suffered from hunger, or thirst, or lack of sleep. Now, suddenly, I fell a victim to it. I was separated from Sartre for days or even weeks at a time. On our Sundays in Tours we were too shy to go up to a hotel bedroom in broad daylight; and besides, I would not have love-making take on the appearance of a concerted enterprise. I was all for liberty, but dead set against deliberation. I refused to admit either that one could yield to desires against one's will, or the possibility of organizing one's pleasures in cold blood. The pleasures of love-making should be as unforeseen and as irresistible as the surge of the sea or a peach tree breaking into blossom. I could not have explained why, but the idea of any discrepancy between my physical emotions and my conscious will I found alarming in the extreme: and it was precisely this split that in fact took place. My body had its own whims, and I was powerless to control them; their violence overrode all my defenses. I found out that missing a person physically is not a mere matter of nostalgia, but an actual *pain*. From the roots of my hair to the soles of my feet a poisoned shirt was woven across my body. I hated suffering; I hated the thought that this suffering was born of my blood, that I was involved in it; I even went so far as to hate the very pulsing of the blood through my veins. Every morning in the Métro, still numb with sleep, I would stare at my fellow travelers, wondering if they too were familiar with this torture, and how it was that no book I knew had ever described its full agony. Gradually the poisoned shirt would dissolve, and I would feel the fresh morning air caressing my closed eyelids. But by nightfall my obsession would rouse itself once more, and thousands of ants would crawl across my lips: the mirror showed me bursting with health, but a hidden disease was rotting the marrow in my very bones.

A shameful disease, too. I had emancipated myself just far enough from my puritanical upbringing to be able to take unconstrained pleasure in my own body, but not so far that I could allow it to cause me any inconvenience. Starved of its sustenance, it begged and pleaded with me: I found it repulsive. I was forced to admit a truth that I had been doing my best to conceal ever since adolescence: my physical appetites were greater than I wanted them to be. In the feverish caresses and love-making that bound me to the man of my choice I could discern the movements of my heart, my freedom as an individual. But that mood of solitary, languorous excitement cried out for anyone, regardless. In the night train from Tours to Paris the touch of an anonymous hand along my leg could arouse feelings—against my conscious will—of quite shattering intensity. I said nothing about these shameful incidents. Now that I had embarked on our policy of absolute frankness, this reticence was, I felt, a kind of touchstone. If I dared not confess such things, it was because they were by definition unavowable. By driving me to such secrecy my body became a stumbling block rather than a bond of union between us, and I felt a burning resentment against it.

Though I had available a whole set of moral precedents which encouraged me to take sexual encounters lightly, I found that my personal experience gave them the lie. I was too convinced a materialist to distinguish, as Alain and his followers did, between body and mind, conceding each its due. To judge from my own case, the mind did *not* exist in isolation from the body, and my body compromised me completely. I might well have inclined toward Claudel's type of su-blimation, and in particular toward that naturalistic optimism which claims to reconcile the rational and instinctive elements in man; but the truth was that for me, at any rate, this "reconciliation" simply did not work. My reason could not come to terms with my tyrannical desires. I learned with my body that humanity does *not* subsist in the calm light of the Good; men suffer the dumb, futile, cruel agonies of defenseless beasts. The face of the earth must have been hellish indeed to judge by the dark and lurid desires that, from time to time, struck me with the force of a thunderbolt.

One day I caught a glimpse of this hell on earth outside myself, in another person. I was not yet inured to such things, and it terrified me. One August afternoon I was at Sainte-Radegonde, reading, on the bank of that overgrown semi-island which I have already referred to. I heard an odd noise behind me: cracking twigs, and an animal panting that sounded like a death rattle. I turned around to find a man crouching in the bushes, a tramp, his eyes fixed on me, masturbating. I fled, panic-stricken. What brutish distress was hinted at in this solitary act of self-relief! For a long while I could not bear to recall the incident.

The notion that I partook of a condition common to all mankind gave me no consolation at all. It wounded my pride to find myself condemned to a subordinate rather than a commanding role where the private movements of my blood were concerned. It was hard for me to decide which of the many complaints I had against myself was the most important: each beyond doubt lent support to the rest. I would have found it easier to accept my unruly physical urges if I had achieved self-contentment with regard to my life as a whole; and my position as intellectual parasite would have bothered me less if I had not felt my freedom being engulfed by the flesh. But these burning pangs of desire, coupled with the pointlessness of my pursuits and my complete surrender to an alien personality, all conspired to fill me with feelings of guilt and disgrace. This emotion was too deep-rooted for me to envisage freeing myself from it by any artificial contrivance. I had no intention of faking my emotions, or feigning, whether by deed or word, a freedom I did not in fact possess. Nor did I pin my hopes upon a sudden conversion. I knew very well that a mere act of will would not suffice to restore my self-confidence, revive my wilting ambitions, or regain a genuine measure of independence. My moral code required me to remain at the center of my life, though instinctively I preferred an existence other than my own. I realized that to restore the balance—without cheating— would mean a long, hard job.

Very soon, however, I would be forced to tackle it, and the prospect restored my equanimity. The atmosphere of happiness in which I was floundering had a somewhat precarious basis, since Sartre anticipated leaving soon for Japan. I made up my mind to go abroad too. I wrote to Fernando asking if he could find me a job in Madrid. He couldn't. But Monsieur Poirier, the headmaster, told me of an institute that would shortly be opened up in Morocco, and Bandi suggested a job at the University of Budapest. This would be exile with a vengeance, a clean break; I would have to take fresh stock of myself then, and no mistake. There was no risk of my slumbering in security forever; yet it would have been very wrong of me not to take full advantage of such opportunities, since they might well be denied me later. The future, then, offered me some sort of self-justification; but I paid a heavy price for it. I was still young enough to regard two years as a lifetime; this great gulf looming up on the horizon put the fear of death into me, and I no longer dared look directly at it. I find myself wondering, all things considered, just what the true reason for my discomposure may have been. Would I—at this stage—have protested against being caught in the toils of complacent happiness unless I was scared that someone might hook me out of it? At all events, guilt and fear, far from canceling one another out, attacked me simultaneously. I surrendered to their assault, in accordance with the dictates of a rhythmical pattern that has governed almost the entire course of my life. I would go weeks on end in a state of euphoria; and then for a few hours I would be ravaged by a kind of tornado that stripped me bare. To justify my condition of despair yet further, I would wallow in an abyss compounded of death, nothingness, and infinity. When the sky cleared again I could never be certain whether I was waking from a nightmare or relapsing into some long sky-blue fantasy, a permanent dream world.

Mary McCarthy

Mary McCarthy was born in Seattle, Washington, in 1912, the first of four children. She was orphaned in the influenza epidemic of 1918, as her family was moving from Seattle to Minneapolis, where her paternal grandfather had grown wealthy in the grain elevator business. For five years, she and her three brothers were raised in Minneapolis by her great-aunt and uncle, a severe and parsimonious couple who "had a positive gift for turning everything sour and ugly." Thinking back on these deprived years, she is convinced that "it was religion that saved me," the "sensuous life" of Catholicism providing a source of beauty and pleasure. In 1923, the McCarthy family agreed to send Mary alone to Seattle to live with "the Protestants," her maternal grandparents. Beginning when she was eleven, her grandparents sent her to the Forest Ridge Convent in Seattle, the Annie Wright Seminary, and Vassar College. By this time she had given up religion.

After graduating from Vassar in 1933, Miss McCarthy worked in a publishing house and began her literary career writing reviews of books and theater productions for *The Nation, The New Republic,* and *Partisan Review.* In the late 1940s she taught English at Bard and Sarah Lawrence. It was through her early critical style, unmistakably sharp, witty, and decisive, that she first gained recognition. "Style is really everything," she believes, "if one means by style the voice, the irreducible and always recognizable and alive thing." In 1938 Edmund Wilson, her second husband, encouraged her to write fiction. Her first published book, *The Company She Keeps* (1942), is a collection of short stories about one woman's experiences, based largely on her own background. Much of her fiction has its source in autobiography. "What I really do," she says, "is take real plums and put them into an imaginary cake." Her novels include *The Oasis* (1949), *The Group* (1963), and *Birds of America* (1971). She has also published art history, political analysis, and collections of theater reviews.

The selection we reprint below, in which Miss McCarthy recalls her two years at the Forest Ridge Convent, is a chapter from *Memories of a Catholic Girlhood* (1957), an autobiography rewritten and enlarged from articles printed in *The New Yorker* and *Harper's Bazaar* from 1946 through 1955. It captures some of the particular anguish and comic misunderstandings (comic after the fact) of early adolescence. The opening discussion on names invites immediate comparison to the reader's own junior high school memories: what names seemed desirable then? What else carried status? Was it better to be different or to be indistinguishable from others? The two episodes that follow are remarkably concrete and specific. The author makes no attempt to generalize or to gloss over the more painful moments— if anything she looks hard where most other people like to squint—and her self-description is not always flattering. But as a result, the narrative becomes both special and universal in a way that it could not have been had she dealt mainly in generalities. The reader may test this seeming paradox by writing a very concrete piece on an incident from his own childhood and seeing if it captures any of the universal quality that Mary McCarthy's does.

Names, from *Memories*
of a Catholic Girlhood

Anna Lyons, Mary Louise Lyons, Mary von Phul, Emilie von Phul, Eugenia McLellan, Marjorie McPhail, Marie-Louise L'Abbé, Mary Danz, Julia Dodge, Mary Fordyce Blake, Janet Preston—these were the names (I can still tell them over like a rosary) of some of the older girls in the convent: the Virtues and Graces. The virtuous ones wore wide blue or green moire good-conduct ribbons, bandoleer-style, across their blue serge uniforms; the beautiful ones wore rouge and powder or at least were reputed to do so. Our class, the eighth grade, wore pink ribbons (I never got one myself) and had names like Patricia ("Pat") Sullivan, Eileen Donohoe, and Joan Kane. We were inelegant even in this respect; the best name we could show, among us, was Phyllis ("Phil") Chatham, who boasted that her father's name, Ralph, was pronounced "Rafe" as in England.

Names had a great importance for us in the convent, and foreign names, French, German, or plain English (which, to us, were foreign, because of their Protestant sound), bloomed like prize roses among a collection of spuds. Irish names were too common in the school to have any prestige either as surnames (Gallagher, Sheehan, Finn, Sullivan, McCarthy) or as Christian names (Kathleen, Eileen). Anything exotic had value: an "olive" complexion, for example. The pet girl of the convent was a fragile Jewish girl named Susie Lowenstein, who had pale red-gold hair and an exquisite retroussé nose, which, if we had had it, might have been called "pug." We liked her name too and the name of a child in the primary grades: Abbie Stuart Baillargeon. My favorite name, on the whole, though, was Emilie von Phul (pronounced "Pool"); her oldest sister, recently graduated, was called Celeste. Another name that appealed to me was Genevieve Albers, Saint Genevieve being the patron saint of Paris who turned back Attila from the gates of the city.

All these names reflected the still-pioneer character of the Pacific Northwest. I had never heard their like in the parochial school in Minneapolis, where "foreign" extraction, in any case, was something to be ashamed of, the whole drive being toward Americanization of first name and surname alike. The exceptions to this were the Irish, who could vaunt such names as Catherine O'Dea and the name of my second

cousin, Mary Catherine Anne Rose Violet McCarthy, while an unfortu-
nate German boy named Manfred was made to suffer for his. But that
was Minneapolis. In Seattle, and especially in the convent of the Ladies
of the Sacred Heart, foreign names suggested not immigration but
emigration—distinguished exile. Minneapolis was a granary; Seattle was
a port, which had attracted a veritable Foreign Legion of adventurers—
soldiers of fortune, younger sons, gamblers, traders, drawn by the
fortunes to be made in virgin timber and shipping and by the Alaska
Gold Rush. Wars and revolutions had sent the defeated out to Puget
Sound, to start a new life; the latest had been the Russian Revolution,
which had shipped us, via Harbin, a Russian colony, complete with
restaurant, on Queen Anne Hill. The English names in the convent,
when they did not testify to direct English origin, as in the case of
"Rafe" Chatham, had come to us from the South and represented a kind
of internal exile; such girls as Mary Fordyce Blake and Mary McQueen
Street (a class ahead of me; her sister was named Francesca) bore their
double-barreled first names like titles of aristocracy from the ante-
bellum South. Not all our girls, by any means, were Catholic; some of
the very prettiest ones—Julia Dodge and Janet Preston, if I remember
rightly—were Protestants. The nuns had taught us to behave with
special courtesy to these strangers in our midst, and the whole effect was
of some superior hostel for refugees of all the lost causes of the past
hundred years. Money could not count for much in such an atmosphere;
the fathers and grandfathers of many of our "best" girls were ruined
men.

Names, often, were freakish in the Pacific Northwest, particularly
girls' names. In the Episcopal boarding school I went to later, in
Tacoma, there was a girl called De Vere Utter, and there was a girl
called Rocena and another called Hermoine. Was Rocena a mistake for
Rowena and Hermoine for Hermione? And was Vere, as we called her,
Lady Clara Vere de Vere? Probably. You do not hear names like those
often, in any case, east of the Cascade Mountains; they belong to the
frontier, where books and libraries were few and memory seems to have
been oral, as in the time of Homer.

Names have more significance for Catholics than they do for other
people; Christian names are chosen for the spiritual qualities of the
saints they are taken from; Protestants used to name their children out
of the Old Testament and now they name them out of novels and plays,
whose heroes and heroines are perhaps the new patron saints of a secular
age. But with Catholics it is different. The saint a child is named for is
supposed to serve, literally, as a model or pattern to imitate; your name
is your fortune and it tells you what you are or must be. Catholic
children ponder their names for a mystic meaning, like birthstones; my
own, I learned, besides belonging to the Virgin and Saint Mary of Egypt,
originally meant "bitter" or "star of the sea." My second name, Therese,
could dedicate me either to Saint Theresa or to the saint called the

Little Flower, Soeur Thérèse of Lisieux, on whom God was supposed to have descended in the form of a shower of roses. At Confirmation, I had added a third name (for Catholics then rename themselves, as most nuns do, yet another time, when they take orders); on the advice of a nun, I had taken "Clementina," after Saint Clement, an early pope—a step I soon regretted on account of "My Darling Clementine" and her number nine shoes. By the time I was in the convent, I would no longer tell anyone what my Confirmation name was. The name I had nearly picked was "Agnes," after a little Roman virgin martyr, always shown with a lamb, because of her purity. But Agnes would have been just as bad, I recognized in Forest Ridge Convent—not only because of the possibility of "Aggie," but because it was subtly, indefinably *wrong*, in itself. Agnes would have made me look like an ass.

The fear of appearing ridiculous first entered my life, as a governing motive, during my second year in the convent. Up to then, a desire for prominence had decided many of my actions and, in fact, still persisted. But in the eighth grade, I became aware of mockery and perceived that I could not seek prominence without attracting laughter. Other people could, but I couldn't. This laughter was proceeding, not from my classmates, but from the girls of the class just above me, in particular from two boon companions, Elinor Heffernan and Mary Harty, a clownish pair—oddly assorted in size and shape, as teams of clowns generally are, one short, plump, and baby-faced, the other tall, lean, and owlish—who entertained the high-school department by calling attention to the oddities of the younger girls. Nearly every school has such a pair of satirists, whose marks are generally low and who are tolerated just because of their laziness and non-conformity; one of them (in this case, Mary Harty, the plump one) usually appears to be half asleep. Because of their low standing, their indifference to appearances, the sad state of their uniforms, their clowning is taken to be harmless, which, on the whole, it is, their object being not to wound but to divert; such girls are bored in school. We in the eighth grade sat directly in front of the two wits in study hall, so that they had us under close observation; yet at first I was not afraid of them, wanting, if anything, to identify myself with their laughter, to be initiated into the joke. One of their specialties was giving people nicknames, and it was considered an honor to be the first in the eighth grade to be let in by Elinor and Mary on their latest invention. This often happened to me; they would tell me, on the playground, and I would tell the others. As their intermediary, I felt myself almost their friend and it did not occur to me that I might be next on their list.

I had achieved prominence not long before by publicly losing my faith and regaining it at the end of a retreat. I believe Elinor and Mary questioned me about this on the playground, during recess, and listened with serious, respectful faces while I told them about my conversations with the Jesuits. Those serious faces ought to have been an omen, but if the two girls used what I had revealed to make fun of me, it must have been behind my back. I never heard any more of it, and yet just at this time I began to feel something, like a cold breath on the nape of my neck, that made me wonder whether the new position I had won for myself in the convent was as secure as I imagined. I would turn around in study hall and find the two girls looking at me with speculation in their eyes.

It was just at this time, too, that I found myself in a perfectly absurd situation, a very private one, which made me live, from month to month, in horror of discovery. I had waked up one morning, in my convent room, to find a few small spots of blood on my sheet; I had somehow scratched a trifling cut on one of my legs and opened it during the night. I wondered what to do about this, for the nuns were fussy about bedmaking, as they were about our white collars and cuffs, and if we had an inspection those spots might count against me. It was best, I decided, to ask the nun on dormitory duty, tall, stout Mother Slattery, for a clean bottom sheet, even though she might scold me for having scratched my leg in my sleep and order me to cut my toenails. You never know what you might be blamed for. But Mother Slattery, when she bustled in to look at the sheet, did not scold me at all; indeed, she hardly seemed to be listening as I explained to her about the cut. She told me to sit down: she would be back in a minute. "You can be excused from athletics today," she added, closing the door. As I waited, I considered this remark, which seemed to me strangely munificent, in view of the unimportance of the cut. In a moment, she returned, but without the sheet. Instead, she produced out of her big pocket a sort of cloth girdle and a peculiar flannel object which I first took to be a bandage, and I began to protest that I did not need or want a bandage; all I needed was a bottom sheet. "The sheet can wait," said Mother Slattery, succinctly, handing me two large safety pins. It was the pins that abruptly enlightened me; I saw Mother Slattery's mistake, even as she was instructing me as to how this flannel article, which I now understood to be a sanitary napkin, was to be put on.

"Oh, no, Mother," I said, feeling somewhat embarrassed. "You don't understand. It's just a little cut, on my leg." But Mother, again, was not listening; she appeared to have grown deaf, as the nuns had a habit of doing when what you were saying did not fit in with their ideas. And now that I knew what was in her mind, I was conscious of a funny constraint; I did not feel it proper to name a natural process, in so many words, to a nun. It was like trying not to think of their going to the bathroom or trying not to see the straggling iron-grey hair coming out of their coifs (the common notion that they shaved their heads was false). On the whole, it seemed better just to show her my cut. But when I offered to do so and unfastened my black stocking, she only glanced at my leg, cursorily. "That's only a scratch, dear," she said. "Now hurry up and put this on or you'll be late for chapel. Have you any pain?" "No, no, Mother!" I cried. "You don't understand!" "Yes, yes, I understand," she replied soothingly, "and you will too, a little later. Mother Superior will tell you about it some time during the morning. There's nothing to be afraid of. You have become a woman."

"I know all about that," I persisted. "Mother, please listen. I just cut my leg. On the athletic field. Yesterday afternoon." But the more excited I grew, the more soothing, and yet firm, Mother Slattery became. There seemed to be nothing for it but to give up and do as I was bid. I was in the grip of a higher authority, which almost had the power to persuade me that it was right and I was wrong. But of course I was not wrong; that would have been too good to be true. While Mother Slattery waited, just outside my door, I miserably donned the equipment she had given me, for there was no place to hide it, on account of drawer inspection. She led me down the hall to where there was a chute and explained how I was to dispose of the flannel thing, by dropping it down the chute into the laundry. (The convent arrangements were very old-fashioned, dating back, no doubt, to the days of Louis Philippe.)

The Mother Superior, Madame MacIllvra, was a sensible woman, and all through my early morning classes, I was on pins and needles, chafing for the promised interview with her which I trusted would clear things up. *"Ma Mère,"* I would begin, "Mother Slattery thinks . . ." Then I would tell her about the cut and the athletic field. But precisely the same impasse confronted me when I was summoned to her office at recess-time. *I* talked about my cut, and *she* talked about becoming a woman. It was rather like a round, in which she was singing "Scotland's burning, Scotland's burning," and I was singing "Pour on water, pour on water." Neither of us could hear the other, or, rather, I could hear her, but she could not hear me. Owing to our different positions in the convent, she was free to interrupt me, whereas I was expected to remain silent until she had finished speaking. When I kept breaking in, she hushed me, gently, and took me on her lap. Exactly like Mother Slattery, she attributed all my references to the cut to a blind fear of this new, unexpected reality that had supposedly entered my life. Many young girls, she reassured me, were frightened if they had not been prepared. "And you, Mary, have lost your dear mother, who could have made this easier for you." Rocked on Madame MacIllvra's lap, I felt paralysis overtake me and I lay, mutely listening, against her bosom, my face being tickled by her white, starched, fluted wimple, while she explained to me how babies were born, all of which I had heard before.

There was no use fighting the convent. I had to pretend to have become a woman, just as, not long before, I had had to pretend to get my faith back—for the sake of peace. This pretense was decidedly awkward. For fear of being found out by the lay sisters downstairs in the laundry (no doubt an imaginary contingency, but the convent was so very thorough), I reopened the cut on my leg, so as to draw a little blood to stain the napkins, which were issued me regularly, not only on this occasion, but every twenty-eight days thereafter. Eventually, I abandoned this bloodletting, for fear of lockjaw, and trusted to fate. Yet I was in awful dread of detection; my only hope, as I saw it, was either to be released from the convent or to become a woman in reality, which might take a year, at least, since I was only twelve. Getting out of athletics once a month was not sufficient compensation for the farce I was going through. It was not my fault; they had forced me into it; nevertheless, it was I who would look silly—worse than silly; half mad— if the truth ever came to light.

I was burdened with this guilt and shame when the nickname finally found me out. "Found me out," in a general sense, for no one ever did learn the particular secret I bore about with me, pinned to the linen band. "We've got a name for you," Elinor and Mary called out to me, one day on the playground. "What is it?" I asked, half hoping, half fearing, since not all their sobriquets were unfavorable. "Cye," they answered, looking at each other and laughing. " 'Si'?" I repeated, supposing that it was based on Simple Simon. Did they regard me as a hick? "C.Y.E.," they elucidated, spelling it out in chorus. "The letters stand for something. Can you guess?" I could not and I cannot now. The closest I could come to it in the convent was "Clean Your Ears." Perhaps that was it, though in later life I have wondered whether it did not stand, simply, for "Clever Young Egg" or "Champion Young Eccentric." But in the convent I was certain that it stood for something horrible, something even worse than dirty ears (as far as I knew, my ears were clean), something I could never guess because it represented some aspect of myself that the world could see and I couldn't, like a sign pinned on my back. Everyone in the convent must have known what the letters stood for, but no one would tell me. Elinor and Mary had made them promise. It was like halitosis; not even my best friend, my deskmate, Louise, would tell me, no matter how much I pleaded. Yet everyone assured me that it was "very good," that is, very apt. And it made everyone laugh.

This name reduced all my pretensions and solidified my sense of *wrongness.* Just as I felt I was beginning to belong to the convent, it turned me into an outsider, since I was the only pupil who was not in the know. I liked the convent, but it did not like me, as people say of certain foods that disagree with them. By this, I do not mean that I was actively unpopular, either with the pupils or with the nuns. The Mother Superior cried when I left and predicted that I would be a novelist, which surprised me. And I had finally made friends; even Emilie von Phul smiled upon me softly out of her bright blue eyes from the far end of the study hall. It was just that I did not fit into the convent pattern; the simplest thing I did, like asking for a clean sheet, entrapped me in consequences that I never could have predicted. I was not bad; I did not consciously break the rules; and yet I could never, not even for a week, get a pink ribbon, and this was something I could not understand, because I was trying as hard as I could. It was the same case as with the hated name; the nuns, evidently, saw something about me that was invisible to me.

The oddest part was all that pretending. There I was, a walking mass of lies, pretending to be a Catholic and going to confession while really I had lost my faith, and pretending to have monthly periods by cutting myself with nail scissors; yet all this had come about without my volition and even contrary to it. But the basest pretense I was driven to was the acceptance of the nickname. Yet what else could I do? In the convent, I could not live it down. To all those girls, I had become "Cye McCarthy." That was who I was. That was how I had to identify myself when telephoning my friends during vacations to ask them to the movies: "Hello, this is Cye." I loathed myself when I said it, and yet I succumbed to the name totally, making myself over into a sort of hearty to go with it—the kind of girl I hated. "Cye" was my new patron saint. This false personality stuck to me, like the name, when I entered public high school, the next fall, as a freshman, having finally persuaded my grandparents to take me out of the convent, although they could never get to the bottom of my reasons, since, as I admitted, the nuns were kind, and I had made many nice new friends. What I wanted was a fresh start, a chance to begin life over again, but the first thing I heard in the corridors of the public high school was that name called out to me, like the warmest of welcomes: "Hi, there, Si!" That was the way they thought it was spelled. But this time I was resolute. After the first weeks, I dropped the hearties who called me "Si" and I never heard it again. I got my own name back and sloughed off Clementina and even Therese—the names that did not seem to me any more to be mine but to have been imposed on me by others. And I preferred to think that Mary meant "bitter" rather than "star of the sea."

Isak Dinesen

Isak Dinesen is the pseudonym of Baroness Karen Blixen, born Karen Dinesen in 1885 in Denmark. Educated by governesses, she studied English literature at Oxford in 1904 and published her first three stories, in Danish, in 1907 and 1909. She recalls that in the following years she "studied painting in Copenhagen and later in Rome, and had much fun."

In 1914 she married her cousin, Baron Blixen, and received from her family as a dowry a six-thousand-acre coffee plantation in Kenya. From the time of her divorce in 1921 until the depression forced her to sell out and return to Denmark in 1931, Baroness Blixen managed the plantation entirely alone. She considered her close relationship with the African natives living on her land "a magnificent enlargment of all my world" and wrote years later that "to my mind the life of a farmer in the East African highlands is near to an ideal existence."

She returned to writing after her years in Africa. Her *Seven Gothic Tales* (1934), extravagantly romantic and mysterious stories, were written in English and greeted in America with high praise and great popularity. Her second book, *Out of Africa* (1937), from which we reprint the chapter below, consists of quiet but spell-binding stories of her life on her Kenya plantation. After the publication of *Winter's Tales* in 1942, she wrote almost nothing for a period of fifteen years. In her seventies she published four more books, including new narratives from her years in Africa in *Shadows in the Grass* (1961), but her literary reputation rests primarily on her three earlier works. She died in 1962.

Many of Isak Dinesen's stories take on a mythical or fairy tale quality that can be seen even in the selection below. The story of Emmanuelson is clear and simple, but she links the facts to archetypal images of actor and wanderer, the stage and the journey, which all come together in the concluding paragraph. And in the process of telling her story, the writer reveals as much about herself as she does about Emmanuelson. Try to put your finger on the qualities that chiefly go into your impression of her.

A Fugitive Rests on the Farm

There was one traveller who came to the farm, slept there for one night, and walked off not to come back, of whom I have since thought from time to time. His name was Emmanuelson; he was a Swede and when I first knew him he held the position of *maître d'hotel* at one of the hotels of Nairobi. He was a fattish young man with a red puffed face, and he was in the habit of standing by my chair when I was lunching at the hotel, to entertain me in a very oily voice of the old country, and of mutual acquaintances there; he was so persistently conversational that after a while I changed over to the only other hotel which in those days we had in the town. I then only vaguely heard of Emmanuelson; he seemed to have a gift for bringing himself into trouble, and also to differ, in his tastes and ideas of the pleasures of life, from the customary. So he had become unpopular with the other Scandinavians of the country. Upon one afternoon he suddenly appeared at the farm, much upset and frightened, and asked me for a loan so as to get off to Tanganyika at once, as otherwise he believed he would be sent to jail. Either my help came too late or Emmanuelson spent it on other things, for a short time after I heard that he had been arrested in Nairobi, he did not go to prison but for some time he disappeared from my horizon.

One evening I came riding home so late that the stars were already out, and caught sight of a man waiting outside my house on the stones. It was Emmanuelson and he announced himself to me in a cordial voice: "Here comes a vagabond, Baroness." I asked him how it was that I should find him there, and he told me that he had lost his way and so been landed at my house. His way to where? To Tanganyika.

That could hardly be true—the Tanganyika road was the great highway and easy to find, my own farm-road took off from it. How was he going to get to Tanganyika? I asked him. He was going to walk, he informed me. That, I answered, was not a possible thing to do for anyone, it would mean three days through the Masai-Reserve without water, and the lions were bad there just now, the Masai had been in the same day to complain about them and had asked me to come out and shoot one for them.

Yes, yes, Emmanuelson knew of all that, but he was going to walk to Tanganyika all the same. For he did not know what else to do. He was wondering now whether, having lost his way, he could bear me company for dinner and sleep at the farm to start early in the morning?—if that was not convenient to me he would set out straight away while the stars were out so bright.

I had remained sitting on my horse while I talked to him, to accentuate that he was not a guest in the house, for I did not want him in to dine with me. But as he spoke, I saw that he did not expect to be invited either, he had no faith in my hospitality or in his own power of persuasion, and he made a lonely figure in the dark outside my house, a man without a friend. His hearty manner was adapted to save not his own face, which was past it, but mine, if now I sent him away it would be no unkindness, but quite all right. This was courtesy in a hunted animal,—I called for my Sice to take the pony, and got off—"Come in, Emmanuelson," I said, "you can dine here and stay over the night."

In the light of the lamp Emmanuelson was a sad sight. He had on a long black overcoat such as nobody wears in Africa, he was unshaven and his hair was not cut, his old shoes were split at the toe. He was bringing no belongings with him to Tanganyika, his hands were empty. It seemed that I was to take the part of the High Priest who presents the goat alive to the Lord, and sends it into the wilderness. I thought that here we needed wine. Berkeley Cole, who generally kept the house in wine, some time ago had sent me a case of a very rare burgundy, and I now told Juma to open a bottle from it. When we sat down for dinner and Emmanuelson's glass was filled he drank half of it, held it towards the lamp and looked at it for a long time like a person attentively listening to music. "*Fameux*" he said, "*fameux*; this is a Chambertin 1906." It was so, and that gave me respect for Emmanuelson.

Otherwise he did not say much to begin with, and I did not know what to say to him. I asked him how it was that he had not been able to find any work at all. He answered that it was because he knew nothing of the things with which people out here occupied themselves. He had been dismissed at the hotel, besides he was not really a maître d'hotel by profession.

"Do you know anything of book-keeping?" I asked him.

"No. Nothing at all," he said, "I have always found it very difficult to add two figures together."

"Do you know about cattle at all?" I went on. "Cows?" he asked. "No, no. I am afraid of cows."

"Can you drive à tractor, then?" I asked. Here a faint ray of hope appeared on his face. "No," he said, "but I think that I could learn that."

"Not on my tractor though," I said, "but tell me, Emmanuelson, what have you ever been doing? What are you in life?"

Emmanuelson drew himself up straight. "What am I?" he exclaimed. "Why, I am an actor."

I thought: Thank God, it is altogether outside my capacity to assist this lost man in any practical way; the time has come for general human conversation. "You are an actor?" I said, "that is a fine thing to be. And which were your favourite parts when you were on the stage?"

"Oh I am a tragic actor," said Emmanuelson, "my favourite parts were that of Armand in 'La Dame aux Camelias' and of Oswald in 'Ghosts'."

We talked for some time of these plays, of the various actors whom we had seen in them and of the way in which we thought that they should be acted. Emmanuelson looked round the room. "You have not," he asked, "by any chance got the plays of Henrik Ibsen here? Then we might do the last scene of 'Ghosts' together, if you would not mind taking the part of Mrs. Alving."

I had not got Ibsen's plays.

"But perhaps you will remember it?" said Emmanuelson warming to his plan. "I myself know Oswald by heart from beginning to end. That last scene is the best. For a real tragic effect, you know, that is impossible to beat."

The stars were out and it was a very fine warm night, there was not long, now, to the big rains. I asked Emmanuelson if he did really mean to walk to Tanganyika.

"Yes," he said, "I am going, now, to be my own prompter."

"It is a good thing for you," I said, "that you are not married."

"Yes," said he, "yes." After a little while he added modestly: "I am married though."

In the course of our talk, Emmanuelson complained of the fact that out here a white man could not hold his own against the competition from the Natives, who worked so much cheaper. "Now in Paris," he said, "I could always, for a short time, get a job as a waiter in some café or other."

"Why did you not stay in Paris, Emmanuelson?" I asked him.

He gave me a swift clear glance. "Paris?" he said, "no, no, indeed. I got out of Paris just at the nick of time."

Emmanuelson had one friend in the world to whom in the course of the evening he came back many times. If he could only get in touch with him again, everything would be different, for he was prosperous and very generous. This man was a conjurer and was travelling all over the world. When Emmanuelson had last heard of him he had been in San Francisco.

From time to time we talked of literature and the theatre and then again we would come back to Emmanuelson's future. He told me how his countrymen out here in Africa had one after another turned him out.

"You are in a hard position, Emmanuelson," I said, "I do not know that I can think of anyone who is, in a way, harder up against things than you are."

"No, I think so myself," he said. "But then there is one thing of which I have thought lately and of which perhaps you have not thought: some person or other will have to be in the worst position of all people."

He had finished his bottle and pushed his glass a little away from him. "This journey," he said, "is a sort of gamble to me, *le rouge et le noir*. I have a chance to get out of things, I may even be getting out of everything. On the other hand if I get to Tanganyika I may get into things."

"I think you will get to Tanganyika," I said, "you may get a lift from one of the Indian lorries travelling on that road."

"Yes, but there are the lions," said Emmanuelson, "and the Masai."

"Do you believe in God, Emmanuelson?" I asked him.

"Yes, yes, yes," said Emmanuelson. He sat in silence for a time. "Perhaps you will think me a terrible sceptic," he said, "if I now say what I am going to say. But with the exception of God I believe in absolutely nothing whatever."

"Look here, Emmanuelson," I said, "have you got any money?"

"Yes, I have," he said, "eighty cents."

"That is not enough," I said, "and I myself have got no money in the house. But perhaps Farah will have some." Farah had got four rupees.

Next morning, some time before sunrise, I told my boys to wake up Emmanuelson and to make breakfast for us. I had thought, in the course of the night, that I should like to take him in my car for the first ten miles of his way. It was no advantage to Emmanuelson, who would still have another eighty miles to walk, but I did not like to see him step straight from the threshold of my house into his uncertain fate, and besides I wished to be, myself, somewhere within this comedy or tragedy of his. I made him up a parcel of sandwiches and hard-boiled eggs, and gave him with it a bottle of the Chambertin 1906 since he appreciated it. I thought that it might well be his last drink in life.

Emmanuelson in the dawn looked like one of those legendary corpses whose beards grow quickly in the earth, but he came forth from his grave with a good grace and was very placid and well-balanced as we drove on. When we had come to the other side of the Mbagathi river, I let him down from the car. The morning air was clear and there was not a cloud in the sky. He was going towards the South-West. As I looked round to the opposite horizon, the sun just came up, dull and red: like the yolk of a hard-boiled egg, I thought. In three or four hours she would be white-hot, and fierce upon the head of the wanderer.

Emmanuelson said good-bye to me; he started to walk, and then came back and said good-bye once more. I sat in the car and watched him, and I think that as he went he was pleased to have a spectator. I believe that the dramatic instinct within him was so strong that he was at this moment vividly aware of being seen leaving the stage, of disappearing, as if he had, with the eyes of his audience, seen himself go. Exit Emmanuelson. Should not the hills, the thorn-trees and the dusty road take pity and for a second put on the aspect of cardboard?

In the morning breeze his long black overcoat fluttered round his legs, the neck of the bottle stuck up from one of its pockets. I felt my heart filling with the love and gratitude which the people who stay at home are feeling for the wayfarers and wanderers of the world, the sailors, explorers and vagabonds. As he came to the top of the hill he turned, took off his hat and waved it to me, his long hair was blown up from his forehead.

Farah, who was with me in the car, asked me: "Where is that Bwana going?" Farah called Emmanuelson a Bwana for the sake of his own dignity, since he had slept in the house.

"To Tanganyika," I said.

"On foot?" asked he.

"Yes," I said.

"Allah be with him," said Farah.

In the course of the day I thought much of Emmanuelson, and went out of the house to look towards the Tanganyika road. In the night, about ten o'clock, I heard the roar of a lion far away to the South-West; half an hour later I heard him again. I wondered if he was sitting upon an old black overcoat. During the following week I tried to get news of Emmanuelson, and told Farah to ask his Indian acquaintances who were running lorries to Tanganyika, whether any lorry had passed or met him on the road. But nobody knew anything of him.

Half a year later I was surprised to receive a registered letter from Dodoma, where I knew no one. The letter was from Emmanuelson. It contained the fifty rupees that I had first lent him when he had been trying to get out of the country, and Farah's four rupees. Apart from this sum,—the last money in all the world that I had expected to see again,— Emmanuelson sent me a long, sensible and charming letter. He had got a job as a bartender in Dodoma, whatever kind of bar they may have there, and was getting on well. He seemed to have in him a talent for gratitude, he remembered everything of his evening on the farm, and came back many times to the fact that there he had felt amongst friends. He told me in detail about his journey to Tanganyika. He had much good to say of the Masai. They had found him on the road and had taken him in, had shown him great kindness and hospitality, and had let him travel with them most of the way, by many circuits. He had, he wrote, entertained them so well, with recounts of his adventures in many countries, that they had not wanted to let him go. Emmanuelson did not know any Masai language, and for his Odyssey he must have fallen back upon pantomime.

It was fit and becoming, I thought, that Emmanuelson should have sought refuge with the Masai, and that they should have received him. The true aristocracy and the true proletariat of the world are both in understanding with tragedy. To them it is the fundamental principle of God, and the key,—the minor key,—to existence. They differ in this way from the bourgeoisie of all classes, who deny tragedy, who will not tolerate it, and to whom the word of tragedy means in itself unpleasantness. Many misunderstandings between the white middle-class immigrant settlers and the Natives arise from this fact. The sulky Masai are both aristocracy and proletariat, they would have recognized at once in the lonely wanderer in black, a figure of tragedy; and the tragic actor had come, with them, into his own.

Frieda and D.H. Lawrence

David Herbert Lawrence (1885-1930) grew up in central England, son of a coal miner and an ex-schoolteacher. He graduated from Nottingham Boys' High School in 1902, and attended University College, Nottingham, for two years to earn a teacher's certificate. Soon after his mother's death in 1910, poor health forced him to give up teaching. The family conflicts of his childhood, his relationship with his mother, and his conviction that modern love is most often destructively possessive are explored in his autobiographical novel, *Sons and Lovers* (1931).

Lawrence met Frieda von Richthofen Weekley in April 1912. Daughter of a German baron and raised in great comfort, Frieda was married to Nottingham University Professor Ernest Weekley and had three children. She eloped with Lawrence on May 3, 1912. The text and letters below from Frieda Lawrence's *"Not I, But the Wind . . ."* (1934) record their meeting, escape from England, and attempt to persuade Ernest Weekley to agree to a divorce. In Metz, only Frieda's sisters at first knew of Lawrence's presence, but when he was arrested on suspicion of spying for the British, Frieda was obliged to ask her father, Baron von Richthofen, to exert his influence to have the charges dropped. Lawrence retreated to Trier and Waldbröl, then rejoined Frieda in Munich in early June. They were married soon after Frieda obtained a divorce in 1914. A collection of D. H. Lawrence's poems, *Look! We Have Come Through!* (1917), traces the first five years of their relationship.

During the years of their marriage, Frieda and D. H. Lawrence traveled extensively, living for shorter or longer periods in Italy, Australia, New Mexico, Mexico, and France. Lawrence wrote profusely until his death at forty-five, producing over forty volumes of fiction, poetry, drama, criticism, and philosophy. He wrote in 1913, "my great religion is a belief in the blood, the flesh, as being wiser than the intellect. We can go wrong in our minds. But what our blood feels and believes and says, is always true." The doctrine is embodied in his novels *The Rainbow* (1915), *Women in Love* (1920), *The Plumed Serpent* (1926), and *Lady Chatterley's Lover* (1928). Frieda Lawrence lived to see critical praise succeed the public outrage with which Lawrence's sexually explicit novels were at first received. Her *Memoirs and Correspondence* was published in 1961, five years after her death.

D. H. Lawrence's letters to Bertrand Russell, Carlo Linati, and Ottoline Morrell are taken from *The Collected Letters of D. H. Lawrence* (ed. Harry T. Moore, 1962). The letter to the mathematician and philosopher Bertrand Russell marks a point near the end of their brief friendship. They met early in 1915, shared feelings of pacifism and horror at England's role in World War I, and planned to give lectures together. Russell prepared a series of lectures, later published as *Principles of Social Reconstruction* (1916), but they proved extremely unpalatable to Lawrence. Russell wrote more than thirty-five years later: "I find it difficult now to understand the devastating effect that this letter had upon me . . . . I supposed that he must be right. For twenty-four hours I thought that I was not fit to live and contemplated committing suicide. But at the end of that time, a healthier reaction set in. . . ."

Russell concluded that Lawrence was expressing his own hatred of mankind. The two men ended their acquaintance after corresponding politely for a few months more.

Carlo Linati, an Italian literary critic who has written about Ezra Pound and D. H. Lawrence, exchanged a few letters with Lawrence in 1925. Lawrence gave Linati information for an essay he was then writing. The novel *Quetzalcoatl* was published as *The Plumed Serpent*. Compare the ideas of Miss Cress (p. 76) on books and life.

Lady Ottoline Morrell, to whom the third letter below is addressed, entertained the Lawrences at her country estate in 1915. Recognizing herself in the monstrous character of Hermione Roddice in the manuscript of *Women in Love*, she broke off relations with Lawrence in 1916 and threatened legal proceedings to stop publication of the novel. They resumed correspondence in 1928, just before the copies of *Lady Chatterley's Lover*, published in Florence, began circulating in England.

D. H. Lawrence's writings unfailingly bring up controversial questions: feeling vs. thought, honesty vs. tact, naturalness vs. restraint, involvement vs. objectivity. Most of them boil down to the one problem of "being born into your own intrinsic self," as Frieda puts it. It is a question taken up by many of the writers in this collection—most notably by Simone de Beauvoir (p. 140).

The letter to Lady Ottoline Morrell raises the question of obscenity in language and may be studied in connection with the remarks of Piri Thomas (p. 52). Frieda's narrative and descriptions, and Lawrence's descriptions, are equally interesting for their simplicity of syntax and their choice of details. The details that Frieda recalls just before she knew she loved Lawrence are especially worth study.

Frieda Lawrence

We Meet

As I look back now it surprises me that Lawrence could have loved me at first sight as he did. I hardly think I could have been a very lovable woman at the time. I was thirty-one and had three children. My marriage seemed a success. I had all a woman can reasonably ask. Yet there I was, all "smock ravelled," to use one of Lawrence's phrases.

I had just met a remarkable disciple of Freud and was full of undigested theories. This friend did a lot for me. I was living like a somnambulist in a conventional set life and he awakened the consciousness of my own proper self.

Being born and reborn is no joke, and being born into your own intrinsic self, that separates and singles you out from all the rest—it's a painful process.

When people talk about sex, I don't know what they mean—as if sex hopped about by itself like a frog, as if it had no relation to the rest of living, one's growth, one's ripening. What people mean by sex will always remain incomprehensible to me, but I am thankful to say sex is a mystery to me.

Theories applied to life aren't any use. Fanatically I believed that if only sex were "free" the world would straightaway turn into a paradise. I suffered and struggled at outs with society, and felt absolutely isolated. The process left me unbalanced. I felt alone. What could I do, when there were so many millions who thought differently from me? But I couldn't give in, I couldn't submit. It wasn't that I felt hostile, only different. I could not accept society. And then Lawrence came. It was an April day in 1912. He came for lunch, to see my husband about a lectureship at a German University. Lawrence was also at a critical period of his life just then. The death of his mother had shaken the foundations of his health for a second time. He had given up his post as a schoolmaster at Croydon. He had done with his past life.

I see him before me as he entered the house. A long thin figure, quick straight legs, light, sure movements. He seemed so obviously simple. Yet he arrested my attention. There was something more than met the eye. What kind of a bird was this?

The half-hour before lunch the two of us talked in my room, French windows open, curtains fluttering in the spring wind, my children playing on the lawn.

He said he had finished with his attempts at knowing women. I was amazed at the way he fiercely denounced them. I had never before heard anything like it. I laughed, yet I could tell he had tried very hard, and had cared. We talked about Oedipus and understanding leaped through our words.

After leaving, that night, he walked all the way to his home. It was a walk of at least five hours. Soon afterwards he wrote to me: "You are the most wonderful woman in all England."

I wrote back: "You don't know many women in England, how do you know?" He told me, the second time we met: "You are quite unaware of your husband, you take no notice of him." I disliked the directness of this criticism.

He came on Easter Sunday. It was a bright, sunny day. The children were in the garden hunting for Easter eggs.

The maids were out and I wanted to make some tea. I tried to turn on the gas but didn't know how. Lawrence became cross at such ignorance. Such a direct critic! It was something my High and Mightiness was very little accustomed to.

Yet Lawrence really understood me. From the first he saw through me like glass, saw how hard I was trying to keep up a cheerful front. I thought it was so despicable and unproud and unclean to be miserable, but he saw through my hard bright shell.

What I cannot understand is how he could have loved me and wanted me at that time. I certainly did have what he called "sex in the head"; a theory of loving men. My real self was frightened and shrank from contact like a wild thing.

So our relationship developed.

One day we met at a station in Derbyshire. My two small girls were with us. We went for a walk through the early-spring woods and fields. The children were running here and there as young creatures will.

We came to a small brook, a little stone bridge crossed it. Lawrence made the children some paper boats and put matches in them and let them float downstream under the bridge. Then he put daisies in the brook, and they floated down with their upturned faces. Crouched by the brook, playing there with the children, Lawrence forgot about me completely.

Suddenly I knew I loved him. He had touched a new tenderness in me. After that, things happened quickly.

He came to see me one Sunday. My husband was away and I said: "Stay the night with me." "No, I will not stay in your husband's house while he is away, but you must tell him the truth and we will go away together, because I love you."

I was frightened. I knew how terrible such a thing would be for my husband, he had always trusted me. But a force stronger than myself made me deal him the blow. I left the next day. I left my son with his father, my two little girls I took to their grandparents in London. I said good-bye to them on Hampstead Heath, blind and blank with pain, dimly feeling I should never again live with them as I had done.

Lawrence met me at Charing Cross Station, to go away with him, never to leave him again.

He seemed to have lifted me body and soul out of all my past life. This young man of twenty-six had taken all my fate, all my destiny, into his hands. And we had known each other barely for six weeks. There had been nothing else for me to do but submit.

Going Away Together

We met at Charing Cross and crossed the grey channel sitting on some ropes, full of hope and agony. There was nothing but the grey sea, and the dark sky, and the throbbing of the ship, and ourselves.

We arrived at Metz where my father was having his fifty-years-of-service jubilee. Prewar Germany: the house was full of grandchildren and relatives, and I stayed in a hotel where Lawrence also stayed. It was a hectic time. Bands were playing in honour of my father, telegrams came flying from England. Lawrence was pulling me on one side, my children on the other. My mother wanted me to stay with her. My father, who loved me, said to me in great distress: "My child, what are you doing? I always thought you had so much sense. I know the world." I answered: "Yes, that may be, but you never knew the best." I meant to know the best.

There was a fair going on at Metz at the moment. I was walking with my sister Johanna through the booths of Turkish Delight, the serpent-men, the ladies in tights, all the pots and pans.

Johanna, or "Nusch," as we called her, was at the height of her beauty and elegance, and was the last word in "chic." Suddenly Lawrence appeared round a corner, looking odd, in a cap and raincoat. What will she think of him, I thought.

He spoke a few words to us and went away. To my surprise, Johanna said: "You can go with him. You can trust him."

At first nobody knew of Lawrence's presence except my sisters. One afternoon Lawrence and I were walking in the fortifications of Metz, when a sentinel touched Lawrence on the shoulder, suspecting him of being an English officer. I had to get my father's help to pull us out of the difficulty. Lo, the cat was out of the bag, and I took Lawrence home to tea.

He met my father only once, at our house. They looked at each other fiercely—my father, the pure aristocrat, Lawrence, the miner's son. My father, hostile, offered a cigarette to Lawrence. That night I dreamt that they had a fight, and that Lawrence defeated my father.

The strain of Metz proved too great for Lawrence and he left, for the Rhineland. I stayed behind in Metz.

Here are some of Lawrence's letters, which show his side of our story up to that time.

D. H. Lawrence

Four Letters To Frieda

Tuesday—

Now I can't stand it any longer, I can't. For two hours I haven't moved a muscle—just sat and thought. I have written a letter to E. . . You needn't, of course, send it. But you must say to him all I have said. No more dishonour, no more lies. Let them do their—silliest—but no more subterfuge, lying, dirt, fear. I feel as if it would strangle me. What is it all but procrastination. No, I can't bear it, because it's bad. I love you. Let us face anything, do anything, put up with anything. But this crawling under the mud I cannot bear.

I'm afraid I've got a fit of heroics. I've tried so hard to work—but I can't. This situation is round my chest like a cord. It *mustn't* continue. I will go right away, if you like. I will stop in Metz till you get E . . .'s answer to the truth. But no, I won't utter or act or willingly let you utter or act, another single lie in the business.

I'm not going to joke, I'm not going to laugh, I'm not going to make light of things for you. The situation tortures me too much. It's the situation, the situation I can't stand—no, and I won't. I love you too much.

Don't show this letter to either of your sisters—no. Let us be good. You are clean, but you dirty your feet. I'll sign myself as you call me—Mr. Lawrence.

Don't be miserable—if I didn't love you I wouldn't mind when you lied.

But I love you, and Lord, I pay for it.

Hotel Rheinischer Hof, Trier
8 May 1912

I am here—I have dined—it seems rather nice. The hotel is little—the man is proprietor, waiter, bureau, and everything else, apparently—speaks English and French and German quite sweetly—has evidently been in swell restaurants abroad—has an instinct for doing things decently, with just a touch of swank—is cheap—his wife (they're a youngish couple) draws the beer—it's awfully nice. The bedroom is two marks fifty per day, including breakfast—per person. That's no more than my room at the Deutscher Hof, and this is much nicer. It's on the second floor—two beds—rather decent. Now, you ought to be here, you ought to be here. Remember, you are to be my wife—see that they don't send you any letters, or only under cover to me. But you aren't here yet. I shall love Trier—it isn't a ghastly medley like Metz—new town, old town, barracks, barracks, cathedral, Montigny. This is nice, old, with trees down the town. I wish you were here. The valley all along coming is full of apple trees in blossom, pink puffs like the smoke of an explosion, and then bristling vine sticks, so that the hills are angry hedgehogs.

I love you so much. No doubt there'll be another dish of tragedy in the morning, and we've only enough money to run us a fortnight, and we don't know where the next will come from, but still I'm happy, I am happy. But I wish you were here. But you'll come, and it isn't Metz. Curse Metz.

They are all men in this hotel—business men. They are the connoisseurs of comfort and moderate price. Be sure men will get the best for the money. I think it'll be nice for you. You don't mind a masculine atmosphere, I know.

I begin to feel quite a man of the world. I ought, I suppose, with this wickedness of waiting for another man's wife in my heart. Never mind, in heaven there is no marriage nor giving in marriage.

I must hurry to post—it's getting late. Come early on Saturday morning. Ask the Black Hussy at Deutscher Hof if there are any letters for me. I love you—and Else—I do more than thank her. Love

D. H. Lawrence

Hotel Rheinischer Hof
Trier—Thursday

Another day nearly gone—it is just sunset. Trier is a nice town. This is a nice hotel. The man is a cocky little fellow, but good. He's lived in every country and swanks about his languages. He really speaks English nicely. He's about thirty-five, I should think. When I came in just now—it is sunset—he said, "You are tired?" It goes without saying I laughed. "A little bit," he added, quite gently. That amuses me. He would do what my men friends always want to do, look after me a bit in the trifling, physical matters.

I have written a newspaper article that nobody on earth will print, because it's too plain and straight. However, I don't care. And I've been a ripping walk—up a great steep hill nearly like a cliff, beyond the river. I will take you on Saturday—so nice: apple blossom everywhere, and the cuckoo, and brilliant beech trees. Beech leaves seem to *rush* out in spring, with *éclat*. You can have coffee at a nice place, and look at the town, like a handful of cinders and rubbish thrown beside the river down below. Then there are the birds always. And I went past a Madonna stuck with flowers, beyond the hilltop, among all the folds and jumble of hills: pretty as heaven. And I smoked a pensive cigarette, and philosophized about love and life and battle, and you and me. And I thought of a theme for my next novel. And I forgot the German for matches, so I had to beg a light from a young priest, in French, and he held me the red end of his cigar. There are not so many soldiers here. I should never hate Trier. There are more priests than soldiers. Of the sort I've seen—not a bit Jesuitical—I prefer them. The cathedral is crazy: a grotto, not a cathedral, inside—baroque, baroque. The town is always pleasant, and the people.

One more day, and you'll be here. Suddenly I see your chin. I love your chin. At this moment, I seem to love you, because you've got such a nice chin. Doesn't it seem ridiculous?

I must go down to supper. I *am* tired. It was a long walk. And then the strain of these days. I dreamed E . . . was frantically furiously wild with me—I won't tell you the details—and then he calmed down, and I had to comfort him. I am a devil at dreaming. It's because I get up so late. One always dreams after seven a.m.

The day is gone. I'll talk a bit to my waiter fellow, and post this. You *will* come on Saturday? By Jove, if you don't! We shall always have to battle with *life,* so we'll never fight with each other, always help.

Bis Samstag—ich liebe dich schwer.

D. H. Lawrence

Waldbröl-Mittwoch

I have had all your three letters quite safely. We are coming on quickly now. Do tell me if you can what is E . . .'s final decision. He will get the divorce, I think, because of his thinking you ought to marry me. That is the result of *my* letter to him. I will crow my little crow, in opposition to you. And then after six months, we will be married—will you? Soon we will go to Munich. But give us a little time. Let us get solid before we set up together. Waldbröl restores me to my decent sanity. Is Metz still bad for you—no? It will be better for me to stay here—shall I say till the end of next week. We must decide what we are going to do, very definitely. If I am to come to Munich next week, what are we going to live on? Can we scramble enough together to last us till my payments come in? I am not going to tell my people anything till you have the divorce. If we can go decently over the first three or four months—financially—I think *I* shall be able to keep us going for the rest. Never mind about the infant. If it should come, we will be glad, and stir ourselves to provide for it—and if it should not come, ever—I shall be sorry. I do not believe, when people love each other, in interfering there. It is wicked, according to my feeling. I want you to have children to me—I don't care how soon. I never thought I should have that definite desire. But you see, we must have a more or less stable foundation if we are going to run the risk of the responsibility of children—not the risk of children, but the risk of the responsibility.

I think after a little while, I shall write to E . . . again. Perhaps he would correspond better with me.

Can't you feel how certainly I love you and how certainly we shall be married? Only let us wait just a short time, to get strong again. Two shaken, rather sick people together would be a bad start. A little waiting, let us have, because I love you. Or does the waiting make you worse?— no, not when it is only a time of preparation. Do you know, like the old knights, I seem to want a certain time to prepare myself—a sort of vigil with myself. Because it is a great thing for me to marry you, not a quick, passionate coming together. I know in my heart "here's my marriage." It feels rather terrible—because it is a great thing in my life— it is *my life*—I am a bit awe-inspired—I want to get used to it. If you think it is fear and indecision, you wrong me. It is *you* who would hurry, who are undecided. It's the very strength and inevitability of the oncoming thing that makes me wait, to get in harmony with it. Dear God, I am marrying you, now, don't you see. It's a far greater thing than ever I knew. Give me till next weekend, at least. If you love me, you will understand.

If I seem merely frightened and reluctant to you—you must forgive me.

I try, I will always try, when I write to you, to write the truth as near the mark as I can get it. It frets me, for fear you are disappointed in me, and for fear you are too much hurt. But you are strong when necessary.

You have got all myself—I don't even flirt—it would bore me very much—unless I got tipsy. It's a funny thing, to feel one's passion—sex desire—no longer a sort of wandering thing, but steady, and calm. I think, when one loves, one's very sex passion becomes calm, a steady sort of force, instead of a storm. Passion, that nearly drives one mad, is far away from real love. I am realizing things that I never thought to realize. Look at that poem I sent you—I would never write that to you. I shall love you all my life. That also is a new idea to me. But I believe it.

Auf Wiedersehen
D. H. Lawrence

Letters to Bertrand Russell, Carlo Linati, and Lady Ottoline Morrell

To Bertrand Russell, from
1 Byron Villas, Hampstead,
14 September 1915

Dear Russell: I'm going to quarrel with you again. You simply don't speak the truth, you simply are not sincere. The article you send me is a plausible lie, and I hate it. If it says some true things, that is not the point. The fact is that you, in the Essay, are all the time a lie.

Your basic desire is the maximum of desire of war, you are really the super-war-spirit. What you want is to jab and strike, like the soldier with the bayonet, only you are sublimated into words. And you are like a soldier who might jab man after man with his bayonet, saying 'This is for ultimate peace.' The soldier would be a liar. And it isn't in the least true that you, your basic self, want ultimate peace. You are satisfying in an indirect, false way your lust to jab and strike. Either satisfy it in a direct and honourable way, saying 'I hate you all, liars and swine, and am out to set upon you,' or stick to mathematics, where you can be true—But to come as the angel of peace—no, I prefer Tirpitz a thousand times in that rôle.

You are simply *full* of repressed desires, which have become savage and anti-social. And they come out in this sheep's clothing of peace propaganda. As a woman said to me, who had been to one of your meetings: 'It seemed so strange, with his face looking so evil, to be talking about peace and love. He can't have *meant* what he said.'

I believe in your inherent power for realizing the truth. But I don't believe in your will, not for a second. Your will is false and cruel. You are too full of devilish repressions to be anything but lustful and cruel. I would rather have the German soldiers with rapine and cruelty, than you with your words of goodness. It is the falsity I can't bear. I wouldn't care if you were six times a murderer, so long as you said to yourself, 'I am this.' The enemy of all mankind, you are, full of the lust of enmity. It is *not* the hatred of falsehood which inspires you. It is the hatred of people, of flesh and blood. It is a perverted, mental blood-lust. Why don't you own it.

Let us become strangers again, I think it is better.

To Carlo Linati, from Aveñida Piño Suarez #43, Oaxaca, 22 January 1925

Dear Carlo Linati: The *Corriere della Sera* with your article on me, wandered in today. It makes me laugh a bit. I never knew I was so *frenètico*. You leave me quite out of breath about myself. Well, well, in a world so anxious for outside tidiness, the critics will tidy me up, so I needn't bother. Myself, I don't care a button for neat works of art. But you read too much of me at once, I think.—And again, I can't help laughing, your article seems such a breathless series of explosions. Do I really seem like that?—all you say?

I have been busy down here in Mexico doing a novel I began last year: it's nearly done—I dread to think of its going out into the world. I call it *Quetzalcoatl.*

But really, Signor Linati, do you think that books should be sort of toys, nicely built up of observations and sensations, all finished and complete?—I don't. To me, even Synge, whom I admire very much indeed, is a bit too rounded off and, as it were, put on the shelf to be looked at. I can't bear art that you can walk round and admire. A book should be either a bandit or a rebel or a man in a crowd. People should either run for their lives, or come under the colours, or say *how do you do?* I hate the actor-and-the-audience business. An author should be in among the crowd, kicking their shins or cheering on to some mischief or merriment. That rather cheap seat in the gods where one sits with fellows like Anatole France and benignly looks down on the foibles, follies, and frenzies of so-called fellow-men, just annoys me. After all the world is *not* a stage—not to me: nor a theatre: nor a show-house of any sort. And art, especially novels, are not little theatres where the reader sits aloft and watches—like a god with a twenty-lira ticket—and sighs, commiserates, condones and smiles.—That's what you want a book to be: because it leaves you so safe and so superior, with your two-dollar ticket to the show. And that's what my books are not and never will be. You need not complain that I don't subject the intensity of my vision—or whatever it is—to some vast and imposing rhythm—by which you mean, isolate it on a stage, so that you can look down on it like a god who has got a ticket to the show. I never will: and you will never have that satisfaction from me. Stick to Synge, Anatole France, Sophocles: they will never kick the footlights even. But whoever reads me will be in the thick of the scrimmage, and if he doesn't like it—if he wants a safe seat in the audience—let him read somebody else.

I think my wife and I will come to Europe in the spring. If we come through Milan I will let you know. Anyhow we leave here in February. If you have anything to write me, will you address me c/o Curtis Brown, 6 Henrietta St, Covent Garden, London, W.C., England. Thank you for the article, and all the interest you took in my works.—I feel like coming to Italy again.

To Lady Ottoline Morrell, from Hôtel Beau Rivage, Bandol, 28 December 1928

My dear Ottoline: I was glad to hear from you again, and very glad to know you are better. Aldous also wrote that you were really wonderfully well, after that bad time. As for me, it's *pòco a pòco*, but I'm really getting better all the time.

We have been down on this coast since October, and I must say it has suited me well, it's a good winter climate. I didn't know Katherine had been here—wonder where she stayed. But I think in a fortnight we shall move on to Spain. From here it's not so very far. We've got to find somewhere to live, now we've given up the Florence house. Frieda gets fidgety, being without a house. But she doesn't really know *where* she wants one. Where does one want to live, finally?

About *Lady C.*—you mustn't think I advocate perpetual sex. Far from it. Nothing nauseates me more than promiscuous sex in and out of season. But I want, with *Lady C.*, to make an *adjustment in consciousness* to the basic physical realities. I realise that one of the reasons why the common people often keep—or kept—the good *natural glow* of life, just warm life, longer than educated people, was because it was still possible for them to say fuck! or shit without either a shudder or a sensation. If a man had been able to say to you when you were young and in love: an' if tha shits, an' if tha pisses, I' glad, I shouldna want a woman who couldna shit nor piss—surely it would have been a liberation to you, and it would have helped to keep your heart warm. Think of poor Swift's insane *But* of horror at the end of every verse of that poem to Celia. But Celia shits!—you see the very fact that it should horrify him, and simply devastate his consciousness, is all wrong, and a bitter shame to poor Celia. It's the awful and truly unnecessary *recoil* from these things that I would like to break. It's a question of conscious acceptance and adjustment—only that. God forbid that I should be taken as urging loose sex activity. There is a brief time for sex, a long time when sex is out of place. But when it is out of place as an activity there still should be the large and quiet space in the consciousness where it lives quiescent. Old people can have a lovely quiescent sort of sex, like apples, leaving the young quite free for *their* sort.

It's such a pity preachers have always dinned in: Go thou and do likewise! That's not the point. The point is: It is so, let it be so, with a generous heart.

Well, forgive all this, but I don't want you to misunderstand me, because I always count on your sympathy somewhere.

Frieda sends her love, and one day I hope we'll have a few quiet chats and laughs together—there's still time for that.

George Orwell

George Orwell (1903-1950) was born Eric Arthur Blair in Bengal, a province of British India. After five years as a scholarship boy at a school which he calls St. Cyprian's in the essay we print here, he won a King's Scholarship to Eton in 1917. Leaving school in 1921, he served with the Indian Imperial Police in Burma for five years. The experience turned him against the "evil despotism" of British colonialism, which he portrayed in *Burmese Days* (1934). When he returned to Europe, Orwell spent several years barely subsisting on odd jobs, a lifestyle which he relates to his experience in Burma: "For five years I had been part of an oppressive system. . . . I was conscious of an immense weight of guilt that I had got to expiate." His first published book, *Down and Out in Paris and London* (1933), is a vivid record of these years.

With financial support from F. J. Warburg's publishing house, Orwell was able to join a Socialist militia unit in the Spanish Civil War in 1936. His *Homage to Catalonia* (1938), which Lionel Trilling calls "one of the important documents of our time," records his experiences and his struggle against the Communist harshness and divisiveness which weakened the revolutionary army. Orwell's opposition to Stalinist communism is given literary treatment in *Animal Farm* (1945), a fable based on the history of the Russian Revolution. His last novel, *Nineteen Eighty-Four* (1949), is a horrifying picture of social control carried to its ultimate extremes.

During his lifetime, Orwell was probably best known for his books, but since his death at forty-six, his reputation as an essayist has risen steadily. George Steiner writes that he "despised generality. It was the specific, local truth which mattered," and notes his "unswerving attention to detail, to the loose ends and broken edges which in fact make up the fabric of human behavior."

"Such, Such Were the Joys" is a long autobiographical sketch, published posthumously in 1953, in which Orwell describes his first school experiences. We reprint here the first and the last of six sections as they appear in his *Collected Essays, Journalism, and Letters* (1968). They are a good example of how Orwell the essayist borrows techniques from fiction, how he relies on narration, description, and dialogue. He is also an unabashed user of the first person singular, but this never prevents him from working his private, personal perceptions into a larger understanding or awareness or idea. Thus in the first section he begins with an account of how he actually felt when he was an eight-year-old boy and concludes with insights drawn from his having long reflected on the experience. Similarly, the last section provides a reflective, idea-laden conclusion to the whole essay. As with most of Orwell's essays, it shows us how the "first person singular" essay that looks inward can at the same time be turned outward to become the expository essay of ideas. The genre invites imitation; nearly everyone has memories that have turned out to be instructive on close examination.

from *"Such, Such Were the Joys"*

Soon after I arrived at St Cyprian's (not immediately, but after a week or two, just when I seemed to be settling into the routine of school life) I began wetting my bed. I was now aged eight, so that this was a reversion to a habit which I must have grown out of at least four years earlier.

Nowadays, I believe, bed-wetting in such circumstances is taken for granted. It is a normal reaction in children who have been removed from their homes to a strange place. In those days, however, it was looked on as a disgusting crime which the child committed on purpose and for which the proper cure was a beating. For my part I did not need to be told it was a crime. Night after night I prayed, with a fervour never previously attained in my prayers, "Please God, do not let me wet my bed! Oh, please God, do not let me wet my bed!", but it made remarkably little difference. Some nights the thing happened, others not. There was no volition about it, no consciousness. You did not properly speaking *do* the deed: you merely woke up in the morning and found that the sheets were wringing wet.

After the second or third offence I was warned that I should be beaten next time, but I received the warning in a curiously roundabout way. One afternoon, as we were filing out from tea, Mrs. W——, the Headmaster's wife, was sitting at the head of one of the tables, chatting with a lady of whom I knew nothing, except that she was on an afternoon's visit to the school. She was an intimidating, masculine-looking person wearing a riding-habit, or something that I took to be a riding-habit. I was just leaving the room when Mrs W—— called me back, as though to introduce me to the visitor.

Mrs W—— was nicknamed Flip, and I shall call her by that name, for I seldom think of her by any other. (Officially, however, she was addressed as Mum, probably a corruption of the "Ma'am" used by public school-boys to their housemasters' wives.) She was a stocky square-built woman with hard red cheeks, a flat top to her head, prominent brows and deep-set, suspicious eyes. Although a great deal of the time she was full of false heartiness, jollying one along with mannish slang (*"Buck* up, old chap!" and so forth), and even using one's Christian name, her eyes never lost their anxious, accusing look. It was very difficult to look her in the face without feeling guilty, even at moments when one was not guilty of anything in particular.

"Here is a little boy," said Flip, indicating me to the strange lady, "who wets his bed every night. Do you know what I am going to do if you wet your bed again?" she added, turning to me. "I am going to get the Sixth Form to beat you."

The strange lady put on an air of being inexpressibly shocked, and exclaimed "I-should-*think*-so!" And here there occurred one of those wild, almost lunatic misunderstandings which are part of the daily experience of childhood. The Sixth Form was a group of older boys who were selected as having "character" and were empowered to beat smaller boys. I had not yet learned of their existence, and I mis-heard the phrase "the Sixth Form" as "Mrs Form". I took it as referring to the strange lady—I thought, that is, that her name was Mrs Form. It was an improbable name, but a child has no judgement in such matters. I imagined, therefore, that it was *she* who was to be deputed to beat me. It did not strike me as strange that this job should be turned over to a casual visitor in no way connected with the school. I merely assumed that "Mrs Form" was a stern disciplinarian who enjoyed beating people (somehow her appearance seemed to bear this out) and I had an immediate terrifying vision of her arriving for the occasion in full riding kit and armed with a hunting-whip. To this day I can feel myself almost swooning with shame as I stood, a very small, round-faced boy in short corduroy knickers, before the two women. I could not speak. I felt that I should die if "Mrs Form" were to beat me. But my dominant feeling was not fear or even resentment: it was simply shame because one more person, and that a woman, had been told of my disgusting offence.

A little later, I forget how, I learned that it was not after all "Mrs Form" who would do the beating. I cannot remember whether it was that very night that I wetted my bed again, but at any rate I did wet it again quite soon. Oh, the despair, the feeling of cruel injustice, after all my prayers and resolutions, at once again waking between the clammy sheets! There was no chance of hiding what I had done. The grim statuesque matron, Margaret by name, arrived in the dormitory specially to inspect my bed. She pulled back the clothes, then drew herself up, and the dreaded words seemed to come rolling out of her like a peal of thunder:

"REPORT YOURSELF to the Headmaster after breakfast!"

I put REPORT YOURSELF in capitals because that was how it appeared in my mind. I do not know how many times I heard that phrase during my early years at St Cyprian's. It was only very rarely that it did not mean a beating. The words always had a portentous sound in my ears, like muffled drums or the words of the death sentence.

When I arrived to report myself, Flip was doing something or other at the long shiny table in the ante-room to the study. Her uneasy eyes searched me as I went past. In the study the Headmaster, nicknamed Sambo, was waiting. Sambo was a round-shouldered, curiously oafish-looking man, not large but shambling in gait, with a chubby face which was like that of an overgrown baby, and which was capable of good humour. He knew, of course, why I had been sent to him, and had already taken a bone-handled riding-crop out of the cupboard, but it was part of the punishment of reporting yourself that you had to proclaim your offence with your own lips. When I had said my say, he read me a short but pompous lecture, then seized me by the scruff of the neck, twisted me over and began beating me with the riding-crop. He had a habit of continuing his lecture while he flogged you, and I remember the words "you dir-ty lit-tle boy" keeping time with the blows. The beating did not hurt (perhaps, as it was the first time, he was not hitting me very hard), and I walked out feeling very much better. The fact that the beating had not hurt was a sort of victory and partially wiped out the shame of the bed-wetting. I was even incautious enough to wear a grin on my face. Some small boys were hanging about in the passage outside the door of the ante-room.

"D'you get the cane?"

"It didn't hurt," I said proudly.

Flip had heard everything. Instantly her voice came screaming after me:

"Come here! Come here this instant! What was that you said?"

"I said it didn't hurt," I faltered out.

"How dare you say a thing like that? Do you think that is a proper thing to say? Go in and REPORT YOURSELF AGAIN!"

This time Sambo laid on in real earnest. He continued for a length of time that frightened and astonished me—about five minutes, it seemed—ending up by breaking the riding-crop. The bone handle went flying across the room.

"Look what you've made me do!" he said furiously, holding up the broken crop.

I had fallen into a chair, weakly snivelling. I remember that this was the only time throughout my boyhood when a beating actually reduced me to tears, and curiously enough I was not even now crying because of the pain. The second beating had not hurt very much either. Fright and shame seemed to have anaesthetised me. I was crying partly because I felt that this was expected of me, partly from genuine repentance, but partly also because of a deeper grief which is peculiar to childhood and not easy to convey: a sense of desolate loneliness and helplessness, of being locked up not only in a hostile world but in a world of good and evil where the rules were such that it was actually not possible for me to keep them.

I knew that the bed-wetting was (a) wicked and (b) outside my control. The second fact I was personally aware of, and the first I did not question. It was possible, therefore, to commit a sin without knowing that you committed it, without wanting to commit it, and without being able to avoid it. Sin was not necessarily something that you did: it might be something that happened to you. I do not want to claim that this idea flashed into my mind as a complete novelty at this very moment, under the blows of Sambo's cane: I must have had glimpses of it even before I left home, for my early childhood had not been altogether happy. But at any rate this was the great, abiding lesson of my boyhood: that I was in a world where it was *not possible* for me to be good. And the double beating was a turning-point, for it brought home to me for the first time the harshness of the environment into which I had been flung. Life was more terrible, and I was more wicked, than I had imagined. At any rate, as I sat snivelling on the edge of a chair in Sambo's study, with not even the self-possession to stand up while he stormed at me, I had a conviction of sin and folly and weakness, such as I do not remember to have felt before.

In general, one's memories of any period must necessarily weaken as one moves away from it. One is constantly learning new facts, and old ones have to drop out to make way for them. At twenty I could have written the history of my schooldays with an accuracy which would be quite impossible now. But it can also happen that one's memories grow sharper after a long lapse of time, because one is looking at the past with fresh eyes and can isolate and, as it were, notice facts which previously existed undifferentiated among a mass of others. Here are two things which in a sense I remembered, but which did not strike me as strange or interesting until quite recently. One is that the second beating seemed to me a just and reasonable punishment. To get one beating, and then to get another and far fiercer one on top of it, for being so unwise as to show that the first had not hurt—that was quite natural. The gods are jealous, and when you have good fortune you should conceal it. The other is that I accepted the broken riding-crop as my own crime. I can still recall my feeling as I saw the handle lying on the carpet—the feeling of having done an ill-bred clumsy thing, and ruined an expensive object. *I* had broken it: so Sambo told me, and so I believed. This acceptance of guilt lay unnoticed in my memory for twenty or thirty years.

So much for the episode of the bed-wetting. But there is one more thing to be remarked. This is that I did not wet my bed again—at least, I did wet it once again, and received another beating, after which the trouble stopped. So perhaps this barbarous remedy does work, though at a heavy price, I have no doubt.

All this was thirty years ago and more. The question is: Does a child at school go through the same kind of experiences nowadays?

The only honest answer, I believe, is that we do not with certainty know. Of course it is obvious that the present-day *attitude* towards education is enormously more humane and sensible than that of the past. The snobbishness that was an integral part of my own education would be almost unthinkable today, because the society that nourished it is dead. I recall a conversation that must have taken place about a year before I left St. Cyprian's. A Russian boy, large and fair-haired, a year older than myself, was questioning me.

"How much a year has your father got?"

I told him what I thought it was, adding a few hundreds to make it sound better. The Russian boy, neat in his habits, produced a pencil and a small note-book and made a calculation.

"My father has over two hundred times as much money as yours," he announced with a sort of amused contempt.

That was in 1915. What happened to that money a couple of years later, I wonder? And still more I wonder, do conversations of that kind happen at preparatory schools now?

Clearly there has been a vast change of outlook, a general growth of "enlightenment", even among ordinary, unthinking middle-class people. Religious belief, for instance, has largely vanished, dragging other kinds of nonsense after it. I imagine that very few people nowadays would tell a child that if it masturbates it will end in the lunatic asylum. Beating, too, has become discredited, and has even been abandoned at many schools. Nor is the underfeeding of children looked on as a normal, almost meritorious act. No one now would openly set out to give his pupils as little food as they could do with, or tell them that it is healthy to get up from a meal as hungry as you sat down. The whole status of children has improved, partly because they have grown relatively less numerous. And the diffusion of even a little psychological knowledge has made it harder for parents and schoolteachers to indulge their aberrations in the name of discipline. Here is a case, not known to me personally, but known to someone I can vouch for, and happening within my own lifetime. A small girl, daughter of a clergyman, continued wetting her bed at an age when she should have grown out of it. In order to punish her for this dreadful deed, her father took her to a large garden party and there introduced her to the whole company as a little girl who wetted her bed: and to underline her wickedness he had previously painted her face black. I do not suggest that Flip and Sambo would actually have done a thing like this, but I doubt whether it would have much surprised them. After all, things do change. And yet—!

The question is not whether boys are still buckled into Eton collars on Sunday, or told that babies are dug up under gooseberry bushes. That kind of thing is at an end, admittedly. The real question is whether it is still normal for a schoolchild to live for years amid irrational terrors and lunatic misunderstandings. And here one is up against the very great difficulty of knowing what a child really feels and thinks. A child which appears reasonably happy may actually be suffering horrors which it cannot or will not reveal. It lives in a sort of alien under-water world which we can only penetrate by memory or divination. Our chief clue is the fact that we were once children ourselves, and many people appear to forget the atmosphere of their own childhood almost entirely. Think for instance of the unnecessary torments that people will inflict by sending a child back to school with clothes of the wrong pattern, and refusing to see that this matters! Over things of this kind a child will sometimes utter a protest, but a great deal of the time its attitude is one of simple concealment. Not to expose your true feelings to an adult seems to be instinctive from the age of seven or eight onwards. Even the affection that one feels for a child, the desire to protect and cherish it, is a cause of misunderstanding. One can love a child, perhaps, more deeply than one can love another adult, but it is rash to assume that the child feels any love in return. Looking back on my own childhood, after the infant years were over, I do not believe that I ever felt love for any mature person, except my mother, and even her I did not trust, in the sense that shyness made me conceal most of my real feelings from her. Love, the spontaneous, unqualified emotion of love, was something I could only feel for people who were young. Towards people who were old—and remember that "old" to a child means over thirty, or even over twenty-five—I could feel reverence, respect, admiration or compunction, but I seemed cut off from them by a veil of fear and shyness mixed up with physical distaste. People are too ready to forget the child's *physical* shrinking from the adult. The enormous size of grown-ups, their ungainly, rigid bodies, their coarse, wrinkled skins, their great relaxed eyelids, their yellow teeth, and the whiffs of musty clothes and beer and sweat and tobacco that disengage from them at every movement! Part of the reason for the ugliness of adults, in a child's eyes, is that the child is usually looking upwards, and few faces are at their best when seen from below. Besides, being fresh and unmarked itself, the child has impossibly high standards in the matter of skin and teeth and complexion. But the greatest barrier of all is the child's misconception about age. A child can hardly envisage life beyond thirty, and in judging people's ages it will make fantastic mistakes. It will think that a person of twenty-five is forty, that a person of forty is sixty-five, and so on. Thus, when I fell in love with Elsie I took her to be grown-up. I met her again, when I was thirteen and she, I think, must have been twenty-three; she now seemed to me a middle-aged woman, somewhat past her best. And the child thinks of growing old as an almost obscene calamity, which for some mysterious reason will never happen to itself. All who have passed the age of thirty are joyless grotesques, endlessly fussing about things of no importance and staying alive without, so far as the child can see, having anything to live for. Only child life is real life. The schoolmaster who imagines that he is loved and trusted by his boys is in fact mimicked and laughed at behind his back. An adult who does not seem dangerous nearly always seems ridiculous.

I base these generalisations on what I can recall of my own childhood outlook. Treacherous though memory is, it seems to me the chief means we have of discovering how a child's mind works. Only by resurrecting our own memories can we realise how incredibly distorted is the child's vision of the world. Consider this, for example. How would St Cyprian's appear to me now, if I could go back, at my present age, and see it as it was in 1915? What should I think of Sambo and Flip, those terrible, all-powerful monsters? I should see them as a couple of silly, shallow, ineffectual people, eagerly clambering up a social ladder which any thinking person could see to be on the point of collapse. I would no more be frightened of them than I would be frightened of a dormouse.

Moreover, in those days they seemed to me fantastically old, whereas—though of this I am not certain—I imagine they must have been somewhat younger than I am now. And how would Johnny Hale appear, with his blacksmith's arms and his red, jeering face? Merely a scruffy little boy, barely distinguishable from hundreds of other scruffy little boys. The two sets of facts can lie side by side in my mind, because those happen to be my own memories. But it would be very difficult for me to see with the eyes of any other child, except by an effort of the imagination which might lead me completely astray. The child and the adult live in different worlds. If that is so, we cannot be certain that school, at any rate boarding school, is not still for many children as dreadful an experience as it used to be. Take away God, Latin, the cane, class distinctions and sexual taboos, and the fear, the hatred, the snobbery and the misunderstanding might still all be there. It will have been seen that my own main trouble was an utter lack of any sense of proportion or probability. This led me to accept outrages and believe absurdities, and to suffer torments over things which were in fact of no importance. It is not enough to say that I was "silly" and "ought to have known better". Look back into your own childhood and think of the nonsense you used to believe and the trivialities which could make you suffer. Of course my own case had its individual variations, but essentially it was that of countless other boys. The weakness of the child is that it starts with a blank sheet. It neither understands nor questions the society in which it lives, and because of its credulity other people can work upon it, infecting it with the sense of inferiority and the dread of offending against mysterious, terrible laws. It may be that everything that happened to me at St Cyprian's could happen in the most "enlightened" school, though perhaps in subtler forms. Of one thing, however, I do feel fairly sure, and that is that boarding schools are worse than day schools. A child has a better chance with the sanctuary of its home near at hand. And I think the characteristic faults of the English upper and middle classes may be partly due to the practice, general until recently, of sending children away from home as young as nine, eight or even seven.

I have never been back to St Cyprian's. Reunions, old boys' dinners and such-like leave me something more than cold, even when my memories are friendly. I have never even been down to Eton, where I was relatively happy, though I did once pass through it in 1933 and noted with interest that nothing seemed to have changed, except that the shops now sold radios. As for St. Cyprian's, for years I loathed its very name so deeply that I could not view it with enough detachment to see the significance of the things that happened to me there. In a way, it is only within the last decade that I have really thought over my schooldays, vividly though their memory has always haunted me. Nowadays, I believe, it would make very little impression on me to see the place again, if it still exists. (I remember hearing a rumour some years ago that it had been burnt down.) If I had to pass through Eastbourne I would not make a detour to avoid the school: and if I happened to pass the school itself I might even stop for a moment by the low brick wall, with the steep bank running down from it, and look across the flat playing field at the ugly building with the square of asphalt in front of it. And if I went inside and smelt again the inky, dusty smell of the big schoolroom, the rosiny smell of the chapel, the stagnant smell of the swimming bath and the cold reek of the lavatories, I think I should only feel what one invariably feels in revisiting any scene of childhood: How small everything has grown, and how terrible is the deterioration in myself! But it is a fact that for many years I could hardly have borne to look at it again. Except upon dire necessity I would not have set foot in Eastbourne. I even conceived a prejudice against Sussex, as the county that contained St Cyprian's, and as an adult I have only once been in Sussex, on a short visit. Now, however, the place is out of my system for good. Its magic works no longer, and I have not even enough animosity left to make me hope that Flip and Sambo are dead or that the story of the school being burnt down was true.

James Thurber

James Thurber (1894-1961) was born and raised in Columbus, Ohio. He began writing and editing for student publications at Ohio State University in 1917. He left college in 1918 to become a code clerk for the State Department until the end of World War I. While planning and writing pieces of his own which didn't sell, he worked for the Columbus *Dispatch,* the Paris edition of the Chicago *Tribune,* and the New York *Evening Post.*

Joining the *New Yorker* staff in 1926, Thurber met E. B. White, with whom he collaborated on a parody of popularized sex books, *Is Sex Necessary?* From the publication of this book in 1929, Thurber's line drawings and his humorous writings became famous. His more than twenty books, from *The Owl in the Attic* (1931) to *Credos and Curios* (1962), have established him as one of America's greatest humorists and cartoonists. A changeable and less than joyous man—he wrote of humorists like himself that "the little wheels of their invention are set in motion by the damp hand of melancholy."

"The Car We Had to Push" is the second chapter of *My Life and Hard Times* (1933). Like much of Thurber's work it is based on his early life in Columbus. This account, despite its apparently relaxed and wandering tone, is extremely artful, one of the most literary in the present book. While ostensibly describing the old car, Thurber deftly sketches a gallery of family portraits, including his own, and sets a mood that well illustrates his characterization of his humor as based on "a kind of emotional chaos told about calmly and quietly in retrospect." In catching the flavor of family life, Thurber edges well over the boundaries of widely accepted fact (consider the disease his uncle Zenas died of!). Is his account therefore essentially untrue? Try to catch the flavor of your own family's life by focusing loosely on the car or some other likely family totem.

The Car We Had to Push

Many autobiographers, among them Lincoln Steffens and Gertrude Atherton, describe earthquakes their families have been in. I am unable to do this because my family was never in an earthquake, but we went through a number of things in Columbus that were a great deal like earthquakes. I remember in particular some of the repercussions of an old Reo we had that wouldn't go unless you pushed it for quite a way and suddenly let your clutch out. Once, we had been able to start the engine easily by cranking it, but we had had the car for so many years that finally it wouldn't go unless you pushed it and let your clutch out. Of course, it took more than one person to do this; it took sometimes as many as five or six, depending on the grade of the roadway and conditions underfoot. The car was unusual in that the clutch and brake were on the same pedal, making it quite easy to stall the engine after it got started, so that the car would have to be pushed again.

My father used to get sick at his stomach pushing the car, and very often was unable to go to work. He had never liked the machine, even when it was good, sharing my ignorance and suspicion of all automobiles of twenty years ago and longer. The boys I went to school with used to be able to identify every car as it passed by: Thomas Flyer, Firestone-Columbus, Stevens Duryea, Rambler, Winton, White Steamer, etc. I never could. The only car I was really interested in was one that the Get-Ready Man, as we called him, rode around town in: a big Red Devil with a door in the back. The Get-Ready Man was a lank unkempt elderly gentleman with wild eyes and a deep voice who used to go about shouting at people through a megaphone to prepare for the end of the world. "GET READY! GET READ-Y" he would bellow. "THE WORLLLD IS COMING TO AN END!" His startling exhortations would come up, like summer thunder, at the most unexpected times and in the most surprising places. I remember once during Mantell's production of "King Lear" at the Colonial Theatre, that the Get-Ready Man added his bawlings to the squealing of Edgar and the ranting of the King and the mouthing of the Fool, rising from somewhere in the balcony to join in. The theatre was in absolute darkness and there were rumblings of thunder and flashes of lightning offstage. Neither father nor I, who were there, ever completely got over the scene, which went something like this:

Edgar: Tom's a-cold.—O, do de, do de, do de!—Bless thee from whirlwinds, star-blasting, and taking . . . the foul fiend vexes!

(Thunder off.)

Lear: What! Have his daughters brought him to this pass?—
Get-Ready Man: Get ready! Get ready!
Edgar: Pillicock sat on Pillicock-hill:—

Halloo, halloo, loo, loo!
(Lightning flashes.)

Get-Ready Man: The Worllld is com-ing to an End!
Fool: This cold night will turn us all to fools and madmen!
Edgar: Take heed o' the foul fiend: obey thy paren—
Get-Ready Man: Get *Rea*-dy!
Edgar: Tom's a-*cold*!
Get-Ready Man: The *Worr*-uld is coming to an end! . . .

They found him finally, and ejected him, still shouting. The Theatre, in our time, has known few such moments.

But to get back to the automobile. One of my happiest memories of it was when, in its eighth year, my brother Roy got together a great many articles from the kitchen, placed them in a square of canvas, and swung this under the car with a string attached to it so that, at a twitch, the canvas would give way and the steel and tin things would clatter to the street. This was a little scheme of Roy's to frighten father, who had always expected the car might explode. It worked perfectly. That was twenty-five years ago, but it is one of the few things in my life I would like to live over again if I could. I don't suppose that I can, now. Roy twitched the string in the middle of a lovely afternoon, on Bryden Road near Eighteenth Street. Father had closed his eyes and, with his hat off, was enjoying a cool breeze. The clatter on the asphalt was tremendously effective: knives, forks, can-openers, pie pans, pot lids, biscuit-cutters, ladles, egg-beaters fell, beautifully together, in a lingering, clamant crash. "Stop the *car!*" shouted father. "I can't," Roy said. "The engine fell out." "God Almighty!" said father, who knew what *that* meant, or knew what it sounded as if it might mean.

It ended unhappily, of course, because we finally had to drive back and pick up the stuff and even father knew the difference between the works of an automobile and the equipment of a pantry. My mother wouldn't have known, however, nor *her* mother. My mother, for instance, thought—or, rather, knew—that it was dangerous to drive an automobile without gasoline: it fried the valves, or something. "Now don't you dare drive all over town without gasoline!" she would say to us when we started off. Gasoline, oil, and water were much the same to her, a fact that made her life both confusing and perilous. Her greatest dread, however, was the Victrola—we had a very early one, back in the "Come Josephine in My Flying Machine" days. She had an idea that the Victrola might blow up. It alarmed her, rather than reassured her, to explain that the phonograph was run neither by gasoline nor by electricity. She could only suppose that it was propelled by some newfangled and untested apparatus which was likely to let go at any minute, making us all the victims and martyrs of the wild-eyed Edison's dangerous experiments. The telephone she was comparatively at peace with, except, of course, during storms, when for some reason or other she always took the receiver off the hook and let it hang. She came naturally by her confused and groundless fears, for her own mother lived the latter years of her life in the horrible suspicion that electricity was dripping invisibly all over the house. It leaked, she contended, out of empty sockets if the wall switch had been left on. She would go around screwing in bulbs, and if they lighted up she would hastily and fearfully turn off the wall switch and go back to her *Pearson's* or *Everybody's,* happy in the satisfaction that she had stopped not only a costly but a dangerous leakage. Nothing could ever clear this up for her.

Our poor old Reo came to a horrible end, finally. We had parked it too far from the curb on a street with a car line. It was late at night and the street was dark. The first streetcar that came along couldn't get by. It picked up the tired old automobile as a terrier might seize a rabbit and drubbed it unmercifully, losing its hold now and then but catching a new grip a second later. Tires booped and whooshed, the fenders queeled and graked, the steering-wheel rose up like a spectre and disappeared in the direction of Franklin Avenue with a melancholy whistling sound, bolts and gadgets flew like sparks from a Catherine wheel. It was a splendid spectacle but, of course, saddening to everybody (except the motorman of the streetcar, who was sore). I think some of us broke down and wept. It must have been the weeping that caused grandfather to take on so terribly. Time was all mixed up in his mind; automobiles and the like he never remembered having seen. He apparently gathered, from the talk and excitement and weeping, that somebody had died. Nor did he let go of this delusion. He insisted, in fact, after almost a week in which we strove mightily to divert him, that it was a sin and a shame and a disgrace on the family to put the funeral off any longer. "Nobody is dead! The automobile is smashed!" shouted my father, trying for the thirtieth time to explain the situation to the old man. "Was he drunk?" demanded grandfather, sternly. "Was who drunk?" asked father. "Zenas," said grandfather. He had a name for the corpse now: it was his brother Zenas, who, as it happened, *was* dead, but not from driving an automobile while intoxicated. Zenas had died in 1866. A sensitive, rather poetical boy of twenty-one when the Civil War broke out, Zenas had gone to South America—"just," as he wrote back, "until it blows over." Returning after the war had blown over, he caught the same disease that was killing off the chestnut trees in those years, and passed away. It was the only case in history where a tree doctor had to be called in to spray a person, and our family had felt it very keenly; nobody else in the United States caught the blight. Some of us have looked upon Zenas' fate as a kind of poetic justice.

Now that grandfather knew, so to speak, who was dead, it became increasingly awkward to go on living in the same house with him as if nothing had happened. He would go into towering rages in which he threatened to write to the Board of Health unless the funeral were held at once. We realized that something had to be done. Eventually, we persuaded a friend of father's, named George Martin, to dress up in the manner and costume of the eighteen-sixties and pretend to be Uncle Zenas, in order to set grandfather's mind at rest. The impostor looked fine and impressive in sideburns and a high beaver hat, and not unlike the daguerreotypes of Zenas in our album. I shall never forget the night, just after dinner, when this Zenas walked into the living-room. Grandfather was stomping up and down, tall, hawk-nosed, round-oathed. The newcomer held out both his hands. "Clem!" he cried to grandfather. Grandfather turned slowly, looked at the intruder, and snorted. "Who air *you*?" he demanded in his deep, resonant voice. "I'm Zenas!" cried Martin. "Your brother Zenas, fit as a fiddle and sound as a dollar."

"Zenas, my foot!" said grandfather. "Zenas died of the chestnut blight in '66!"

Grandfather was given to these sudden, unexpected, and extremely lucid moments; they were generally more embarrassing than his other moments. He comprehended before he went to bed that night that the old automobile had been destroyed and that its destruction had caused all the turmoil in the house. "It flew all to pieces, Pa," my mother told him, in graphically describing the accident. "I knew 'twould," growled grandfather. "I allus told ye to git a Pope-Toledo."

Vladimir Nabokov

Vladimir Nabokov was born in 1899 in St. Petersburg (now Leningrad), one of five children of a wealthy Russian family. He was educated by tutors and, from 1910 to 1917, at the Prince Tenishev School, learned to read English before Russian and to read and speak French as well. He received his B.A. from Trinity College, Cambridge, in 1922. As a result of the 1917 Russian Revolution, his family lost its fortune and emigrated in 1919. His father, a liberal reformer, was assassinated in Berlin in 1922. From 1922 until 1937 Nabokov lived in Berlin, giving lessons in English and tennis, writing novels and plays, and contributing poetry and crossword puzzles to the Russian emigré newspapers. After three years in Paris, he came to the United States in 1940 and became a United States citizen in 1945. He has taught Russian literature and creative writing at several American universities and has researched and published extensively in his second specialty, the classification of butterflies.

Nabokov published his first book of verse, in Russian, when he was thirteen. His first novel, *Mashen'ka*, was written in 1926. He has translated many of his early Russian works into English and often translates his English works into Russian. His fifteen novels, along with short stories, plays, and criticism, have since brought him widespread popularity and a reputation as one of the finest contemporary English stylists. *Lolita* (1955) created a near scandal, although Nabokov himself considers the story neither satirical nor immoral, but rather "like the composition of a beautiful puzzle." The experimental form and polished language of *Pale Fire* (1962) led Mary McCarthy to hail it as "one of the very great works of art of this century."

Nabokov seems not to believe in the social significance of art; he says that for him "the work of fiction exists only in so far as it affords me what I shall bluntly call aesthetic bliss; that is, a sense of being somehow, somewhere connected with other states of being where art (curiosity, tenderness, kindness, ecstasy) is the norm."

In many of his works, Nabokov strives to overcome conventional time and to reach what he calls "a flowering of the present," in which the past is fully re-created and revived in art. "I confess I do not believe in time," he writes. "I like to fold my magic carpet, after use, in such a way as to superimpose one part of the pattern upon another. Let visitors trip." This approach to time informs his autobiography, originally written in separate chapters and published in magazines from 1936 through 1951. The first complete version, *Conclusive Evidence: A Memoir* (1951), he then translated into Russian with some additions in 1953. The revised Russian text formed the basis for a new English version, *Speak, Memory,* in 1966. It is from this second English version that the following passage is taken.

The passage is highly characteristic of Nabokov's tone and style, and many readers will find it difficult to decide what to feel about him. His passion for rare words ("fatidic," "praedormitary," "hypnagogic," "palpebral"!) is like his passion for collecting rare moths and butterflies and may at first seem merely exhibitionistic. His tone is that of an egoist (in the largest sense), and his utter freedom and self-possession in the face of his reader (e.g., "I hasten to complete my list . . . ."

[p. 193]) may intimidate the latter as much as it attracts him. The reader will have to decide whether the feeling of being occasionally played with is compensated for by the pleasure of sharing Nabokov's experience in its unrivalled concreteness, freshness, and tenderness. This passage will particularly repay appreciation of the range of Nabokov's vocabulary, the originality of his metaphors and similes, his mastery of prolonged rhythmical spells, and his capacity to draw whole scenes and episodes from a single remembered image.

My Mother,
from *Speak, Memory*

1

As far back as I remember myself (with interest, with amusement, seldom with admiration or disgust), I have been subject to mild hallucinations. Some are aural, others are optical, and by none have I profited much. The fatidic accents that restrained Socrates or egged on Joaneta Darc have degenerated with me to the level of something one happens to hear between lifting and clapping down the receiver of a busy party-line telephone. Just before falling asleep, I often become aware of a kind of one-sided conversation going on in an adjacent section of my mind, quite independently from the actual trend of my thoughts. It is a neutral, detached, anonymous voice, which I catch saying words of no importance to me whatever—an English or a Russian sentence, not even addressed to me, and so trivial that I hardly dare give samples, lest the flatness I wish to convey be marred by a molehill of sense. This silly phenomenon seems to be the auditory counterpart of certain praedormitary visions, which I also know well. What I mean is not the bright mental image (as, for instance, the face of a beloved parent long dead) conjured up by a wing-stroke of the will; *that* is one of the bravest movements a human spirit can make. Nor am I alluding to the so-called *muscae volitantes*—shadows cast upon the retinal rods by motes in the vitreous humor, which are seen as transparent threads drifting across the visual field. Perhaps nearer to the hypnagogic mirages I am thinking of is the colored spot, the stab of an afterimage, with which the lamp one has just turned off wounds the palpebral night. However, a shock of this sort is not really a necessary starting point for the slow, steady development of the visions that pass before my closed eyes. They come and go, without the drowsy observer's participation, but are essentially different from dream pictures for he is still master of his senses. They are often grotesque. I am pestered by roguish profiles, by some coarse-featured and florid dwarf with a swelling nostril or ear. At times, however, my photisms take on a rather soothing *flou* quality, and then I see—projected, as it were, upon the inside of the eyelid—gray figures walking between beehives, or small black parrots gradually vanishing among mountain snows, or a mauve remoteness melting beyond moving masts.

On top of all this I present a fine case of colored hearing. Perhaps "hearing" is not quite accurate, since the color sensation seems to be produced by the very act of my orally forming a given letter while I imagine its outline. The long *a* of the English alphabet (and it is this alphabet I have in mind farther on unless otherwise stated) has for me the tint of weathered wood, but a French *a* evokes polished ebony. This black group also includes hard *g* (vulcanized rubber) and *r* (a sooty rag being ripped). Oatmeal *n*, noodle-limp *l*, and the ivory-backed hand mirror of *o* take care of the whites. I am puzzled by my French *on* which I see as the brimming tension-surface of alcohol in a small glass. Passing on to the blue group, there is steely *x*, thundercloud *z*, and huckleberry *k*. Since a subtle interaction exists between sound and shape, I see *q* as browner than *k*, while *s* is not the light blue of *c*, but a curious mixture of azure and mother-of-pearl. Adjacent tints do not merge, and diphthongs do not have special colors of their own, unless represented by a single character in some other language (thus the fluffy-gray, three-stemmed Russian letter that stands for *sh*, a letter as old as the rushes of the Nile, influences its English representation).

I hasten to complete my list before I am interrupted. In the green group, there are alder-leaf *f*, the unripe apple of *p*, and pistachio *t*. Dull green, combined somehow with violet, is the best I can do for *w*. The yellows comprise various *e*'s and *i*'s, creamy *d*, bright-golden *y*, and *u*, whose alphabetical value I can express only by "brassy with an olive sheen." In the brown group, there are the rich rubbery tone of soft *g*, paler *j*, and the drab shoelace of *h*. Finally, among the reds, *b* has the tone called burnt sienna by painters, *m* is a fold of pink flannel, and today I have at last perfectly matched *v* with "Rose Quartz" in Maerz and Paul's *Dictionary of Color*. The word for rainbow, a primary, but decidedly muddy, rainbow, is in my private language the hardly pronounceable: *kzspygv*. The first author to discuss *audition colorée* was, as far as I know, an albino physician in 1812, in Erlangen.

The confessions of a synesthete must sound tedious and pretentious to those who are protected from such leakings and drafts by more solid walls than mine are. To my mother, though, this all seemed quite normal. The matter came up, one day in my seventh year, as I was using a heap of old alphabet blocks to build a tower. I casually remarked to her that their colors were all wrong. We discovered then that some of her letters had the same tint as mine and that, besides, she was optically

affected by musical notes. These evoked no chromatisms in me whatsoever. Music, I regret to say, affects me merely as an arbitrary succession
of more or less irritating sounds. Under certain emotional circumstances
I can stand the spasms of a rich violin, but the concert piano and all
wind instruments bore me in small doses and flay me in larger ones.
Despite the number of operas I was exposed to every winter (I must have
attended *Ruslan* and *Pikovaya Dama* at least a dozen times in the
course of half as many years), my weak responsiveness to music was
completely overrun by the visual torment of not being able to read over
Pimen's shoulder or of trying in vain to imagine the hawkmoths in the
dim bloom of Juliet's garden.

My mother did everything to encourage the general sensitiveness I
had to visual stimulation. How many were the aquarelles she painted for
me; what a revelation it was when she showed me the lilac tree that
grows out of mixed blue and red! Sometimes, in our St. Petersburg
house, from a secret compartment in the wall of her dressing room (and
my birth room), she would produce a mass of jewelry for my bedtime
amusement. I was very small then, and those flashing tiaras and chokers
and rings seemed to me hardly inferior in mystery and enchantment to
the illumination in the city during imperial fêtes, when, in the padded
stillness of a frosty night, giant monograms, crowns, and other armorial
designs, made of colored electric bulbs—sapphire, emerald, ruby—glowed
with a kind of charmed constraint above snow-lined cornices on
housefronts along residential streets.

2

My numerous childhood illnesses brought my mother and me still
closer together. As a little boy, I showed an abnormal aptitude for
mathematics, which I completely lost in my singularly talentless youth.
This gift played a horrible part in tussles with quinsy or scarlet fever,
when I felt enormous spheres and huge numbers swell relentlessly in my
aching brain. A foolish tutor had explained logarithms to me much too
early, and I had read (in a British publication, the *Boy's Own Paper,* I
believe) about a certain Hindu calculator who in exactly two seconds
could find the seventeenth root of, say, 352947114576027513230
1897342055866171392 (I am not sure I have got this right; anyway the
root was 212). Such were the monsters that thrived on my delirium, and
the only way to prevent them from crowding me out of myself was to
kill them by extracting their hearts. But they were far too strong, and I
would sit up and laboriously form garbled sentences as I tried to explain
things to my mother. Beneath my delirium, she recognized sensations
she had known herself, and her understanding would bring my expanding
universe back to a Newtonian norm.

The future specialist in such dull literary lore as autoplagiarism will
like to collate a protagonist's experience in my novel *The Gift* with the

original event. One day, after a long illness, as I lay in bed still very weak, I found myself basking in an unusual euphoria of lightness and repose. I knew my mother had gone to buy me the daily present that made those convalescences so delightful. What it would be this time I could not guess, but through the crystal of my strangely translucent state I vividly visualized her driving away down Morskaya Street toward Nevski Avenue. I distinguished the light sleigh drawn by a chestnut courser. I heard his snorting breath, the rhythmic clacking of his scrotum, and the lumps of frozen earth and snow thudding against the front of the sleigh. Before my eyes and before those of my mother loomed the hind part of the coachman, in his heavily padded blue robe, and the leather-encased watch (twenty minutes past two) strapped to the back of his belt, from under which curved the pumpkin-like folds of his huge stuffed rump. I saw my mother's seal furs and, as the icy speed increased, the muff she raised to her face—that graceful, winter-ride gesture of a St. Petersburg lady. Two corners of the voluminous spread of bearskin that covered her up to the waist were attached by loops to the two side knobs of the low back of her seat. And behind her, holding on to these knobs, a footman in a cockaded hat stood on his narrow support above the rear extremities of the runners.

Still watching the sleigh, I saw it stop at Treumann's (writing implements, bronze baubles, playing cards). Presently, my mother came out of this shop followed by the footman. He carried her purchase, which looked to me like a pencil. I was astonished that she did not carry so small an object herself, and this disagreeable question of dimensions caused a faint renewal, fortunately very brief, of the "mind dilation effect" which I hoped had gone with the fever. As she was being tucked up again in the sleigh, I watched the vapor exhaled by all, horse included. I watched, too, the familiar pouting movement she made to distend the network of her close-fitting veil drawn too tight over her face, and as I write this, the touch of reticulated tenderness that my lips used to feel when I kissed her veiled cheek comes back to me—*flies* back to me with a shout of joy out of the snow-blue, blue-windowed (the curtains are not yet drawn) past.

A few minutes later, she entered my room. In her arms she held a big parcel. It had been, in my vision, greatly reduced in size—perhaps, because I subliminally corrected what logic warned me might still be the dreaded remnants of delirium's dilating world. Now the object proved to be a giant polygonal Faber pencil, four feet long and correspondingly thick. It had been hanging as a showpiece in the shop's window, and she presumed I had coveted it, as I coveted all things that were not quite purchasable. The shopman had been obliged to ring up an agent, a "Doctor" Libner (as if the transaction possessed indeed some pathological import). For an awful moment, I wondered whether the point was made of real graphite. It was. And some years later I satisfied myself, by drilling a hole in the side, that the lead went right through the whole length—a perfect case of art for art's sake on the part of Faber and Dr. Libner since the pencil was far too big for use and, indeed, was not meant to be used.

"Oh, yes," she would say as I mentioned this or that unusual sensation. "Yes, I know all that," and with a somewhat eerie ingenuousness she would discuss such things as double sight, and little raps in the woodwork of tripod tables, and premonitions, and the feeling of the *déjà vu*. A streak of sectarianism ran through her direct ancestry. She went to church only at Lent and Easter. The schismatic mood revealed itself in her healthy distaste for the ritual of the Greek Catholic Church and for its priests. She found a deep appeal in the moral and poetical side of the Gospels, but felt no need in the support of any dogma. The appalling insecurity of an afterlife and its lack of privacy did not enter her thoughts. Her intense and pure religiousness took the form of her having equal faith in the existence of another world and in the impossibility of comprehending it in terms of earthly life. All one could do was to glimpse, amid the haze and the chimeras, something real ahead, just as persons endowed with an unusual persistence of diurnal cerebration are able to perceive in their deepest sleep, somewhere beyond the throes of an entangled and inept nightmare, the ordered reality of the waking hour.

3

To love with all one's soul and leave the rest to fate, was the simple rule she heeded. "*Vot zapomni* [now remember]," she would say in conspiratorial tones as she drew my attention to this or that loved thing in Vyra—a lark ascending the curds-and-whey sky of a dull spring day, heat lightning taking pictures of a distant line of trees in the night, the palette of maple leaves on brown sand, a small bird's cuneate footprints on new snow. As if feeling that in a few years the tangible part of her world would perish, she cultivated an extraordinary consciousness of the various time marks distributed throughout our country place. She cherished her own past with the same retrospective fervor that I now do her image and my past. Thus, in a way, I inherited an exquisite simulacrum—the beauty of intangible property, unreal estate—and this proved a splendid training for the endurance of later losses. Her special tags and imprints became as dear and as sacred to me as they were to her. There was the room which in the past had been reserved for her mother's pet hobby, a chemical laboratory; there was the linden tree marking the spot, by the side of the road that sloped up toward the village of Gryazno (accented on the ultima), at the steepest bit where one preferred to take one's "bike by the horns" *(bīka za roga)* as my father, a dedicated cyclist, liked to say, and where he had proposed; and there was, in the so-called "old" park, the obsolete tennis court, now a region of moss, mole-heaps, and mushrooms, which had been the scene of gay rallies in the eighties and nineties (even her grim father would shed his coat and give the heaviest racket an appraisive shake, but which, by the time I was ten, nature had effaced with the thoroughness of a felt eraser wiping out a geometrical problem.

By then, an excellent modern court had been built at the end of the "new" part of the park by skilled workmen imported from Poland for that purpose. The wire mesh of an ample enclosure separated it from the flowery meadow that framed its clay. After a damp night the surface acquired a brownish gloss and the white lines would be repainted with liquid chalk from a green pail by Dmitri, the smallest and oldest of our gardeners, a meek, black-booted, red-shirted dwarf slowly retreating, all hunched up, as his paintbrush went down the line. A pea-tree hedge (the "yellow acacia" of northern Russia), with a midway opening, corresponding to the court's screen door, ran parallel to the enclosure and to a path dubbed *tropinka Sfinksov* ("path of the Sphingids") because of the hawkmoths visiting at dusk the fluffy lilacs along the border that faced the hedge and likewise broke in the middle. This path formed the bar of a great T whose vertical was the alley of slender oaks, my mother's coevals, that traversed (as already said) the new park through its entire length. Looking down that avenue from the base of the T near the drive one could make out quite distinctly the bright little gap five hundred yards away—or fifty years away from where I am now. Our current tutor or my father, when he stayed with us in the country, invariably had my brother for partner in our temperamental family doubles. "Play!" my mother would cry in the old manner as she put her little foot forward and bent her white-hatted head to ladle out an assiduous but feeble serve. I got easily cross with her, and she, with the ballboys, two barefooted peasant lads (Dmitri's pug-nosed grandson and the twin brother of pretty Polenka, the head coachman's daughter). The northern summer became tropical around harvest time. Scarlet Sergey would stick his racket between his knees and laboriously wipe his glasses. I see my butterfly net propped against the enclosure—just in case. Wallis Myers' book on lawn tennis lies open on a bench, and after every exchange my father (a first-rate player, with a cannonball service of the Frank Riseley type and a beautiful "lifting drive") pedantically inquires of my brother and me whether the "follow-through," that state of grace, has descended upon us. And sometimes a prodigious cloudburst would cause us to huddle under a shelter at the corner of the court while old Dmitri would be sent to fetch umbrellas and raincoats from the house. A quarter of an hour later he would reappear under a mountain of clothing in the vista of the long avenue which as he advanced would regain its leopard spots with the sun blazing anew and his huge burden unneeded.

She loved all games of skill and gambling. Under her expert hands, the thousand bits of a jigsaw puzzle gradually formed an English hunting scene; what had seemed to be the limb of a horse would turn out to belong to an elm and the hitherto unplaceable piece would snugly fill up a gap in the mottled background, affording one the delicate thrill of an abstract and yet tactile satisfaction. At one time, she was very fond of poker, which had reached St. Petersburg society via diplomatic circles, so that some of the combinations came with pretty French names—*brelan* for "three of a kind," *couleur* for "flush," and so on. The game in use was the regular "draw poker," with, occasionally, the additional tingle of jackpots and an omnivicarious joker. In town, she often played poker at the houses of friends until three in the morning, a society recreation in the last years before World War One; and later, in exile, she used to imagine (with the same wonder and dismay with which she recalled old Dmitri) the chauffeur Pirogov who still seemed to be waiting for her in the relentless frost of an unending night, although, in his case, rum-laced tea in a hospitable kitchen must have gone a long way to assuage those vigils.

One of her greatest pleasures in summer was the very Russian sport of *hodit' po gribï* (looking for mushrooms). Fried in butter and thickened with sour cream, her delicious finds appeared regularly on the dinner table. Not that the gustatory moment mattered much. Her main delight was in the quest, and this quest had its rules. Thus, no agarics were taken; all she picked were species belonging to the edible section of the genus *Boletus* (tawny *edulis,* brown *scaber,* red *aurantiacus,* and a few close allies), called "tube mushrooms" by some and coldly defined by mycologists as "terrestrial, fleshy, putrescent, centrally stipitate fungi." Their compact pilei—tight-fitting in infant plants, robust and appetizingly domed in ripe ones—have a smooth (not lamellate) undersurface and a neat, strong stem. In classical simplicity of form, boletes differ considerably from the "true mushroom," with its preposterous gills and effete stipal ring. It is, however, to the latter, to the lowly and ugly agarics, that nations with timorous taste buds limit their knowledge and appetite, so that to the Anglo-American lay mind the aristocratic boletes are, at best, reformed toadstools.

Rainy weather would bring out these beautiful plants in profusion under the firs, birches and aspens in our park, especially in its older part, east of the carriage road that divided the park in two. Its shady recesses would then harbor that special boletic reek which makes a Russian's nostrils dilate—a dark, dank, satisfying blend of damp moss, rich earth, rotting leaves. But one had to poke and peer for a goodish while among the wet underwood before something really nice, such as a family of bonneted baby *edulis* or the marbled variety of *scaber,* could be discovered and carefully teased out of the soil.

On overcast afternoons, all alone in the drizzle, my mother, carrying a basket (stained blue on the inside by somebody's whortleberries), would set out on a long collecting tour. Toward dinnertime, she could be seen emerging from the nebulous depths of a park alley, her small figure cloaked and hooded in greenish-brown wool, on which countless droplets of moisture made a kind of mist all around her. As she came nearer from under the dripping trees and caught sight of me, her face would show an odd, cheerless expression, which might have spelled poor luck, but which I knew was the tense, jealously contained beatitude of the successful hunter. Just before reaching me, with an abrupt, drooping movement of the arm and shoulder and a "Pouf!" of magnified exhaustion, she would let her basket sag, in order to stress its weight, its fabulous fullness.

Near a white garden bench, on a round garden table of iron, she would lay out her boletes in concentric circles to count and sort them. Old ones, with spongy, dingy flesh, would be eliminated, leaving the young and the crisp. For a moment, before they were bundled away by a servant to a place she knew nothing about, to a doom that did not interest her, she would stand there admiring them, in a glow of quiet contentment. As often happened at the end of a rainy day, the sun might cast a lurid gleam just before setting, and there, on the damp round table, her mushrooms would lie, very colorful, some bearing traces of extraneous vegetation—a grass blade sticking to a viscid fawn cap, or moss still clothing the bulbous base of a dark-stippled stem. And a tiny looper caterpillar would be there, too, measuring, like a child's finger and thumb, the rim of the table, and every now and then stretching upward to grope, in vain, for the shrub from which it had been dislodged.

Gertrude Stein

Gertrude Stein (1874-1946), novelist, poet, dramatist, and critic, grew up in Oakland, California. She recalls that she spent her youth "mostly eating fruit and reading books," devouring Shakespeare at the age of eight and sometimes worrying "lest in a few years more she would have read everything and there should be nothing unread to read." Her experiences at Radcliffe College and at medical school are recounted in the first passage below. In 1902, after she lost interest in medicine and failed to gain her degree, she moved to London to live with her brother Leo. They moved to Paris together in the following year. In 1906, on a brief trip to California, she met Alice B. Toklas, a native San Franciscan who followed her back to Paris and soon became her typist, editor, and lifelong companion.

Gertrude Stein and Alice Toklas set up in their various dwellings a salon that was to become famous in modern art history as a meeting place for avant-garde artists and writers. Miss Stein was particularly acute in her taste for post-impressionist painting; as the second passage below shows, she and her brother began collecting Cézanne and Gaugin (and Matisse and Picasso) long before it became fashionable to do so.

The passages illustrate the unusual form Miss Stein adopted for her autobiography, completed when the two women had been living together for twenty-five years. Entitling the book *The Autobiography of Alice B. Toklas* (1933), she wrote about herself as if through the eyes of her friend—an exercise in attempting to see and write about oneself objectively that is worth trying.

Gertrude Stein is famous for unconventional, experimental writing of all sorts, and the *Autobiography* is one of the easiest of her works to read. Her first published book, *Three Lives* (1909), represents the inner lives of three women through the language rhythms and modes of speech suited to each of them. Other works of original style are her *The Making of Americans* (written 1906-1908), and *Four Saints in Three Acts* (1934), an opera with music by Virgil Thompson.

from *The Autobiography of Alice B. Toklas*

Gertrude Stein Before She Came to Paris

. . . . Life in California came to its end when Gertrude Stein was about seventeen years old. The last few years had been lonesome ones and had been passed in an agony of adolescence. After the death of first her mother and then her father she and her sister and one brother left California for the East. They came to Baltimore and stayed with her mother's people. There she began to lose her lonesomeness. She has often described to me how strange it was to her coming from the rather desperate inner life that she had been living for the last few years to the cheerful life of all her aunts and uncles. When later she went to Radcliffe she described this experience in the first thing she ever wrote. Not quite the first thing she ever wrote. She remembers having written twice before. Once when she was about eight and she tried to write a Shakespearean drama in which she got as far as a stage direction, the courtiers make witty remarks. And then as she could not think of any witty remarks gave it up.

The only other effort she can remember must have been at about the same age. They asked the children in the public schools to write a description. Her recollection is that she described a sunset with the sun going into a cave of clouds. Anyway it was one of the half dozen in the school chosen to be copied out on beautiful parchment paper. After she had tried to copy it twice and the writing became worse and worse she was reduced to letting some one else copy it for her. This, her teacher considered a disgrace. She does not remember that she herself did.

As a matter of fact her handwriting has always been illegible and I am very often able to read it when she is not.

She has never been able or had any desire to indulge in any of the arts. She never knows how a thing is going to look until it is done, in arranging a room, a garden, clothes or anything else. She cannot draw anything. She feels no relation betweeen the object and the piece of paper. When at the medical school, she was supposed to draw anatomical things she never found out in sketching how a thing was made concave or convex. She remembers when she was very small she was to learn to draw and was sent to a class. The children were told to take a cup and saucer at home and draw them and the best drawing would have as its reward a stamped leather medal and the next week the same medal would again be given for the best drawing. Gertrude Stein went home, told her brothers and they put a pretty cup and saucer before her and each one explained to her how to draw it. Nothing happened. Finally one of them drew it for her. She took it to the class and won the leather medal. And on the way home in playing some game she lost the leather medal. That was the end of the drawing class.

She says it is a good thing to have no sense of how it is done in the things that amuse you. You should have one absorbing occupation and as for the other things in life for full enjoyment you should only contemplate results. In this way you are bound to feel more about it than those who know a little of how it is done.

She is passionately addicted to what the french call mé⁺ier and she contends that one can only have one métier as one can only have one language. Her métier is writing and her language is english.

Observation and construction make imagination, that is granting the possession of imagination, is what she has taught many young writers. Once when Hemingway wrote in one of his stories that Gertrude Stein always knew what was good in a Cézanne, she looked at him and said, Hemingway, remarks are not literature.

The young often when they have learnt all they can learn accuse her of an inordinate pride. She says yes of course. She realises that in english literature in her time she is the only one. She has always known it and now she says it.

She understands very well the basis of creation and therefore her advice and criticism is invaluable to all her friends. How often I have heard Picasso say to her when she has said something about a picture of his and then illustrated by something she was trying to do, racontez-moi cela. In other words tell me about it. These two even to-day have long solitary conversations. They sit in two little low chairs up in his apartment studio, knee to knee and Picasso says, expliquez-moi cela. And they explain to each other. They talk about everything, about pictures, about dogs, about death, about unhappiness. Because Picasso is a spaniard and life is tragic and bitter and unhappy. Gertrude Stein often comes down to me and says, Pablo has been persuading me that I am as unhappy as he is. He insists that I am and with as much cause. But are you, I ask. Well I don't think I look it, do I, and she laughs. He says, she says, that I don't look it because I have more courage, but I don't think I am, she says, no I don't think I am.

And so Gertrude Stein having been in Baltimore for a winter and having become more humanised and less adolescent and less lonesome went to Radcliffe. There she had a very good time.

She was one of a group of Harvard men and Radcliffe women and they all lived very closely and very interestingly together. One of them, a young philosopher and mathematician who was doing research work in psychology left a definite mark on her life. She and he together worked out a series of experiments in automatic writing under the direction of Münsterberg. The result of her own experiments, which Gertrude Stein wrote down and which was printed in the Harvard Psychological Review was the first writing of hers ever to be printed. It is very interesting to read because the method of writing to be afterwards developed in Three Lives and Making of Americans already shows itself.

The important person in Gertrude Stein's Radcliffe life was William James. She enjoyed her life and herself. She was the secretary of the philosophical club and amused herself with all sorts of people. She liked making sport of question asking and she liked equally answering them. She liked it all. But the really lasting impression of her Radcliffe life came through William James.

It is rather strange that she was not then at all interested in the work of Henry James for whom she now has a very great admiration and whom she considers quite definitely as her forerunner, he being the only nineteenth century writer who being an american felt the method of the twentieth century. Gertrude Stein always speaks of America as being now the oldest country in the world because by the methods of the civil war and the commercial conceptions that followed it America created the twentieth century, and since all the other countries are now either living or commencing to be living a twentieth century life, America having begun the creation of the twentieth century in the sixties of the nineteenth century is now the oldest country in the world.

In the same way she contends that Henry James was the first person in literature to find the way to the literary methods of the twentieth century. But oddly enough in all of her formative period she did not read him and was not interested in him. But as she often says one is always naturally antagonistic to one's parents and sympathetic to one's grandparents. The parents are too close, they hamper you, one must be alone. So perhaps that is the reason why only very lately Gertrude Stein reads Henry James.

William James delighted her. His personality and his teaching and his way of amusing himself with himself and his students all pleased her. Keep your mind open, he used to say, and when some one objected, but Professor James, this that I say, is true. Yes, said James, it is abjectly true.

Gertrude Stein never had subconscious reactions, nor was she a successful subject for automatic writing. One of the students in the psychological seminar of which Gertrude Stein, although an undergraduate was at William James' particular request a member, was carrying on a series of experiments on suggestions to the subconscious. When he read his paper upon the result of his experiments, he began by explaining that one of the subjects gave absolutely no results and as this much lowered the average and made the conclusion of his experiments false he wished to be allowed to cut this record out. Whose record is it, said James. Miss Stein's, said the student. Ah, said James, if Miss Stein gave no response I should say that it was as normal not to give a response as to give one and decidedly the result must not be cut out.

It was a very lovely spring day, Gertrude Stein had been going to the opera every night and going also to the opera in the afternoon and had been otherwise engrossed and it was the period of the final examinations, and there was the examination in William James' course. She sat down with the examination paper before her and she just could not. Dear Professor James, she wrote at the top of her paper. I am so sorry but really I do not feel a bit like an examination paper in philosophy to-day, and left.

The next day she had a postal card from William James saying, Dear Miss Stein, I understand perfectly how you feel I often feel like that myself. And underneath it he gave her work the highest mark in his course.

When Gertrude Stein was finishing her last year at Radcliffe, William

James one day asked her what she was going to do. She said she had no idea. Well, he said, it should be either philosophy or psychology. Now for philosophy you have to have higher mathematics and I don't gather that that has ever interested you. Now for psychology you must have a medical education, a medical education opens all doors, as Oliver Wendell Holmes told me and as I tell you. Gertrude Stein had been interested in both biology and chemistry and so medical school presented no difficulties.

There were no difficulties except that Gertrude Stein had never passed more than half of her entrance examinations for Radcliffe, having never intended to take a degree. However with considerable struggle and enough tutoring that was accomplished and Gertrude Stein entered Johns Hopkins Medical School.

Some years after when Gertrude Stein and her brother were just beginning knowing Matisse and Picasso, William James came to Paris and they met. She went to see him at his hotel. He was enormously interested in what she was doing, interested in her writing and in the pictures she told him about. He went with her to her house to see them. He looked and gasped. I told you, he said, I always told you that you should keep your mind open.

Only about two years ago a very strange thing happened. Gertrude Stein received a letter from a man in Boston. It was evident from the letter head that he was one of a firm of lawyers. He said in his letter that he had not long ago in reading in the Harvard library found that the library of William James had been given as a gift to the Harvard library. Among these books was the copy of Three Lives that Gertrude Stein had dedicated and sent to James. Also on the margins of the book were notes that William James had evidently made when reading the book. The man then went on to say that very likely Gertrude Stein would be very interested in these notes and he proposed, if she wished, to copy them out for her as he had appropriated the book, in other words taken it and considered it as his. We were very puzzled what to do about it. Finally a note was written saying that Gertrude Stein would like to have a copy of William James' notes. In answer came a manuscript the man himself had written and of which he wished Gertrude Stein to give him an opinion. Not knowing what to do about it all, Gertrude Stein did nothing.

After having passed her entrance examinations she settled down in Baltimore and went to the medical school. She had a servant named Lena and it is her story that Gertrude Stein afterwards wrote as the first story of the Three Lives.

The first two years of the medical school were alright. They were purely laboratory work and Gertrude Stein under Llewelys Barker immediately betook herself to research work. She began a study of all the brain tracts, the beginning of a comparative study. All this was later embodied in Llewelys Barker's book. She delighted in Doctor Mall, professor of anatomy, who directed her work. She always quotes his answer to any student excusing him or herself for anything. He would look reflective and say, yes that is just like our cook. There is always a reason. She never brings the food to the table hot. In summer of course she can't because it is too hot, in winter of course she can't because it is too cold, yes there is always a reason. Doctor Mall believed in everbody developing their own technique. He also remarked, nobody teaches anybody anything, at first every student's scalpel is dull and then later every student's scalpel is sharp, and nobody has taught anybody anything.

These first two years at the medical school Gertrude Stein liked well enough. She always liked knowing a lot of people and being mixed up in a lot of stories and she was not awfully interested but she was not too bored with what she was doing and besides she had quantities of pleasant relatives in Baltimore and she liked it. The last two years at the medical school she was bored, frankly openly bored. There was a good deal of intrigue and struggle among the students, that she liked, but the practice and theory of medicine did not interest her at all. It was fairly well known among all her teachers that she was bored, but as her first two years of scientific work had given her a reputation, everybody gave her the necessary credits and the end of her last year was approaching. It was then that she had to take her turn in the delivering of babies and it was at that time that she noticed the negroes and the places that she afterwards used in the second of the Three Lives stories, Melanctha Herbert, the story that was the beginning of her revolutionary work.

As she always says of herself, she has a great deal of inertia and once started keeps going until she starts somewhere else.

As the graduation examinations drew near some of her professors were getting angry. The big men like Halstead, Osler etcetera knowing her reputation for original scientific work made the medical examinations merely a matter of form and passed her. But there were others who were not so amiable. Gertrude Stein always laughed, and this was difficult. They would ask her questions although as she said to her friends, it was foolish of them to ask her, when there were so many eager and anxious to answer. However they did question her from time to time and as she said, what could she do, she did not know the answers and they did not believe that she did not know them, they thought that she did not answer because she did not consider the professors worth answering. It was a difficult situation, as she said, it was impossible to apologise and explain to them that she was so bored she could not remember the things that of course the dullest medical student could not forget. One of the professors said that although all the big men were ready to pass her he intended that she should be given a lesson and he refused to give her a pass mark and so she was not able to take her degree. There was great excitement in the medical school. Her very close friend Marion Walker pleaded with her, she said, but Gertrude Gertrude remember the cause of women, and Gertrude Stein said, you don't know what it is to be bored.

The professor who had flunked her asked her to come to see him. She did. He said, of course Miss Stein all you have to do is to take a summer course here and in the fall naturally you will take your degree. But not at all, said Gertrude Stein, you have no idea how grateful I am to you. I have so much inertia and so little initiative that very possibly if you had not kept me from taking my degree I would have, well, not taken to the practice of medicine, but at any rate to pathological psychology and you don't know how little I like pathological psychology, and how all medicine bores me. The professor was completely taken aback and that was the end of the medical education of Gertrude Stein. . . .

Gertrude Stein in Paris

During Gertrude Stein's last two years at the Medical School, Johns Hopkins, Baltimore, 1900–1903, her brother was living in Florence. There he heard of a painter named Cézanne and saw paintings by him owned by Charles Loeser. When he and his sister made their home in Paris the following year they went to Vollard's the only picture dealer who had Cézannes for sale, to look at them.

Vollard was a huge dark man who lisped a little. His shop was on the rue Laffitte not far from the boulevard. Further along this short street was Durand-Ruel and still further on almost at the church of the Martyrs was Sagot the ex-clown. Higher up in Montmartre on the rue Victor-Massé was Mademoiselle Weill who sold a mixture of pictures, books and bric-à-brac and in entirely another part of Paris on the rue Faubourg-Saint-Honoré was the ex-café keeper and photographer Druet. Also on the rue Laffitte was the confectioner Fouquet where one could console oneself with delicious honey cakes and nut candies and once in a while instead of a picture buy oneself strawberry jam in a glass bowl.

The first visit to Vollard has left an indelible impression on Gertrude Stein. It was an incredible place. It did not look like a picture gallery. Inside there were a couple of canvases turned to the wall, in one corner was a small pile of big and little canvases thrown pell mell on top of one another, in the center of the room stood a huge dark man glooming. This was Vollard cheerful. When he was really cheerless he put his huge frame against the glass door that led to the street, his arms above his head, his hands on each upper corner of the portal and gloomed darkly into the street. Nobody thought then of trying to come in.

They asked to see Cézannes. He looked less gloomy and became quite polite. As they found out afterward Cézanne was the great romance of Vollard's life. The name Cézanne was to him a magic word. He had first learned about Cézanne from Pissarro the painter. Pissarro indeed was the man from whom all the early Cézanne lovers heard about Cézanne. Cézanne at that time was living gloomy and embittered at Aix-en-Provence. Pissarro told Vollard about him, told Fabry, a Florentine, who told Loeser, told Picabia, in fact told everybody who knew about Cézanne at that time.

There were Cézannes to be seen at Vollard's. Later on Gertrude Stein wrote a poem called Vollard and Cézanne, and Henry McBride printed it in the New York Sun. This was the first fugitive piece of Gertrude Stein's to be so printed and it gave both her and Vollard a great deal of pleasure. Later on when Vollard wrote his book about Cézanne, Vollard at Gertrude Stein's suggestion sent a copy of the book to Henry McBride. She told Vollard that a whole page of one of New York's big daily papers would be devoted to his book. He did not believe it possible, nothing like that had ever happened to anybody in Paris. It did happen and he was deeply moved and unspeakably content. But to return to that first visit.

They told Monsieur Vollard they wanted to see some Cézanne landscapes, they had been sent to him by Mr. Loeser of Florence. Oh yes, said Vollard looking quite cheerful and he began moving about the room, finally he disappeared behind a partition in the back and was heard heavily mounting the steps. After a quite long wait he came down again and had in his hand a tiny picture of an apple with most of the canvas unpainted. They all looked at this thoroughly, then they said, yes but you see what we wanted to see was a landscape. Ah yes, sighed Vollard and he looked even more cheerful, after a moment he again disappeared and this time came back with a painting of a back, it was a beautiful painting there is no doubt about that but the brother and sister were not yet up to a full appreciation of Cézanne nudes and so they returned to the attack. They wanted to see a landscape. This time after even a longer wait he came back with a very large canvas and a very little fragment of a landscape painted on it. Yes that was it, they said, a landscape but what they wanted was a smaller canvas but one all covered. They said, they thought they would like to see one like that. By this time the early winter evening of Paris was closing in and just at this moment a very aged charwoman came down the same back stairs, mumbled, bon soir monsieur et madame, and quietly went out of the door, after a moment another old charwoman came down the same stairs, murmured, bon soir messieurs et mesdames and went quietly out of the door. Gertrude Stein began to laugh and said to her brother, it is all nonsense, there is no Cézanne. Vollard goes upstairs and tells these old women what to paint and he does not understand us and they do not understand him and they paint something and he brings it down and it is a Cézanne. They both began to laugh uncontrollably. Then they recovered and once more explained about the landscape. They said what they wanted was one of those marvellously yellow sunny Aix landscapes of which Loeser had several examples. Once more Vollard went off and this time he came back with a wonderful small green landscape. It was lovely, it covered all the canvas, it did not cost much and they bought it. Later on Vollard explained to every one that he had been visited by two crazy americans and they laughed and he had been much annoyed but gradually he found out that when they laughed most they usually bought something so of course he waited for them to laugh.

From that time on they went to Vollard's all the time. They had soon the privilege of upsetting his piles of canvases and finding what they liked in the heap. They bought a tiny little Daumier, head of an old woman. They began to take an interest in Cézanne nudes and they finally bought two tiny canvases of nude groups. They found a very very small Manet painted in black and white with Forain in the foreground and bought it, they found two tiny little Renoirs. They frequently bought in twos because one of them usually liked one more than the other one did, and so the year wore on. In the spring Vollard announced a show of Gauguin and they for the first time saw some Gauguins. They were rather awful but they finally liked them, and bought two Gauguins. Gertrude Stein liked his sun-flowers but not his figures and her brother preferred the figures. It sounds like a great deal now but in those days these things did not cost much. And so the winter went on.

There were not a great many people in and out of Vollard's but once Gertrude Stein heard a conversation there that pleased her immensely. Duret was a well known figure in Paris. He was now a very old and a very handsome man. He had been a friend of Whistler, Whistler had painted him in evening clothes with a white opera cloak over his arm. He was at Vollard's talking to a group of younger men and one of them Roussel, one of the Vuillard, Bonnard, the post impressionist group, said something complainingly about the lack of recognition of himself and his friends, that they were not even allowed to show in the salon. Duret looked at him kindly, my young friend, he said, there are two kinds of art, never forget this, there is art and there is official art. How can you, my poor young friend, hope to be official art. Just look at yourself. Supposing an important personage came to France, and wanted to meet the representative painters and have his portrait painted. My dear young friend, just look at yourself, the very sight of you would terrify him. You are a nice young man, gentle and intelligent, but to the important personage you would not seem so, you would be terrible. No they need as representative painter a medium sized, slightly stout man, not too well dressed but dressed in the fashion of his class, neither bald or well brushed hair and a respectful bow with it. You can see that you would not do. So never say another word about official recognition, or if you do look in the mirror and think of important personages. No, my dear young friend there is art and there is official art, there always has been and there always will be.

Before the winter was over, having gone so far Gertrude Stein and her brother decided to go further, they decided to buy a big Cézanne and then they would stop. After that they would be reasonable. They convinced their elder brother that this last outlay was necessary, and it was necessary as will soon be evident. They told Vollard that they wanted to buy a Cézanne portrait. In those days practically no big Cézanne portraits had been sold. Vollard owned almost all of them. He was enormously pleased with this decision. They now were introduced into the room above the steps behind the partition where Gertrude Stein had been sure the old charwomen painted the Cézannes and there they spent days deciding which portrait they would have. There were about eight to choose from and the decision was difficult. They had often to go and refresh themselves with honey cakes at Fouquet's. Finally they narrowed the choice down to two, a portrait of a man and a portrait of a woman, but this time they could not afford to buy twos and finally they chose the portrait of the woman.

Vollard said of course ordinarily a portrait of a woman always is more expensive than a portrait of a man but, said he looking at the picture very carefully, I suppose with Cézanne it does not make any difference. They put it in a cab and they went home with it. It was this picture that Alfy Maurer used to explain was finished and that you could tell that it was finished because it had a frame.

It was an important purchase because in looking and looking at this picture Gertrude Stein wrote Three Lives. . . .

Rainer Maria Rilke

Rainer Maria Rilke, the extraordinary lyric poet, was born in Prague in 1875. He had a troubled childhood: he was the only surviving child, his parents separated when he was nine years old, and two years later he was enrolled in a military academy. The chaplain at the academy remembered him as a thin, pale boy, quiet and serious, "who liked to keep to himself" and "patiently endured the compulsions of boarding-school life." He graduated to Military College, but in 1891, at sixteen, he left because of ill health. After a year in a Commercial Academy in Linz, Rilke joined his father in Prague and enrolled as a student first at the University of Prague, then at Munich and Berlin; but he had already decided to be a writer and was writing both prose and poetry steadily during this period. In 1901 he married Clara Westhoff, a young sculptress and a pupil of Auguste Rodin; they had one child but soon separated. Rilke spent many years in Paris, for a time as secretary to Rodin, but much of his life he spent wandering from one place to another. He died of leukemia in 1926, when he was fifty-one. Among his works are a book on Rodin (1907); but he is best known for his poetry written in German, particularly the *Duino Elegies* (1922) and *Sonnets to Orpheus* (1922).

In 1902, Franz Xaver Kappus, an aspiring poet, discovered that Rilke had also attended the military academy he was then enrolled in. Kappus decided to send his poetry to Rilke, asking for his opinion. Rilke answered, and thus began a correspondence that lasted five years. It has been published in English as *Letters to a Young Poet* (trans. M. D. Herter Norton, 1934). The two letters we print below, written when Rilke was twenty-seven years old, offer some of the sternest and gentlest advice ever given aspiring artists, and in many ways the hardest to follow. The second letter, on love and sex and creation, might be called lyrical poetry in prose form. They are both remarkable for their calm wisdom. Yet in a later letter Rilke writes, "Do not believe that he who seeks to comfort you lives untroubled among the simple and quiet words that sometimes do you good. His life has much difficulty and sadness. . . . Were it otherwise, he would never have been able to find those words."

Two Letters
to a Young Poet

Paris, February 17th, 1903

My Dear Sir,

Your letter only reached me a few days ago. I want to thank you for its great and kind confidence. I can hardly do more. I cannot go into the nature of your verses; for all critical intention is too far from me. With nothing can one approach a work of art so little as with critical words: they always come down to more or less happy misunderstandings. Things are not all so comprehensible and expressible as one would mostly have us believe; most events are inexpressible, taking place in a realm which no word has ever entered, and more inexpressible than all else are works of art, mysterious existences, the life of which, while ours passes away, endures.

After these prefatory remarks, let me only tell you further that your verses have no individual style, although they do show quiet and hidden beginnings of something personal. I feel this most clearly in the last poem, "My Soul." There something of your own wants to come through to word and melody. And in the lovely poem "To Leopardi" there does perhaps grow up a sort of kinship with that great solitary man. Nevertheless the poems are not yet anything on their own account, nothing independent, even the last and the one to Leopardi. Your kind letter, which accompanied them, does not fail to make clear to me various shortcomings which I felt in reading your verses without however being able specifically to name them.

You ask whether your verses are good. You ask me. You have asked others before. You send them to magazines. You compare them with other poems, and you are disturbed when certain editors reject your efforts. Now (since you have allowed me to advise you) I beg you to give up all that. You are looking outward, and that above all you should not do now. Nobody can counsel and help you, nobody. There is only one single way. Go into yourself. Search for the reason that bids you write; find out whether it is spreading out its roots in the deepest places of your heart, acknowledge to yourself whether you would have to die if it were denied you to write. This above all—ask yourself in the stillest hour of your night: *must* I write? Delve into yourself for a deep answer. And if this should be affirmative, if you may meet this earnest question with a strong and simple *"I must,"* then build your life according to this necessity; your life even into its most indifferent and slightest hour must be a sign of this urge and a testimony to it. Then draw near to

Nature. Then try, like some first human being, to say what you see and experience and love and lose. Do not write love-poems; avoid at first those forms that are too facile and commonplace: they are the most difficult, for it takes a great, fully matured power to give something of your own where good and even excellent traditions come to mind in quantity. Therefore save yourself from these general themes and seek those which your own everyday life offers you; describe your sorrows and desires, passing thoughts and the belief in some sort of beauty—describe all these with loving, quiet, humble sincerity, and use, to express yourself, the things in your environment, the images from your dreams, and the objects of your memory. If your daily life seems poor, do not blame it; blame yourself, tell yourself that you are not poet enough to call forth its riches; for to the creator there is no poverty and no poor indifferent place. And even if you were in some prison the walls of which let none of the sounds of the world come to your senses—would you not then still have your childhood, that precious, kingly possession, that treasure-house of memories? Turn your attention thither. Try to raise the submerged sensations of that ample past; your personality will grow more firm, your solitude will widen and will become a dusky dwelling past which the noise of others goes by far away.—And if out of this turning inward, out of this absorption into your own world *verses* come, then it will not occur to you to ask anyone whether they are good *verses*. Nor will you try to interest magazines in your poems: for you will see in them your fond natural possession, a fragment and a voice of your life. A work of art is good if it has sprung from necessity. In this nature of its origin lies the judgment of it: there is no other. Therefore, my dear sir, I know no advice for you save this: to go into yourself and test the deeps in which your life takes rise; at its source you will find the answer to the question whether you *must* create. Accept it, just as it sounds, without inquiring into it. Perhaps it will turn out that you are called to be an artist. Then take that destiny upon yourself and bear it, its burden and its greatness, without ever asking what recompense might come from outside. For the creator must be a world for himself and find everything in himself and in Nature to whom he has attached himself.

But perhaps after this descent into yourself and into your inner solitude you will have to give up becoming a poet; (it is enough, as I have said, to feel that one could live without writing: then one must not attempt it at all). But even then this inward searching which I ask of you will not have been in vain. Your life will in any case find its own ways thence, and that they may be good, rich and wide I wish you more than I can say.

What more shall I say to you? Everything seems to me to have its just emphasis; and after all I do only want to advise you to keep growing quietly and seriously throughout your whole development; you cannot disturb it more rudely than by looking outward and expecting from outside replies to questions that only your inmost feeling in your most hushed hour can perhaps answer.

It was a pleasure to me to find in your letter the name of Professor Horaček; I keep for that lovable and learned man a great veneration and a gratitude that endures through the years. Will you, please, tell him how I feel; it is very good of him still to think of me, and I know how to appreciate it.

The verses which you kindly entrusted to me I am returning at the same time. And I thank you once more for your great and sincere confidence, of which I have tried, through this honest answer given to the best of my knowledge, to make myself a little worthier than, as a stranger, I really am.

Yours faithfully and with all sympathy:
Rainer Maria Rilke

Worpswede, near Bremen,
July 16th, 1903

Some ten days ago I left Paris, quite ill and tired, and journeyed into a great northerly plain whose breadth and stillness and sky are to make me well again. But I came into a long spell of rain that today for the first time shows signs of clearing a little over the restlessly wind-blown land; and I am using this first moment of brightness to greet you, dear sir.

Very dear Mr. Kappus: I have left a letter from you long unanswered, not that I had forgotten it—on the contrary: it was of the sort that one reads again, when one finds them among one's correspondence, and I recognized you in it as though you had been close at hand. It was the letter of May 2nd, and you surely remember it. When I read it, as now, in the great quiet of these distances, I am touched by your beautiful concern about life, more even than I had felt it in Paris, where everything resounds and dies away differently because of the too great noise that makes things vibrate. Here, where an immense country lies about me, over which the winds pass coming from the seas, here I feel that no human being anywhere can answer for you those questions and feelings that deep within them have a life of their own; for even the best err in words when they are meant to mean most delicate and almost inexpressible things. But I believe nevertheless that you will not have to remain without a solution if you will hold to objects that are similar to those from which my eyes now draw refreshment. If you will cling to Nature, to the simple in Nature, to the little things that hardly anyone sees, and that can so unexpectedly become big and beyond measuring; if you have this love of inconsiderable things and seek quite simply, as one who serves, to win the confidence of what seems poor: then everything will become easier, more coherent and somehow more conciliatory for you, not in your intellect, perhaps, which lags marveling behind, but in your inmost consciousness, waking and cognizance. You are so young, so before all beginning, and I want to beg you, as much as I can, dear sir, to be patient toward all that is unsolved in your heart and to try to love the *questions themselves* like locked rooms and like books that are written in a very foreign tongue. Do not now seek the answers, which cannot be given you because you would not be able to live them. And the point is, to live everything. *Live* the questions now. Perhaps you will then gradually, without noticing it, live along some distant day into the answer. Perhaps you do carry within yourself the possibility of shaping and forming as a particularly happy and pure way of living; train yourself to it—but take whatever comes with great trust, and if only it comes out of your own will, out of some need of your inmost being, take it upon yourself and hate nothing. Sex is difficult; yes. But they are difficult things with which we have been charged; almost everything serious is difficult, and everything is serious. If you only recognize this and manage, out of yourself, out of your *own* nature and ways, out of your *own* experience and childhood and strength to achieve a relation to sex wholly your own (*not* influenced by convention and custom), then you need no longer be afraid of losing yourself and becoming unworthy of your best possession.

Physical pleasure is a sensual experience no different from pure seeing or the pure sensation with which a fine fruit fills the tongue; it is a great unending experience, which is given us, a knowing of the world, the fullness and the glory of all knowing. And not our acceptance of it is bad; the bad thing is that most people misuse and squander this experience and apply it as a stimulant at the tired spots of their lives and as distraction instead of a rallying toward exalted moments. Men have made even eating into something else: want on the one hand, superfluity upon the other, have dimmed the distinctness of this need, and all the deep, simple necessities in which life renews itself have become similarly dulled. But the individual can clarify them for himself and live them clearly (and if not the individual, who is too dependent, then at least the solitary man). He can remember that all beauty in animals and plants is a quiet enduring form of love and longing, and he can see animals, as he sees plants, patiently and willingly uniting and increasing and growing, not out of physical delight, not out of physical suffering, but bowing to necessities that are greater than pleasure and pain and more powerful than will and withstanding. O that man might take this secret, of which the world is full even to its littlest things, more humbly to himself and bear it, endure it, more seriously and feel how terribly difficult it is, instead of taking it lightly. That he might be more reverent toward his fruitfulness, which is but *one,* whether it seems mental or physical; for intellectual creation too springs from the physical, is of one nature with it and only like a gentler, more ecstatic and more everlasting repetition of physical delight. "The thought of being creator, of procreating, of making" is nothing without its continuous great confirmation and realization in the world, nothing without the thousandfold concordance from things and animals—and enjoyment of it is so indescribably beautiful and rich only because it is full of inherited memories of the begetting and the bearing of millions. In one creative thought a thousand forgotten nights of love revive, filling it with sublimity and exaltation. And those who come together in the night and are entwined in rocking delight do an earnest work and gather sweetnesses, gather depth and strength for the song of some coming poet, who will arise to speak of ecstasies beyond telling. And they call up the future; and though they err and embrace blindly, the future comes all the same, a new human being rises up, and on the ground of that chance which here seems consummated, awakes the law by which a resistant vigorous seed forces its way through to the egg-cell that moves open toward it. Do not be bewildered by the surfaces; in the depths all becomes law. And those who live the secret wrong and badly (and they are very many), lose it only for themselves and still hand it on, like a sealed letter, without knowing it. And do not be confused by the multiplicity of names and the complexity of cases. Perhaps over all there is a great motherhood, as common longing. The beauty of the virgin, a being that (as you so beautifully say) "has not yet achieved anything," is motherhood that begins to sense itself and to prepare, anxious and yearning. And the mother's beauty is ministering motherhood, and in the old woman there is a great remembering. And even in the man there is motherhood, it seems to me, physical and spiritual; his procreating is also a kind of giving birth, and giving birth it is when he creates out of inmost fullness. And perhaps the sexes are more related than we think, and the great renewal of the world will perhaps consist in this, that man and maid, freed of all false feelings and reluctances, will seek each other not as opposites, but as brother and sister, as neighbors, and will come together as human beings, in order simply, seriously and patiently to bear in common the difficult sex that has been laid upon them.

But everything that may some day be possible to many the solitary man can now prepare and build with his hands, that err less. Therefore, dear sir, love your solitude and bear with sweet-sounding lamentation the suffering it causes you. For those who are near you are far, you say, and that shows it is beginning to grow wide about you. And when what is near you is far, then your distance is already among the stars and very large; rejoice in your growth, in which you naturally can take no one with you, and be kind to those who remain behind, and be sure and calm before them and do not torment them with your doubts and do not frighten them with your confidence or joy, which they could not understand. Seek yourself some sort of simple and loyal community with them, which need not necessarily change as you yourself become different and again different; love in them life in an unfamiliar form and be considerate of aging people, who fear that being-alone in which you trust. Avoid contributing material to the drama that is always stretched taut between parents and children; it uses up much of the children's energy and consumes the love of their elders, which is effective and warming even if it does not comprehend. Ask no advice from them and count upon no understanding; but believe in a love that is being stored up for you like an inheritance and trust that in this love there is a strength and a blessing, out beyond which you do not have to step in order to go very far!

It is good that you are presently entering a profession that will make you independent and set you entirely on your own in every sense. Wait patiently to find out whether your inner life feels cramped by the form of this profession. I consider it very difficult and very exacting, as it is burdened with great conventions and scarcely leaves room for a personal conception of its problems. But your solitude will be a hold and home for you even amid very unfamiliar conditions and from there you will find all your ways. All my wishes are ready to accompany you, and my confidence is with you.

Yours:
Rainer Maria Rilke

Leonard Woolf

Leonard Woolf (1880-1969) was born in Victorian London. He won a scholarship to St. Paul's in 1894 and a classical scholarship to Trinity College, Cambridge, in 1899. From 1904 until 1912 he worked in the Ceylon Civil Service, leaving it a thorough enemy of colonialism. After his return to England, he married Virginia Stephen, who became one of the century's finest novelists. During World War I, using a single small hand press, they founded the Hogarth Press, which soon developed into a major publishing house.

The Woolfs were important figures in the Bloomsbury group, an informal group of intellectuals from different professions, who dominated British literary thought of the time with their search for aesthetic beauty and their reaction against Victorian hypocrisy and sentimentality. After the war Leonard Woolf became a Fabian socialist and his interests became primarily sociological and political. His autobiography begins in *Sowing* (1960), from which the following passage is taken, and continues in *Growing* (1961) and *Beginning Again* (1964).

Throughout his career and writings, Leonard Woolf reveals a gentle and decent, but also a rational, even detached, approach to life. In *Sowing* he attributes some of this attitude of "sceptical tolerance" to childhood experiences such as the two described below. His style is spare and direct, yet these two incidents manage to evoke in the reader the writer's feeling of "cosmic despair." The passage can be profitably examined for the actual words and details that help to convey that feeling.

Weltschmerz, from *Sowing*

. . . . In my view happiness and unhappiness are of immense importance, perhaps the most important things in life and, therefore, in an autobiography. It is curious that so little is known about them, particularly the happiness and unhappiness of children. I have pointed out in a serious book on politics, *Principia Politica,* that the apparently innate and profound unhappiness of the human infant, who will go into loud paroxysms of misery without provocation, is unknown in the young of other animals. This primeval pessimism of man must have great psychological and social importance, but autobiographically it is irrelevant, for, as far as I am concerned, I cannot remember anything about my infancy. At the time when my memories begin we were a cheerful and happy family of children, certainly above the average intellectually. But I can vividly recall two occasions when, at a very early age, I was suddenly stricken with an acute pang of cosmic rather than personal unhappiness.

My first experience of *Weltschmerz,* if that is what it was, must have come to me at the very early age of five or six. Behind the house in Lexham Gardens was a long parallelogram enclosed by the house on the north and on the other three sides by three grimy six-foot walls. It was a typical London garden of that era, consisting of a worn parallelogram of grass surrounded by narrow gravel paths and then narrow beds of sooty, sour London soil against the walls. Each child was given a few feet of bed for his own personal "garden" and there we sowed seeds or grew pansies bought off barrows in the Earls Court Road. I was very fond of this garden and of my "garden" and it was here that I first experienced a wave of that profound, cosmic melancholia which is hidden in every human heart and can be heard at its best—or should one say worst?—in the infant crying in the night and with no language but a cry. It happened in this way.

Every year in the last week of July or the first of August, the whole Woolf family went away for a summer holiday to the country. It was a large-scale exodus. First my mother went off and looked at houses. Then we were told that a house had been "taken." When the day came, six, seven, eight, and eventually nine children, servants, dogs, cats, canaries, and at one time two white rats in a bird-cage, mountains of luggage were transported in an omnibus to the station and then in a reserved "saloon" railway carriage to our destination. I can remember country houses in Wimbledon, Kenley, Tenby, Penmaenmawr, Speldhurst, and Whitby which carry me back in memory to my fifth year. And I can remember returning one late, chilly September afternoon to Lexham Gardens from our holiday and rushing out eagerly to see the back garden. There it lay in its grimy solitude. There was not a breath of air. There were no flowers; a few spindly lilac bushes drooped in the beds. The grimy ivy drooped on the grimy walls. And all over the walls from ivy leaf to ivy leaf were large or small spider-webs, dozens and dozens of them, quite motionless, and motionless in the centre of each web sat a large or a small, a fat or a lean spider. I stood by myself in the patch of scurfy grass and contemplated the spiders; I can still smell the smell of sour earth and ivy; and suddenly my whole mind and body seemed to be over-whelmed in melancholy. I did not cry, though there were, I think, tears in my eyes; I had experienced for the first time, without understanding it, that sense of cosmic unhappiness which comes upon us when those that look out of the windows be darkened, when the daughters of music are laid low, the doors are shut in the street, the sound of the grinding is low, the grasshopper is a burden, and desire fails.

There is another curious fact connected with my passion among the spiders in the garden. Forty years later, when I was trying to teach myself Russian, I read Aksakov and the memories of his childhood. His description of the garden and the raspberry canes recalled to me most vividly my spider-haunted London garden and the despair which came upon me that September afternoon. I felt that what I had experienced among the spiders and ivy he must have experienced half a century before among the raspberries in Russia.

The second occasion on which I felt the burden of a hostile universe weigh down my spirit must have been when I was about eight years old. We had arrived in Whitby for our summer holidays and found ourselves in a large, new red-brick house on a cliff overlooking the sea. After tea I wandered out by myself to explore the garden. The house and garden were quite new, for the garden was almost bare. Along the side facing the sea ran a long low mound or rampart. I sat there in the sunshine looking down on the sparkling water. It smelt and felt so good after the long hours in the stuffy train. And then suddenly quite near me out of a hole in the bank came two large black and yellow newts. They did not notice me and stretched themselves out to bask in the sun. They entranced me and I forgot everything, including time, as I sat there with those strange, beautiful creatures surrounded by blue sky, sunshine, and sparkling sea. I do not know how long I had sat there when, all at once, I felt afraid. I looked up and saw that an enormous black thunder cloud had crept up and now covered more than half of the sky. It was just blotting out the sun, and, as it did so, the newts scuttled back into their hole. It was terrifying and, no doubt, I was terrified. But I felt something more powerful than fear, once more that sense of profound, passive, cosmic despair, the melancholy of a human being, eager for happiness and beauty, powerless in face of a hostile universe. As the great raindrops began to fall and the thunder to mutter and growl over the sea, I crept back into the house with a curious muddle of fear, contempt, scepticism, and fatalism in my childish mind. . . .

Lincoln Steffens

Lincoln Steffens (1866-1936) is remembered primarily as a journalist and reformer. Born in Sacramento, California, he spent his youth largely with horses rather than books and failed to pass grammar school. "My parents did not bring me up," he writes. "They sent me to school, they gave me teachers of music, drawing; they offered me every opportunity in their reach. But also they gave me liberty. . . ." A great admirer of Napoleon, Steffens was enrolled at a military academy at fifteen and hoped to become a soldier: "I read about Napoleon as if I were reading up on my own future," he remembers. He acquired an interest in philosophy at the University of California, and subsequently studied in Germany, Paris, and London, returning to the United States in 1892. Steffens then began his career as a reporter for the New York *Evening Post*. After the turn of the century, he became closely associated with the muckraker movement, exposing municipal corruption and inefficiency in numerous magazine articles and in books such as *The Shame of the Cities* (1904).

As the public impact of muckraking lessened, Steffens dropped from the public eye and gradually lost faith in reform as an effective means of change. He supported the Mexican Revolution in 1914 and wrote extensively on the successes of the Russian Revolution and the Communist regime. After twenty years spent in relative obscurity, the publication of *The Autobiography of Lincoln Steffens* in 1931 brought him renewed public interest and acclaim.

When Steffens failed the entrance requirements for the University of California, his father engaged Mr. Evelyn Nixon as a private tutor. For Steffens, Nixon was the first teacher "who interested me in what I had to learn." Nixon apparently realized this and invited him to his home where, on Saturday evenings, he met with a group of friends, all displaced English athletes and scholars, "a maddening lot of cultivated minds" who discussed "any and all subjects with knowledge, with the precise information of scholarship, but with no common opinions on anything apparently." These Saturday nights became Steffens' prep school and whetted his appetite for college.

The passage below, two chapters from the *Autobiography,* records his expectations as well as his disappointment at what he actually found at the university and invites comparison with student expectations and disappointments today. What, one might ask, has changed since 1885? The second chapter, which deals with his liberating discovery that "everything in the world remains to be done over," that "nothing is known," is particularly suited for retesting today. The reader may also want to compare Steffens' experience and ideas with those of Gertrude Stein (p. 201), who writes of another unconventional college career, or better still, to examine his own hopes, his own pleasant and unpleasant discoveries, in the light of those of Steffens or of Stein.

I Go to College

Going to college is, to a boy, an adventure into a new world, and a very strange and complete world too. Part of his preparation for it is the stories he hears from those that have gone before; these feed his imagination, which cannot help trying to picture the college life. And the stories and the life are pretty much the same for any college. The University of California was a young, comparatively small institution when I was entered there in 1885 as a freshman. Berkeley, the beautiful, was not the developed villa community it is now; I used to shoot quail in the brush under the oaks along the edges of the college grounds. The quail and the brush are gone now, but the oaks are there and the same prospect down the hill over San Francisco Bay out through the Golden Gate between the low hills of the city and the high hills of Marin County. My class numbered about one hundred boys and girls, mostly boys, who came from all parts of the State and represented all sorts of people and occupations. There was, however, a significant uniformity of opinion and spirit among us, as there was, and still is, in other, older colleges. The American is molded to type early. And so are our college ways. We found already formed at Berkeley the typical undergraduate customs, rights, and privileged vices which we had to respect ourselves and defend against the faculty, regents, and the State government.

One evening, before I had matriculated, I was taken out by some upper classmen to teach the president a lesson. He had been the head of a private preparatory school and was trying to govern the private lives and the public morals of university "men" as he had those of his schoolboys. Fetching a long ladder, the upper classmen thrust it through a front window of Prexy's house and, to the chant of obscene songs, swung it back and forth, up and down, round and round, till everything breakable within sounded broken and the drunken indignation outside was satisfied or tired.

This turned out to be one of the last battles in the war for liberty against that president. He was allowed to resign soon thereafter and I noticed that not only the students but many of the faculty and regents rejoiced in his downfall and turned with us to face and fight the new president when, after a lot of politics, he was appointed and presented. We learned somehow a good deal about the considerations that governed our college government. They were not only academic. The government of a university was—like the State government and horse-racing and so many other things—not what I had been led to expect. And a college education wasn't either, nor the student mind.

Years later, when I was a magazine editor, I proposed a series of articles to raise and answer the question: Is there any intellectual life in our colleges? My idea sprang from my remembered disappointment at what I found at Berkeley and some experiences I was having at the time with the faculties and undergraduates of the other older colleges in the east. Berkeley, in my day, was an Athens compared with New Haven, for example, when I came to know Yale undergraduates.

My expectations of college life were raised too high by Nixon's Saturday nights. I thought, and he assumed, that at Berkeley I would be breathing in an atmosphere of thought, discussion, and some scholarship; working, reading, and studying for the answers to questions which would be threshed out in debate and conversation. There was nothing of the sort. I was primed with questions. My English friends never could agree on the answers to any of the many and various questions they disputed. They did not care; they enjoyed their talks and did not expect to settle anything. I was more earnest. I was not content to leave things all up in the air. Some of those questions were very present and personal to me, as some of those Englishmen meant them to be. William Owen was trying to convert me to the anarchistic communism in which he believed with all his sincere and beautiful being. I was considering his arguments. Another earnest man, who presented the case for the Roman Catholic Church, sent old Father Burchard and other Jesuits after me. Every conversation at Mr. Nixon's pointed some question, academic or scientific, and pointed them so sharp that they drove me to college with an intense desire to know. And as for communism or the Catholic Church, I was so torn that I could not answer myself. The Jesuits dropped me and so did Owen, in disgust, when I said I was going to wait for my answer till I had heard what the professors had to say and had learned what my university had to teach me upon the questions underlying the questions Oxford and Cambridge and Rome quarreled over and could not agree on. Berkeley would know.

There were no moot questions in Berkeley. There was work to do, knowledge and training to get, but not to answer questions. I found myself engaged, as my classmates were, in choosing courses. The choice was limited and within the limits, had to be determined by the degree we were candidates for. My questions were philosophical, but I could not take philosophy, which fascinated me, till I had gone through a lot of higher mathematics which did not interest me at all. If I had been allowed to take philosophy, and so discovered the need and the relation of mathematics, I would have got the philosophy and I might have got the mathematics which I miss now more than I do the Hegelian metaphysics taught at Berkeley. Or, if the professor who put me off had taken the pains to show me the bearing of mathematical thought on theoretical logic, I would have undertaken the preparation intelligently. But no one ever developed for me the relation of any of my required subjects to those that attracted me; no one brought out for me the relation of anything I was studying to anything else, except, of course, to that wretched degree. Knowledge was absolute, not relative, and it was stored in compartments, categorical and independent. The relation of knowledge to life, even to student life, was ignored, and as for questions, the professors asked them, not the students; and the students, not the teachers, answered them—in examinations.

The unknown is the province of the student; it is the field for his life's adventure, and it is a wide field full of beckonings. Curiosity about it would drive a boy as well as a child to work through the known to get at the unknown. But it was not assumed that we had any curiosity or the potential love of skill, scholarship, and achievement or research. And so far as I can remember now, the professors' attitude was right for most of the students who had no intellectual curiosity. They wanted to be told not only what they had to learn, but what they had to want to learn—for the purpose of passing. That came out in the considerations which decided the choice among optional courses. Students selected subjects or teachers for a balance of easy and hard, to fit into their time and yet "get through." I was the only rebel of my kind, I think. The nearest to me in sympathy were the fellows who knew what they wanted to be: engineers, chemists, professional men, or statesmen. They grunted at some of the work required of them, studies that seemed useless to their future careers. They did not understand me very well, nor I them, because I preferred those very subjects which they called useless, highbrow, cultural. I did not tell them so; I did not realize it myself definitely; but I think now that I had had as a boy an exhausting experience of *being* something great. I did not want now to be but rather to know things. . . .

I Become a Student

It is possible to get an education at a university. It has been done; not often, but the fact that a proportion, however small, of college students do get a start in interested, methodical study, proves my thesis, and the two personal experiences I have to offer illustrate it and show how to circumvent the faculty, the other students, and the whole college system of mind-fixing. My method might lose a boy his degree, but a degree is not worth so much as the capacity and the drive to learn, and the undergraduate desire for an empty baccalaureate is one of the holds the educational system has on students. Wise students some day will refuse to take degrees, as the best men (in England, for instance) give, but do not themselves accept, titles.

My method was hit on by accident and some instinct. I specialized. With several courses prescribed, I concentrated on the one or two that interested me most, and letting the others go, I worked intensively on my favorites. In my first two years, for example, I worked at English and political economy and read philosophy. At the beginning of my junior year I had several cinches in history. Now I liked history; I had neglected it partly because I rebelled at the way it was taught, as positive knowledge unrelated to politics, art, life, or anything else. The professors gave us chapters out of a few books to read, con, and be quizzed on. Blessed as I was with a "bad memory," I could not commit to it anything that I did not understand and intellectually need. The bare record of the story of man, with names, dates, and irrelative events, bored me. But I had discovered in my readings of literature, philosophy, and political economy that history had light to throw upon unhistorical questions. So I proposed in my junior and senior years to specialize in history, taking all the courses required and those also that I had flunked in. With this in mind I listened attentively to the first introductory talk of Professor William Cary Jones on American constitutional history. He was a dull lecturer, but I noticed that, after telling us what pages of what books we must be prepared in, he mumbled off some other references "for those that may care to dig deeper."

When the rest of the class rushed out into the sunshine, I went up to the professor and, to his surprise, asked for this memorandum. He gave it me. Up in the library I ran through the required chapters in the two different books, and they differed on several points. Turning to the other authorities, I saw that they disagreed on the same facts and also on others. The librarian, appealed to, helped me search the book-shelves till the library closed, and then I called on Professor Jones for more references. He was astonished, invited me in, and began to approve my industry, which astonished me. I was not trying to be a good boy; I was better than that: I was a curious boy. He lent me a couple of his books, and I went off to my club to read them. They only deepened the mystery, clearing up the historical question, but leaving the answer to be dug for and written.

The historians did not know! History was not a science, but a field for research, a field for me, for any young man, to explore, to make discoveries in and write a scientific report about. I was fascinated. As I went on from chapter to chapter, day after day, finding frequently essential differences of opinion and of fact, I saw more and more work to do. In this course, American constitutional history, I hunted far enough to suspect that the Fathers of the Republic who wrote our sacred Constitution of the United States not only did not, but did not want to, establish a democratic government, and I dreamed for a while—as I used as a child to play I was Napoleon or a trapper—I promised myself to write a true history of the making of the American Constitution. I did not do it; that chapter has been done or well begun since by two men: Smith of the University of Washington and Beard (then) of Columbia (afterward forced out, perhaps for this very work). I found other events, men, and epochs waiting for students. In all my other courses, in ancient, in European, and in modern history, the disagreeing authorities carried me back to the need of a fresh search for (or of) the original documents or other clinching testimony. Of course I did well in my classes. The history professors soon knew me as a student and seldom put a question to me except when the class had flunked it. Then Professor Jones would say, "Well, Steffens, tell them about it."

Fine. But vanity wasn't my ruling passion then. What I had was a quickening sense that I was learning a method of studying history and that every chapter of it, from the beginning of the world to the end, is crying out to be rewritten. There was something for Youth to do; these superior old men had not done anything, finally.

Years afterward I came out of the graft prosecution office in San Francisco with Rudolph Spreckels, the banker and backer of the investigation. We were to go somewhere, quick, in his car, and we couldn't. The chauffeur was trying to repair something wrong. Mr. Spreckels smiled; he looked closely at the defective part, and to my silent, wondering inquiry he answered: "Always, when I see something badly done or not done at all, I see an opportunity to make a fortune. I never kick at bad work by my class: there's lots of it and we suffer from it. But our failures and neglects are chances for the young fellows coming along and looking for work."

Nothing is done. Everything in the world remains to be done or done over. "The greatest picture is not yet painted, the greatest play isn't written (not even by Shakespeare), the greatest poem is unsung. There isn't in all the world a perfect railroad, nor a good government, nor a sound law." Physics, mathematics, and especially the most advanced and exact of the sciences, are being fundamentally revised. Chemistry is just becoming a science; psychology, economics, and sociology are awaiting a Darwin, whose work in turn is awaiting an Einstein. If the rah-rah boys in our colleges could be told this, they might not all be such specialists in football, petting parties, and unearned degrees. They are not told it, however; they are told to learn what is known. This is nothing, philosophically speaking.

Somehow or other in my later years at Berkeley, two professors, Moses and Howison, representing opposite schools of thought, got into a controversy, probably about their classes. They brought together in the house of one of them a few of their picked students, with the evident intention of letting us show in conversation how much or how little we had understood of their respective teachings. I don't remember just what the subject was that they threw into the ring, but we wrestled with it till the professors could stand it no longer. Then they broke in, and while we sat silent and highly entertained, they went at each other hard and fast and long. It was after midnight when, the debate over, we went home. I asked the other fellows what they had got out of it, and their answers showed that they had seen nothing but a fine, fair fight. When I laughed, they asked me what I, the D.S., had seen that was so much more profound.

I said that I had seen two highly-trained, well-educated Masters of Arts and Doctors of Philosophy disagreeing upon every essential point of thought and knowledge. They had all there was of the sciences; and yet they could not find any knowledge upon which they could base an acceptable conclusion. They had no test of knowledge; they didn't know what is and what is not. And they have no test of right and wrong; they have no basis for even an ethics.

Well, and what of it? They asked me that, and that I did not answer. I was stunned by the discovery that it was philosophically true, in a most literal sense, that nothing is known; that it is precisely the foundation that is lacking for science; that all we call knowledge rested upon assumptions which the scientists did not all accept; and that, likewise, there is no scientific reason for saying, for example, that stealing is wrong. In brief: there was no scientific basis for an ethics. No wonder men said one thing and did another; no wonder they could settle nothing either in life or in the academies.

I could hardly believe this. Maybe these professors, whom I greatly respected, did not know it all. I read the books over again with a fresh eye, with a real interest, and I could see that, as in history, so in other branches of knowledge, everything was in the air. And I was glad of it. Rebel though I was, I had got the religion of scholarship and science; I was in awe of the authorities in the academic world. It was a release to feel my worship cool and pass. But I could not be sure. I must go elsewhere, see and hear other professors, men these California professors quoted and looked up to as their high priests. I decided to go as a student to Europe when I was through Berkeley, and I would start with the German universities.

My father listened to my plan, and he was disappointed. He had hoped I would succeed him in his business; it was for that that he was staying in it. When I said that, whatever I might do, I would never go into business, he said, rather sadly, that he would sell out his interest and retire. And he did soon after our talk. But he wanted me to stay home and, to keep me, offered to buy an interest in a certain San Francisco daily paper. He had evidently had this in mind for some time. I had always done some writing, verse at the poetical age of puberty, then a novel which my mother alone treasured. Journalism was the business for a boy who liked to write, he thought, and he said I had often spoken of a newspaper as my ambition. No doubt I had in the intervals between my campaigns as Napoleon. But no more. I was now going to be a scientist, a philosopher. He sighed; he thought it over, and with the approval of my mother, who was for every sort of education, he gave his consent.

Katie Rowe

Katie Rowe was eighty-eight years old and living in Tulsa, Oklahoma, with her married daughter at the time she was interviewed for the reminiscences printed below. Born a slave near Washington, Hempstead County, Arkansas, she was freed on June 4, 1865, when she must have been sixteen or seventeen years old; she remembers back three generations, so that her narrative actually spans more than one hundred and fifty years.

The interview was undertaken by the Federal Writers' Project, which provided jobs for unemployed writers, researchers, editors, and newspaper reporters during the depression of the 1930s. From 1936 to 1938, the Writers' Project undertook "to study the needs and collect the testimony of ex-slaves" in eighteen states. With tape recording unavailable, the interviewers set down the autobiographies of their informants by hand. The resulting Slave Narrative Collection, composed of photographs and document transcriptions as well as personal histories, contains the narratives of about two thousand persons who remembered their own slavery or slaveholding. B. A. Botkin, folklore editor for the Writers' Project in 1938, prepared from these 10,000 manuscript pages a short collection of the most readable and representative narratives, entitled *Lay My Burden Down* (1945), for the general reader.

Katie Rowe's matter of fact report of what slavery was like in its living form—not as an abstraction or myth—shows how, if you know what you are talking about, if you mean and feel what you are saying, your account will come out right. You do not need to use formal school language in order to achieve eloquence. For the master's point of view on slavery, examine the diary entries by William Byrd (p. 295).

Slavery Days

I can set on the gallery, where the sunlight shine bright, and sew a powerful fine seam when my grandchildren wants a special pretty dress for the school doings, but I ain't worth much for nothing else, I reckon.

These same old eyes seen powerful lot of tribulations in my time, and when I shuts 'em now I can see lots of little children just like my grandchildren, toting hoes bigger than they is, and they poor little black hands and legs bleeding where they scratched by the brambledy weeds, and where they got whippings 'cause they didn't git out all the work the overseer set out for 'em.

I was one of them little slave gals my own self, and I never seen nothing but work and tribulations till I was a grownup woman, just about.

The niggers had hard traveling on the plantation where I was born and raised, 'cause Old Master live in town and just had the overseer on the place, but iffen he had lived out there hisself I 'speck it been as bad, 'cause he was a hard driver his own self.

He git biling mad when the Yankees have that big battle at Pea Ridge and scatter the 'Federates all down through our country all bleeding and tied up and hungry, and he just mount on his hoss and ride out to the plantation where we all hoeing corn.

He ride up and tell old man Saunders—that the overseer—to bunch us all up round the lead row man—that my own uncle Sandy—and then he tell us the law!

"You niggers been seeing the 'Federate soldiers coming by here looking pretty raggedy and hurt and wore out," he say, "but that no sign they licked!"

"Them Yankees ain't gwine git this far, but iffen they do, you all ain't gwine git free by 'em, 'cause I gwine free you before that. When they git here they gwine find you already free, 'cause I gwine line you up on the bank of Bois d'Arc Creek and free you with my shotgun! Anybody miss just one lick with the hoe, or one step in the line, or one clap of that bell, or one toot of the horn, and he gwine be free and talking to the devil long before he ever see a pair of blue britches!"

That the way he talk to us, and that the way he act with us all the time.

We live in the log quarters on the plantation, not far from Washington, Arkansas, close to Bois d'Arc Creek, in the edge of the Little River bottom.

Old Master's name was Dr. Isaac Jones, and he live in the town, where he keep four-five house niggers, but he have about two hundred on the plantation, big and little, and Old Man Saunders oversee 'em at the time of the war. Old Mistress' name was Betty, and she had a daughter name Betty about grown, and then they was three boys, Tom, Bryan, and Bob, but they was too young to go to the war. I never did see 'em but once or twice till after the war.

Old Master didn't got to the war, 'cause he was a doctor and the onliest one left in Washington, and pretty soon he was dead anyhow.

Next fall after he ride out and tell us that he gwine shoot us before he let us free, he come out to see how his steam gin doing. The gin box was a little old thing 'bout as big as a bedstead, with a long belt running through the side of the ginhouse out to the engine and boiler in the yard. The boiler burn cordwood, and it have a little crack in it where the nigger ginner been trying to fix it.

Old Master come out, hopping mad 'cause the gin shut down, and ast the ginner, Old Brown, what the matter. Old Brown say the boiler weak and it liable to bust, but Old Master jump down offen his hoss and go round to the boiler and say, "Cuss fire to your black heart! That boiler all right! Throw on some cordwood, cuss fire to your heart!"

Old Brown start to the woodpile, grumbling to hisself, and Old Master stoop down to look at the boiler again, and it blow right up and him standing right there!

Old Master was blowed all to pieces, and they just find little bitsy chunks of his clothes and parts of him to bury.

The woodpile blow down, and Old Brown land 'way off in the woods, but he wasn't killed.

Two wagons of cotton blowed over, and the mules run away, and all the niggers was scared nearly to death 'cause we knowed the overseer gwine be a lot worse, now that Old Master gone.

Before the war when Master was a young man, the slaves didn't have it so hard, my mammy tell me. Her name was Fanny and her old mammy's name was Nanny. Grandma Nanny was alive during the war yet.

How she come in the Jones family was this way: Old Mistress was just a little girl, and her older brother bought Nanny and give her to her. I think his name was Littlejohn; anyways we called him Master Littlejohn. He drawed up a paper what say that Nanny always belong to Miss Betty and all the children Nanny ever have belong to her, too, and nobody can't take 'em for a debt and things like that. When Miss Betty marry, Old Master he can't sell Nanny or any of her children neither.

That paper hold good too, and Grandmammy tell me about one time it hold good and keep my own mammy on the place.

Grandmammy say Mammy was just a little gal and was playing out in the road with three-four other little children when a white man and Old Master rid up. The white man had a paper about some kind of a debt, and Old Master say take his pick of the nigger children and give him back the paper.

Just as Grandmammy go to the cabin door and hear him say that, the man git off his hoss and pick up my mammy and put her up in front of him and start to ride off down the road.

Pretty soon Mr. Littlejohn come riding up and say something to Old Master, and see Grandmammy standing in the yard screaming and crying. He just job the spurs in his hoss and go kiting off down the road after that white man.

Mammy say he catch up with him just as he git to Bois d'Arc Creek and start to wade the hoss across. Mr. Littlejohn holler to him to come back with that little nigger 'cause the paper don't cover that child, 'cause she Old Mistress' own child, and when the man just ride on, Mr. Littlejohn throw his big old long hoss-pistol down on him and make him come back.

The man hopping mad, but he have to give over my mammy and take one the other children on the debt paper.

Old Master always kind of touchy 'bout Old Mistress having niggers he can't trade or sell, and one day he have his whole family and some more white folks out at the plantation. He showing 'em all the quarters when we all come in from the field in the evening, and he call all the niggers up to let the folks see 'em.

He make Grandmammy and Mammy and me stand to one side and then he say to the other niggers, "These niggers belong to my wife but you belong to me, and I'm the only one you is to call Master. This is Tom, and Bryan, and Bob, and Miss Betty, and you is to call 'em that, and don't you ever call one of 'em Young Master or Young Mistress, cuss fire to your black hearts!" All the other white folks look kind of funny, and Old Mistress look 'shamed of Old Master.

My own pappy was in that bunch, too. His name was Frank, and after the war he took the name of Frank Henderson, 'cause he was born under that name, but I always went by Jones, the name I was born under.

'Long about the middle of the war, after Old Master was killed, the soldiers begin coming round the place and camping. They was Southern soldiers, and they say they have to take the mules and most the corn to git along on. Just go in the barns and cribs and take anything they want, and us niggers didn't have no sweet 'taters nor Irish 'taters to eat on when they gone neither.

One bunch come and stay in the woods across the road from the overseer's house, and they was all on hosses. They lead the hosses down to Bois d'Arc Creek every morning at daylight and late every evening to git water. When we going to the field and when we coming in, we always see them leading big bunches of hosses.

They bugle go just 'bout the time our old horn blow in the morning, and when we come in they eating supper, and we smell it and sure git hungry!

Before Old Master died he sold off a whole lot of hosses and cattle, and some niggers too. He had the sales on the plantation, and white men from around there come to bid, and some traders come. He had a big stump where he made the niggers stand while they was being sold, and the men and boys had to strip off to the waist to show they muscle and iffen they had any scars or hurt places, but the women and gals didn't have to strip to the waist.

The white men come up and look in the slave's mouth just like he was a mule or a hoss.

After Old Master go, the overseer hold one sale, but mostly he just trade with the traders what come by. He make the niggers git on the stump, though. The traders all had big bunches of slaves, and they have 'em all strung out in a line going down the road. Some had wagons and the children could ride, but not many. They didn't chain or tie 'em 'cause they didn't have no place they could run to anyway.

I seen children sold off and the mammy not sold, and sometimes the mammy sold and a little baby kept on the place and give to another woman to raise. Them white folks didn't care nothing 'bout how the slaves grieved when they tore up a family.

Old Man Saunders was the hardest overseer of anybody. He would git mad and give a whipping sometime, and the slave wouldn't even know what it was about.

My Uncle Sandy was the lead row nigger, and he was a good nigger and never would touch a drap of liquor. One night some the niggers git hold of some liquor somehow, and they leave the jug half full on the step of Sandy's cabin. Next morning Old Man Saunders come out in the field so mad he was pale.

He just go to the lead row and tell Sandy to go with him and start toward the woods along Bois d'Arc Creek, with Sandy following behind. The overseer always carry a big heavy stick, but we didn't know he was so mad, and they just went off in the woods.

Pretty soon we hear Sandy hollering, and we know old overseer pouring it on, then the overseer come back by hisself and go on up to the house.

Come late evening he come and see what we done in the day's work, and go back to the quarters with us all. When he git to Mammy's cabin, where Grandmammy live too, he say to Grandmammy, "I sent Sandy down in the woods to hunt a hoss, he gwine come in hungry pretty soon. You better make him a extra hoecake," and he kind of laugh and go on to his house.

Just soon as he gone, we all tell Grandmammy we think he got a whipping, and sure 'nough he didn't come in.

The next day some white boys finds Uncle Sandy where that overseer done killed him and throwed him in a little pond, and they never done nothing to Old Man Saunders at all!

When he go to whip a nigger he make him strip to the waist, and he take a cat-o'-nine-tails and bring the blisters, and then bust the blisters with a wide strap of leather fastened to a stick handle. I seen the blood running outen many a back, all the way from the neck to the waist!

Many the time a nigger git blistered and cut up so that we have to git a sheet and grease it with lard and wrap 'em up in it, and they have to wear a greasy cloth wrapped around they body under the shirt for three-four days after they git a big whipping!

Later on in the war the Yankees come in all around us and camp, and the overseer git sweet as honey in the comb! Nobody git a whipping all the time the Yankees there!

They come and took all the meat and corn and 'taters they want too, and they tell us, "Why don't you poor darkies take all the meat and molasses you want? You made it and it's yours much as anybody's!" But we know they soon be gone, and then we git a whipping iffen we do. Some niggers run off and went with the Yankees, but they had to work just as hard for them, and they didn't eat so good and often with the soldiers.

I never forget the day we was set free!

That morning we all go to the cotton field early, and then a house nigger come out from Old Mistress on a hoss and say she want the overseer to come into town, and he leave and go in. After while the old horn blow up at the overseer's house, and we all stop and listen, 'cause it the wrong time of day for the horn.

We start chopping again, and there go the horn again.

The lead row nigger holler, "Hold up!" And we all stop again. "We better go on in. That our horn," he holler at the head nigger, and the head nigger think so too, but he say he afraid we catch the devil from the overseer iffen we quit without him there, and the lead row man say maybe he back from town and blowing the horn hisself, so we line up and go in.

When we git to the quarters, we see all the old ones and the children up in the overseer's yard, so we go on up there. The overseer setting on the end of the gallery with a paper in his hand, and when we all come up he say come and stand close to the gallery. Then he call off everybody's name and see we all there.

Setting on the gallery in a hide-bottom chair was a man we never see before. He had on a big broad black hat like the Yankees wore, but it didn't have no yellow string on it like most the Yankees had, and he was in store clothes that wasn't homespun or jeans, and they was black. His hair was plumb gray and so was his beard, and it come 'way down here on his chest, but he didn't look like he was very old, 'cause his face was kind of fleshy and healthy-looking. I think we all been sold off in a bunch, and I notice some kind of smiling, and I think they sure glad of it.

The man say, "You darkies know what day this is?" He talk kind, and smile.

We all don't know, of course, and we just stand there and grin. Pretty soon he ask again and the head man say, "No, we don't know."

"Well, this is the fourth day of June, and this is 1865, and I want you all to 'member the date, 'cause you always gwine 'member the day. Today you is free, just like I is, and Mr. Saunders and your mistress and all us white people," the man say.

"I come to tell you," he say, "and I wants to be sure you all understand, 'cause you don't have to git up and go by the horn no more. You is your own bosses now, and you don't have to have no passes to go and come."

We never did have no passes, nohow, but we knowed lots of other niggers on other plantations got 'em.

"I wants to bless you and hope you always is happy and tell you you got all the right and lief that any white people got," the man say, and then he git on his hoss and ride off.

We all just watch him go on down the road, and then we go up to Mr. Saunders and ask him what he want us to do. He just grunt and say do like we damn please, he reckon, but git off that place to do it, lessen any of us wants to stay and make the crop for half of what we make.

None of us know where to go, so we all stay, and he split up the fields and show us which part we got to work in, and we go on like we was, and make the crop and git it in, but they ain't no more horn after that day. Some the niggers lazy and don't git in the field early, and they git it took away from 'em, but they plead around and git it back and work better the rest of that year.

But we all gits fooled on that first go-out! When the crop all in, we don't git half! Old Mistress sick in town, and the overseer was still on the place, and he charge us half the crop for the quarters and the mules and tools and grub!

Then he leave, and we gits another white man, and he sets up a book, and give us half the next year, and take out for what we use up, but we all got something left over after that first go-out.

Old Mistress never git well after she lose all her niggers, and one day the white boss tell us she just drap over dead setting in her chair, and we know her heart just broke.

Next year the children sell off most the place and we scatter off, and I and Mammy go into Little Rock and do work in the town. Grand-mammy done dead.

I git married to John White in Little Rock, but he died, and we didn't have no children. Then in four-five years I marry Billy Rowe. He was a Cherokee citizen, and he had belonged to a Cherokee name Dave Rowe, and lived east of Tahlequah before the war. We married in Little Rock, but he had land in the Cherokee Nation, and we come to east of Tahlequah and lived till he died, and then I come to Tulsa to live with my youngest daughter.

Billy Rowe and me had three children—Ellie, John, and Lula. Lula married a Thomas, and it's her I lives with.

Lots of old people like me say that they was happy in slavery and that they had the worst tribulations after freedom, but I knows they didn't have no white master and overseer like we all had on our place. They both dead now, I reckon, and they no use talking 'bout the dead, but I know I been gone long ago iffen that white man Saunders didn't lose his hold on me.

It was the fourth day of June in 1865 I begins to live, and I gwine take the picture of that old man in the big black hat and long whiskers, setting on the gallery and talking kind to us, clean into my grave with me.

No, bless God, I ain't never seen no more black boys bleeding all up and down the back under a cat-o'-nine-tails, and I never go by no cabin and hear no poor nigger groaning, all wrapped up in a lardy sheet no more!

I hear my children read about General Lee, and I know he was a good man. I didn't know nothing about him then, but I know now he wasn't fighting for that kind of white folks.

Maybe they that kind still yet, but they don't show it up no more, and I got lots of white friends too. All my children and grandchildren been to school, and they git along good, and I know we living in a better world, where they ain't nobody cussing fire to my black heart!

I sure thank the good Lord I got to see it.

Henry D. Thoreau

Henry David Thoreau (1817-1862), individualist, essayist, and prophet, spent most of his life in and around his native village, Concord, Massachusetts. After graduating from Harvard in 1837, he returned home, taught school for some years, then became intermittently a philosopher, lecturer, handyman, helper in the family pencil business, and a writer—one of the most influential that America has produced. His writings express his passion for social justice and for a life, close to nature, of honesty and simplicity. The greatest of his books, *Walden,* is a descriptive and philosophical record of an experiment in living that Thoreau began on July 4, 1845, when he took up residence alone in a small house he had built in the woods near Walden Pond on land belonging to his friend Ralph Waldo Emerson. He lived in the house over two years and there wrote a preliminary version of his experiences, which he repeatedly expanded and reshaped before its publication in 1854.

For *Walden,* as for all his works, Thoreau depended heavily on the journal that he had been keeping since his first year of college and was to continue for the rest of his life. We present below selections from the journal (printed in lefthand column) with the corresponding passages from the final version of *Walden* in parallel. Together they provide an illustration of one of the uses of a journal and an insight into the composition of an American classic. Each of Thoreau's revisions, additions, and rearrangements may be studied for its effect on meaning, rhythm, and feeling. The reader should keep in mind that Thoreau was not attempting merely to report what happened at Walden, but to provide an "imaginative recreation" of it, with significant observations drawn from his experience at other times and places. For a full account of his methods, see the study by J. Lyndon Shanley, *The Making of Walden* (1957).

The only other book Thoreau published in his lifetime was *A Week on the Concord and Merrimack Rivers* (1849), recording a trip taken with his brothers in 1839. Among his many articles and essays the most famous is "Civil Disobedience" (1849). It was writtten to justify his refusal to pay a tax levied by the government during the Mexican War, which he considered unjust.

The Journal and *Walden:*
Parallel Passages

. . . . So many autumn days spent outside the town, trying to hear what was in the wind, to hear it and carry it express. I well-nigh sunk all my capital in it, and lost my own breath into the bargain, by running in the face of it. Depend upon it, if it had concerned either of the parties, it would have appeared in the yeoman's gazette, the *Freeman,* with other earliest intelligence.

For many years I was self-appointed inspector of snow-storms and rain-storms, and did my duty faithfully, though I never received one cent for it.

Surveyor, if not of higher ways, then of forest paths and all across-lot routes, keeping many open ravines bridged and passable at all seasons, where the public heel had testified to the importance of the same, all not only without charge, but even at considerable risk and inconvenience. Many a mower would have forborne to complain had he been aware of the invisible public good that was in jeopardy.

So I went on, I may say without boasting, I trust, faithfully minding my own business without a partner, till it became more and more evident that my townsmen would not, after all, admit me into the list of town officers, nor make the place a sinecure with moderate allowance.

I have looked after the wild stock of the town, which pastures in common, and every one knows that these cattle give you a good

So many autumn, ay, and winter days, spent outside the town, trying to hear what was in the wind, to hear and carry it express! I well-nigh sunk all my capital in it, and lost my own breath into the bargain, running in the face of it. If it had concerned either of the political parties, depend upon it, it would have appeared in the Gazette with the earliest intelligence. At other times watching from the observatory of some cliff or tree, to telegraph any new arrival; or waiting at evening on the hilltops for the sky to fall, that I might catch something, though I never caught much, and that, manna-wise, would dissolve again in the sun.

For a long time I was reporter to a journal, of no very wide circulation, whose editor has never yet seen fit to print the bulk of my contributions, and, as is too common with writers, I got only my labor for my pains. However, in this case my pains were their own reward.

For many years I was self-appointed inspector of snow storms and rain storms, and did my duty faithfully; surveyor, if not of highways, then of forest paths and all across-lot routes, keeping them open, and ravines bridged and passable at all seasons, where the public heel had testified to their utility.

I have looked after the wild stock of the town, which give a faithful herdsman a good deal of deal of trouble in the way of leap- ing fences. I have counted and reg- istered all the eggs I could find at least, and have had an eye to all nooks and corners of the farm, though I did n't always know whether Jonas or Solomon worked in a particular field to-day; that was none of my business. I only knew him for one of the men, and trusted that he was as well em- ployed as I was. I had to make my daily entries in the general farm book, and my duties may sometimes have made me a little stubborn and unyielding.

Many a day spent on the hilltops waiting for the sky to fall, that I might catch something, though I never caught much, only a little, manna-wise, that would dissolve again in the sun.

My accounts, indeed, which I can swear to have been faithfully kept, I have never got audited, still less accepted, still less paid and settled. However, I have n't set my heart upon *that*.

I have watered the red huckleberry and the sand cherry and the hoopwood [?] tree, and the cornel and spoonhunt and yellow violet, which might have withered else in dry seasons. The white grape.

To find the bottom of Walden Pond, and what inlet and outlet it might have.

I found at length that, as they were not likely to offer me any office in the court-house, any curacy or living anywhere else, I must shift for myself, I must fur- nish myself with the necessaries of life.

trouble by leaping fences; and I have had an eye to the un- frequented nooks and corners of the farm; though I did not always know whether Jonas or Solomon worked in a particular field to-day; that was none of my business. I have watered the red huckleberry, the sand cherry and the nettle tree, the red pine and the black ash, the white grape and the yel- low violet, which might have withered else in dry seasons.

In short, I went on thus for a long time (I may say it without boasting), faithfully minding my business, till it became more and more evident that my townsmen would not after all admit me into the list of town officers, nor make my place a sinecure with a moder- ate allowance. My accounts, which I can swear to have kept faithfully, I have, indeed, never got audited, still less accepted, still less paid and settled. However, I have not set my heart on that.

Not long since, a strolling Indian went to sell baskets at the house of a well-known lawyer in my neigh- borhood. "Do you wish to buy any baskets?" he asked. "No, we do not want any," was the reply. "What!" exclaimed the Indian as he went out the gate, "do you mean to starve us?" Having seen his indus- trious white neighbors so well off,—that the lawyer had only to weave arguments, and by some magic wealth and standing fol- lowed,—he had said to himself: I will go into business; I will weave baskets; it is a thing which I can do. Thinking that when he had made the baskets he would have

Now watching from the observatory of the Cliffs or Annursnack to telegraph any new arrival, to see if Wachusett, Watatic, or Monadnock had got any nearer. Climbing trees for the same purpose. I have been reporter for many years to one of the journals of no very wide circulation, and, as is too common, got only my pains for my labor. Literary contracts are little binding. . . .

done his part, and then it would be the white man's to buy them. He had not discovered that it was necessary for him to make it worth the other's while to buy them or at least make him think that it was so, or to make something else which it would be worth his while to buy. I too had woven a kind of basket of a delicate texture, but I had not made it worth any one's while to buy them. Yet not the less, in my case, did I think it worth my while to weave them, and instead of studying how to make it worth men's while to buy my baskets, I studied rather how to avoid the necessity of selling them. The life which men praise and regard as successful is but one kind. Why should we exaggerate any one kind at the expense of the others?

Finding that my fellow-citizens were not likely to offer me any room in the court house, or any curacy or living anywhere else, but I must shift for myself, I turned my face more exclusively than ever to the woods, where I was better known. I determined to go into business at once, and not wait to acquire the usual capital, using such slender means as I had already got. My purpose in going to Walden Pond was not to live cheaply nor to live dearly there, but to transact some private business with the fewest obstacles; to be hindered from accomplishing which for want of a little common sense, a little enterprise and business talent, appeared not so sad as foolish.

There are scores of pitch pines in my field, from one to three inches in diameter, girdled by the mice last winter. A Norwegian winter it was for them, for the snow lay long and deep, and they had to mix much pine meal with their usual diet. Yet these trees have not many of them died, even in midsummer, and laid bare for a foot, but have grown a foot. They seem to do all their gnawing beneath the snow. There is not much danger of the mouse tribe becoming extinct in hard winters, for their granary is a cheap and extensive one.

Here is one has had her nest under my house, and came when I took my luncheon to pick the crumbs at my feet. It had never seen the race of man before, and so the sooner became familiar. It ran over my shoes and up my pantaloons inside, clinging to my flesh with its sharp claws. It would run up the side of the room by short impulses like a squirrel, which [it] resembles, coming between the house mouse and the former. Its belly is a little reddish, and its ears a little longer. At length, as I leaned my elbow on the bench, it ran over my arm and round the paper which contained my dinner. And when I held it a piece of cheese, it came and nibbled between my fingers, and then cleaned its face and paws like a fly.

The mice which haunted my house were not the common ones, which are said to have been introduced into the country, but a wild native kind not found in the village. I sent one to a distinguished naturalist, and it interested him much. When I was building, one of these had its nest underneath the house, and before I had laid the second floor, and swept out the shavings, would come out regularly at lunch time and pick up the crumbs at my feet. It probably had never seen a man before; and it soon became quite familiar, and would run over my shoes and up my clothes. It could readily ascend the sides of the room by short impulses, like a squirrel, which it resembled in its motions. At length, as I leaned with my elbow on the bench one day, it ran up my clothes, and along my sleeve, and round and round the paper which held my dinner, while I kept the latter close, and dodged and played at bo-peep with it; and when at last I held still a piece of cheese between my thumb and finger, it came and nibbled it, sitting in my hand, and afterward cleaned its face and paws, like a fly, and walked away.

September 29, 1843

The first sparrow of spring. The year beginning with younger hope than ever. The faint [first?] silvery warblings heard over the bare dank fields as if the last flakes of winter tinkled. What then are histories, chronologies—traditions, and written revelations. Flakes of warm sunlight fall on the congealed earth—the brooks and rills sing carols and glees for the spring. The marsh hawk already seeks the first slimy life that awakes—The sough of melting snow is heard in the dells of the wood, by the sunny river banks, and the ice dissolves in the seething ponds, evaporating hourly. The earth sends forth as it were an inward green heat and the grass flames up on the warm hill sides like a green spring fire. Methinks the sight of the first sod of fresh grass in the spring would make the reformer reconsider his schemes, the faithless and despairing man revive—The grass blade is a perpetual growth a long green ribbon—streaming from the sod into the summer—checked indeed by the frost—but anon pushing on again lifting its withered hay with fresh life below.—I have seen where early in spring the clumps of grass stood with their three inches of new green upholding their withered spears of the last autumn, and from year to year the herds browse and the mower cuts from this never failing outwelling supply—what their needs require. So the human life but dies down to the surface, but puts forth a green blade to eternity.

The first sparrow of spring! The year beginning with younger hope than ever! The faint silvery warblings heard over the partially bare and moist fields from the bluebird, the song-sparrow, and the red-wing, as if the last flakes of winter tinkled as they fell! What at such a time are histories, chronologies, traditions, and all written revelations? The brooks sing carols and glees to the spring. The marsh-hawk sailing low over the meadow is already seeking the first slimy life that awakes. The sinking sound of melting snow is heard in all dells, and the ice dissolves apace in the ponds. The grass flames up on the hillsides like a spring fire,—"et primitus oritur herba imbribus primoribus evocata,"[and for the first time the grass appears, called forth by the first rains]—as if the earth sent forth an inward heat to greet the returning sun; not yellow but green is the color of its flame;—the symbol of perpetual youth, the grass-blade, like a long green ribbon, streams from the sod into the summer, checked indeed by the frost, but anon pushing on again, lifting its spear of last year's hay with the fresh life below. It grows as steadily as the rill oozes out of the ground. It is almost identical with that, for in the growing days of June, when the rills are dry, the grass blades are their channels, and from year to year the herds drink at this perennial green stream, and the mower draws from it betimes their winter supply. So our human

The grass blade is as steady a growth as the rill which leaks out of the ground—indeed it is almost identical with that, for in the vigorous fertile days of June when the rills are dry the grass blades are their channel.

life but dies down to its root, and still puts forth its green blade to eternity.

March 26, 1846

The change from foul weather to fair, from dark, sluggish hours to serene, elastic ones, is a memorable crisis which all things proclaim. The change from foulness to serenity is instantaneous. Suddenly an influx of light, though it was late, filled my room. I looked out and saw that the pond was already calm and full of hope as on a summer evening, though the ice was dissolved but yesterday. There seemed to be some intelligence in the pond which responded to the unseen serenity in a distant horizon. I heard a robin in the distance,—the first I had heard this spring,—repeating the assurance. The green pitch [pine] suddenly looked brighter and more erect, as if now entirely washed and cleansed by the rain. I knew it would not rain any more. A serene summer-evening sky seemed darkly reflected in the pond, though the clear sky was nowhere visible overhead. It was no longer the end of a season, but the begin-

The change from storm and winter to serene and mild weather, from dark and sluggish hours to bright and elastic ones, is a memorable crisis which all things proclaim. It is seemingly instantaneous at last. Suddenly an influx of light filled my house, though the evening was at hand, and the clouds of winter still overhung it, and the eaves were dripping with sleety rain. I looked out the window, and lo! where yesterday was cold gray ice there lay the transparent pond already calm and full of hope as in a summer evening, reflecting a summer evening sky in its bosom, though none was visible overhead, as if it had intelligence with some remote horizon. I heard a robin in the distance, the first I had heard for many a thousand years, methought, whose note I shall not forget for many a thousand more,— the same sweet and powerful song as of yore. O the evening robin, at the end of a New England summer day! If I could ever find the twig

ning. The pines and shrub oaks, which had before drooped and cowered the winter through with myself, now recovered their several characters and in the landscape revived the expression of an immortal beauty. Trees seemed all at once to be fitly grouped, to sustain new relations to men and to one another. There was somewhat cosmical in the arrangement of nature. O the evening robin, at the close of a New England day! If I could ever find the twig he sits upon! Where does the minstrel really roost? We perceive it is not the bird of the ornithologist that is heard,—the *Turdus migratorius.*

The signs of fair weather are seen in the bosom of ponds before they are recognized in the heavens. It is easy to tell by looking at any twig of the forest whether its winter is past or not.

he sits upon! I mean *he;* I mean *the twig.* This at least is not the *Turdus migratorius.* The pitch-pines and shrub-oaks about my house, which had so long drooped, suddenly resumed their several characters, looked brighter, greener, and more erect and alive, as if effectually cleansed and restored by the rain. I knew that it would not rain any more. You may tell by looking at any twig of the forest, ay, at your very wood-pile, whether its winter is past or not. . . .

John Stuart Mill

John Stuart Mill (1806-1873) was educated entirely by his father, James Mill, in an intense and rigorous fashion. He began Greek at the age of three, Latin at seven, and by the age of fourteen had worked extensively in the classics, mathematics and calculus, logic, history, and political economy: "an amount of knowledge," he remarks in his *Autobiography*, ". . . which is seldom acquired (if acquired at all) until the age of manhood." Mill recognizes the unusual rigor of his childhood, recalling that his father's weapons were anger and scorn, that he was without tenderness, that he kept his son almost completely isolated from other children, and that he allowed no holidays "lest the habit of work should be broken, and a taste for idleness acquired." In spite of these severities, Mill expresses admiration for his father's diligence, and respect for an education which was not "crammed with mere facts, and with the opinions and phrases of other people," as public school educations may be, but which strove to communicate understanding rather than facts, and to develop the power of independent thought.

By the time he was sixteen, Mill's formal education was complete. In this year he founded the Utilitarian Society, a small group dedicated to discussion and debate concerning the philosophy of utilitarianism, originally formulated by Jeremy Bentham. This strictly rational philosophy holds that whatever is useful is good, so that usefulness should determine questions of right and wrong. In 1823, he and his father began writing for the *Westminister Review,* a utilitarian journal founded by Bentham; and by 1825 he had organized and extensively edited manuscripts of Bentham's *Treatise Upon Evidence* amounting to five published volumes.

In the next year, when he was twenty years old, Mill suffered the period of uncertainty and depression described in the following passage from his *Autobiography* (1873). Mill's biographers attribute this mental crisis to overwork, or to overstimulation, or to the tremendous pressures of his childhood. Mill himself at first wrote that he was depressed "probably from physical causes (connected perhaps merely with the time of year)," but he later deleted this phrase in his manuscript and attributed his condition wholly to weaknesses in his personal philosophy.

After the time described in this passage, Mill became interested in the poetry of Wordsworth, Coleridge, and Goethe and expanded the bounds of his political philosophy to include elements of socialism, French liberalism, and the fight for women's rights. His works include *A System of Logic, Ratiocinative and Inductive* (1843), *Principles of Political Economy* (1848), and *On Liberty* (1859). His autobiography, begun in 1853, was published in the year of his death.

An interesting question to post-Freudian readers of this passage is whether Mill himself fully realizes the importance of his relationship with his father in the mental crisis described. Mill does not speculate, as a modern autobiographer might, on the full meaning of the resolution of the crisis. The passage also raises important issues in educational theory, particularly on the rival claims of analytic thought and of feeling, and on the validity of "associationist" (today we might call it "behaviorist" or "Skinnerian") psychology.

Mill's writing is as straight and lucid as his mind, and it continually produces

250 John Stuart Mill

phrases that ask to be tested for their truth. "If I had loved any one sufficiently to make confiding my griefs a necessity, I should not have been in the condition I was" (p. 251); "ask yourself whether you are happy, and you cease to be so" (p. 255). Though Mill concludes that "the cultivation of the feelings became one of the cardinal points in my ethical and philosophic creed" (p. 255), there is some question whether his new creed ever penetrated his mature writing style, of which this is a good example. Compare this passage with one of Nabokov's, or D. H. Lawrence's or Dorothy Wordsworth's, for its evocation of feelings.

A Crisis in My Mental History

For some years after this I wrote very little, and nothing regularly, for publication: and great were the advantages which I derived from the intermission. It was of no common importance to me, at this period, to be able to digest and mature my thoughts for my own mind only, without any immediate call for giving them out in print. Had I gone on writing, it would have much disturbed the important transformation in my opinions and character, which took place during those years. The origin of this transformation, or at least the process by which I was prepared for it, can only be explained by turning some distance back.

From the winter of 1821, when I first read Bentham, and especially from the commencement of the Westminster Review, I had what might truly be called an object in life; to be a reformer of the world. My conception of my own happiness was entirely identified with this object. The personal sympathies I wished for were those of fellow labourers in this enterprise. I endeavoured to pick up as many flowers as I could by the way; but as a serious and permanent personal satisfaction to rest upon, my whole reliance was placed on this; and I was accustomed to felicitate myself on the certainty of a happy life which I enjoyed, through placing my happiness in something durable and distant, in which some progress might be always making, while it could never be exhausted by complete attainment. This did very well for several years, during which the general improvement going on in the world and the idea of myself as engaged with others in struggling to promote it, seemed enough to fill up an interesting and animated existence. But the time came when I awakened from this as from a dream. It was in the autumn of 1826. I was in a dull state of nerves, such as everybody is occasionally liable to; unsusceptible to enjoyment or pleasurable excitement; one of those moods when what is pleasure at other times, becomes insipid or indifferent; the state, I should think, in which converts to Methodism usually are, when smitten by their first "conviction of sin." In this frame of mind it occurred to me to put the question directly to myself: "Suppose that all your objects in life were realized; that all the changes in institutions and opinions which you are looking forward to, could be completely effected at this very instant; would this be a great joy and happiness to you?" And an irrepressible self-consciousness distinctly answered, "No!" At this my heart sank within me: the whole foundation on which my life was constructed fell down. All my happiness was to have been found in the continual pursuit of this end. The end had ceased to charm, and how could there ever again be any interest in the means? I seemed to have nothing left to live for.

At first I hoped that the cloud would pass away of itself; but it did not. A night's sleep, the sovereign remedy for the smaller vexations of life, had no effect on it. I awoke to a renewed consciousness of the woful fact. I carried it with me into all companies, into all occupations. Hardly anything had power to cause me even a few minutes oblivion of it. For some months the cloud seemed to grow thicker and thicker. The lines in Coleridge's "Dejection"—I was not then acquainted with them—exactly describe my case:

"A grief without a pang, void, dark and drear,
A drowsy, stifled, unimpassioned grief,
Which finds no natural outlet of relief
In word, or sigh, or tear."

In vain I sought relief from my favourite books; those memorials of past nobleness and greatness from which I had always hitherto drawn strength and animation. I read them now without feeling, or with the accustomed feelings *minus* all its charm; and I became persuaded, that my love of mankind, and of excellence for its own sake, had worn itself out. I sought no comfort by speaking to others of what I felt. If I had loved any one sufficiently to make confiding my griefs a necessity, I should not have been in the condition I was. I felt, too, that mine was not an interesting, or in any way respectable distress. There was nothing in it to attract sympathy. Advice, if I had known where to seek it, would have been most precious. The words of Macbeth to the physician often occurred to my thoughts. But there was no one on whom I could build the faintest hope of such assistance. My father, to whom it would have been natural to me to have recourse in any practical difficulties, was the last person to whom, in such a case as this, I looked for help. Everything convinced me that he had no knowledge of any such mental state as I was suffering from, and that even if he could be made to understand it, he was not the physician who could heal it. My education, which was wholly his work, had been conducted without any regard to the possibility of its ending in this result; and I saw no use in giving him the pain of thinking that his plans had failed, when the failure was probably irremediable, and, at all events, beyond the power of *his* remedies. Of other friends, I had at that time none to whom I had any hope of making my condition intelligible. It was however abundantly intelligible to myself; and the more I dwelt upon it, the more hopeless it appeared.

My course of study had led me to believe, that all mental and moral feelings and qualities, whether of a good or of a bad kind, were the results of association; that we love one thing, and hate another, take pleasure in one sort of action or contemplation, and pain in another sort, through the clinging of pleasurable or painful ideas to those things, from the effect of education or of experience. As a corollary from this, I had always heard it maintained by my father, and was myself convinced, that the object of education should be to form the strongest possible associations of the salutary class; associations of pleasure with all things beneficial to the great whole, and of pain with all things hurtful to it. This doctrine appeared inexpugnable; but it now seemed to me, on retrospect, that my teachers had occupied themselves but superficially with the means of forming and keeping up these salutary associations. They seemed to have trusted altogether to the old familiar instruments, praise and blame, reward and punishment. Now, I did not doubt that by these means, begun early, and applied unremittingly, intense associations of pain and pleasure, especially of pain, might be created, and might produce desires and aversions capable of lasting undiminished to the end of life. But there must always be something artificial and casual in associations thus produced. The pains and pleasures thus forcibly associated with things, are not connected with them by any natural tie; and it is, therefore, I thought, essential to the durability of these associations, that they should have become so intense and inveterate as to be practically indissoluble, before the habitual exercise of the power of analysis had commenced. For I now saw, or thought I saw, what I had always before received with incredulity—that the habit of analysis has a tendency to wear away the feelings: as indeed it has, when no other mental habit is cultivated, and the analysing spirit remains without its natural complements and correctives. The very excellence of analysis (I argued) is that it tends to weaken and undermine whatever is the result of prejudice; that it enables us mentally to separate ideas which have only casually clung together: and no associations whatever could ultimately resist this dissolving force, were it not that we owe to analysis our clearest knowledge of the permanent sequences in nature; the real connexions between Things, not dependent on our will and feelings; natural laws, by virtue of which, in many cases, one thing is inseparable from another in fact; which laws, in proportion as they are clearly perceived and imaginatively realized, cause our ideas of things which are always joined together in Nature, to cohere more and more closely in our thoughts. Analytic habits may thus even strengthen the associations between causes and effects, means and ends, but tend altogether to weaken those which are, to speak familiarly, a *mere* matter of feeling. They are therefore (I thought) favourable to prudence and clear-sightedness, but a perpetual worm at the root both of the passions and of the virtues; and, above all, fearfully undermine all desires, and all pleasures, which are the effects of association, that is, according to the theory I held, all except the purely physical and organic; of the entire insufficiency of which to make life desirable, no one had a stronger conviction than I had. These were the laws of human nature, by which, as it seemed to me, I had been brought to my present state. All those to whom I looked up, were of opinion that the pleasure of sympathy with human beings, and the feelings which made the good of others, and especially of mankind on a large scale, the object of existence, were the greatest and surest sources of happiness. Of the truth of this I was convinced, but to know that a feeling would make me happy if I had it, did not give me the feeling. My education, I thought, had failed to create these feelings in sufficient strength to resist the dissolving influence of analysis, while the whole course of my intellectual cultivation had made precocious and premature analysis the inveterate habit of my mind. I was thus, as I said to myself, left stranded at the commencement of my voyage, with a well-equipped ship and a rudder, but no sail; without any real desire for the ends which I had been so carefully fitted out to work for: no delight in virtue, or the general good, but also just as little in anything else. The fountains of vanity and ambition seemed to have dried up within me, as completely as those of benevolence. I had had (as I reflected) some gratification of vanity at too early an age: I had obtained some distinction, and felt myself of some importance, before the desire of distinction and of importance had grown into a passion: and little as it was which I had attained, yet having been attained too early, like all pleasures enjoyed too soon, it had made me *blasé* and indifferent to the pursuit. Thus neither selfish nor unselfish pleasures were pleasures to me. And there seemed no power in nature sufficient to begin the formation of my character anew, and create in a mind now irretrievably analytic, fresh associations of pleasure with any of the objects of human desire.

These were the thoughts which mingled with the dry heavy dejection of the melancholy winter of 1826-7. During this time I was not incapable of my usual occupations. I went on with them mechanically, by the mere force of habit. I had been so drilled in a certain sort of mental exercise, that I could still carry it on when all the spirit had gone out of it. I even composed and spoke several speeches at the debating society, how, or with what degree of success, I know not. Of four years continual speaking at that society, this is the only year of which I remember next to nothing. Two lines of Coleridge, in whom alone of all writers I have found a true description of what I felt, were often in my thoughts, not at this time (for I had never read them), but in a later period of the same mental malady:

"Work without hope draws nectar in a sieve,
And hope without an object cannot live."

In all probability my case was by no means so peculiar as I fancied it, and I doubt not that many others have passed through a similar state; but the idiosyncrasies of my education had given to the general phenomenon a special character, which made it seem the natural effect of causes that it was hardly possible for time to remove. I frequently asked myself, if I could, or if I was bound to go on living, when life must be passed in this manner. I generally answered to myself, that I did not think I could possibly bear it beyond a year. When, however, not more than half that duration of time had elapsed, a small ray of light broke in upon my gloom. I was reading, accidentally, Marmontel's "Mémoires," and came to the passage which relates his father's death, the distressed position of the family, and the sudden inspiration by which he, then a mere boy, felt and made them feel that he would be everything to them—would supply the place of all that they had lost. A vivid conception of the scene and its feelings came over me, and I was moved to tears. From this moment my burthen grew lighter. The oppression of the thought that all feeling was dead within me, was gone. I was no longer hopeless: I was not a stock or a stone. I had still, it seemed, some of the material out of which all worth of character, and all capacity for happiness, are made. Relieved from my ever present sense of ir-remediable wretchedness, I gradually found that the ordinary incidents of life could again give me some pleasure; that I could again find enjoyment, not intense, but sufficient for cheerfulness, in sunshine and sky, in books, in conversation, in public affairs; and that there was, once more, excitement, though of a moderate kind, in exerting myself for my opinions, and for the public good. Thus the cloud gradually drew off, and I again enjoyed life: and though I had several relapses, some of which lasted many months, I never again was as miserable as I had been.

The experiences of this period had two very marked effects on my opinions and character. In the first place, they led me to adopt a theory of life, very unlike that on which I had before acted, and having much in common with what at that time I certainly had never heard of, the anti-self-consciousness theory of Carlyle. I never, indeed, wavered in the conviction that happiness is the test of all rules of conduct, and the end of life. But I now thought that this end was only to be attained by not making it the direct end. Those only are happy (I thought) who have their minds fixed on some object other than their own happiness; on the happiness of others, on the improvement of mankind, even on some art or pursuit, followed not as a means, but as itself an ideal end. Aiming thus at something else, they find happiness by the way. The enjoyments of life (such was now my theory) are sufficient to make it a pleasant thing, when they are taken *en passant,* without being made a principal object. Once make them so, and they are immediately felt to be insufficient. They will not bear a scrutinizing examination. Ask yourself whether you are happy, and you cease to be so. The only chance is to treat, not happiness, but some end external to it, as the purpose of life. Let your self-consciousness, your scrutiny, your self-interrogation, exhaust themselves on that; and if otherwise fortunately circumstanced you will inhale happiness with the air you breathe, without dwelling on it or thinking about it, without either forestalling it in imagination, or putting it to flight by fatal questioning. This theory now became the basis of my philosophy of life. And I still hold to it as the best theory for all those who have but a moderate degree of sensibility and of capacity for enjoyment, that is, for the great majority of mankind.

The other important change which my opinions at this time underwent, was that I, for the first time, gave its proper place, among the prime necessities of human well-being, to the internal culture of the individual. I ceased to attach almost exclusive importance to the ordering of outward circumstances, and the training of the human being for speculation and for action.

I had now learnt by experience that the passive susceptibilities needed to be cultivated as well as the active capacities, and required to be nourished and enriched as well as guided. I did not, for an instant, lose sight of, or undervalue, that part of the truth which I had seen before; I never turned recreant to intellectual culture, or ceased to consider the power and practice of analysis as an essential condition both of individual and social improvement. But I thought that it had consequences which required to be corrected, by joining other kinds of cultivation with it. The maintenance of a due balance among the faculties, now seemed to me of primary importance. The cultivation of the feelings became one of the cardinal points in my ethical and philosophical creed. And my thoughts and inclinations turned in an increasing degree towards whatever seemed capable of being instrumental to that object. . . .

Dorothy and William Wordsworth

Dorothy Wordsworth was born on Christmas day, 1771, a year and a half after her brother William, the great English poet. Her mother died when she was six years old, and she was raised apart from her brother by a succession of relatives. The two children remained devoted to one another throughout their separation and planned for years to live together. After 1794, their hopes were at last realized in Dorset, Somerset, and finally Grasmere in England's Lake District. There they immersed themselves in nature through gardening and extensive country walks.

Although Dorothy Wordsworth did not consider herself a poet (at one point she wrote "I tried to write verses—alas!"), her intense poetic responsiveness to nature strongly affected William Wordsworth's sensitivity: "She gave me eyes, she gave me ears," he declares. Their friend the poet Samuel Taylor Coleridge wrote that "her manners are simple, ardent, impressive . . . Her eye watchful in the minutest observation of nature." At Alfoxden in Somerset, and at Grasmere after 1800, Dorothy kept journals of her life with William that reveal a poetical as well as personal interaction between them. Her Grasmere journal, written "to please William," often records a day's experience together with the birth of a poem by William arising from the experience, as in the April 16 entry reprinted below. Dorothy's descriptions in the April 15 entry record the feeling that William recollected two years later to write "I wandered lonely as a cloud." Her entry on July 29 is intimately related to William's sonnet "Upon Westminster Bridge." We print the poems with the journal entries to provide an unrivaled occasion for the comparison between verse and prose.

The first few days covered in the journal entries include William's return from arranging his marriage to Mary Hutchinson and the return of William and Dorothy on foot from Eusmere to their home in Grasmere fifteen miles away. The engagement of William and Mary was very painful to Dorothy, but in the course of the following weeks she was reassured of her brother's continuing need of her. At the end of May she wrote, with her accustomed combination of strong feeling and plainness, "My tooth broke today. They will soon be gone. Let that pass, I shall be beloved—I want no more." She lived all her life with William and his family, sadly afflicted with illness and mental degeneration in her later years, and died in 1855.

Dorothy Wordsworth

from *The Grasmere Journal (1802)*

April 13th, Tuesday. I had slept ill and was not well and obliged to go to bed in the afternoon—Mrs. C. waked me from sleep with a letter from Coleridge. After tea I went down to see the bank and walked along the Lakeside to the field where Mr. Smith thought of building his house. The air was become still, the lake was of a bright slate colour, the hills darkening. The bays shot into the low fading shores. Sheep resting. All things quiet. When I returned Jane met me—*William* was come. The suprise shot through me. He looked well, but he was tired and went soon to bed after a dish of tea.

[*April*] *14th, Wednesday.* William did not rise till dinner time. I walked with Mrs. C. I was ill, out of spirits, disheartened. Wm. and I took a long walk in the rain.

[*April*] *15th, Thursday.* It was a threatening, misty morning, but mild. We set off after dinner from Eusemere. Mrs. Clarkson went a short way with us, but turned back. The wind was furious, and we thought we must have returned. We first rested in the large boat-house, then under a furze bush opposite Mr. Clarkson's. Saw the plough going in the field. The wind seized our breath. The Lake was rough. There was a boat by itself floating in the middle of the bay below Water Millock. We rested again in the Water Millock Lane. The hawthorns are black and green, the birches here and there greenish, but there is yet more of purple to be seen on the twigs. We got over into a field to avoid some cows—people working. A few primroses by the roadside—woodsorrel flower, the anemone, scentless violets, strawberries, and that starry, yellow flower which Mrs. C. calls pile wort. When we were in the woods beyond Gowbarrow Park we saw a few daffodils[1] close to the water-side. We fancied that the lake had floated the seeds ashore, and that the little colony had so sprung up. But as we went along there were more and yet more; and at last, under the boughs of the trees, we saw that there was a long belt of them along the shore, about the breadth of a country turnpike road. I never saw daffodils so beautiful. They grew among the mossy stones about and about them; some rested their heads upon these stones as on a pillow for weariness; and the rest tossed and reeled and danced, and seemed as if they verily laughed with the wind, that blew upon them over the lake; they looked so gay, ever glancing, ever

---

[1] See William Wordsworth's poem "I Wandered Lonely as a Cloud" on page 261.

changing. This wind blew directly over the lake to them. There was here and there a little knot, and a few stragglers a few yards higher up; but they were so few as not to disturb the simplicity, unity, and life of that one busy highway. We rested again and again. The bays were stormy, and we heard the waves at different distances, and in the middle of the water, like the sea. Rain came on—we were wet when we reached Luff's, but we called in. Luckily all was chearless and gloomy, so we faced the storm—we *must* have been wet if we had waited—put on dry clothes at Dobson's. I was very kindly treated by a young woman, the landlady looked sour, but it is her way. She gave us a goodish supper, excellent ham and potatoes. We paid 7/- when we came away. William was sitting by a bright fire when I came downstairs. He soon made his way to the library, piled up in a corner of the window. He brought out a volume of Enfield's *Speaker*, another miscellany, and an odd volume of Congreve's plays. We had a glass of warm rum and water. We enjoyed ourselves, and wished for Mary. It rained and blew, when we went to bed. N.B. Deer in Gowbarrow Park like skeletons.

April 16th, Friday (Good Friday). When I undrew my curtains in the morning, I was much affected by the beauty of the prospect, and the change. The sun shone, the wind had passed away, the hills looked chearful, the river was very bright as it flowed into the lake. The church rises up behind a little knot of rocks, the steeple not so high as an ordinary three-story house. Trees in a row in the garden under the wall. After Wm. had shaved we set forward; the valley is at first broken by little rocky woody knolls that make retiring places, fairy valleys in the vale; the river winds along under these hills, travelling, not in a bustle but not slowly, to the lake. We saw a fisherman in the flat meadow on the other side of the water. He came towards us, and threw his line over the two-arched bridge. It is a bridge of a heavy construction, almost bending inwards in the middle, but it is grey, and there is a look of ancientry in the architecture of it that pleased me. As we go on the vale opens out more into one vale, with somewhat of a cradle bed. Cottages, with groups of trees, on the side of the hills. We passed a pair of twin Children, 2 years old. Sate on the next bridge which we crossed—a single arch. We rested again upon the turf, and looked at the same bridge. We observed arches in the water, occasioned by the large stones sending it down in two streams. A sheep came plunging through the river, stumbled up the bank, and passed close to us, it had been frightened by an insignificant little dog on the other side. Its fleece dropped a glittering shower under its belly. Primroses by the road-side, pile wort that shone like stars of gold in the sun, violets, strawberries, retired and half-buried among the grass. When we came to the foot of Brothers Water, I left William sitting on the bridge, and went along the path on the right side of the Lake through the wood. I was delighted with what I saw. The water under the boughs of the bare old trees, the simplicity of the mountains, and the exquisite beauty of the path. There was one grey cottage. I repeated *The Glow-worm,* as I walked along. I hung over the gate, and thought I could have stayed for ever. When I returned, I found William writing a poem descriptive of the sights and sounds we saw and heard.[2] There was the gentle flowing of the stream, the glittering, lively lake, green fields without a living creature to be seen on them, behind us, a flat pasture with 42 cattle feeding; to our left, the road leading to the hamlet. No smoke there, the sun shone on the bare roofs. The people were at work ploughing, harrowing, and sowing; lasses spreading dung, a dog's barking now and then, cocks crowing, birds twittering, the snow in patches at the top of the highest hills, yellow palms, purple and green twigs on the birches, ashes with their glittering spikes quite bare. The hawthorn a bright green, with black stems under the oak. The moss of the oak glossy. We then went on, passed two sisters at work *(they first passed us),* one with two pitchforks in her hand, the other had a spade. We had some talk with them. They laughed aloud after we were gone, perhaps half in wantonness, half boldness. William finished his poem before we got to the foot of Kirkstone. There we ate our dinner. There were hundreds of cattle in the vale. The walk up Kirkstone was very interesting. The becks among the rocks were all alive. Wm. showed me the little mossy streamlet which he had before loved when he saw its bright green track in the snow. The view above Ambleside very beautiful. There we sate and looked down on the green vale. We watched the crows at a little distance from us become white as silver as they flew in the sunshine, and when they went still further, they looked like shapes of water passing over the green fields. The whitening of Ambleside church is a great deduction from the beauty of it, seen from this point. We called at the Luffs, the Boddingtons there. Did not go in, and went round by the fields. I pulled off my stockings, intending to wade the beck, but I was obliged to put them on, and we climbed over the wall at the bridge. The post passed us. No letters! Rydale Lake was in its own evening brightness: the Islands and Points distinct. Jane Ashburner came up to us when we were sitting upon the wall. We rode in her cart to Tom Dawson's. All well. The garden looked pretty in the half-moonlight, half-daylight. As we went up the vale of Brother's Water more and more cattle feeding, 100 of them.

[April] 17th, Saturday. A mild warm rain. We sate in the garden all the morning. William dug a little. I transplanted a honey-suckle. The lake was still. The sheep on the island, reflected in the water, like the grey deer we saw in Gowbarrow park. We walked after tea by moonlight. I had been in bed in the afternoon, and William had slept in his chair. We walked towards Rydale first, then backwards and forwards below Mr. Olliff's. The village was beautiful in the moonlight. Helm Crag we observed very distinct. The dead hedge round Benson's field bound together at the top by an interlacing of ash sticks, which made a chain

[2] See Wordsworth's poem "The Cock Is Crowing" on page 262.

of silver when we faced the moon. A letter from C. and also from S. H. I saw a robin chacing a scarlet butterfly this morning.

[*July*] . . . On Thursday morning, 29th, we arrived in London. Wm. left me at the Inn. I went to bed, etc. etc. After various troubles and disasters, we left London on Saturday morning at 1/2-past 5 or 6, the 31st of July. (I have forgot which.) We mounted the Dover Coach at Charing Cross. It was a beautiful morning. The city, St. Paul's, with the river and a multitude of little boats, made a most beautiful sight as we crossed Westminster Bridge.[3] The houses were not overhung by their cloud of smoke, and they were spread out endlessly, yet the sun shone so brightly, with such a fierce light, that there was even something like the purity of one of nature's own grand spectacles. . . .

William Wordsworth

Three Poems

I Wandered Lonely as a Cloud

I wandered lonely as Cloud
That floats on high o'er Vales and Hills,
When all at once I saw a crowd
A host of dancing Daffodills;
Along the Lake, beneath the trees,
Ten thousand dancing in the breeze.

The waves beside them danced, but they
Outdid the sparkling waves in glee:—
A Poet could not but be gay
In such a laughing company:
I gaz'd—and gaz'd—but little thought
What wealth the shew to me had brought:

For oft when on my couch I lie
In vacant or in pensive mood,
They flash upon that inward eye
Which is the bliss of solitude,
And then my heart with pleasure fills,
And dances with the Daffodils.

---

[3] See Wordsworth's "Sonnet Composed Upon Westminster Bridge" on page 262.

The Cock Is Crowing

The cock is crowing,
The stream is flowing,
The small birds twitter,
The lake doth glitter,
The green field sleeps in the sun;
The oldest and youngest
Are at work with the strongest;
The cattle are grazing,
Their heads never raising;
There are forty feeding like one!

Like an army defeated
The Snow hath retreated,
And now doth fare ill
On the top of the bare hill;
The Plough-boy is whooping—anon—anon:
There's joy in the mountains;
There's life in the fountains;
Small clouds are sailing,
Blue sky prevailing;
The rain is over and gone!

Sonnet Composed Upon Westminster Bridge

Earth has not any thing to shew more fair:
Dull would he be of soul who could pass by
A sight so touching in its majesty:
This City now doth like a garment wear
The beauty of the morning; silent, bare,
Ships, towers, domes, theatres, and temples lie
Open unto the fields, and to the sky;
All bright and glittering in the smokeless air.
Never did sun more beautifully steep
In his first splendor valley, rock or hill;
Ne'er saw I, never felt, a calm so deep!
The river glideth at his own sweet will:
Dear God! the very houses seem alseep;
And all that mighty heart is lying still!

Abigail Adams

Abigail Smith Adams was born in 1744 in Massachusetts. "I never was sent to any school," she recalls. "I was always sick. Female education, in the best families, went no further than writing and arithmetic; in some few and rare instances, music and dancing." She was tutored to some extent by her parents and her grandmother, whose "happy method of mixing instruction and amusement together" she remembered many years later. She began writing letters to relatives as a child and kept up a continuous and varied correspondence with friends and government officials throughout her life.

In 1764 she married John Adams. During the Revolutionary War, she and her four children were frequently separated from Mr. Adams, a situation which she remembered on her fiftieth wedding anniversary as "the greatest source of unhappiness I have known." These years are recorded in vivid and fascinating detail in the letters she wrote to her husband, published in *Familiar Letters of John Adams and His Wife Abigail Adams* (1876).

In 1784 Mrs. Adams traveled to Europe to join her husband, who had been negotiating the Revolutionary War settlement in Paris. After a brief visit in England, she lived eight months in Paris and three years in London. A few of her letters to relatives, written from just after her arrival in Paris in 1784, are reprinted below from *Letters of Mrs. Adams* (1840).

Mr. and Mrs. Adams returned to America in 1787. Quickly nominated to be the first Vice President of the United States, John Adams wrote to his wife, "My country has in its wisdom contrived for me the most insignificant office that ever the invention of man contrived or his imagination conceived." He served two terms as Vice President and one as President (1797-1801). In the following years, increasing ill health forced Mrs. Adams to withdraw from Philadelphia society to her country home. "You will find your father in his fields, attending to his hay-makers," she wrote to her son, "and your mother busily occupied in the domestic concerns of her family." She died in 1818 at the age of seventy-four.

Letters from Abigail Adams were greatly praised during her lifetime. Her grandson, Charles Francis Adams, first edited her letters many years after her death, in 1840 and 1876. He reveals that "It was the habit of the writer to make first a rough draft of what she intended to say, and from this to form a fair copy for her correspondent; but in the process she altered so much of the original that, in every instance where the two have been compared, they are by no means the same thing." Abigail Adams herself considered her writing "heedless and inaccurate," not sufficiently sophisticated or learned to attract readers. To a request to publish some of her correspondence she replied in 1817, "You terrify me, my dear sir, when you ask for letters of mine to publish. . . . *Style* I never studied. My Language is . . . the spontaneous effusions of friendship."

That these "spontaneous effusions of friendship" also have "style" is illustrated by the richly descriptive quality and the clear voice in the following three letters. Most of us tend to note most vividly the details that strike us first, especially when we are away from home and see with new eyes, not dulled by habit. What we see (as well as what we don't see) in turn reveals our attitudes and values and frequently also hints at our way of life. Mrs. Adams' word pictures convey her own attitudes, her almost comic dismay at the lady with whom she dines (what, one wonders, might Benjamin Franklin's attitude have been?), her discomfort at the multiplicity of servants, her mixed feelings at the dancing on the French stage. The reader might ask himself how he responds to Mrs. Adams, and why. What kind of person emerges for him? He may also wish to try writing a letter from a new locale, a new neighborhood, where he can see his surroundings with the eyes of the foreigner.

Three Letters from France

To Miss Lucy Cranch
Auteuil, 5 September, 1784

My Dear Lucy,

I promised to write to you from the Hague, but your uncle's unexpected arrival at London prevented me. Your uncle purchased an excellent travelling coach in London, and hired a post-chaise for our servants. In this manner we travelled from London to Dover, accommodated through England with the best of horses, postilions, and good carriages; clean, neat apartments, genteel entertainment, and prompt attendance. But no sooner do you cross from Dover to Calais, than every thing is reversed, and yet the distance is very small between them.

The cultivation is by no means equal to that of England; the villages look poor and mean, the houses all thatched, and rarely a glass window in them; their horses, instead of being handsomely harnessed, as those in England are, have the appearance of so many old cart-horses. Along you go, with seven horses tied up with ropes and chains, rattling like trucks; two ragged postilions, mounted, with enormous jack-boots, add to the comic scene. And this is the style in which a duke or a count travels through this kingdom. You inquire of me how I like Paris. Why, they tell me I am no judge, for that I have not seen it yet. One thing, I know, and that is that I have smelt it. If I was agreeably disappointed in London, I am as much disappointed in Paris. It is the very dirtiest place I ever saw. There are some buildings and some squares, which are tolerable; but in general the streets are narrow, the shops, the houses, inelegant and dirty, the streets full of lumber and stone, with which they build. Boston cannot boast so elegant public buildings; but, in every other respect, it is as much superior in my eyes to Paris, as London is to Boston. To have had Paris tolerable to me, I should not have gone to London. As to the people here, they are more given to hospitality than in England it is said. I have been in company with but one French lady since I arrived; for strangers here make the first visit, and nobody will know you until you have waited upon them in form.

This lady I dined with at Dr. Franklin's. She entered the room with a careless, jaunty air; upon seeing ladies who were strangers to her, she bawled out, "Ah! mon Dieu, where is Franklin? Why did you not tell me there were ladies here?" You must suppose her speaking all this in French. "How I look!" said she, taking hold of a chemise made of tiffany, which she had on over a blue lutestring, and which looked as much upon the decay as her beauty, for she was once a handsome woman; her hair was frizzled; over it she had a small straw hat, with a dirty gauze half-handkerchief round it, and a bit of dirtier gauze, than ever my maids wore, was bowed on behind. She had a black gauze scarf thrown over her shoulders. She ran out of the room; when she returned, the Doctor entered at one door, she at the other; upon which she ran forward to him, caught him by the hand, "Helas! Franklin;" then gave him a double kiss, one upon each cheek, and another upon his forehead. When we went into the room to dine, she was placed between the Doctor and Mr. Adams. She carried on the chief of the conversation at dinner, frequently locking her hand into the Doctor's, and sometimes spreading her arms upon the backs of both the gentlemen's chairs, then throwing her arm carelessly upon the Doctor's neck.

I should have been greatly astonished at this conduct, if the good Doctor had not told me that in this lady I should see a genuine Frenchwoman, wholly free from affectation or stiffness of behaviour, and one of the best women in the world. For this I must take the Doctor's word; but I should have set her down for a very bad one, although sixty years of age, and a widow. I own I was highly disgusted, and never wish for an acquaintance with any ladies of this cast. After dinner she threw herself upon a settee, where she showed more than her feet. She had a little lap-dog, who was, next to the Doctor, her favorite. This she kissed, and when he wet the floor she wiped it up with her chemise. This is one of the Doctor's most intimate friends, with whom he dines once every week, and she with him. She is rich, and is my near neighbour; but I have not yet visited her. Thus you see, my dear, that manners differ exceedingly in different countries. I hope, however, to find amongst the French ladies manners more consistent with my ideas of decency, or I shall be a mere recluse.

You must write to me, and let me know all about you; marriages, births, and preferments; every thing you can think of. Give my respects to the Germantown family. I shall begin to get letters for them by the next vessel.

Good night. Believe me   Your most affectionate aunt,

A. A.

To Mrs. Shaw
Auteuil, 14 December, 1784

My Dear Sister,

From the interest you take in every thing which concerns your friends, I hear you inquiring how I do, how I live, whom I see, where I visit, who visit me. I know not whether your curiosity extends so far as the color of the house, which is white stone, and to the furniture of the chamber where I sleep. If it does, you must apply to Betsey Cranch for information, whose fancy has employed itself so busily as to seek for intelligence even in the minutiae; and, although they look trifling upon paper, yet, if our friends take an interest in them, that renders them important; and I am the rather tempted to a compliance from the recollection, that, when I have received a sentimental letter from an absent friend, I have passed over the sentiment at the first reading, and hunted for that part, which more particularly related to themselves.

This village, where we reside, is four miles from Paris, and is famous for nothing that I know of, but the learned men who have inhabited it. Such were Boileau, Molière, D'Aguesseau, and Helvétius. The first and last lived near this hotel, and Boileau's garden is preserved as a choice relic. As to my own health, it is much as usual. I suffer through want of exercise, and grow too fat. I cannot persuade myself to walk an hour in the day, in a long entry which we have, merely for exercise; and as to the streets, they are continually a quagmire. No walking there without boots or wooden shoes, neither of which are my feet calculated for. Mr. Adams makes it his constant practice to walk several miles every day, without which he would not be able to preserve his health, which at best is but infirm. He professes himself so much happier for having his family with him, that I feel amply gratified in having ventured across the ocean. He is determined, that nothing but the inevitable stroke of death shall in future separate him at least from one part of it; so that I know not what climates I may yet have to visit,—more, I fear, than will be agreeable to either of us.

If you want to know the manners and customs of this country, I answer you, that pleasure is the business of life, more especially upon a Sunday. We have no days with us or rather with you, by which I can give you any idea of them, except Commencements and Elections. We have a pretty wood within a few rods of this house, which is called the Bois de Boulogne. This is cut into many regular walks, and during the summer months, upon Sundays, it looked like Boston and Cambridge

Commons upon the public days I have mentioned. Paris is a horrid dirty city, and I know not whether the inhabitants could exist, if they did not come out one day in the week to breathe a fresh air. I have sat at my window of a Sunday, and seen whole cartloads of them at a time. I speak literally; for those, who neither own a coach nor are able to hire one, procure a cart, which in this country is always drawn by horses. Sometimes they have a piece of canvass over it. There are benches placed in them, and in this vehicle you will see as many well-dressed women and children as can possibly pile in, led out by a man, or driven. Just at the entrance of the wood they descend. The day is spent in music, dancing, and every kind of play. It is a very rare thing to see a man with a hat anywhere but under his arm, or a woman with a bonnet upon her head. This would brush off the powder, and spoil the elegant *toupet*. They have a fashion of wearing a hood or veil either of gauze or silk. If you send for a tailor in this country, your servant will very soon introduce to you a gentleman full dressed in black, with his head as white as a snow-bank, and which a hat never rumpled. If you send to a mantuamaker, she will visit you in the same style, with her silk gown and petticoat, her head in ample order, though, perhaps, she lives up five pair of stairs, and eats nothing but bread and water, as two thirds of these people do. We have a servant in our family, who dresses more than his young master, and would not be guilty of tending table *unfrizzed,* upon any consideration. He dresses the hair of his young master, but has his own dressed by a hair-dresser. By the way, I was guilty of a sad mistake in London. I desired the servant to procure me a barber. The fellow stared, and was loth to ask for what purpose I wanted him. At last he said, "You mean a hair-dresser, Madam, I believe?" "Ay," says I, "I want my hair dressed." "Why, barbers, Madam, in this country, do nothing but shave."

When I first came to this country, I was loth to submit to such an unnecessary number of domestics, as it appeared to me, but I soon found that they would not let me do without them; because, every one having a fixed and settled department, they would not lift a pin out of it, although two thirds of the time they had no employment. We are however thankful that we are able to make eight do for us, though we meet with some difficulties for want of a ninth. Do not suppose from this, that we live remarkably nice. I never put up in America with what I do here. I often think of Swift's High Dutch bride, who had so much nastiness, and so much pride.

Adieu. Most affectionately yours,
A. A.

To Mrs. Cranch
Auteuil, 20 February, 1785

My Dear Sister,

This day eight months I sailed for Europe, since which many new and interesting scenes have presented themselves before me. I have seen many of the beauties, and some of the deformities, of this old world. I have been more than ever convinced, that there is no summit of virtue, and no depth of vice, which human nature is not capable of rising to, on the one hand, or sinking into, on the other. I have felt the force of an observation, which I have read, that daily example is the most subtile of poisons. I have found my taste reconciling itself to habits, customs, and fashions, which at first disgusted me. The first dance which I saw upon the stage shocked me; the dresses and beauty of the performers were enchanting; but, no sooner did the dance commence, than I felt my delicacy wounded, and I was ashamed to be seen to look at them. Girls, clothed in the thinnest silk and gauze, with their petticoats short, springing two feet from the floor, poising themselves in the air, with their feet flying, and as perfectly showing their garters and drawers as though no petticoat had been worn, was a sight altogether new to me. Their motions are as light as air, and as quick as lightning; they balance themselves to astonishment. No description can equal the reality. They are daily trained to it, from early infancy, at a royal academy, instituted for this purpose. You will very often see little creatures, not more than seven or eight years old, as undauntedly performing their parts as the eldest among them. Shall I speak a truth, and say that repeatedly seeing these dances has worn off that disgust, which I at first felt, and that I see them now with pleasure? Yet, when I consider the tendency of these things, the passions they must excite, and the known character, even to a proverb, which is attached to an opera girl, my abhorrence is not lessened, and neither my reason nor judgment has accompanied my sensibility in acquiring any degree of callousness. The art of dancing is carried to the highest degree of perfection that it is capable of. At the opera, the house is neither so grand, nor of so beautiful architecture, as the French theatre, but it is more frequented by the *beau monde,* who had rather be amused than instructed. The scenery is more various and more highly decorated, the dresses more costly and rich. And O! the music, vocal and instrumental, it has a soft, persuasive power, and a dying sound. Conceive a highly decorated building, filled with youth, beauty, grace, ease, clad in all the most pleasing and various ornaments of dress, which fancy can form; these objects singing like cherubs to the best tuned instruments, most skilfully handled, the softest, tenderest strains; every attitude corresponding with the music; full of the god or goddess whom they celebrate; the female voices accompanied by an equal number of Adonises. Think you that this city can fail of becoming a Cythera and this house the temple of Venus?

"When music softens, and when dancing fires,"

it requires the immortal shield of the invincible Minerva, to screen youth from the arrows which assail them on every side.

As soon as a girl sets her foot upon the floor of the opera, she is excommunicated by the Church, and denied burial in holy ground. She conceives nothing worse can happen to her; all restraint is thrown off, and she delivers herself to the first who bids high enough for her. But let me turn from a picture, of which the outlines are but just sketched; I would willingly veil the rest, as it can only tend to excite sentiments of horror. . . .

Very affectionately yours,

A. A.

James Boswell

James Boswell (1740-1795), lawyer, author, and personality, was until the 1920s and 1930s best known for having written one of the greatest biographies in English, *The Life of Samuel Johnson* (1791); then the mass of his private papers was rediscovered, including most of the voluminous journals he had kept since his late teens. The publication of these journals, now going on, makes Boswell one of the most intimately known men who ever lived, a fascinating character in his own right, and adds another masterpiece to his credit.

Boswell attended high school and university in Edinburgh, Scotland. Much of his early maturity was spent in a struggle against the desire of his father, a supreme court judge, to make him a lawyer. Boswell would have preferred a dashing career in the army and spent as much time as he could pursuing his strong natural inclination toward women, the theatre, literature, and good conversation. After a number of preliminary skirmishes, his father gave him permission to go to London in November 1762, to seek an officer's commission in the Guards—in those days a matter of finding and using the recommendations of noblemen influential at Court. He failed to get the commission, and in August 1763 he was forced to go to Utrecht to study law. Meanwhile, however, he had lived the life of a playboy, had met the great Dr. Johnson, whose biography he was to write, and had recorded all his doings in a journal. From this journal we have abstracted entries mostly describing the first part of his affair with Mrs. Anne Lewis, a young actress.

In studying this passage, the reader should keep in mind that Boswell did not write his journal everyday, nor was it written for his eyes alone. He sent weekly installments of it to his friend John Johnston in Edinburgh, and in writing up some of the events of a given day he must often have known how the next day or two were going to go. Boswell was nothing if not frank; there is no reason to doubt his account, but it should be read as the conscious literary work that it is, and not as if it were a more spontaneous, unpolished piece of composition. It is, in fact, one of the most artistic of journals and took up some of the spare time of which Boswell had plenty in London. It may be examined for dialogue and characterization much like a short novel.

We have ended our selection just short of its climax and denouement, mostly to lure the reader to the book itself, *Boswell's London Journal, 1762-1763* (ed. Frederick A. Pottle), which became a best-seller on its publication in 1950. Readers of the book will not only find out how the story ends, but will be treated to a fuller and fairer view of Boswell's character than any excerpt could provide. It is, perhaps, for the writer's self-characterization that the journal is most worth studying. Professor Pottle has with his associates published a number of additional volumes of Boswell's *Journals,* and is author of a biography, *James Boswell, The Earlier Years, 1740-1769* (1966), where he writes: "He had an enormous zest for living. The workings of his own mind fascinated him, and he relished every other variety of human nature. But the experience was not complete, not lived through, not wholly *realized,* until he had explored it verbally and had written it down. 'I should live no more than I can record,' he once wrote, 'as one should not have more corn growing than one can get in.' "

The Courtship of Louisa, from *The London Journal*

Tuesday 14 December

It is very curious to think that I have now been in London several weeks without ever enjoying the delightful sex, although I am surrounded with numbers of freehearted ladies of all kinds: from the splendid Madam at fifty guineas a night, down to the civil nymph with white-thread stockings who tramps along the Strand and will resign her engaging person to your honour for a pint of wine and a shilling. Manifold are the reasons for this my present wonderful continence. I am upon a plan of economy, and therefore cannot be at the expense of first-rate dames. I have suffered severely from the loathsome distemper, and therefore shudder at the thoughts of running any risk of having it again. Besides, the surgeons' fees in this city come very high. But the greatest reason of all is that fortune, or rather benignant Venus, has smiled upon me and favoured me so far that I have had the most delicious intrigues with women of beauty, sentiment, and spirit, perfectly suited to my romantic genius.

Indeed, in my mind, there cannot be higher felicity on earth enjoyed by man than the participation of genuine reciprocal amorous affection with an amiable woman. There he has a full indulgence of all the delicate feelings and pleasures both of body and mind, while at the same time in this enchanting union he exults with a consciousness that he is the superior person. The dignity of his sex is kept up. These paradisial scenes of gallantry have exalted my ideas and refined my taste, so that I really cannot think of stooping so far as to make a most intimate companion of a groveling-minded, ill-bred, worthless creature, nor can my delicacy be pleased with the gross voluptuousness of the stews. I am therefore walking about with a healthful stout body and a cheerful mind, in search of a woman worthy of my love, and who thinks me worthy of hers, without any interested views, which is the only sure way to find out if a woman really loves a man. If I should be a single man for the whole winter, I will be satisfied. I have had as much elegant pleasure as I could have expected would come to my share in many years.

However, I hope to be more successful. In this view, I had now called several times for a handsome actress of Covent Garden Theatre, whom I was a little acquainted with, and whom I shall distinguish in this my journal by the name of Louisa. This lady had been indisposed and saw no company, but today I was admitted. She was in a pleasing undress and looked very pretty. She received me with great politeness. We chatted on the common topics. We were not easy—there was a constraint upon us—we did not sit right on our chairs, and we were unwilling to look at one another. I talked to her on the advantage of having an agreeable acquaintance, and hoped I might see her now and then. She desired me to call in whenever I came that way, without ceremony. "And pray," said she, "when shall I have the pleasure of your company at tea?" I fixed Thursday, and left her, very well satisfied with my first visit. . . .

Wednesday 15 December

The enemies of the people of England who would have them considered in the worst light represent them as selfish, beef-eaters, and cruel. In this view I resolved today to be a true-born Old Englishman. I went into the City to Dolly's Steak-house in Paternoster Row and swallowed my dinner by myself to fulfill the charge of selfishness; I had a large fat beefsteak to fulfill the charge of beef-eating; and I went at five o'clock to the Royal Cockpit in St. James's Park and saw cock-fighting for about five hours to fulfill the charge of cruelty.

A beefsteak-house is a most excellent place to dine at. You come in there to a warm, comfortable, large room, where a number of people are sitting at table. You take whatever place you find empty; call for what you like, which you get well and cleverly dressed. You may either chat or not as you like. Nobody minds you, and you pay very reasonably. My dinner (beef, bread and beer and waiter) was only a shilling. The waiters make a great deal of money by these pennies. Indeed. I admire the English for attending to small sums, as many smalls make a great, according to the proverb.

At five I filled my pockets with gingerbread and apples (quite the method), put on my old clothes and laced hat, laid by my watch, purse, and pocket-book, and with oaken stick in my hand sallied to the pit. I was too soon there. So I went into a low inn, sat down amongst a parcel of arrant blackguards, and drank some beer. The sentry near the house had been very civil in showing me the way. It was very cold. I bethought myself of the poor fellow, so I carried out a pint of beer myself to him. He was very thankful and drank my health cordially. He told me his name was Hobard, that he was a watch-maker but in distress for debt, and enlisted that his creditors might not touch him.

I then went to the Cockpit, which is a circular room in the middle of which the cocks fight. It is seated round with rows gradually rising. The pit and the seats are all covered with mat. The cocks, nicely cut and dressed and armed with silver heels, are set down and fight with amazing bitterness and resolution. Some of them were quickly dispatched. One pair fought three quarters of an hour. The uproar and noise of betting is prodigious. A great deal of money made a very quick circulation from hand to hand. There was a number of professed gamblers there. An old cunning dog whose face I had seen at Newmarket sat by me a while. I told him I knew nothing of the matter. "Sir," said he, "you have as good a chance as anybody." He thought I would be a good subject for him. I was young-like. But he found himself balked. I was shocked to see the distraction and anxiety of the betters. I was sorry for the poor cocks. I looked round to see if any of the spectators pitied them when mangled and torn in a most cruel manner, but I could not observe the smallest relenting sign in any countenance. I was therefore not ill pleased to see them endure mental torment. Thus did I complete my true English day, and came home pretty much fatigued and pretty much confounded at the strange turn of this people.

Thursday 16 December

. . . .In the afternoon I went to Louisa's. . . .

We chatted pretty easily. We talked of love as a thing that could not be controlled by reason, as a fine passion. I could not clearly discern how she meant to behave to me. She told me that a gentleman had come to her and offered her £50, but that her brother knocked at the door and the man run out of the house without saying a word. I said I wished he had left his money. We joked much about the £50. I said I expected some night to be surprised with such an offer from some decent elderly gentlewoman. I made just a comic parody to her story. I sat till past eight. She said she hoped it would not be long before she had the pleasure of seeing me again.

This night I made no visible progress in my amour, but I in reality was doing a great deal. I was getting well acquainted with her. I was appearing an agreeable companion to her; I was informing her by my looks of my passion for her.

Friday 17 December

I engaged in this amour just with a view of convenient pleasure but the god of pleasing anguish now seriously seized my breast. I felt the fine delirium of love. I waited on Louisa at one, found her alone, told her that her goodness in hoping to see me *soon* had brought me back: that it appeared long to me since I saw her. I was a little bashful. However, I took a good heart and talked with ease and dignity. "I hope, Madam, you are at present a single woman." "Yes, sir." "And your affections are not engaged?" "They are not, Sir." "But this is leading me into a strange confession. I assure you, Madam, my affections are engaged." "Are they, Sir?" "Yes, Madam, they are engaged to you." (She looked soft and beautiful.) "I hope we shall be better acquainted and like one another better." "Come, Sir, let us talk no more of that now." "No, Madam, I will not. It is like giving the book in the preface." "Just so, Sir, telling in the preface what should be in the middle of the book." (I think such conversations are best written in the dialogue way.) "Madam, I was very happy to find you. From the first time that I saw you, I admired you." "O, Sir." "I did, indeed. What I like beyond everything is an agreeable female companion, where I can be at home and have tea and genteel conversation. I was quite happy to be here." "Sir, you are welcome here as often as you please. Every evening, if you please." "Madam I am infinitely obliged to you."

This is just what I wanted. I left her, in good spirits, and dined at Sheridan's. . . .

Monday 20 December

I went to Louisa's after breakfast. "Indeed," said I, "it was hard upon me to leave you so soon yesterday. I am quite happy in your company." "Sir," said she, "you are very obliging. But," said she, "I am in bad humour this morning. There was a person who professed the greatest friendship for me; I now applied for their assistance, but was shifted. It was such a trifle that I am sure they could have granted it. So I have been railing against my fellow-creatures." "Nay, dear Madam, don't abuse them all on account of an individual. But pray what was this favour? Might I know?" (She blushed.) "Why, Sir, there is a person has sent to me for a trifling debt. I sent back word that it was not convenient for me to let them have it just now, but in six weeks I should pay it."

I was a little confounded and embarrassed here. I dreaded bringing myself into a scrape. I did not know what she might call a trifling sum. I half-resolved to say no more. However, I thought that she might now be trying my generosity and regard for her, and truly this was the real test. I thought I would see if it was in my power to assist her.

"Pray, Madam, what was the sum?" "Only two guineas, Sir." Amazed and pleased, I pulled out my purse. "Madam," said I, "if I can do you any service, you may command me. Two guineas is at present all that I have, but a trifle more. There they are for you. I told you that I had very little, but yet I hope to live. Let us just be honest with one another. Tell me when you are in any little distress, and I will tell you what I can do." She took the guineas. "Sir, I am infinitely obliged to you. As soon as it is in my power, I shall return them. Indeed I could not have expected this from you." Her gratitude warmed my heart. "Madam! though I have little, yet as far as ten guineas, you may apply to me. I would live upon nothing to serve one that I regarded."

I did not well know what to think of this scene. Sometimes I thought it artifice, and that I was taken in. And then again, I viewed it just as a circumstance that might very easily happen. Her mentioning returning the money looked well. My naming the sum of ten guineas was rash; however, I considered that it cost me as much to be cured of what I contracted from a whore, and that ten guineas was but a moderate expense for women during the winter.

I had all along treated her with a distant politeness. On Saturday I just kissed her hand. She now sung to me. I got up in raptures and kissed her with great warmth. She received this very genteelly. I had a delicacy in presuming too far, lest it should look like demanding goods for my money. I resumed the subject of love and gallantry. She said, "I pay no regard to the opinion in the world so far as contradicts my own sentiments." "No Madam, we are not to mind the arbitrary rules imposed by the multitude." "Yet, Sir, there is a decency to be kept with the public. And I must do so, whose bread depends upon them." "Certainly, Madam. But when may I wait upon you? Tomorrow evening?" "Sir, I am obliged to be all day with a lady who is not well." "Then next day, Madam." "What! to drink a dish of tea, Sir?" "No, no, not to drink a dish of tea." (Here I looked sheepish.) "What time may I wait upon you?" "Whenever you please, Sir." I kissed her again, and went away highly pleased with the thoughts of the affair being settled.
. . .

Sunday 2 January

I had George Home at breakfast with me. He is a good honest fellow and applies well to his business as a merchant. He had seen me all giddiness at his father's, and was astonished to find me settled on so prudent a plan. As I have made it a rule to dine every Sunday at home, and have got my landlady to give us regularly on that day a piece of good roast beef with a warm apple-pie, I was a little difficulted today, as our time of dining is three o'clock, just my hour of assignation. However, I got dinner to be at two, and at three I hastened to my charmer.

Here a little speculation on the human mind may well come in. For here was I, a young man full of vigour and vivacity, the favourite lover of a handsome actress and going to enjoy the full possession of my warmest wishes. And yet melancholy threw a cloud over my mind. I could relish nothing. I felt dispirited and languid. I approached Louisa with a kind of an uneasy tremor. I sat down. I toyed with her. Yet I was not inspired by Venus. I felt rather a delicate sensation of love than a violent amorous inclination for her. I was very miserable. I thought myself feeble as a gallant, although I had experienced the reverse many a time. Louisa knew not my powers. She might imagine me impotent. I sweated almost with anxiety, which made me worse. She behaved extremely well; did not seem to remember the occasion of our meeting at all. I told her I was very dull. Said she, "People cannot always command their spirits." The time of church was almost elapsed when I began to feel that I was still a man. I fanned the flame by pressing her alabaster breasts and kissing her delicious lips. I then barred the door of her dining-room, led her all fluttering into her bedchamber, and was just making a triumphal entry when we heard her landlady coming up. "O Fortune why did it happen thus?" would have been the exclamation of a Roman bard. We were stopped most suddenly and cruelly from the fruition of each other. She ran out and stopped the landlady from coming up. Then returned to me in the dining-room. We fell into each other's arms, sighing and panting, "O dear, how hard this is." "O Madam, see what you can contrive for me." "Lord, Sir, I am so frightened."

Her brother then came in. I recollected that I had been at no place of worship today. I begged pardon for a little and went to Covent Garden Church, where there is evening service between five and six. I heard a few prayers and then returned and drank tea. She entertained us with her adventures when travelling through the country. Some of them were excellent. I told her she might make a novel. She said if I would put them together that she would give me material. I went home at seven. I was unhappy at being prevented from the completion of my wishes, and yet I thought that I had saved my credit for prowess, that I might through anxiety have not acted a vigorous part; and that we might contrive a meeting where I could love with ease and freedom.

Tuesday 4 January

Louisa told me that she would go with me to pass the night when she was sure that she would not be wanted at the playhouse next day; and she mentioned Saturday as most convenient, being followed by Sunday, on which nothing is done. "But, Sir," said she, "may not this be attended with expense? I hope you'll excuse me." There was something so kind and so delicate in this hint that it charmed me. "No, Madam, it cannot be a great expense, and I can save on other articles to have money for this.". . .

I then bethought me of a place to which Louisa and I might safely go. I went to my good friend Hayward's at the Black Lion, told him that I had married, and that I and my wife, who was to be in town on Saturday, would sleep in his house till I got a lodging for her. The King of Prussia says in one of his poems that gallantry comprises every vice. That of lying it certainly does, without which intrigue can never be carried on. But as the proverb says, in love and war all is fair. I who am a lover and hope to be a soldier think so. In this instance we could not be admitted to any decent house except as man and wife. Indeed, we are so if union of hearts be the principal requisite. We are so, at least for a time. How cleverly this can be done here. In Scotland it is impossible. We should be married with a vengeance. I went home and dined. I thought my slender diet weakened me. I resolved to live hearty and be stout. This afternoon I became very low-spirited. I sat in close. I hated all things. I almost hated London. O miserable absurdity! I could see nothing in a good light. I just submitted and hoped to get the better of this.

Philip Dormer Stanhope, 4th Earl of Chesterfield

Philip Dormer Stanhope (1694-1773), Fourth Earl of Chesterfield, in many ways epitomizes the eighteenth-century English gentleman: elegant and witty, associate of Addison and Gay, Pope and Arbuthnot, correspondent of Voltaire and Montesquieu, he lived a long public life as diplomat and member of Parliament, and enjoyed a long retirement with his garden, his books, and his correspondence. Chesterfield's mother died shortly after he was born, and his father generally neglected him. His education was left to the care of his grandmother, who engaged the appropriate tutors until at eighteen he entered Cambridge, where he lived a typical undergraduate life and studied rhetoric and oratory. "When I first went to the University," he writes in a letter to his son, "I drank and smoked, notwithstanding the aversion I had to wine and tobacco, only because I though it genteel, and that it made me look like a man." Two years later he went on the customary foreign tour, visited The Hague, "where gaming was much in fashion," and spent some time in Paris. On his return in 1715, he entered the House of Commons as a Whig member, the party opposed to the Jacobite persuasions of his father; he remained in public life until his retirement. In 1726, the death of his father made him an Earl and brought him a seat in the House of Lords, which he referred to as a "hospital for incurables." He served as ambassador to Holland and later as an exemplary Lord Lieutenant of Ireland.

While he was ambassador to Holland between 1728 and 1732, Chesterfield had an affair with a Frenchwoman, Elisabeth du Bouchet, who bore him a son, Philip, in 1732. He returned to England that year and the following year married the Countess of Walsingham, but there were no children; Philip remained his only son. In 1737, he began the famous correspondence from which we print three letters below and which was to continue until the death of Philip in 1767, when he was thirty-five years old. In this correspondence, Chesterfield undertook the education of his son; the early letters include lessons in history and geography and etymology, as well as moral instruction stressing industry and attention. But later letters take on more worldly advice. When Philip was fourteen the world became his classroom, and he began his grand tour under the tutelage of the Reverend Walter Hare; the first letter below, on learning and knowledge, was written at that time. Chesterfield hoped for a distinguished career for his son, but his advice notwithstanding, Philip remained no more than a minor diplomat until his death. He left behind a wife and two sons from a marriage kept secret from his father. His wife then sold the letters against the wishes of her husband's family, and thus they became public documents.

In reading the letters below, the reader should try to evaluate Chesterfield's advice and to come to terms with his tone and personality. One way might be to identify with Philip and to write Chesterfield a reply. The final letter raises a general question about the use of language which every speaker and writer must settle for himself.

Three Letters to His Son

Bath, 4 October 1746

Dear Boy,

Though I employ so much of my time in writing to you, I confess I have often my doubts whether it is to any purpose. I know how unwelcome advice generally is; I know that those who want it most, like it and follow it least; and I know, too, that the advice of parents, more particulary, is ascribed to the moroseness, the imperiousness, or the garrulity of old age. But then, on the other hand, I flatter myself, that as your own reason, though too young as yet to suggest much to you of itself, is however, strong enough to enable you, both to judge of, and receive plain truths; I flatter myself (I say) that your own reason, young as it is, must tell you, that I can have no interest but yours in the advice I give you; and that consequently you will at least weigh and consider it well: in which case, some of it will, I hope, have its effect. Do not think that I mean to dictate as a parent; I only mean to advise as a friend, and an indulgent one too: and do not apprehend that I mean to check your pleasures; of which, on the contrary, I only desire to be the guide, not the censor. Let my experience supply your want of it, and clear your way, in the progress of your youth, of those thorns and briars which scratched and disfigured me in the course of mine. I do not, therefore, so much as hint to you, how absolutely dependent you are upon me; that you neither have, nor can have a shilling in the world but from me; and that, as I have no womanish weakness for your person, your merit must and will be the only measure of my kindness. I say, I do not hint these things to you, because I am convinced that you will act right, upon more noble and generous principles: I mean, for the sake of doing right, and out of affection and gratitude to me.

I have so often recommended to you attention and application to whatever you learn, that I do not mention them now as duties; but I point them out to you as conducive, nay, absolutely necessary to your pleasures; for can there be a greater pleasure than to be universally allowed to excel those of one's own age and manner of life? And, consequently, can there be anything more mortifying than to be excelled by them? In this latter case, your shame and regret must be greater than anybody's, because everybody knows the uncommon care which has been taken of your education, and the opportunities you have had of knowing more than others of your age. I do not confine the application which I recommend, singly to the view and emulation of excelling others (though that is a very sensible pleasure and a very warrantable pride); but I mean likewise to excel in the thing itself; for, in my mind, one may as well not know a thing at all, as know it but imperfectly. To know a little of anything, gives neither satisfaction nor credit; but often brings disgrace or ridicule.

Mr. Pope says, very truly,

> A little knowledge is a dangerous thing.
> Drink deep, or taste not the Castalian spring.

And what is called a *smattering* of everything; infallibly constitutes a coxcomb. I have often, of late, reflected what an unhappy man I must now have been, if I had not acquired in my youth some fund and taste of learning. What could I have done with myself, at this age, without them? I must, as many ignorant people do, have destroyed my health and faculties by sotting away the evenings; or, by wasting them frivolously in the tattle of women's company, must have exposed myself to the ridicule and contempt of those very women; or, lastly, I must have hanged myself, as a man once did, for weariness of putting on and pulling off his shoes and stockings every day. My books, and only my books, are now left me; and I daily find what Cicero says of learning, to be true: '*Haec studia* (says he) *adolescentiam alunt, senectutem oblectant, secundas res ornant, adversis perfugium ac solatium praebent, delectant domi, non impediunt foris, pernoctant nobiscum, peregrinantur, rusticantur.*' [These studies nourish youth, delight old age, adorn success, offer refuge and solace in adversity, please at home, are no hindrance abroad, pass the night with us, travel about, and stay with us in the country.]

I do not mean, by this, to exclude conversation out of the pleasures of an advanced age; on the contrary, it is a very great and a very rational pleasure, at all ages; but the conversation of the ignorant is no conversation, and gives even them no pleasure: they tire of their own sterility, and have not matter enough to furnish them with words to keep up a conversation.

Let me, therefore, most earnestly recommend to you to hoard up, while you can, a great stock of knowledge; for though, during the dissipation of your youth, you may not have occasion to spend much of it, yet you may depend upon it, that a time will come when you will want it to maintain you. Public granaries are filled in plentiful years; not that it is known that the next, or the second, or third year will prove a scarce one; but because it is known, that, sooner or later, such a year will come, in which the grain will be wanted.

I will say no more to you upon this subject; you have Mr. Harte with you to enforce it; you have Reason to assent to the truth of it; so that, in short, 'you have Moses and the Prophets; if you will not believe them, neither will you believe, though one rose from the dead.' Do not imagine that the knowledge which I so much recommend to you, is confined to books, pleasing, useful, and necessary as that knowledge is: but I comprehend in it the great knowledge of the world, still more necessary than that of books. In truth, they assist one another reciprocally; and no man will have either perfectly, who has not both. The knowledge of the world is only to be acquired in the world, and not in a closet. Books alone will never teach it you; but they will suggest many things to your observation, which might otherwise escape you; and your own observations upon mankind, when compared with those which you will find in books, will help you to fix the true point.

To know mankind well, requires full as much attention and application as to know books, and, it may be, more sagacity and discernment. I am at this time acquainted with many elderly people, who have all passed their whole lives in the great world, but with such levity and inattention, that they know no more of it now, than they did at fifteen. Do not flatter yourself, therefore, with the thoughts that you can acquire this knowledge in the frivolous chit-chat of idle companies; no, you must go much deeper than that. You must look into people, as well as at them. Almost all people are born with all the passions, to a certain degree; but almost every man has a prevailing one, to which the others are subordinate. Search every one for that ruling passion; pry into the recesses of his heart, and observe the different workings of the same passion in different people. And, when you have found out the prevailing passion of any man, remember never to trust him where that passion is concerned. Work upon him by it, if you please; but be upon your guard yourself against it, whatever professions he may make you.

I would desire you to read this letter twice over, but that I much doubt whether you will read once to the end of it. I will trouble you no longer now; but we will have more upon this subject hereafter. Adieu.

I have this moment received your letter from Schaffhausen: in the date of it you forgot the month.

London, 27 March 1747

Dear Boy,

Pleasure is the rock which most young people split upon; they launch out with crowded sails in quest of it, but without a compass to direct their course, or reason sufficient to steer the vessel; for want of which, pain and shame, instead of pleasure, are the returns of their voyage. Do not think that I mean to snarl at pleasure, like a Stoic, or to preach against it, like a parson; no, I mean to point it out, and recommend it to you, like an Epicurean: I wish you a great deal; and my only view is to hinder you from mistaking it.

The character which most young men first aim at is, that of a man of pleasure; but they generally take it upon trust; and, instead of consulting their own taste and inclinations, they blindly adopt whatever those, with whom they chiefly converse, are pleased to call by the name of pleasure; and a *man of pleasure,* in the vulgar acceptation of that phrase, means only a beastly drunkard, an abandoned whore-master, and a profligate swearer and curser. As it may be of use to you, I am not unwilling, though at the same time ashamed, to own, that the vices of my youth proceeded much more from my silly resolution of being what I heard called a man of pleasure, than from my own inclinations. I always naturally hated drinking; and yet I have often drunk, with disgust at the time, attended by great sickness the next day, only because I then considered drinking as a necessary qualification for a fine gentleman, and a man of pleasure.

The same as to gaming. I did not want money, and consequently had no occasion to play for it; but I thought play another necessary ingredient in the composition of a man of pleasure, and accordingly I plunged into it without desire, at first; sacrificed a thousand real pleasures to it; and made myself solidly uneasy by it, for thirty the best years of my life.

I was even absurd enough, for a little while, to swear, by way of adorning and completing the shining character which I affected; but this folly I soon laid aside, upon finding both the guilt and the indecency of it.

Thus seduced by fashion, and blindly adopting nominal pleasures, I lost real ones; and my fortune impaired, and my constitution shattered, are, I must confess, the just punishment of my errors.

Take warning then by them; choose your pleasures for yourself, and do not let them be imposed upon you. Follow nature, and not fashion: weigh the present enjoyment of your pleasures against the necessary consequences of them, and then let your own common sense determine your choice.

Were I to begin the world again, with the experience which I now have of it, I would lead a life of real, not of imaginary, pleasure. I would enjoy the pleasures of the table, and of wine; but stop short of the pains inseparably annexed to an excess in either. I would not, at twenty years, be a preaching missionary of abstemiousness and sobriety; and I should let other people do as they would, without formally and sententiously rebuking them for it: but I would be most firmly resolved not to destroy my own faculties and constitution, in compliance to those who have no regard to their own. I would play to give me pleasure, but not to give me pain; that is, I would play for trifles, in mixed companies, to amuse myself, and conform to custom: but I would take care not to venture for sums, which, if I won, I should not be the better for; but, if I lost, should be under a difficulty to pay; and, when paid, would oblige me to retrench in several other articles. Not to mention the quarrels which deep play commonly occasions.

I would pass some of my time in reading, and the rest in the company of people of sense and learning, and chiefly those above me; and I would frequent the mixed companies of men and women of fashion, which, though often frivolous, yet they unbend and refresh the mind, not uselessly, because they certainly polish and soften the manners.

These would be my pleasures and amusements, if I were to live the last thirty years over again: they are rational ones; and moreover, I will tell you, they are really the fashionable ones: for the others are not, in truth, the pleasures of what I call people of fashion, but of those who only call themselves so. Does good company care to have a man reeling drunk among them? Or to see another tearing his hair, and blaspheming for having lost, at play, more than he is able to pay? Or a whore-master with half a nose, and crippled by coarse and infamous debauchery? No; those practices, and, much more, those who brag of them, make no part of good company, and are most unwillingly, if ever, admitted into it. A real man of fashion and pleasure observes decency; at least, neither borrows nor affects vices; and, if he unfortunately has any, he gratifies them with choice, delicacy, and secrecy.

I have not mentioned the pleasures of the mind (which are the solid and permanent ones), because they do not come under the head of what people commonly call pleasures, which they seem to confine to the senses. The pleasure of virtue, of charity, and of learning, is true and lasting pleasure; which I hope you will be well and long acquainted with. Adieu!

London, 9 December 1749

Dear Boy,

It is now above forty years since I have never spoken nor written one single word, without giving myself at least one moment's time to consider, whether it was a good one or a bad one, and whether I could not find out a better in its place. An unharmonious and rugged period, at this time, shocks my ears; and I, like all the rest of the world, will willingly exchange, and give up some degree of rough sense, for a good degree of pleasing sound. I will freely and truly own to you, without either vanity or false modesty, that whatever reputation I have acquired as a speaker, is more owing to my constant attention to my diction, than to my matter, which was necessarily just the same as other people's. When you come into Parliament, your reputation as a speaker will depend much more upon your words, and your periods, than upon the subject. The same matter occurs equally to everybody of common sense, upon the same question; the dressing it well, is what excites the attention and admiration of the audience.

It is in Parliament that I have set my heart upon your making a figure; it is there that I want to have you justly proud of yourself, and to make me justly proud of you. This means that you must be a good speaker there; I use the word *must,* because I know you may if you will. The vulgar, who are always mistaken, look upon a speaker and a comet with the same astonishment and admiration, taking them both for preternatural phenomena. This error discourages many young men from attempting that character; and good speakers are willing to have their talent considered as something very extraordinary, if not a peculiar gift of God to His elect. But let you and I analyse and simplify this good speaker; let us strip him of those adventitious plumes, with which his own pride, and the ignorance of others have decked him, and we shall find the true definition of him to be no more than this: A man of good common sense, who reasons justly, and expresses himself elegantly on that subject upon which he speaks. There is, surely, no witchcraft in this. A man of sense, without a superior and astonishing degree of parts, will not talk nonsense upon any subject; nor will he, if he has the least taste or application, talk inelegantly. What then does all this mighty art and mystery of speaking in Parliament amount to? Why, no more than this, That the man who speaks in the House of Commons, speaks in that House, and to four hundred people, that opinion, upon a given subject, which he would make no difficulty of speaking in any house in England, round the fire, or at table, to any fourteen people whatsoever; better judges, perhaps, and severer critics of what he says, than any fourteen gentlemen of the House of Commons.

I have spoken frequently in Parliament, and not always without some applause; and therefore I can assure you, from my experience, that there is very little in it. The elegancy of the style, and the turn of the periods, make the chief impression upon the hearers. Give them but one or two round and harmonious periods in a speech, which they will retain and repeat, and they will go home as well satisfied, as people do from an opera, humming all the way one or two favourite tunes that have struck their ears and were easily caught. Most people have ears, but few have judgment; tickle those ears, and, depend upon it, you will catch their judgments, such as they are.

Cicero, conscious that he was at the top of his profession (for in his time Eloquence was a profession), in order to set himself off, defines, in his Treatise *de Oratore,* an orator to be such a man as never was, or never will be; and by this fallacious argument, says, that he must know every art and science whatsoever, or how shall he speak upon them? But with submission to so great an authority, my definition of an orator is extremely different from, and, I believe, much truer than his. I call that man an orator, who reasons justly, and expresses himself elegantly upon whatever subject he treats. Problems in geometry, equations in algebra, processes in chemistry, and experiments in anatomy, are never, that I have heard of, the objects of eloquence; and therefore I humbly conceive, that a man may be a very fine speaker, and yet know nothing of geometry, algebra, chemistry, or anatomy. The subjects of all Parliamentary debates, are subjects of common sense singly.

Thus I write whatever occurs to me, that I may contribute either to form or inform you. May my labour not be in vain! and it will not, if you will but have half the concern for yourself, that I have for you. Adieu!

Jonathan Edwards

Jonathan Edwards, only son of a Congregational minister, was born in 1703 in East Windsor, Connecticut. From his childhood he was intensely devoted to religion, praying secretly five times a day and discussing religion and praying with other children as well. Although he suffered lapses from his self-imposed disciplines, he recalled later in life that from his childhood he occasionally attained an ecstatic state, "a calm, sweet abstraction of soul from all the concerns of this world; and sometimes a kind of vision, or fixed ideas and imaginations, of being alone in the mountains, or some solitary wilderness, far from all mankind, sweetly conversing with Christ, and wrapt and swallowed up in God." Tutored by his parents, he learned precociously, entered Yale at the age of twelve, and graduated in 1720. After two years of theological study, he was given the ministry of a Presbyterian church in New York, but withdrew two years later because of insufficient financial support from the small congregation.

During his New York ministry, which he began when he was nineteen, Edwards wrote the greater part of his seventy "resolutions" for a virtuous life and began keeping a diary, whose first few entries are reprinted below. Reflecting on his two years in New York almost twenty years later, Edwards writes that he was at that time seeking holiness "with far greater diligence and earnestness, than ever I pursued any thing in my life; but yet with too great a dependence on my own strength. . . . My experience had not then taught me, as it has done since, my extreme feebleness and impotence, every manner of way; and the bottomless depths of secret corruption and deceit, there was in my heart."

In 1726, Edwards joined his grandfather in the ministry of a small Congregational church in Northampton, Massachusetts. Strongly opposed to this congregation's gradual acceptance of the Anglican doctrine that human worth rather than God's grace alone can affect salvation, Edwards preached fiery sermons on the natural depravity of all men and the astounding mercy of a God who saves a few of them. In 1734 and 1735, his preaching and his church were the center of a widerspread revival of religious enthusiasm. His "Narrative of Surprising Conversions" is a vivid record of these months.

Edwards remained with his Northampton congregation until 1750, when his rigorous examination of applicants for membership in the congregation led to his dismissal by a council of ten churches. He explained his position in *The Great Christian Doctrine of Original Sin Defended* (1758). From 1751 until just before his death in 1758, he was a minister and missionary to the Indians in Stockbridge, Massachusetts.

The diary entries below record a particular quality of religious feeling, which can be compared and contrasted with those expressed by St. Augustine (p. 326), St. Teresa (p. 309), and Thomas Merton (p. 118). The undermining of more positive feelings by those of dullness, depression, or melancholy is common to quite a few of the other writers in this book: it may be found in such different personalities as Mill,

Boswell, Simone de Beauvoir, and Leonard Woolf. How much of Jonathan Edwards' ethic remains in the American character? The question may be answered in terms of his attitudes toward time, pleasure, improvement, business, and friendship, as well as toward God and sin.

from *The Diary*

Dec. 18. [*1722*] This day made the 35th Resolution. [*Resolved,* Whenever I so much question whether I have done my duty, as that my quiet and calm is thereby disturbed, to set it down, and also how the question was resolved.] The reason why I, in the least, question my interest in God's love and favour, is,—1. Because I cannot speak so fully to my experience of that preparatory work, of which divines speak:—2. I do not remember that I experienced regeneration, exactly in those steps, in which divines say it is generally wrought:—3. I do not feel the christian graces sensibly enough, particularly faith. I fear they are only such hypocritical outside affections, which wicked men may feel, as well as others. They do not seem to be sufficiently inward, full, sincere, entire and hearty. They do not seem so substantial, and so wrought into my very nature, as I could wish.—4. Because I am sometimes guilty of sins of omission and commission. Lately I have doubted, whether I do not transgress in evil speaking. This day, resolved, No.

Dec. 19. This day made the 36th Resolution. [*Resolved,* Never to speak evil of any, except I have some particular good call to it.] Lately, I have been very much perplexed, by seeing the doctrine of different degrees in glory questioned; but now have almost got over the difficulty.

Dec. 20. This day somewhat questioned, whether I had not been guilty of negligence yesterday, and this morning; but resolved, No.

Dec. 21, Friday. This day, and yesterday, I was exceedingly dull, dry and dead.

Dec. 22, Saturday. This day, revived by God's Holy Spirit; affected with the sense of the excellency of holiness; felt more exercise of love to Christ, than usual. Have, also, felt sensible repentance for sin, because it was committed against so merciful and good a God. This night made the 37th Resolution. [*Resolved,* To enquire every night, as I am going to bed, Wherein I have been negligent,—What sin I have committed,—and wherein I have denied myself;—also, at the end of every week, month and year.]

Sabbath-night, Dec. 23. Made the 38th Resolution. [*Resolved,* Never to utter any thing that is sportive, or matter of laughter, on a Lord's day.]

Monday, Dec. 24. Higher thoughts than usual of the excellency of

Christ and his kingdom.—Concluded to observe, at the end of every month, the number of breaches of Resolutions, to see whether they increase or diminish, to begin from this day, and to compute from that the weekly account, my monthly increase, and, out of the whole, my yearly increase, beginning from new year days.

Wednesday, Dec. 26. Early in the morning yesterday, was hindered by the head-ache all day; though I hope I did not lose much. Made an addition to the 37th Resolution, concerning weeks, months and years. *At night;* made the 39th Resolution. [*Resolved,* Never to do anything, of which I so much question the lawfulness, as that I intend, at the same time, to consider and examine afterwards, whether it be lawful or not; unless I as much question the lawfulness of the omission.]

Saturday, Dec. 29. About sunset this day, dull and lifeless.

Tuesday, Jan. 1. [*1723*] Have been dull for several days. Examined whether I have not been guilty of negligence to-day; and resolved, No.

Wednesday, Jan. 2. Dull. I find, by experience, that, let me make Resolutions, and do what I will, with never so many inventions, it is all nothing, and to no purpose at all, without the motions of the Spirit of God; for if the Spirit of God should be as much withdrawn from me always, as for the week past, notwithstanding all I do, I should not grow, but should languish, and miserably fade away. I perceive, if God should withdraw his Spirit a little more, I should not hesitate to break my Resolutions, and should soon arrive at my old state. There is no dependence on myself. Our resolutions may be at the highest one day, and yet, the next day, we may be in a miserable dead condition, not at all like the same person who resolved. So that it is to no purpose to resolve, except we depend on the grace of God. For, if it were not for his mere grace, one might be a very good man one day, and a very wicked one the next. I find also by experience, that there is no guessing out the ends of Providence, in particular dispensations towards me—any otherwise than as afflictions come as corrections for sin, and God intends when we meet with them, to desire us to look back on our ways, and see wherein we have done amiss, and lament that particular sin, and all our sins, before him:—knowing this, also, that all things shall work together for our good; not knowing in what way, indeed, but trusting in God.

Saturday evening, Jan. 5. A little redeemed from a long dreadful dulness, about reading the Scriptures. This week, have been unhappily low in the weekly account:—and what are the reasons of it?—abundance of listlessness and sloth; and, if this should continue much longer, I perceive that other sins will begin to discover themselves. It used to appear to me, that I had not much sin remaining; but now, I perceive that there are great remainders of sin. Where may it not bring me to, if God should leave me? Sin is not enough mortified. Without the influences of the Spirit of God, the old serpent would begin to rouse up himself from his frozen state, and would come to life again. *Resolved,*

That I have been negligent in two things:—in not striving enough in duty; and in not forcing myself upon religious thoughts.

Sabbath, Jan. 6. At night; Much concerned about the improvement of precious time. Intend to live in continual mortification, without ceasing, and even to weary myself thereby, as long as I am in this world, and never to expect or desire any worldly ease or pleasure.

Monday, Jan. 7. At night, made the 40th Resolution. [*Resolved,* To enquire every night, before I go to bed, whether I have acted in the best way I possibly could, with respect to eating and drinking.]

Tuesday, Jan. 8. In the morning, had higher thoughts than usual of the excellency of Christ, and felt an unusual repentance of sin therefrom.

Wednesday, Jan. 9. At night: Decayed. I am sometimes apt to think, that I have a great deal more of holiness than I really have. I find now and then that abominable corruption, which is directly contrary to what I read of eminent christians. I do not seem to be half so careful to improve time, to do every thing quick, and in as short a time as I possibly can, nor to be perpetually engaged to think about religion, as I was yesterday and the day before, nor indeed as I have been at certain times, perhaps a twelve month ago. If my resolutions of that nature, from that time, had always been kept alive and awake, how much better might I have been, than I now am. How deceitful is my heart! I take up a strong resolution, but how soon doth it weaken.

Thursday, Jan. 10, about noon. Recovering. It is a great dishonour to Christ, in whom I hope I have an interest, to be uneasy at my worldly state and condition; or, when I see the prosperity of others, and that all things go easy with them, the world is smooth to them, and they are very happy in many respects, and very prosperous, or are advanced to much honour; to grudge them their prosperity, or envy them on account of it, or to be in the least uneasy at it, to wish and long for the same prosperity, and to desire that it should ever be so with me. Wherefore, concluded always to rejoice in every one's prosperity, and not to pretend to expect or desire it for myself, and to expect no happiness of that nature, as long as I live; but to depend on afflictions, and to betake myself entirely to another happiness.—I think I find myself much more sprightly and healthy, both in body and mind, for my self-denial in eating, drinking and sleeping. I think it would be advantageous, every morning to consider my business and temptations, and the sins to which I shall be exposed on that day, and to make a resolution how to improve the day, and avoid those sins, and so at the beginning of every week, month and year. I never knew before what was meant, by not setting our hearts on those things. It is, not to care about them, nor to depend upon them, nor to afflict ourselves with the fear of losing them, nor to please ourselves with the expectation of obtaining them, or with the hopes of their continuance.—*At night;* made the 41st Resolution. [*Resolved,* To ask myself, at the end of every day, week, month and year, wherein I could possibly, in any respect, have done better.]

Saturday, Jan. 12. In the morning. I have this day, solemnly renewed my baptismal covenant and self-dedication, which I renewed, when I was taken into the communion of the church. I have been before God, and have given myself, all that I am, and have, to God; so that I am not, in any respect, my own. I can challenge no right in this understanding, this will, these affections, which are in me. Neither have I any right to this body, or any of its members—no right to this tongue, these hands, these feet; no right to these senses, these eyes, these ears, this smell, or this taste. I have given myself clear away, and have not retained any thing, as my own. I gave myself to God, in my baptism, and I have been this morning to him, and told him, that I gave myself *wholly* to him. I have given every power to him; so that for the future, I'll challenge no right in myself, in no respect whatever. I have expressly promised him, and I do now promise Almighty God, that by his grace, I will not. I have this morning told him, that I did take Him for my whole portion and felicity, looking on nothing else, as any part of my happiness, nor acting as if it were; and his Law, for the constant rule of my obedience; and would fight, with all my might, against the world, the flesh and the devil, to the end of my life; and that I did believe in Jesus Christ, and did receive him as a Prince and Saviour; and that I would adhere to the faith and obedience of the Gospel, however hazardous and difficult, the confession and practice of it may be; and that I did receive the blessed Spirit, as my Teacher, Sanctifier, and only Comforter, and cherish all his motions to enlighten, purify, confirm, comfort and assist me. This, I have done; and I pray God, for the sake of Christ, to look upon it as a self-dedication, and to receive me now, as entirely his own, and to deal with me, in all respects, as such, whether he afflicts me, or prospers me, or whatever he pleases to do with me, who am his. Now, henceforth, I am not to act, in any respect, as my own.—I shall act as my own, if I ever make use of any of my powers, to any thing, that is not to the glory of God, and do not make the glorifying of him, my whole and entire business:—if I murmur in the least at affliction; if I grieve at the prosperity of others; if I am in any way uncharitable; if I am angry, because of injuries; if I revenge them; if I do any thing, purely to please myself, or if I avoid any thing, for the sake of my own case; if I omit any thing, because it is great self-denial; if I trust to myself; if I take any of the praise of any good that I do, or that God doth by me; or if I am in any way proud. This day, made the 42d and 43d Resolutions:—Whether or no, any other end ought to have any influence at all, on any of my actions; or, whether any action ought to be any otherwise, in any respect, than it would be, if nothing else but religion had the least influence on my mind. [*Resolved,* Frequently to renew the dedication of myself to God, which was made at my baptism, which I solemnly renewed, when I was received into the communion of the church, and which I have solemnly re-made this 12th day of January, 1723. *Resolved,* Never, henceforward, till I die, to act as if I were any way my own, but entirely and altogether God's; agreeably to what is to be found in Saturday, Jan. 12th.] Wherefore, I make the 44th Resolution. [*Resolved,* That no other end but religion, shall have any influence at all on any of my actions; and that no action shall be, in the least circumstance, any otherwise than the religious end will carry it.]

Query: Whether any delight, or satisfaction, ought to be allowed, because any other end is obtained, beside a religious one. In the afternoon, I answer, Yes; because, if we should never suffer ourselves to rejoice, but because we have obtained a religious end, we should never rejoice at the sight of friends, we should not allow ourselves any pleasure in our food, whereby the animal spirits would be withdrawn, and good digestion hindered. But the query is to be answered thus:—We never ought to allow any joy or sorrow, but what helps religion. Wherefore, I make the 45th Resolution. [*Resolved,* Never to allow any pleasure or grief, joy or sorrow, nor any affection at all, nor any degree of affection, nor any circumstance relating to it, but what helps Religion.]

The reason why I so soon grow lifeless, and unfit for the business I am about, I have found out, is only because I have been used to suffer myself to leave off, for the sake of ease, and so, I have acquired a habit of expecting ease; and therefore, when I think I have exercised myself a great while, I cannot keep myself to it any longer, because I expect to be released, as my due and right. And then, I am deceived, as if I were really tired and weary. Whereas, if I did not expect ease, and was resolved to occupy myself by business, as much as I could; I should continue with the same vigour at my business, without vacation time to rest. Thus, I have found it in reading the scriptures; and thus, I have found it in prayer; and thus, I believe it to be in getting sermons by heart, and in other things.

At night. This week, the weekly account rose higher than ordinary. It is suggested to me, that too constant a mortification, and too vigorous application to religion, may be prejudicial to health; but nevertheless, I will plainly feel it and experience it, before I cease, on this account. It is no matter how much tired and weary I am, if my health is not impaired.

Sabbath day, Jan. 13. I plainly feel, that if I should continue to go on, as from the beginning of the last week hitherto, I should continually grow and increase in grace. After the afternoon meeting, made an addition to the 45th Resolution. *At noon;* I remember I thought that I loved to be a member of Christ, and not any thing distinct, but only a part, so as to have no separate interest, or pleasure of my own. *At night,* resolved to endeavour fully to understand 1 Cor. vii. 29—32, and to act according to it.

Monday, Jan. 14. About 10 o'clock in the morning, made this book, and put these papers in it.* The dedication, which I made of myself to

---

*He refers to slips of paper on which the first part of the Diary is written; as far as Jan. 15, *at night.*

God, on Saturday last, has been exceedingly useful to me. I thought I had a more spiritual insight into the scriptures, when reading the 8th of Romans, than ever before. *At night.* Great instances of mortification, are deep wounds, given to the body of sin; hard blows, which make him stagger and reel. We thereby get strong ground and footing against him, he is the weaker ever after, and we have easier work with him the next time. He grows cowardly; and we can easily cause him to give way, until at length, we find it easy work with him, and can kill him at pleasure. While we live without great instances of mortification and self-denial, the old man keeps about where he was; for he is sturdy and obstinate, and will not stir for small blows. This, without doubt, is one great reason why many christians do not sensibly increase in grace. After the greatest mortifications, I always find the greatest comfort. Wrote the 63d Resolution. [On the supposition, that there never was to be but one individual in the world, at any one time, who was properly a complete christian, in all respects of a right stamp, having christianity always shining in its true lustre, and appearing excellent and lovely, from whatever part and under whatever character viewed: *Resolved,* To act just as I would do, if I strove with all my might to be that one, who should live in my time.] Such little things as Christians commonly do, will not evince much increase of grace. We must do great things for God.—It will be best, when I find that I have lost any former ancient good motions or actions, to take notice of it, if I can remember them.

Tuesday, Jan. 15.—About two or three o'clock. I have been all this time decaying. It seemed yesterday, the day before, and Saturday, that I should always retain the same resolutions to the same height. But alas! how soon do I decay! O how weak, how infirm, how unable to do any thing of myself! What a poor inconsistent being! What a miserable wretch, without the assistance of the Spirit of God! While I stand, I am ready to think that I stand by my own strength, and upon my own legs; and I am ready to triumph over my spiritual enemies, as if it were I myself, that caused them to flee:—when alas! I am but a poor infant, upheld by Jesus Christ; who holds me up, and gives me liberty to smile, to see my enemies flee, when he drives them before me. And so I laugh, as though I myself did it, when it is only Jesus Christ leads me along, and fights himself against my enemies. And now the Lord has a little left me, how weak do I find myself. O let it teach me to depend less on myself, to be more humble, and to give more of the praise of my ability to Jesus Christ! The heart of man is deceitful above all things and desperately wicked: who can know it!—The occasion of my decaying, is a little melancholy. My spirits are depressed, because I fear that I lost some friendship the last night; and, my spirits being depressed, my resolutions have lost their strength. I differ to-day from yesterday, in these things. I do not resolve any thing to-day, half so strongly. I am not so perpetually thinking of renewing my resolutions, as I was then. I am not half so vigorous as I was then; nor am I half so careful to do every thing with vigour. Then, I kept continually acting; but now, I do things slowly, and satisfy myself by thinking of religion in the mean time. I am not so careful to go from one business to another.—I felt humiliation, about sunset. What shall I do, in order that I may, with a good grace, fall into christian discourse and conversation. *At night.*—The next time I am in such a lifeless frame, I will force myself to go rapidly from one thing to another, and to do those things with vigour, in which vigour would ever be useful. The things, which take off my mind, when bent on religion, are commonly some remarkable change or alteration—journies, change of place, change of business, change of studies, and change of other circumstances; or something that makes me melancholy; or some sin.

Thursday, Jan. 17. About three o'clock, overwhelmed with melancholy.

William Byrd

William Byrd was born into a wealthy and powerful Virginia family in 1674. He was sent to England as a child to receive his education at Felsted Grammar School and in the Middle Temple, studying law. Returning briefly to Virginia in 1692, he was immediately elected to the House of Burgesses, of which his father was a member. In England again, he studied the classics, Hebrew, law, and mathematics, and became a Fellow of the Royal Society. When the death of his father, the elder William Byrd, brought him back to Virginia in 1705, he was the most polished gentleman in the colony and one of the most influential. He owned several plantations totaling 179,000 acres, among them Falling Creek plantation and the Falls, mentioned in the passage below. Although his political ambitions were damaged by conflicts with Governor Alexander Spotswood, William Byrd commanded militia units, was receiver-general of the royal revenues for ten years, and served in the very powerful Council of State from 1708 until his death in 1744.

In the fashion of gentlemen, Byrd wrote humorous poems and prose pieces which he circulated among his friends in manuscript form for their amusement. *The History of the Dividing Line* (published 1841), his account of the surveying of the boundary between Virginia and North Carolina in 1728, is such a piece of writing. In addition, during most of his adult years Byrd kept a journal of his daily life, written in a difficult shorthand and intended for his eyes alone. The selections below (printed here with the unclear words in brackets) begin with a journey from the colonial capital of Williamsburg back to Byrd's plantation home.

This kind of diary, containing facts of the day with relatively little reflective comment, is one of the easiest kinds to keep. Yet, kept faithfully, it takes on various kinds of value. It is a valuable historical record—here of upper-class life in colonial Virginia—and becomes a self-characterization in spite of its apparent objectivity. From it we learn not only of Byrd's peculiar fondness for milk, his practice of a calisthenic dance, and his tempestuous relations with his wife. Here and there we can read deeper elements of his character in his relations with his friends and employees, not the least with the slaves whose presence is so incidentally and coolly recorded in these pages.

from *The Secret Diary*

[December, 1711]

26. I rose about 7 o'clock and read nothing because I prepared for my journey. However I said my prayers and ate boiled milk for breakfast. It

was cold and threatened rain or snow. About 9 I took leave and rode towards home and between Captain Stith's and home I met my wife and Mrs. Dunn going to Williamsburg to see what was become of me, but they turned back with me home where I found all well, thank God Almighty, except old Jane who was very ill of a fever. About 3 o'clock we went to dinner and I ate some wild goose. In the afternoon I looked about and found all things in good order. Mr. Anderson dined with me and after dinner gave old Jane the Sacrament. He stayed with me till the evening and then returned home. I inquired of my people how everything was and they told me well. Then I gave them some rum and cider to be merry with and afterwards read some Italian and wrote two letters to my overseers. I said my prayers and had good health, and good thoughts, and good humor, thank God Almighty. I rogered my wife [lustily].

27. I rose about 7 o'clock and read nothing because I put my things in order, but I wrote in my journal. I should have said my prayers but as soon as I had eaten boiled milk for breakfast Colonel Hill and Mrs. Anderson came to see us. My wife had [c-s] some of her [f-x]. The Colonel inquired how matters went below and I acquainted him with everything I knew concerning it. The weather was more moderate than it had been lately. Mr. Anderson would have come likewise but he was obliged to go to marry a couple of his parishioners. About 1 o'clock we went to dinner and I ate some roast beef. The company stayed with me till 4 o'clock and then went away. Then I danced my dance and said my prayers devoutly and then walked in my library because the ground was wet. In the evening I wrote in my journal and caused several of my people to be let blood by way of prevention. Then I read some Latin in Terence till 10 o'clock. I said my prayers and had good health, good thoughts, and good humor, thank God Almighty. I rogered my wife [lustily].

28. I rose about 7 o'clock and read two chapters in Hebrew and some Greek in Lucian. I said my prayers and ate boiled milk for breakfast. The weather was warm but cloudy. I danced my dance. I wrote some accounts and put several matters in order. Poor old Jane was very ill. We had several of the people let blood by way of prevention and Jenny for a sore throat. I ate boiled beef for dinner. In the afternoon settled several accounts till the evening and then I took a walk about the plantation and found matters pretty well, thank God. At night I wrote in my journal and read some Latin in Terence till 10 o'clock. It snowed a little this evening. I said my prayers and had good health, good thoughts, and good humor, thank God Almighty. About 8 o'clock came Mr. G-r-l and George Smith by whom I learned that all was well at Falling Creek and the coal-pit.

29. I rose about 7 o'clock and read two chapters in Hebrew and some Greek in Lucian. I said my prayers and ate boiled milk for breakfast. I had abundance of talk with Mr. G-r-l about the affairs of Falling Creek

and he told me some of his wants and so did George Smith, which I endeavored to supply as well as I could. I gave John G-r-l leave to go visit his mother. Poor old Jane died this morning about 9 o'clock and I caused her to be buried as soon as possible because she stank very much. It was not very cold today. I danced my dance. Mr. G-r-l and George Smith went away about 12 o'clock. I ate some broiled goose for dinner. In the afternoon I set my razor, and then went out to shoot with bow and arrow till the evening and then I ran to breathe myself and looked over everything. At night I read some Latin in Terence till about 10 o'clock. I said my prayers and had good health, good thoughts, and good humor, thank God Almighty.

30. I rose about 7 o'clock and read a chapter in Hebrew and three chapters in the Greek Testament. I said my prayers very devoutly and ate boiled milk for breakfast. The weather was very clear and warm so that my wife walked out with Mrs. Dunn and forgot dinner, for which I had a little quarrel with her and another afterwards because I was not willing to let her have a book out of the library. About 12 o'clock came Mr. Bland from Williamsburg but brought no news. He stayed to dinner and I ate some roast beef. In the afternoon we sat and talked till about 4 o'clock and then I caused my people to set him over the river and then I walked with the women about the plantation till they were very weary. At night we ate some eggs and drank some Virginia beer and talked very gravely without reading anything. However I said my prayers and spoke with all my people. I had good health, good thoughts, and good humor, thank God Almighty. I danced my dance in the morning.

31. I rose about 7 o'clock and read a chapter in Hebrew and six leaves in Lucian. I said my prayers and ate boiled milk for breakfast. The weather continued warm and clear. I settled my accounts and wrote several things till dinner. I danced my dance. I ate some turkey and chine for dinner. In the afternoon I weighed some money and then read some Latin in Terence and then Mr. Mumford came and told me my man Tony had been very sick but he was recovered again, thank God. He told me Robin Bolling had been like to die and that he denied that he was the first to mention the imposition on skins which he certainly did. Then he and I took a walk about the plantation. When I returned I was out of humor to find the negroes all at work in our chambers. At night I ate some broiled turkey with Mr. Mumford and we talked and were merry all the evening. I said my prayers and had good health, good thoughts, and good humor, thank God Almighty. My wife and I had a terrible quarrel about whipping Eugene while Mr. Mumford was there but she had a mind to show her authority before company but I would not suffer it, which she took very ill; however for peace sake I made the first advance towards a reconciliation which I obtained with some difficulty and after abundance of crying. However it spoiled the mirth of the evening, but I was not conscious that I was to blame in that quarrel.

January, 1712

1. I lay abed till 9 o'clock this morning to bring my wife into temper again and rogered her by way of reconciliation. I read nothing because Mr. Mumford was here, nor did I say my prayers, for the same reason. However I ate boiled milk for breakfast, and after my wife tempted me to eat some pancakes with her. Mr. Mumford and I went to shoot with our bows and arrows but shot nothing, and afterwards we played at billiards till dinner, and when we came we found Ben Harrison there, who dined with us. I ate some partridge for dinner. In the afternoon we played at billiards again and I won two bits. I had a letter from Colonel Duke by H-l the bricklayer who came to offer his services to work for me. Mr. Mumford went away in the evening and John Bannister with him to see his mother. I took a walk about the plantation and at night we drank some mead of my wife's making which was very good. I gave the people some cider and a dram to the negroes. I read some Latin in Terence and had good health, good thoughts, and good humor, thank God Almighty. I said my prayers.

2. I rose about 7 o'clock and read two chapters in Hebrew and some Greek in Lucian. I said my prayers and ate boiled milk for breakfast. I danced my dance. It rained pretty much in the night and was cloudy this morning. I settled several accounts and wrote a letter to Colonel Duke. About 12 o'clock came Colonel Eppes but could not stay because he was obliged to go to court. A little before dinner came Ben Harrison in his best clothes, because he happened to come yesterday in his worst. He dined with us and I ate roast beef and before we had done Colonel Hill and Mrs. Harrison came and the Colonel ate some pudding with us, but Mrs. Harrison ate nothing. They went away about 4 o'clock and then my wife and I went to walk about the plantation and saw some young trees that Tom had planted this day. At night I read some Terence till almost 10 o'clock. I said my prayers and had good health, good thoughts, and good humor, thank God Almighty. My mulatto Jacky came from Falling Creek with a very sore arm and told me all was well there, thank God.

3. I rose about 7 o'clock and read two chapters in Hebrew and some Greek in Lucian. I said my prayers and ate boiled milk for breakfast. I danced my dance and then settled several accounts. The weather was very clear and cold. Mr. Bland's sloop brought two hogsheads of cider and 66 hides from Williamsburg which were put ashore. I read some Latin till dinner and then I ate some roast pork. I gave Anaka a good scolding for letting Billy Brayne have a hole in his stocking. In the afternoon I set my razor and then went to prune the trees in the young orchard and then I took a walk about the plantation and my wife and Mrs. Dunn came to walk with me. At night I read some Latin in Terence and then we drank some cider. I said my prayers and had good health, good thoughts, and good humor, thank God Almighty. . . .

5. I rose about 7 o'clock and read nothing because Tom Turpin was here. He came with 30 hogs from the Falls. He told me all was well above. I said my prayers and ate boiled milk for breakfast. I danced my dance. About 9 o'clock came Major Harrison and the captain of the "Pelican." I gave them a bottle of sack. Then we played at billiards and I won 7 shillings, and sixpence. About one o'clock we went to dinner and I ate some boiled beef. In the afternoon we were merry and made the Quaker captain drink the Queen's health on his knees. About 2 o'clock came my brother and sister Custis and sat down to dinner. They brought no news. My sister was much tired. In the evening the captain and Major Harrison went away to Mrs. Harrison's where I understood that Mr. Clayton was come. We drank a bottle of wine at night. This day a negro of mine at Falling Creek had a tree fall on his head and had his brains beat out. I neglected to say my prayers and had good health, good thoughts, and good humor, thank God Almighty. . . .

6. I rose about 8 o'clock because my wife made me lie in bed and I rogered her. I read nothing and neglected to say my prayers but had boiled milk for breakfast. About 10 o'clock came Mr. Clayton and brought me two English letters without any news because they were of an old date. I gave him a dram and about 11 o'clock we walked to church where we heard a good sermon from Mr. Anderson. I invited Colonel Hill to dine with me and ate wild goose for dinner. In the afternoon it rained so that Colonel Hill agreed to stay all night. In the evening we drank a supper bottle and were merry with nonsense but Colonel Hill's head ached a little. However it did not mar the supper or conversation. The Colonel is a man of good sense and good principles notwithstanding what has been said of him. I neglected to say my prayers but had good health, good thoughts, and good humor, thank God Almighty.

7. I rose about 7 o'clock and read nothing because we prepared to go to Colonel Hill's. I ate chocolate for breakfast. I said a short prayer. About 10 o'clock our ladies made a shift to get dressed, when we got on horseback and my horse was very frolicsome. The weather was cold and very clear. We called at Captain Llewellyn's, and took Lew Eppes and his wife with us to Colonel Hill's, where we found all well. We were as merry as we could be, considering there was but little [w—]. About 2 o'clock we went to dinner and I ate some boiled pork for dinner. In the afternoon we went to see the ship and found them far advanced. Then we returned and saw my sloop bringing to at the Hundred, where my people left behind 50 bushels of wheat from G-r-l. In the evening we were very merry and the women offered violence to me because I would not dance and my wife quarrelled with her sister because she would not dance. About 10 o'clock we went to bed. I recommended myself and family to the protection of Almighty God, and had good health, good thoughts, and good humor, thank God Almighty. . . .

9. I rose about 7 o'clock and found the weather exceedingly cold. I

neglected to say my prayers because of the company. However I drank chocolate for breakfast and ate some cake. After breakfast we went to [p-l-y] and I won £10 at cards. About 10 o'clock Major Harrison and his brother Harry went away but the rest of the company was persuaded to stay a day longer, only Parson Finney, who went away likewise. Mr. Clayton and I took a walk till dinner and then I ate some roast mutton which was very good. My sloop went away this morning to Falling Creek. In the afternoon we were merry without drinking but did not venture out because of the [. . .] cold weather. In the evening Peter came from the Falls and told me all was well, thank God. We drank some of my best wine and were merry but would not let the women part from us. About 10 we ate some bread and cheese and drank a bottle on it, and about 11 we went to bed. My wife had got some cold and was disordered in her hip. I neglected to say my prayers but had good health, good thoughts, and good humor, thank God Almighty, only I was a little displeased at a story somebody had told the Governor that I had said that no Governor ought to be trusted with £20,000. Little Peter brought a wild goose with him and two ducks.

10. I rose about 7 o'clock and found it terribly cold. My wife was a little better. I neglected my prayers and ate boiled milk for breakfast but the company ate some chicken pie. About 11 o'clock my company took leave and went away and then I could do everything which too much company had hindered me from. I read this day no Hebrew nor Greek in Lucian but read my English letters and settled some accounts. Mr. Chamberlayne came from Appomattox and told me all was well there, thank God. He would dine with me whether I asked him or not and I ate roast beef. In the afternoon I weighed some money and settled some accounts till the evening and then took a walk about the plantation. Redskin Peter pretended he fell and hurt himself but it was dissimulation. I had a cow die this day. At night I read some Latin in Terence. Then I said my prayers and had good health, good thoughts, and good humor, thank God Almighty.

11. I rose about 7 o'clock and read two chapters in Hebrew and some Greek in Lucian. I said my prayers and ate boiled milk for breakfast. I danced my dance. It was not so cold as it has been because the wind came to south. My wife was a little indisposed with a cold. I settled several accounts and put many things in order till dinner. I ate some raspberries for dinner. In the afternoon I set my razor and then went into the new orchard and trimmed the trees till the evening and then I took a walk about the plantation. Redskin Peter was very well again after he had worn the bit 24 hours and went to work very actively. Before I came in I took a run for my health. At night I read some Latin in Terence. I said my prayers and had thoughts [sic], good health, and good humor, thank God Almighty.

Girolamo Cardano

Girolamo Cardano (1501-1576) was born in Pavia, Italy, and studied there and at Milan and at Padua, where he received his degree in medicine in 1526. He was a man of enormously broad interests. When for political reasons the college of doctors in Milan barred him from practice there and he could not earn enough as a village doctor, he turned to teaching mathematics, and in 1539 published two textbooks on it. The same year he was admitted by the college of doctors after publishing an attack on their bad medical practices. Cardano soon became one of the most well-known scholars in Europe, became professor of medicine at Padua, and wrote prolifically, almost always in Latin, on a wide range of topics.

At the peak of Cardano's career, in 1560, his son Giambatista was executed for poisoning his unfaithful wife. Crushed by this event, Cardano retreated to Bologna, where he joined the university faculty and was made an honorary citizen. But bad luck pursued him in the criminal activities of his second son, Aldo; and in 1570 Cardano was imprisoned for some months by the inquisition on the charge of heresy. He was no heretic, but so prolific and scientific an author could easily fall under suspicion during the Counter-Reformation. He was released on condition that he give up teaching and publishing. Taken to Rome by his former student and faithful friend, Rodolfo Silvestri, he continued to write if not to publish, and there he produced his final book, the autobiography *De propria vita*, from which we print the passages below.

Cardano, a true "renaissance man," wrote on an astonishing range of topics, from astrology and astronomy on through the sciences, philosophy, and beyond. An inveterate gambler as well as mathematician, he wrote the first study of the principles of probability, *De ludo alcae (On Games of Chance*, trans. 1953); his book of consolation, translated into renaissance English as *Comforte* (1573), may be the very book that we are to suppose that Hamlet is reading before his "To be or not to be" soliloquy; his *Ars Magna* (1543, trans. 1968) is a landmark in the history of algebra; his encyclopedic discussions on science and natural philosophy, *De subtilitate rerum* (1547) and *De rerum varietate* (1557) had very wide audiences in the sixteenth century. Of the 131 printed works he mentions (not to speak of 111 in manuscript!) over half were on medical topics. Yet it is likely that the autobiography is the most important work of all for the history of Western culture. In it he not only gives an insight into a complex and curious personality, but to our knowledge gives for the first time an objective, realistic, portrayal of an individual self. For this reason Cardano's work is historically more interesting than the famous autobiography of his contemporary, Benvenuto Cellini. Cardano carried over his scientific bent into the description of himself. The apparently commonplace reports below thus mark a revolution in the history of individualism. In ages previous, men had written of themselves for the general laws and moral example that could be drawn from their experiences, and rarely if ever dealt with the specific and often trivial traits that made themselves unique. Cardano's purpose is to find his way to the plain facts: "I merely lay bare the truth." It seems like a simple exercise, but is, in fact, still intensely difficult, as the reader will find if he tries it.

from *The Book of My Life*

Stature and Appearance

I am a man of medium height; my feet are short, wide near the toes, and rather too high at the heels, so that I can scarcely find well-fitting shoes; it is usually necessary to have them made to order. My chest is somewhat narrow and my arms slender. The thickly fashioned right hand has dangling fingers, so that chiromantists have declared me a rustic; it embarrasses them to know the truth. The line of life upon my palm is short, while the line called Saturn's is extended and deep. My left hand, on the contrary, is truly beautiful with long, tapering, well-formed fingers and shining nails.

A neck a little long and inclined to be thin, cleft chin, full pendulous lower lip, and eyes that are very small and apparently half-closed; unless I am gazing at something . . . such are my features. Over the eyebrow of my left eye is a blotch or wart, like a small lentil, which can scarcely be noticed. The wide forehead is bald at the sides where it joins the temples. My hair and beard were blonde; I am wont to go rather closely clipped. The beard, like my chin, is divided, and the part of it beneath my chin always was thick and long, seeming to have a more abundant growth thereunder. Old age has wrought changes in this beard of mine, but not much in my hair.

A rather too shrill voice draws upon me the censure of those who pretend to be my friends, for my tone is harsh and high; yet when I am lecturing it cannot be heard at any distance. I am not inclined to speak in the least suavely, and I speak too often.

I have a fixed gaze as if in meditation. My complexion varies, turning from white to red. An oval face, not too well filled out, the head shaped off narrowly behind and delicately rounded, complete a picture so truly commonplace that several painters who have come from afar to make my portrait have found no feature by which they could so characterize me, that I might be distinguished. Upon the lower part of my throat is a swelling like a hard ball, not at all conspicuous, and coming to me as an inheritance from my mother.

Manner of Life

It is my custom to remain in bed ten hours, and, if I am well and of fair and proper strength, to sleep eight hours; in periods of ill-health I can sleep but four or five hours. I arise at the second hour of the day. If insomnia troubles me, I get up, walk around the bed and count to a thousand many times. I also diet, cutting down on my food by more than half. At such times I make small use of medication beyond a little poplar ointment or bear's grease or oil of water lilies. With this I anoint seventeen places: the thighs, the soles of my feet, the cervix, the elbows, the wrists, the temples, the regions of the jugular, heart, and liver, and last of all my upper lip. I was especially troubled with early morning wakefulness.

Breakfast was always a lighter meal than dinner. After my fiftieth year I was satisfied in the morning with bread steeped in broth, or even at first, with bread and water, and with those large Cretan grapes called Zibbibos or red raisins. Later in the day I followed a more varied menu, desiring for the midday meal simply an egg-yolk with two ounces of bread or a little more, and a mild draught of sweet wine, or none at all. Or if the day happen to be Friday, or Saturday, I try a small piece of meat with bread and cockle broth or crab soup. I consider nothing better than firm young veal, beaten tender with the back of a butcher knife and pot-roasted without any liquors save its own. In this dish I take great satisfaction; it has a way of drawing its own drippings, than which nothing is better; and thus the meat is far more juicy and much richer than meat roasted on a spit.

For supper I order a dish of beets, a little rice, a salad of endive; but I like even better the wide-leafed spiny sow-thistle, or the root of the white endive. I eat more freely of fish than of meat, but only wholesome fresh fish. I love firm meat, the breast of veal or of wild boar roasted, and finely cut with sharp knives. And it seems good to me to eat my meal by the fire. At this repast I delight also in sweet new wine, about six ounces with double, or even more, the amount of water. I find especially good the wings, livers, and giblets of young fowl and pigeons.

I am especially fond of river crabs, because, while my mother carried me, she ate so many of them. Likewise I delight in cockles and oysters. I prefer fish to meat, and eat them with much more benefit than the latter: sole, turbot, flatfish, gudgeon, land-turtles, chub, mullet, or red mullet, roach, sea bream, the merluce or seacod, the spigola or wolf-fish, tilefish, and grayling.

Of the freshwater fish, I prefer pike, carp, perch, and both varieties of sargo. Also, I like loach, squalus, tunny, and herrings, the latter fresh, salted, or best of all, dried. It is surprising that I eat cockles as a very agreeable dish, and turn away from the palatable conger eel, and the mussels as if they were poison, as I do from snails unless they are well cleaned. Freshwater crabs and other crustaceans please me; sea-crabs are

too tough, and eels and frogs I find too disgusting, as is the case with
fungi.

I take great delight in honey, in cane sugar, dried grapes, ripe grapes,
melons—after I learned of their medicinal properties—figs, cherries,
peaches, and fruit syrup; nor do these cause me the least distress, even at
my present age. Above all, I find olive oil delicious, mixed with salt and
ripe olives. Garlic does me good; and bitter rue has always seemed to
have special properties, both when I was a boy and since I am grown, of
protecting my health and, besides, serving as an antidote against all
poisons. By experiment I have found *absinthium Romanum* or worm-
wood, beneficial.

I was never immoderately addicted to venery, nor have I been harmed
much by excesses in this respect; now, however, it plainly results in
abdominal nervousness.

The white meat of the smaller fishes, when they are fresh and tender
and cooked on the grill, I enjoy and find beneficial. Nor do I turn up my
nose at a good sheepcheese. Above all eatables, I prefer a carp of from
three to seven pounds, but of the choicest flesh. From the large fishes I
remove the head and the entrails, and from the little ones the backbone
and the tail. The head is always cooked in boiling water, and, in the case
of the larger fishes, all remaining parts either fried or broiled on the
gridiron. Small fishes may be fried until tender, or boiled not too much.
. . .

Customs, Vices, and Errors

An account of this nature is by its own character a most difficult thing
to write, and so much the more for me as I reflect that those who have
been wont to read the autobiographical books of writers are not used to
seeing such a straightforward narrative set down as I purpose to publish.

Some have committed themselves to writing as they think they ought
to be, like Antoninus; others have, indeed, given true accounts, but with
all their shortcomings carefully suppressed, as did Josephus. But I prefer
to do service to truth, though well aware that he who transgresses the
conventions cannot offer the same excuses as suffice for other mistakes.
Yet who constrains me? Shall I not be, therefore, like that leper who, of
the ten healed, alone returned to acknowledge the Lord?

By this reasoning physicians and astrologers find the origins of our
moral natures in our innate qualities, and of our voluntary acts in
education, interests, and conversations. These all are present in every
man, but peculiarly adapted to each appropriate epoch of his life, yet
with variations, nevertheless, even in similar instances. It is necessary,
consequently, to exercise choice, and to select with care from all these
influences one principle whereby we may get understanding. For myself,

as far as I could judge, the well known γνῶϑι σαυτόν [know thyself] seemed the best guide.

My nature, as a result, has ever been manifest to me: high-tempered, straightforward, and devoted to the pleasures of passion. From these beginnings, as it were, have issued bitterness, contentious obstinacy, lack of amenity, hasty judgment, anger, and an intense desire for revenge—to say nothing of headstrong will; that which many damn, by word at least, was my delight. "At vindicta bonum vita iucundius ipsa." [Yet vengeance is sweeter to me than life itself.] On the whole I was not inclined to deviate from the ways of rectitude even though it is commonly said, "Natura nostra prona est ad malum." [Our nature is prone to evil.]

Yet I am a truthful man; I am mindful of benefits conferred, attached to my own people, a lover of justice, and a contemner of money. Zeal for undying fame has captured my devotion, and rendered me wont to despise mediocrity, to say nothing of petty concerns. Aware nevertheless, how greatly very insignificant matters affect any circumstance from its outset, I am accustomed to minimize no occasions. By nature I am prone to every vice and every evil save ambition; I recognize my shortcomings as well as anyone.

For the rest, because of my veneration for God, and because I clearly recognize how vain all these things are, I deliberately let pass many an offered opportunity for revenge. Timid of spirit, I am cold of heart, warm of brain, and given to never-ending meditation; I ponder over ideas, many and weighty, and even over things which can never come to pass. I am able to admit two distinct trains of thought to my mind at the same time.

Any who cast aspersions upon the praises I have enjoyed by intimating that I am boastful and extravagant, accuse me of faults of others, for those sins are not mine. I resent such, and defend myself; I attack no one. Why then do I trouble to make this examination of myself when I have given testimony so many times of the emptiness of life? My excuse is the praise spoken by some, who think that a man who has attained so much distinction does not have his shortcomings.

I have accustomed my features always to assume an expression quite contrary to my feelings: thus I am able to feign outwardly, yet within know nothing of dissimulation. This habit is easy if compared to the practice of hoping for nothing, which I have bent my efforts toward acquiring for fifteen successive years, and have at last succeeded. And now, trained to pretenses of a sort, I sometimes go forth clad in rags, but just as often elegantly dressed; sometimes I am taciturn, and sometimes talkative; sometimes gay, sometimes sad. From these moods all things acquire double aspects.

In youth I spent little and only occasional care upon the appearance of my head because of my eagerness to be at things I was more interested in. My movements are irregular, now quick, now slow. At home I go about with my legs bare to the ankles.

I am lacking in reverence and have a far from continent tongue; and I have such a quick temper that I am often shamed and embarrassed thereby. Though I may be led to repent, I have, nevertheless, paid heavy penalties, as I have elsewhere stated, for my sins; even so I atoned for the debaucheries of that Sardanapalian life I led the year I was rector of the University at Padua. Yet wisely and patiently to have carried and corrected one's fault, is praise even in disgrace, and virtue even in sin. Necessity may pardon me for speaking thus in my own praise; yet even if I were inclined to pass over in silence the gifts of God toward me, I should be an ingrate indeed to complain of the loss which I suffered without acknowledging the kind of life I was leading at the time. Frankness is, moreover, the simpler course inasmuch as my personal affairs are not as highly esteemed as men commonly value their own interests—vain, empty affairs like those great clouds seen in the wake of the sunset which are meaningless and soon pass away. If anyone would like to pass unprejudiced judgment on these actions and to reflect how easy it is to yield, he will understand in what spirit of mind, and urged by what necessity, or by what occasion I acted, and with what great grief I was afflicted through those deeds of my youth.

It is a fact that some, without scruple, are guilty of faults much worse than those; who, far from confessing them publicly, are silent even in private. They are people who are not mindful of benefits conferred upon them—who entirely forget that favors have ever been done them. Perhaps these people will be somewhat more charitable in judging me.

But let us get on. This I recognize as unique and outstanding among my faults—the habit, which I persist in, of preferring to say above all things what I know to be displeasing to the ears of my hearers. I am aware of this, yet I keep it up wilfully, in no way ignorant of how many enemies it makes for me. So strongly are our natures fettered to long-standing habits! Yet I avoid this practice in the presence of my benefactors and of my superiors. It is enough not to fawn upon these, or at least not to flatter them.

I used to be just as immoderate in living when I well knew what course was most expedient to follow, and what I ought to do; scarcely another man could be found so obstinate in a fault of the sort.

I am alone as much as I can be, although I know that this way of living has been condemned by Aristotle. For he said, "Homo solitarius aut bestia aut deus." [The solitary man partakes of the nature of the beasts or of the gods.] But for this I have rendered an excuse.

By a similar foolishness, and with no small loss to myself, I retained those domestics whom I knew to be utterly useless to me, or even a cause for shame. I become the owner of all sorts of little animals that get attached to me: kids, lambs, hares, rabbits, and storks. They litter up the whole house. I have troubled myself with the poverty of friends, especially my faithful friends.

And I have committed many, nay, numberless blunders, wherever I wished to mingle with my fellows; whatever these were, whether great or small, timely or untimely, I was conscious of them; and I even went so far as to wound those whom it had been my intention to praise. Among these was Aimar de Ranconet, a president of the Parliament of Paris, a most devoted scholar and a Frenchman. On this occasion I blundered, almost unavoidably, not solely because of lack of deliberation, and an ignorance of foreign manners and customs, but because I did not duly regard certain of those conventions which I learned about long afterwards, and with which cultivated men, for the most part, are acquainted.

In deliberating, I am too precipitate, and therefore frequently make rash decisions. In any sort of transaction, I am impatient of delay. My rivals, observing that I was not easily taken in, if I had time to think, did their best to hurry me on. I detected them plainly enough, since I am on my guard against my competitors, and deem that I can justly hold them as my enemies. But if I had not been wont never to regret any action I voluntarily undertook, even something that came to a bad end, I should have lived most unhappily.

Truly the cause of a great part of my misery was the stupidity of my sons, connected as it was with actual shame, the folly of my kinsfolk, and the jealousy existing among them, which was a vice peculiar to our family. Indeed, it is a fault common to many a group!

From my youth, I was immoderately given to gambling; and in this way I became known to Francesco Sforza, a prince of Milan, and made many friendships for myself among the nobles. And since for many years—almost forty—I applied myself assiduously to gambling, it is not easy to say how greatly the status of my private affairs suffered, and with nothing to show for it. The dice turned out to be far worse, and once my sons were instructed in the attractions of games of chance, our home too frequently was thrown open to gamblers. For this gaming habit I have naught but a worthless excuse to offer—the poverty of my early life, a certain shrewdness in hazards, and something of skill in play.

This is mortal frailty, then, but some will not admit it; others are even intolerant of it. Are they better, or wiser?

What if one should address a word to the kings of the earth and say, "Not one of you but eats lice, flies, bugs, worms, fleas—nay the very filth of your servants!" With what an attitude would they listen to such statements, though they be truths? What is this complacency then but an ignoring of conditions, a pretense of not being aware of what we know exists, or a will to set aside a fact by force? And so it is with our sins and everything else foul, vain, confused and untrue in our lives. On a rotting tree are rotten apples! It is nothing new that I proclaim; I merely lay bare the truth.

Those Things in Which I Take Pleasure

Among the things which please me greatly are stilettos, or *stili* for writing; for them I have spent more than twenty gold crowns, and much money besides for other sorts of pens. I daresay the writing materials which I have got at one time and another could not be bought for two hundred crowns. Besides these, I take great pleasure in gems, in metal bowls, in vessels of copper or silver, in painted glass globes and in rare books.

I enjoy swimming a little and fishing very much. I was devoted to the art of angling as long as I remained at Pavia and I am sorry I ever changed.

The reading of history gives me extraordinary satisfaction, as well as readings in philosophy, in Aristotle and Plotinus, and the study of treatises on the revelations of mysteries, and especially treatises on medical questions.

In the Italian poets, Petrarch and Luigi Pulci, I find great delight.

I prefer solitude to companions, since there are so few men who are trustworthy, and almost none truly learned. I do not say this because I demand scholarship in all men—although the sum total of men's learning is small enough; but I question whether we should allow anyone to waste our time. The wasting of time is an abomination.

St. Teresa of Avila

St. Teresa (1515-1582) was born in Avila, Spain, and attended a convent school in that town. At eighteen she entered the Carmelite convent of the Incarnation, and, except for severe illnesses, led an unremarkable religious life for many years. Then in 1554, at the age of thirty-nine, she experienced a kind of conversion in the presence of an image of the wounded Christ; from then on she lost every worldly desire and devoted herself to spiritual perfection. She also began to have the ever-deepening mystical experiences, especially of the presence of Christ, that went on all the rest of her life. In the period 1558 to 1560 she had visions of a sort described in the passages below. The passages are taken from the twenty-seventh and thirty-second chapters of the autobiography that she wrote, in colloquial Spanish, between 1562 and 1565.

The book was written at the behest of her confessors, her spiritual directors, in an attempt to make clear the history and quality of her experiences, especially those received in prayer. St. Teresa's visions were by no means universally accepted by her sisters and superiors; many thought them the work of the devil. Her natural humility led her to accept this possibility and to subject her own mind and spirit to the most rigorous analysis. The result is a remarkable piece of psychological self-examination. The quality of St. Teresa's attitude toward God and Christ can be compared with those of St. Augustine (p. 326), Jonathan Edwards (p. 288), and Thomas Merton (p. 118). Her account of the mystical experience may lead the reader—whether he is a believer or not—to compare his own knowledge of the life beyond ordinary perception and to try to express his understanding of it in equally plain language.

St. Teresa's ideals led her to the founding of a reformed branch of the Carmelites—called the Descalzos or Barefoots. The last twenty years of her life were spent in establishing its convents and monasteries all over Spain, often against an opposition from inside and outside her Order that severely tested her determination and her great administrative ability. She continued also to write, enlarging and deepening her study of the spiritual life in *The Way of Perfection* (about 1565) and *The Interior Castle* (1577).

Visions, from
The Life Written by Herself

I now resume the story of my life. I was in great pain and distress; and many prayers, as I said, were made on my behalf, that our Lord would lead me by another and a safer way; for this, they told me, was so suspicious. The truth is, that though I was praying to God for this, and wished I had a desire for another way, yet, when I saw the progress I was making, I was unable really to desire a change,—though I always prayed for it,—excepting on those occasions when I was extremely cast down by what people said to me, and by the fears with which they filled me.

I felt that I was wholly changed; I could do nothing but put myself in the hands of God: He knew what was expedient for me; let Him do with me according to His will in all things. I saw that by this way I was directed heavenwards, and that formerly I was going down to hell. I could not force myself to desire a change, nor believe that I was under the influence of Satan. Though I was doing all I could to believe the one and to desire the other, it was not in my power to do so. I offered up all my actions, if there should be any good in them, for this end; I had recourse to the Saints for whom I had a devotion, that they might deliver me from the evil one; I made novenas; I commended myself to St. Hilarion, to the Angel St. Michael, to whom I had recently become devout, for this purpose; and many other Saints I importuned, that our Lord might show me the way,—I mean, that they might obtain this for me from His Majesty.

At the end of two years spent in prayer by myself and others for this end, namely, that our Lord would either lead me by another way, or show the truth of this,—for now the locutions of our Lord were extremely frequent,—this happened to me. I was in prayer one day,—it was the feast of the glorious St. Peter,—when I saw Christ close by me, or, to speak more correctly, felt Him; for I saw nothing with the eyes of the body, nothing with the eyes of the soul. He seemed to me to be close beside me; and I saw, too, as I believe, that it was He who was speaking to me. As I was utterly ignorant that such a vision was possible, I was extremely afraid at first, and did nothing but weep; however, when He spoke to me but one word to reassure me, I recovered myself, and was, as usual, calm and comforted, without any fear whatever. Jesus Christ seemed to be by my side continually, and, as the vision was not imaginary, I saw no form; but I had a most distinct feeling that He was always on my right hand, a witness of all I did; and never at any time, if I was but slightly recollected, or not too much distracted, could I be ignorant of His near presence.

I went at once to my confessor, in great distress, to tell him of it. He asked in what form I saw our Lord. I told him I saw no form. He then said: "How did you know that it was Christ?" I replied, that I did not know how I knew it; but I could not help knowing that He was close beside me,—that I saw Him distinctly, and felt His presence,—that the recollectedness of my soul was deeper in the prayer of quiet, and more continuous,—that the effects thereof were very different from what I had hitherto experienced,—and that it was most certain. I could only make comparisons in order to explain myself; and certainly there are no comparisons, in my opinion, by which visions of this kind can be described. Afterwards I learnt from Friar Peter of Alcantara, a holy man of great spirituality,—of whom I shall speak by and by,—and from others of great learning, that this vision was of the highest order, and one with which Satan can least interfere; and therefore there are no words whereby to explain,—at least, none for us women, who know so little: learned men can explain it better.

For if I say that I see Him neither with the eyes of the body, nor with those of the soul,—because it was not an imaginary vision,—how is it that I can understand and maintain that He stands beside me, and be more certain of it than if I saw Him? If it be supposed that it is as if a person were blind, or in the dark, and therefore unable to see another who is close to him, the comparison is not exact. There is a certain likelihood about it, however, but not much, because the other senses tell him who is blind of that presence: he hears the other speak or move, or he touches him; but in these visions there is nothing like this. The darkness is not felt; only He renders Himself present to the soul by a certain knowledge of Himself which is more clear than the sun. I do not mean that we now see either a sun or any brightness, only that there is a light not seen, which illumines the understanding so that the soul may have the fruition of so great a good. This vision brings with it great blessings.

It is not like that presence of God which is frequently felt, particularly by those who have attained to the prayer of union and of quiet, when we seem, at the very commencement of our prayer, to find Him with whom we would converse, and when we seem to feel that He hears us by the effects and the spiritual impressions of great love and faith of which we are then conscious, as well as by the good resolutions, accompanied by sweetness, which we then make. This is a great grace from God; and let him to whom He has given it esteem it much, because it is a very high degree of prayer; but it is not vision. God is understood to be present there by the effects He works in the soul: that is the way His Majesty makes His presence felt; but here, in this vision, it is seen clearly that Jesus Christ is present, the Son of the Virgin. In the prayer of union and of quiet, certain inflowings of the Godhead are present; but in the vision, the Sacred Humanity also, together with them, is pleased to be our visible companion, and to do us good.

My confessor next asked me, who told me it was Jesus Christ. I replied that He often told me so Himself; but, even before He told me so, there was an impression on my understanding that it was He; and before this He used to tell me so, and I saw Him not. If a person whom I had never seen, but of whom I had heard, came to speak to me, and I were blind or in the dark, and told me who he was, I should believe him; but I could not so confidently affirm that he was that person, as I might do if I had seen him. But in this vision I could do so, because so clear a knowledge is impressed on the soul that all doubt seems impossible, though He is not seen. Our Lord wills that this knowledge be so graven on the understanding, that we can no more question His presence than we can question that which we see with our eyes: not so much even; for very often there arises a suspicion that we have imagined things we think we see; but here, though there may be a suspicion in the first instant, there remains a certainty so great, that the doubt has no force whatever. So also is it when God teaches the soul in another way, and speaks to it without speaking, in the way I have described.

There is so much of heaven in this language, that it cannot well be understood on earth, though we may desire ever so much to explain it, if our Lord will not teach it experimentally. Our Lord impresses in the innermost soul that which He wills that soul to understand; and He manifests it there without images or formal words, after the manner of the vision I am speaking of. Consider well this way in which God works, in order that the soul may understand what He means—His great truths and mysteries; for very often what I understand, when our Lord explains to me the vision, which it is His Majesty's pleasure to set before me, is after this manner; and it seems to me that this is a state with which the devil can least interfere, for these reasons; but if these reasons are not good, I must be under a delusion. The vision and the language are matters of such pure spirituality, that there is no turmoil of the faculties, or of the senses, out of which—so it seems to me—the devil can derive any advantage.

It is only at intervals, and for an instant, that this occurs; for generally—so I think—the senses are not taken away, and the faculties are not suspended: they preserve their ordinary state. It is not always so in contemplation; on the contrary, it is very rarely so; but when it is so, I say that we do nothing whatever ourselves: no work of ours is then possible; all that is done is apparently the work of our Lord. It is as if food had been received into the stomach which had not first been eaten, and without our knowing how it entered; but we do know well that it is there, though we know not its nature, nor who it was that placed it there. In this vision, I know who placed it; but I do not know how He did it. I neither saw it, nor felt it; I never had any inclination to desire it, and I never knew before that such a thing was possible. . . .

Some considerable time after our Lord had bestowed upon me the graces I have been describing, and others also of a higher nature, I was one day in prayer when I found myself in a moment, without knowing how, plunged apparently into hell. I understood that it was our Lord's will I should see the place which the devils kept in readiness for me, and which I had deserved by my sins. It was but a moment, but it seems to me impossible I should ever forget it even if I were to live many years.

The entrance seemed to be by a long narrow pass, like a furnace, very low, dark, and close. The ground seemed to be saturated with water, mere mud, exceedingly foul, sending forth pestilential odours, and covered with loathsome vermin. At the end was a hollow place in the wall, like a closet, and in that I saw myself confined. All this was even pleasant to behold in comparison with what I felt there. There is no exaggeration in what I am saying.

But as to what I then felt, I do not know where to begin, if I were to describe it; it is utterly inexplicable. I felt a fire in my soul. I cannot see how it is possible to describe it. My bodily sufferings were unendurable. I have undergone most painful sufferings in this life, and, as the physicians say, the greatest that can be borne, such as the contraction of my sinews when I was paralysed, without speaking of others of different kinds, yea, even those of which I have also spoken, inflicted on me by Satan; yet all these were as nothing in comparison with what I felt then, especially when I saw that there would be no intermission, nor any end to them.

These sufferings were nothing in comparison with the anguish of my soul, a sense of oppression, of stifling, and of pain so keen, accompanied by so hopeless and cruel an infliction, that I know not how to speak of it. If I said that the soul is continually being torn from the body, it would be nothing, for that implies the destruction of life by the hands of another; but here it is the soul itself that is tearing itself in pieces. I cannot describe that inward fire or that despair, surpassing all torments and all pain. I did not see who it was that tormented me, but I felt myself on fire, and torn to pieces, as it seemed to me; and, I repeat it, this inward fire and despair are the greatest torments of all.

Left in that pestilential place, and utterly without the power to hope for comfort, I could neither sit nor lie down: there was no room. I was placed as it were in a hole in the wall; and those walls, terrible to look on of themselves, hemmed me in on every side. I could not breathe. There was no light, but all was thick darkness. I do not understand how it is; though there was no light, yet everything that can give pain by being seen was visible.

Our Lord at that time would not let me see more of hell. Afterwards, I had another most fearful vision, in which I saw the punishment of certain sins. They were most horrible to look at; but, because I felt none of the pain, my terror was not so great. In the former vision, our Lord made me really feel those torments, and that anguish of spirit, just as if I had been suffering them in the body there. I know not how it was, but I understood distinctly that it was a great mercy that our Lord would have me see with mine own eyes the very place from which His compassion saved me. I have listened to people speaking of these things, and I have at other times dwelt on the various torments of hell, though not often, because my soul made no progress by the way of fear; and I have read of the diverse tortures, and how the devils tear the flesh with red-hot pincers. But all is as nothing before this; it is a wholly different matter. In short, the one is a reality, the other a picture; and all burning here in this life is as nothing in comparison with the fire that is there.

I was so terrified by that vision,—and that terror is on me even now while I am writing,—that, though it took place nearly six years ago, the natural warmth of my body is chilled by fear even now when I think of it. And so, amid all the pain and suffering which I may have had to bear, I remember no time in which I do not think that all we have to suffer in this world is as nothing. It seems to me that we complain without reason. I repeat it, this vision was one of the grandest mercies of our Lord. It has been to me of the greatest service, because it has destroyed my fear of trouble and of the contradiction of the world, and because it has made me strong enough to bear up against them, and to give thanks to our Lord, who has been my Deliverer, as it now seems to me, from such fearful and everlasting pains. . . .

Peter Abelard

Peter Abelard (1079-1142) was the eldest son of a noble family of Brittany; early in life he gave up his patrimony and the expected military career to pursue instead the study of philosophy. In the manner of the period, he wandered from school to school, listening to lectures, disputing with the professors, and often overthrowing them by the vigor and cogency of his arguments. At twenty-two, barred by jealous authorities from teaching, he opened his own school; but at length he was given the chair at the cathedral school of Notre Dame in Paris. There he acquired an unrivaled reputation for his lectures in philosophy and theology, attracting students from all over Europe. It was at this time, in the period about 1117, that occurred his famous love affair with Heloise, a brilliant girl then in her teens, which is described by Abelard in the passage below.

From the shattering consequences of the love affair, Abelard first retired to a monastery, then he reopened his school and resumed teaching and writing. On top of his notoriety and his reputation for arrogance, Abelard's ideas engendered fierce hostility among more orthodox thinkers. For the times he had a highly sceptical and rationalistic mind and a severe devotion to logic. While he accepted faith, he gave reason an unprecedentedly important place beside it. Although they laid important groundwork for the great scholastic philosophy of the next century, his writings smacked of heresy to such powerful churchmen as St. Bernard. In 1121 Abelard's work on theology was ordered to be burned. Twenty years later, not long before his death, he was condemned by a Church council and then by the Pope.

Abelard's theological difficulties were accompanied by personal ones; he spent much of the latter part of his life either in posts that he found unpleasant or in prolonged wanderings in search of a livable situation. While he was Abbot of St. Gildas in Brittany, about 1132, he wrote a long letter to a friend, entitled *Historia Calamitatum (The Story of My Calamities)*, designed as a work of consolation. "In comparing your trials with mine," he writes, "you may find that yours are nothing, or at best trivial, and so you will be able to endure them more easily." Whatever the intent, the *Historia* is one of the few works of the Middle Ages that can be called autobiography. It is supposed that it shortly fell into the hands of Heloise (then a nun), who wrote to Abelard and thus initiated the brief but famous exchange of letters between them. Both the *Historia* and the letters have been called thirteenth-century forgeries. The authenticity of the *Historia* seems to us more reliable than that of the letters, however, and so we have chosen our passage from it, in the translation by J. T. Muckle (1964).

The only part of the passage that may puzzle the modern reader is that concerning the argument over the marriage and its secrecy. The case against marriage made by Heloise contains arguments from antifeminist writings that every medieval student would have known. What is surprising is that Heloise, according to Abelard's account, should have identified herself so completely with the overpower-ingly male-oriented point of view of the period. At this time Abelard was not a priest but a "cleric and canon," a minor official in the Church. While marriage was permitted in such an office, it might have resulted in the loss of the income of the office. In any case, publicity about a "shotgun" marriage could not have helped the career of a famous lecturer on logic and theology.

from *The Story of My Calamities*

After a few days I returned to Paris and for some years enjoyed peaceful possession of the school of which, though long ago it had been yielded and turned over to me, I had been deprived. As soon as I took over there, I was eager to finish the commentary on Ezechiel begun at Laon. My lectures proved so popular with my hearers that they considered I had acquired no less charm in lecturing in divinity than they had witnessed in philosophy. Through desire for lectures in both branches, my students increased greatly in number, and the financial gain and glory which accrued to me you know well from report. But success always puffs up fools and worldly repose weakens the strength of one's mind and readily loosens its fiber through carnal allurement. At a time when I considered that I was the one philosopher in the world and had nothing to fear from others, I, who up to that time had lived most chastely, began to relax the reins on my passions. And the more success I had in philosophy and sacred science, the more I withdrew from philosophers and divines through an unclean life. For it is well known that philosophers, not to speak of divines—I mean men attentive to the lessons of sacred scripture—were especially adorned with the virtue of chastity. And while I was laboring under my pride and lechery, God's grace provided a cure for each, though I willed it not, first for my lechery by depriving me of the organs by which I practised it, then for my pride which my scholarship especially nursed in me in accordance with the saying of St. Paul: *Knowledge puffs up.* This was accomplished by humiliating me through the burning of the book which was my special glory.

I would have you know correctly the story of each cure, just as it occurred, from the facts and not from hearsay. I had always detested unclean harlots and my constant attention to my books had kept me from frequent association with women of nobility and I knew little of society among women in the world. But perverse fortune, as the saying goes, by her blandishments found an easier way to cast me down from the height of my glory, or rather God in His goodness claimed me for Himself, a humbled man instead of one most proud and forgetful of the grace he had received.

There lived in Paris a maiden named Heloise, the niece of a canon named Fulbert, who from his deep love for her was eager to have her advanced in all literary pursuits possible. She was a lady of no mean appearance while in literary excellence she was the first. And as the gift of letters is rare among women, so it had gained favor for her and made her the most renowned woman in the whole kingdom.

I considered all the qualities which usually inspire lovers and decided she was just the one for me to join in love. I felt that this would be very easy to accomplish; I then enjoyed such renown and was so outstanding for my charm of youth that I feared no repulse by any woman whom I should deign to favor with my love. And I felt that this maiden would all the more readily yield to me as I knew she possessed and cherished a knowledge of letters; thereby we, though separated, could through interchange of missives live in each other's presence and, by writing more boldly than conversation permits, we could constantly engage in pleasant talks.

And so, all on fire with love for her, I sought opportunity to enable me to make her familiar with me by private and daily association, the more easily to win her over. To effect this, through the intervention of some friends, I arranged with her uncle to receive me at his own price into his home which was near my school on the pretext that the care of my household greatly interfered with my studies and proved too heavy a financial burden. He was a very avaricious man and also most anxious that his niece advance in her literary studies. Because of these two traits, I easily gained his assent and got what I desired since he was all eager for the money and considered that his niece would profit from my teaching. On this latter point he strongly urged me beyond my fondest hopes, acceding to my wishes and furthering my love. He put his niece entirely under my control that whenever I was free upon returning from school I might devote myself night and day to teaching her, telling me to use pressure if I found her remiss. I was astonished at his simplicity in this matter and would have been no more astounded if he had been giving over a tender lamb to a ravenous wolf. For when he handed her over to me not only to teach but to discipline, what else was he doing but giving free rein to my designs, and opportunity, even if I were not seeking it, easily to subdue her by threats and stripes if blandishments did not work? Two factors especially kept him from suspecting any wrongdoing, namely his fondness for his niece and my own reputation in the past for chastity.

What was the result? We were first together in one house and then one in mind. Under the pretext of work we made ourselves entirely free for love and the pursuit of her studies provided the secret privacy which love desired. We opened our books but more words of love than of the lesson asserted themselves. There was more kissing than teaching; my hands found themselves at her breasts more often than on the book. Love brought us to gaze into each other's eyes more than reading kept them on the text. And the better to prevent suspicion, I sometimes struck her not through anger or vexation but from love and affection which were beyond the sweetness of every ointment. No sign of love was omitted by us in our ardor and whatever unusual love could devise, that was added too. And the more such delights were new to us, the more ardently we indulged in them, and the less did we experience satiety. And the more these pleasures engaged me, the less time I had for philosophy and the less attention I gave to my school. It became wearisome for me to go there and equally hard to stay when I was using nightly vigils for love and the days for study. I became negligent and indifferent in my lectures so that nothing I said stemmed from my talent but I repeated everything from rote. I came simply to say again what had been said long ago and, if I composed any verses, the theme was of love and not of the secrets of philosophy. Many of these songs, as you yourself know, are still popular in various places and sung by people of like tastes. It is not easy even to realize the sadness, the expressed regrets and sorrow of my students when they saw the preoccupation and disturbance of my mind with such things.

Such a course could have escaped the notice of very few and of no one at all, I feel, except the man most disgraced by such base conduct, I mean the uncle of the maiden. When it was suggested to him at times by some, he could not believe it on account of his extreme love of his niece noted above and of my well-known chastity in the past. For it is hard for us to suspect those we love and the taint of suspicion of evil cannot exist along with strong affection. As St. Jerome says in his letter to Sabinianus:

"We are usually the last to know of the scandal in our own household and the sins of our wife and children remain hidden from us although they are the common gossip of the neighbors."

But at length we come to find out and recognize it and what is common knowledge cannot easily be kept from just one person.

And in the course of several months that is what happened with regard to us. Imagine his bitter sorrow when her uncle found it out. Imagine the grief of us lovers at being separated; how I was filled with shame and remorse over the maiden's trouble. Imagine the sadness which flooded her soul from my sense of shame. Neither one of us complained of our own trials or bewailed our own misfortune but those of the other. The bodily separation became a strong link to bind our hearts together and our love became the more inflamed, denied opportunity. But shame gradually disappeared and made us more shameless and it became less as acts became easier. What the poet tells us of Mars and Venus caught in the act happened also to us. For not long afterwards the girl noticed that she was pregnant and she wrote me about it with great exultation and asked what I thought should be done. One night, when her uncle was away, I secretly took her from his house, as we had arranged, and had her taken directly to my native place. There she stayed with my sister until she gave birth to a boy whom she named Astralabe.

Upon his return, her uncle almost went mad and no one could appreciate except from experience the anguish which wrenched him or the shame he felt. He did not know what to do to me or by what plan he could waylay me. He was very much afraid that, if he maimed or killed me, his dear niece would pay for it in my native place. He could not get hold of me and coerce me anywhere against my will especially since I was very much on my guard for I had no doubt that he would quickly attack me if he could or dared to. After a while I began to sympathize with him in his extreme anxiety and blamed myself for the deceit which love had wrought which was, as it were, a base betrayal. I went to see him and, begging forgiveness, promised to make whatever amends he decided on. I told him that whoever had felt the force of love or recalled to what a crash women from the beginning have brought even the greatest men would not be surprised at my fall. And further to appease him, I made an offer beyond his fondest hopes to make satisfaction by marrying her whom I had defiled, provided this be done secretly so that my reputation would not be damaged. He agreed both by his own word and kiss of peace and by that of his backers. He thereby became on good terms with me which was what I asked but he did it only the more easily to betray me.

I straightway returned to my native land and brought back my beloved to marry her. She disapproved of the plan and tried to dissuade me from it on two counts, the risk involved and the disgrace I should incur. She stated with an oath that her uncle could never be placated by such satisfaction, as we afterwards found out. What glory, she asked, would she derive from me since she would bring me to disgrace and humiliate both of us alike. What punishment would the world demand of her if she deprived it of such a shining light? What curses, what loss to the Church, what weeping among philosophers would ensue from our marriage; how disgraceful, how lamentable would it be, if I, whom nature had produced for all, should devote myself to a woman and submit to such baseness! She utterly abhorred such a marriage which would prove a disgrace and a burden to me. She pointed out both the loss of my reputation and the hardships of marriage, which latter the Apostle exhorts us to avoid when he says:

"*Art thou freed from a wife? Do not seek a wife. But if thou takest a wife, thou hast not sinned. And if a virgin marry, she has not sinned. Yet such will have tribulation of the flesh. But I spare you that . . . I would have you free from care, etc.*"

But if I would not heed the advice of the Apostle and the exhortations

of the saints on the great burden of marriage, she said, I should at least
listen to the philosophers and pay attention to what has been written by
them or of them on this matter. The saints in general have carefully
done this to rebuke us. One instance is St. Jerome in his first book
Against Jovinianus when he recalls how Theophrastus carefully set
forth in great detail the unbearable troubles and constant cares of
marriage and confirmed by patent proofs his declaration that a philosopher should not marry and concludes his reasons based on the exhortation of philosophers by saying: "When Theophrastus so reasons . . .
what Christian should not blush, etc.?" And again in the same work St.
Jerome goes on:

"When Cicero, after divorcing Terentia, was requested by Hirtius to marry
his sister, he emphatically declined saying that he could not devote himself
to a wife and philosophy alike."

He did not say simply 'to devote himself' but added 'alike', not wishing
to do anything which would compete with his zeal for philosophy.

To say no more about the hindrance to the study of philosophy, she
went on, consider the status of the dignified life. What could there be in
common between scholars and wetnurses, writing desks and cradles,
books, writing tablets and distaffs, styles, pens and spindles? Or who is
there who is bent on sacred or philosophical reflection who could bear
the wailing of babies, the silly lullabies of nurses to quiet them, the
noisy horde of servants, both male and female; who could endure the
constant degrading defilement of infants? You will say that the rich can
do it whose palaces or mansions have private rooms, and who with their
wealth do not feel expense and are not troubled with daily anxieties. But
I answer that the status of philosophers is not that of millionaires and of
those who, engrossed in riches and entangled in worldly cares, will have
no time for sacred or philosophical studies.

And so it is true to say that the great philosophers of old utterly
despising the world fled rather than retired from it and renounced all
pleasures that they might repose in the embrace of philosophy alone.
The greatest of them, Seneca, says in instructing Lucilius:

"You are not to pursue philosophy simply in your free time. Everything else
is to be given up that we may devote ourselves to it for no length of time is
long enough . . . It makes little difference whether you give up or interrupt
the study of philosophy for, once it is interrupted, it does not abide . . . We
must resist occupations which are not simply to be regulated but avoided."

What those among us who truly bear the name of monks endure for love
of God, that they, the esteemed philosophers among the pagans, endured
for love of philosophy. For among every people, whether Jew, Gentile or
Christian, there have always been some who were outstanding for their
faith and uprightness of life and who cut themselves off from the rank

and file by their distinguished chastity and abstinence. Among the Jews of old there were the Nazarenes who consecrated themselves to the Lord according to the Law. And there were also the sons of the Prophets, the followers of Elias and Eliseus who, as St. Jerome witnesses, are called monks in the Old Testament. Later on there were three classes of philosophers whom Josephus distinguishes in his *Antiquities* calling some Pharisees, others Sadducees, still others Essenes. Among us there are the monks who imitate the common life of the apostles or the earlier life of solitude of John the Baptist. And among the Gentiles, as we have mentioned, there are the philosophers. For the term wisdom or philosophy was used to refer not so much to acquisition of knowledge as to a religious life as we learn from the first use of it and from the testimony of the saints themselves.

In line with this, St. Augustine in the eighth book of his *City of God* distinguishes the classes of philosophers:

"The Italians had Pythagoras of Samos as the founder of their school who, it is said, first used the term philosophy. For before him, anyone who appeared to be outstanding by a praiseworthy manner of life was called a sage. But when he was asked what his profession was, he answered that he was a philosopher, that is to say, one who pursues and loves wisdom; it seemed to him that to say that such a one was already a wise man would be the height of arrogance."

And so in this passage where he says "appeared to be outstanding by a praiseworthy manner of life, etc.," he clearly shows that the wise men, that is, the philosophers, among the Gentiles were so called in praise of their life rather than of their knowledge. How temperately and chastely they lived is not for me to adduce from instances lest I appear to teach Minerva herself.

Now, she continued, if lay people and pagans so lived, men who were bound by no religious profession, what should you, a cleric and canon, do to avoid preferring base pleasure to sacred duties lest such a Charybdis drag you down headlong and you shamelessly and irrevocably swamp yourself in such obscenities. And if you do not regard the privilege of cleric, at least uphold the dignity of philosopher. If you despise reverence for God, let the love of uprightness at least restrain your shamelessness. Recall that Socrates had a wife, and the degrading incident by which he atoned for this defilement of philosophy to put others on their guard by his experience. Jerome himself in his first book *Against Jovinianus* brings this out when writing of Socrates:

"Once, after he had withstood numberless words of invective which Xanthippe hurled against him from the upper story, she threw some filthy water down upon him; Socrates wiped his head and exclaimed: 'I knew that a shower would follow such rumblings'."

Heloise went on to point out what a risk it would be for me to take her back and that it would be dearer to her and more honorable to me to be called my lover than my wife so that her charm alone would keep me for her, not the force of a nuptial bond; she also stated that the joys of our meeting after separation would be the more delightful as they were rare. When she could not divert me from my mad scheme by such arguments of exhortation and discussion and could not bear to offend me, she sighed deeply and in tears ended her final appeal as follows: "If we do this, one fate finally awaits us: we shall both be ruined and sorrow will thereby pierce our hearts equal in intensity to the love with which they are now aflame." And, as all the world knows, she was possessed of the spirit of prophecy in this statement.

And so when the infant was born we entrusted it to my sister and returned secretly to Paris. After a few days, we spent a night in a secret vigil of prayer in a church and early on the following day we were joined by the nuptial blessing in the presence of her uncle and some of his and our friends. We straightway separated and left secretly. After that we saw each other only rarely and then on the quiet, hiding by dissimulation what we had done.

But her uncle and the members of his household seeking solace for his disgrace began to make our marriage public and thereby to break the word they had given regarding it. Heloise on her part cursed and swore that it was a lie. He uncle became strongly aroused and kept heaping abuse upon her. When I found this out, I sent her to the convent of nuns in a town near Paris called Argenteuil where as a young girl she had been brought up and received instruction. I had a religious habit, all except the veil, made for her and had her vested in it.

When her uncle and his kinsmen heard of this they considered that now I had fooled them and that by making her a nun I wanted easily to get rid of her. They became strongly incensed against me and formed a conspiracy. One night when I was sound asleep in an inner room of my lodgings, by bribing my attendant they wrought vengeance upon me in a cruel and shameful manner and one which the world with great astonishment abhorred, namely, they cut off the organs by which I had committed the deed which they deplored. They immediately fled but two of them were caught and had their eyes put out and were castrated; one of these was my servant already mentioned who while in my service was brought by greed to betray me.

When morning came, the whole city flocked to me and it is hard, yes impossible, to describe the astonishment which stunned them, the wailing they uttered, the shouting which irritated me and the moaning which upset me. The clerics and especially my students by their excessive lamentation and wailing pained me so that I endured more from their expression of sympathy than from the suffering caused by the mutilation. I felt the embarrassment more than the wound and the shame was harder to bear than the pain. I fell to thinking how great had been my renown and in how easy and base a way this had been brought low and utterly destroyed; how by a just judgment of God I had been afflicted in that part of my body by which I had sinned; how just was the betrayal by which he whom I had first betrayed paid me back; how my rivals would extol such a fair retribution; how great would be the sorrow and lasting grief which my mutilation would cause my parents and friends; with what speed the news of this extraordinary mark of disgrace would spread throughout the world; what course could I follow; how could I face the public to be pointed at by all with a finger of scorn, to be insulted by every tongue and to become a monstrosity and a spectacle to all the world.

This also caused me no little confusion that according to the letter of the Law, which kills, God so abominated eunuchs that men who had their testicles cut off or bruised were forbidden as offensive and unclean to enter a congregation and in sacrifice animals of like character were utterly rejected (*Lev.* chapter XXII):·

"You shall not offer to the Lord any beast that hath the testicles bruised or crushed or cut and taken away. (Deuteronomy, chapter XXIII). An eunuch, whose testicles are broken or cut away or cut off shall not enter into the Church of the Lord."

Filled as I was with such remorse, it was, I confess, confusion springing from shame rather than devotion the result of conversion, which drove me to the refuge of monastic cloister. Heloise meanwhile at my order had consented to take the veil and entered the convent. Both of us alike took the holy habit, I in the abbey of St. Denis, she in the convent at Argenteuil mentioned above. I recall that many of her sympathizers tried to keep her, young as she was, from submitting to the yoke of monastic rule as an intolerable punishment. But it was in vain. Amid tears and sighs she broke forth as best she could into the famous complaint of Cornelia:

"O mighty husband, too good for such a wife, had Fortune such power over one so great? Why am I guilty of marrying you, if I was to bring you misery? Now accept the penalty— a penalty I willingly pay."

And while uttering these lines she hastened to the altar and straightway took from it the veil blessed by the bishop and bound herself in the presence of all to religious life. . . .

St. Augustine

St. Augustine, Bishop of Hippo, lived during the last years of the Roman Empire and the first years of the dominance of the Christian Church over paganism. Of his writing it is said, *"Mentitur qui se totum legisse fatetur:* He lies who says that he has read all of his works." Of one hundred and thirteen books, two hundred and eighteen letters, and over five hundred sermons that survive today, a great part seek to establish the truth of Christian teaching against paganism and Judaism and against the attacks of heretical Christian sects such as the Manicheans, the Donatists, and the Pelagians. In his antiheretical writings Augustine wielded large and permanent influence over the development of orthodox Christian doctrine. In addition to works directed against specific heresies, he wrote many works which are still widely enjoyed today. *On Christian Doctrine* is a short introduction to reading and interpreting the Bible. The *City of God* (a philosophical approach to the problem of history) is based on the idea that all men are divided into two "cities" or groups of loyalty, one devoted to love of the world and its sins, and the other devoted to God and life in heaven. Finally, Augustine's *Confessions* (written between 397 and 400 A.D.), addressed to God, provides a moving account of his spiritual development from childhood to conversion, at the age of thirty-two, from conscious sinfulness to Christian asceticism.

Augustine was born in 354 in Thagaste, an agricultural village in North Africa. Since he showed great intellectual promise, his father, a minor official in the local Roman government, sent him to school in Madauros, a nearby college town, when he was eleven. Remembering his childhood thefts of food and his dishonesty at games, Augustine asks, "Is this boyish innocence? It is not, O Lord, it is not . . . For these are the practises that pass from tutors and teachers, and from nuts and balls and birds, to governors and kings, and to money and estates and slaves." In his seventeenth year he entered school in Carthage, "where a cauldron of shameful loves seethed and sounded about me." Here he joined the Manichean sect and took a mistress by whom he had a son when he was eighteen. He acquired at this time a deep interest in philosophy and spent the next thirteen years of his life teaching in Thagaste, Carthage, Rome, and Milan.

After hearing St. Ambrose, Bishop of Milan, preaching in 384, Augustine became gradually convinced that he should convert to Christianity. He recalls the day of his conversion in the passages below from the eighth book of his *Confessions* (trans. from the Latin by F. J. Sheed, 1943). He was baptized in 387 and returned to Thagaste to establish a religious community. In 391 he traveled to Hippo, a large African port, and was drafted by the Christian congregation to be an assistant to Bishop Valerius. For nearly four decades after the death of Valerius in 396, Augustine as Bishop of Hippo combatted heresies in public and written debates, presided in civil law cases, and was responsible for all the instruction and spiritual care of the church in a large surrounding territory. He died in 430.

Regarded with the greatest respect in his own lifetime, he resisted pride in his reputation to the last year of his life, when in answer to a flattering letter he sent a copy of his *Confessions* with the note, "In these behold me, that you may not praise me beyond what I am; in these believe what is said of me, not by others, but by myself; in these contemplate me, and see what I have been, in myself by myself. . . . For 'He hath made us and not we ourselves,' indeed, we had destroyed ourselves, but He who made us had made us anew."

The present collection provides a number of comparisons by which to define and appreciate the quality of Augustine's feeling: St. Teresa (p. 309) for the mystical element; Jonathan Edwards (p. 288) for the consciousness of sin; Thomas Merton (p. 118) for the relief of conversion; even the much more "secular" crisis of Mill (p. 250) may be compared, especially for the mechanism by which the crisis finds its resolution.

Conversion, from *The Confessions*

Now, O Lord, my Helper and my Redeemer, I shall tell and confess to Your name how You delivered me from the chain of that desire of the flesh which held me so bound, and the servitude of worldly things. . . .

On a certain day—Nebridius was away for some reason I cannot recall—there came to Alypius and me at our house one Ponticianus, a fellow countryman of ours, being from Africa, holder of an important post in the emperor's court. There was something or other he wanted of us and we sat down to discuss the matter. As it happened he noticed a book on a gaming table by which we were sitting. He picked it up, opened it, and found that it was the apostle Paul, which surprised him because he had expected that it would be one of the books I wore myself out teaching. Then he smiled a little and looked at me, and expressed pleasure but surprise too at having come suddenly upon that book, and only that book, lying before me. For he was a Christian and a devout Christian; he knelt before You in church, O our God, in daily prayer and many times daily. I told him that I had given much care to these writings. Whereupon he began to tell the story of the Egyptian monk Antony, whose name was held in high honour among Your servants, although Alypius and I had never heard it before that time. When he learned this, he was the more intent upon telling the story, anxious to introduce so great a man to men ignorant of him, and very much marvelling at our ignorance. But Alypius and I stood amazed to hear of Your wonderful works, done in the true faith and in the Catholic Church so recently, practically in our own times, and with such numbers of witnesses. All three of us were filled with wonder, we because the deeds we were now hearing were so great, and he because we had never heard them before.

From this story he went on to the great groups in the monasteries, and their ways all redolent of You, and the fertile deserts of the wilderness, of all of which we knew nothing. There was actually a monastery at Milan, outside the city walls. It was full of worthy brethren and under the care of Ambrose. And we had not heard of it. He continued with his discourse and we listened in absolute silence. It chanced that he told how on one occasion he and three of his companions—it was at Treves, when the emperor was at the chariot races in the Circus—had gone one afternoon to walk in the gardens close by the city walls. As it happened they fell into two groups, one of the others staying with him, and the other two likewise walking their own way. But as those other two strolled on they came into a certain house, the dwelling of some servants of Yours, poor in spirit, of whom is the kingdom of God. There they found a small book in which was written the life of Antony. One of them began to read it, marvelled at it, was inflamed by it. While he was actually reading he had begun to think how he might embrace such a life, and give up his worldly employment to serve You alone. For the two men were both state officials. Suddenly the man who was doing the reading was filled with a love of holiness and angry at himself with righteous shame. He looked at his friend and said to him: "Tell me, please, what is the goal of our ambition in all these labours of ours? What are we aiming at? What is our motive in being in the public service? Have we any higher hope at court than to be friends of the emperor? And at that level, is not everything uncertain and full of perils? And how many perils must we meet on the way to this greater peril? And how long before we are there? But if I should choose to be a friend of God, I can become one now." He said this, and all troubled with the pain of the new life coming to birth in him, he turned back his eyes to the book. He read on and was changed inwardly, where You alone could see; and the world dropped away from his mind, as soon appeared outwardly. For while he was reading and his heart thus tossing on its own flood, at length he broke out in heavy weeping, saw the better way and chose it for his own. Being now Your servant he said to his friend, "Now I have broken from that hope we had and have decided to serve God; and I enter upon that service from this hour, in this place. If you have no will to imitate me, at least do not try to dissuade me."

The other replied that he would remain his companion in so great a service for so great a prize. So the two of them, now Your servants, built a spiritual tower at the only cost that is adequate, the cost of leaving all things and following You. Then Ponticianus and the man who had gone walking with him in another part of the garden came looking for them in the same place, and when they found them suggested that they should return home as the day was now declining. But they told their decision and their purpose, and how that will had arisen in them and was now settled in them; and asked them not to try to argue them out of their decision, even if they would not also join them. Ponticianus and his friend, though not changed from their former state, yet wept for themselves, as he told us, and congratulated them in God and commended themselves to their prayers. Then with their own heart trailing in the dust they went off to the palace, while the other two, with their heart fixed upon heaven, remained in the hut. Both these men, as it happened, were betrothed, and when the two women heard of it they likewise dedicated their virginity to You.

This was the story Ponticianus told. But You, Lord, while he was speaking, turned me back towards myself, taking me from behind my own back where I had put myself all the time that I preferred not to see myself. And You set me there before my own face that I might see how vile I was, how twisted and unclean and spotted and ulcerous. I saw myself and was horrified; but there was no way to flee from myself. If I tried to turn my gaze from myself, there was Ponticianus telling what he was telling; and again You were setting me face to face with myself, forcing me upon my own sight, that I might see my iniquity and loathe it. I had known it, but I had pretended not to see it, had deliberately looked the other way and let it go from my mind.

But this time, the more ardently I approved those two as I heard of their determination to win health for their souls by giving themselves up wholly to Your healing, the more detestable did I find myself in comparison with them. For many years had flowed by—a dozen or more—from the time when I was nineteen and was stirred by the reading of Cicero's Hortensius to the study of wisdom; and here was I still postponing the giving up of this world's happiness to devote myself to the search for that of which not the finding only but the mere seeking is better than to find all the treasures and kingdoms of men, better than all the body's pleasures though they were to be had merely for a nod. But I in my great worthlessness—for it was greater thus early—had begged You for chastity, saying: "Grant me chastity and continence, but not yet." For I was afraid that You would hear my prayer too soon, and too soon would heal me from the disease of lust which I wanted satisfied rather than extinguished. So I had gone wandering in my sacrilegious superstition through the base ways of the Manicheans: not indeed that I was sure they were right but that I preferred them to the Christians, whom I did not inquire about in the spirit of religion but simply opposed through malice.

I had thought that my reason for putting off from day to day the following of You alone to the contempt of earthly hopes was that I did not see any certain goal towards which to direct my course. But now the day was come when I stood naked in my own sight and my conscience accused me: "Why is my voice not heard? Surely you are the man who used to say that you could not cast off vanity's baggage for an uncertain truth. Very well: now the truth is certain, yet you are still carrying the load. Here are men who have been given wings to free their shoulders from the load, though they did not wear themselves out in searching nor spend ten years or more thinking about it."

Thus was I inwardly gnawed at. And I was in the grip of the most horrible and confounding shame, while Ponticianus was telling his story. He finished the tale and the business for which he had come; and he went his way, and I to myself. What did I not say against myself, with what lashes of condemnation did I not scourge my soul to make it follow me now that I wanted to follow You! My soul hung back. It would not follow, yet found no excuse for not following. All its arguments had already been used and refuted. There remained only trembling silence: for it feared as very death the cessation of that habit of which in truth it was dying.

In the midst of that great tumult of my inner dwelling place, the tumult I had stirred up against my own soul in the chamber of my heart, I turned upon Alypius, wild in look and troubled in mind, crying out: "What is wrong with us? What is this that you heard? The unlearned arise and take heaven by force, and here are we with all our learning, stuck fast in flesh and blood! Is there any shame in following because they have gone before us, would it not be a worse shame not to follow at once?" These words and more of the same sort I uttered, then the violence of my feeling tore me from him while he stood staring at me thunderstruck. For I did not sound like myself. My brow, cheeks, eyes, flush, the pitch of my voice, spoke my mind more powerfully than the words I uttered. There was a garden attached to our lodging, of which we had the use, as indeed we had of the whole house: for our host, the master of the house, did not live there. To this garden the storm in my breast somehow brought me, for there no one could intervene in the fierce suit I had brought against myself, until it should reach its issue: though what the issue was to be, You knew, not I: but there I was, going mad on my way to sanity, dying on my way to life, aware how evil I was, unaware that I was to grow better in a little while. So I went off to the garden, and Alypius close on my heels: for it was still privacy for me to have him near, and how could he leave me to myself in that state? We found a seat as far as possible from the house. I was frantic in mind, in a frenzy of indignation at myself for not going over to Your law and Your covenant, O my God, where all my bones cried out that I should be, extolling it to the skies. The way was not by ship or chariot or on foot: it was not as far as I had gone when I went from the house to the place where we sat. For I had but to will to go, in order not merely to go but to arrive; I had only to will to go—but to will powerfully and wholly, not to turn and twist a will half-wounded this way and that, with the part that would rise struggling against the part that would keep to the earth. . . .

Thus I was sick at heart and in torment, accusing myself with a new intensity of bitterness, twisting and turning in my chain in the hope that it might be utterly broken, for what held me was so small a thing! But it still held me. And You stood in the secret places of my soul, O Lord, in the harshness of Your mercy redoubling the scourges of fear and shame lest I should give way again and that small slight tie which remained should not be broken but should grow again to full strength and bind me closer even than before. For I kept saying within myself: "Let it be now, let it be now," and by the mere words I had begun to move towards the resolution. I almost made it, yet I did not quite make it. But I did not fall back into my original state, but as it were stood near to get my breath. And I tried again and I was almost there, and now I could all but touch it and hold it: yet I was not quite there, I did not touch it or hold it. I still shrank from dying unto death and living unto life. The lower condition which had grown habitual was more powerful than the better condition which I had not tried. The nearer the point of time came in which I was to become different, the more it struck me with horror; but it did not force me utterly back nor turn me utterly away, but held me there between the two.

Those trifles of all trifles, and vanities of vanities, my one-time mistresses, held me back, plucking at my garment of flesh and murmuring softly: "Are you sending us away?" And "From this moment shall we not be with you, now or forever?" And "From this moment shall this or that not be allowed you, now or forever?" What were they suggesting to me in the phrase I have written "this or that," what were they suggesting to me, O my God? Do you in your mercy keep from the soul of Your servant the vileness and uncleanness they were suggesting. And now I began to hear them not half so loud; they no longer stood against me face to face, but were softly muttering behind my back and, as I tried to depart, plucking stealthily at me to make me look behind. Yet even that was enough, so hesitating was I, to keep me from snatching myself free, from shaking them off and leaping upwards on the way I was called: for the strong force of habit said to me: "Do you think you can live without them?"

But by this time its voice was growing fainter. In the direction towards which I had turned my face and was quivering in fear of going, I could see the austere beauty of Continence, serene and indeed joyous but not evilly, honourably soliciting me to come to her and not linger, stretching forth loving hands to receive and embrace me, hands full of multitudes of good examples. With her I saw such hosts of young men and maidens, a multitude of youth and of every age, gray widows and women grown old in virginity, and in them all Continence herself, not barren but the fruitful mother of children, her joys, by You, Lord, her Spouse. And she smiled upon me and her smile gave courage as if she were saying: "Can you not do what these men have done, what these

women have done? Or could men or women have done such in themselves, and not in the Lord their God? The Lord their God gave me to
them. Why do you stand upon yourself and so not stand at all? Cast
yourself upon Him and be not afraid; He will not draw away and let you
fall. Cast yourself without fear, He will receive you and heal you."

Yet I was still ashamed, for I could still hear the murmuring of those
vanities, and I still hung hesitant. And again it was as if she said: "Stop
your ears against your unclean members, that they may be mortified.
They tell you of delights, but not of such delights as the law of the Lord
your God tells." This was the controversy raging in my heart, a
controversy about myself against myself. And Alypius stayed by my side
and awaited in silence the issue of such agitation as he had never seen in
me.

When my most searching scrutiny had drawn up all my vileness from
the secret depths of my soul and heaped it in my heart's sight, a mighty
storm arose in me, bringing a mighty rain of tears. That I might give
way to my tears and lamentations, I rose from Alypius: for it struck me
that solitude was more suited to the business of weeping. I went far
enough from him to prevent his presence from being an embarrassment
to me. So I felt, and he realized it. I suppose I had said something and
the sound of my voice was heavy with tears. I arose, but he remained
where we had been sitting, still in utter amazement. I flung myself down
somehow under a certain fig tree and no longer tried to check my tears,
which poured forth from my eyes in a flood, *an acceptable sacrifice to
Thee.* And much I said not in these words but to this effect: *"And
Thou, O, Lord, how long? How long, Lord; wilt Thou be angry forever?
Remember not our former iniquities."* For I felt that I was still bound
by them. And I continued my miserable complaining: "How long, how
long shall I go on saying tomorrow and again tomorrow? Why not now,
why not have an end to my uncleanness this very hour?"

Such things I said, weeping in the most bitter sorrow of my heart.
And suddenly I heard a voice from some nearby house, a boy's voice or a
girl's voice, I do not know: but it was a sort of sing-song, repeated again
and again, "Take and read, take and read." I ceased weeping and
immediately began to search my mind most carefully as to whether
children were accustomed to chant these words in any kind of game, and
I could not remember that I had ever heard any such thing. Damming
back the flood of my tears I arose, interpreting the incident as quite
certainly a divine command to open my book of Scripture and read the
passage at which I should open. For it was part of what I had been told
about Anthony, that from the Gospel which he happened to be reading
he had felt that he was being admonished as though what he read was
spoken directly to himself: *Go, sell what thou hast and give to the poor
and thou shalt have treasure in heaven; and come follow Me.* By this
experience he had been in that instant converted to You. So I was

moved to return to the place where Alypius was sitting, for I had put down the Apostle's book there when I arose. I snatched it up, opened it and in silence read the passage upon which my eyes first fell: *Not in rioting and drunkenness, not in chambering and impurities, not in contention and envy, but put ye on the Lord Jesus Christ and make not provision for the flesh in its concupiscenses. [Romans xiii, 13.]* I had no wish to read further, and no need. For in that instant, with the very ending of the sentence, it was as though a light of utter confidence shone in all my heart, and all the darkness of uncertainty vanished away. Then leaving my finger in the place or marking it by some other sign, I closed the book and in complete calm told the whole thing to Alypius and he similarly told me what had been going on in himself, of which I knew nothing. He asked to see what I had read. I showed him, and he looked further than I had read. I had not known what followed. And this is what followed: *"Now him that is weak in faith, take unto you."* He applied this to himself and told me so. And he was confirmed by this message, and with no troubled wavering gave himself to God's good-will and purpose—a purpose indeed most suited to his character, for in these matters he had been immeasurably better than I.

Then we went in to my mother and told her, to her great joy. We related how it had come about: she was filled with triumphant exultation, and praised You who are mighty beyond what we ask or conceive: for she saw that You had given her more than with all her pitiful weeping she had ever asked. For You converted me to Yourself so that I no longer sought a wife nor any of this world's promises, but stood upon that same rule of faith in which You had shown me to her so many years before. Thus You changed her mourning into joy, a joy far richer than she had thought to wish, a joy much dearer and purer than she had thought to find in grandchildren of my flesh.

Author and Title Index

Rhetorical and Topical Index

The rhetorical entries are printed in boldface; the topical entries in roman.

ANALYTIC GENERALIZATION: Jackson (May 28, 1970); Cress; Agee (November 19); Merton; D. H. Lawrence (to Lady. . .); Orwell; Rilke; Woolf; Steffens; Mill; Chesterfield; Edwards; Cardano; Abelard. **See also de Beauvoir; Stein; Thoreau; St. Teresa**

ANGER: Jackson; Cress; Orwell; Rowe. See also D. H. Lawrence (to Russell, to Linati); Adams (5 September); Abelard

ARGUMENTATION: Jackson (July, 1965); Cress; D. H. Lawrence (to Linati, to Lady. . .); Rilke; Chesterfield; Abelard

ART (see also Literary Matters): Cress; Stein; Rilke. See also Adams; Chesterfield

AUTOBIOGRAPHY (Genre): Kerouac; Baez; Thomas; Angelou; Merton; de Beauvoir; McCarthy; Dinesen; Thurber; Nabokov; Stein; Woolf; Steffens; Thoreau (Walden); Mill; Cardano; St. Teresa; Abelard; St. Augustine

BARRIO CULTURE (Spanish Harlem): Thomas. Compare de Jesus

BECOMING—see CHANGES. . .; CHILDHOOD. . .; PUBERTY; TURNING POINT. . .

BIG WORDS: Nabokov. **See also Blake; Mill; Chesterfield; and compare Baez; Rowe**

BLACK CULTURE (Minority Experience): Parks; Jackson (July, 1965, May 28, 1970); Angelou; Rowe. See also Blake; Byrd

BROTHER-SISTER: Angelou; D. & W. Wordsworth. See also Stein

CATALOGUES (long lists or series): Kerouac; McCarthy; Nabokov; Cardano. **See also Thurber; D. Wordsworth; Abelard**

CENTRALITY OF SELF: Kerouac (Belief & Technique); Rilke; Mill; Cardano. See also de Beauvoir; Boswell; and compare Steffens; Edwards

CHANGES IN ATTITUDE: Parks; Thomas; Jackson (July 15, 1957); Cress; Frank; Camus; de Beauvoir; Woolf; Steffens; Mill; Chesterfield (27 March); Edwards. See also Baez (My Father); Adams (20 February)

CHARACTER PORTRAYAL (see also Self-Characterization): Adams; Baez (My Father); Blake; Angelou; Camus; Dinesen; F. Lawrence; Orwell; Nabokov. **See also Boswell; Cardano**

CHILDHOOD & SCHOOL YEARS: Baez; Frank; Angelou; McCarthy; Orwell; Nabokov; Woolf. See also Chau; Thurber; Rowe

CITY LIFE (compare Nature): Kerouac; de Jesus; Thomas; Adams; W. Wordsworth (sonnet). See Thoreau

COLLOQUIAL OR VERNACULAR LANGUAGE: Thomas; Blake; Rowe. Compare Nabokov

DESCRIPTIVE DETAIL: Kerouac (Paris); Chau; Castaneda; Blake; Angelou; Merton; Camus; Nin; Dinesen; F. & D. H. Lawrence; Orwell; Thurber; Nabokov; Woolf; Thoreau; D. & W. Wordsworth; Adams; Boswell; Cardano. See also de Jesus; Thomas; Frank; McCarthy; Stein; St. Teresa

DESPONDENCY OR DEPRESSION: Agee; de Beauvoir; Woolf; Mill; Boswell; Edwards; St. Teresa; St. Augustine. See also Baez (Morning Devils); de Jesus; Cress

DIALOGUE: Chau; Castaneda; Angelou; Dinesen; Orwell; Boswell

DIARY OR JOURNAL (Genre—see also Notebook): Parks; de Jesus; Frank; Senesh; Thoreau; D. Wordsworth; Boswell; Edwards; Byrd. See also Camus; Nin

DISTINCTIVE VOICE: de Jesus; Blake; Cress; D. H. Lawrence; Nabokov; Stein; Adams; Boswell

DREAMS (compare Inward Experience, Visionary Experience): Frank (6 January). See also Jackson (May 28, 1970); F. & D. H. Lawrence; and compare Nabokov

DRUGS (compare Visionary Experience): Thomas; Blake. See also Baez; Castaneda

EDUCATION (see Teacher-Student): Castaneda; Orwell; Stein; Steffens; Mill; Chesterfield. See also Baez; McCarthy

ESSAY (Genre): Orwell

FAMILY—see BROTHER-SISTER; FAMILY LIFE; FATHER-DAUGHTER; FATHER-SON; HETEROSEXUAL LOVE; MOTHER-DAUGHTER; MOTHER-SON

FAMILY LIFE: Baez (My Father); de Jesus; Angelou; Thurber; Nabokov; Byrd. See also Chau; Frank; Woolf; Rowe; and compare McCarthy

FANTASY—see DREAMS; INWARD EXPERIENCE

FATHER-DAUGHTER: Baez (My Father). See also Frank

FATHER-SON: Jackson (July, 1965, etc.); Mill; Chesterfield. See also Thurber; and compare Agee

FIGURATIVE LANGUAGE: Chau; Thomas; Blake; Cress; Angelou; Agee; Merton; Camus; Nin; de Beauvoir; McCarthy; Dinesen; F. & D. H. Lawrence; Orwell; Thurber; Nabokov; Thoreau; D. & W. Wordsworth; St. Augustine. See also Baez (Morning Devils); Chesterfield; St. Teresa

FRIENDSHIP: Cress; Frank; McCarthy. See also de Jesus; Agee; Dinesen; Orwell; Mill

GENRE—see AUTOBIOGRAPHY; DIARY OR JOURNAL; ESSAY; LETTERS; NOTEBOOK

HETEROSEXUAL LOVE: Thomas; Frank (6, 7, & 12 January); Senesh (July 5-26, February 25); de Beauvoir; F. & D. H. Lawrence; Rilke (2nd letter); Boswell; Abelard. See also Jackson (May 28, 1970); Byrd

HOMOSEXUALITY: Blake

HUMOR (wit, comedy): Angelou; McCarthy; Orwell; Thurber; Stein; Boswell. See also Byrd

INWARD EXPERIENCE (compare Dreams, Religion, Visionary Experience): Baez (Morning Devils); Thomas; Frank; Senesh; Merton; Camus; Nin; de Beauvoir; Nabokov; Woolf; Mill; Edwards; St. Augustine. See also Rilke; St. Teresa

JEWRY & ANTI-SEMITISM (Minority Experience): Senesh. See also Frank

JOURNAL—see DIARY

LETTERS (Genre): Jackson; Blake; Cress; Agee; D. H. Lawrence; Rilke; Adams; Chesterfield. See also Frank

LITERARY MATTERS (style, form, technique, methods, goals, etc.)—see ORATORY...; RIGHT USE...; SPONTANEOUS...; WRITING.... See also OBSCENITY

LONELINESS: Cress; Senesh; Camus; Rilke; Woolf; Mill. See also Baez; Thomas; Frank; Dinesen; W. Wordsworth; Edwards

LOVE—see FAMILY LIFE; FATHER-DAUGHTER; FATHER-SON; FRIENDSHIP; HETEROSEXUAL LOVE; HOMOSEXUALITY; etc.

METIER; FINDING ONE'S OWN PLACE (compare Turning Point, Writing): Thomas; Senesh; Thoreau. See also Castaneda

MILITARY TRAINING (see Violence & War): Parks. Compare Orwell

MINORITY EXPERIENCE—see BARRIO CULTURE; BLACK CULTURE; JEWRY.... See also POVERTY; WOMAN'S ROLE

MOTHER-DAUGHTER: Frank (2, 5, & 12 January). Compare McCarthy

MOTHER-SON: Nabokov. See also Thurber; St. Augustine

NARRATIVE STRUCTURE: Chau; Castaneda; Thomas; Merton; McCarthy; Dinesen; F. Lawrence; Orwell; Nabokov; Stein; Woolf; Steffens; Boswell; Abelard; St. Augustine. See also Baez; Parks; Blake; de Beauvoir; Thurber; Rowe; Mill; Byrd

NATURE (compare City Life): Camus; Thoreau; D. & W. Wordsworth. See also Chau; Senesh

NOTEBOOK (Genre—see also Diary): Camus. See also Thoreau; D. Wordsworth

OBSCENITY (see Literary Matters): Thomas; D. H. Lawrence (to Lady...)

ORATORY & ORATORS (Literary Matters): Chesterfield (9 December)

PACIFISM (compare Violence & War): Baez (My Father); D. H. Lawrence (to Russell)

PERSONAL RELATIONS—see BROTHER-SISTER; FAMILY LIFE; FATHER-DAUGHTER; FATHER-SON; FRIENDSHIP; HETEROSEXUAL LOVE; HOMOSEXUALITY; MOTHER-DAUGHTER; MOTHER-SON; TEACHER-STUDENT

PLAIN STYLE: Baez; Parks; Stein; Cardano. See also Byrd

POVERTY: Chau; de Jesus; Thomas; Jackson (July, 1965); Cress; Rowe. See also Blake; Woolf; and compare Nabokov; Adams; Byrd

PRISONS (physical & psychological): Thomas; Jackson (July 15, 1967, October 17, 1967); Blake; Cress; Frank; Nin; Orwell; Rowe

PUBERTY: Frank (5 January, etc.); McCarthy. See also Baez (Morning Devils)

RELIGION (compare Sin): Merton; Edwards; St. Teresa; St. Augustine. See also Senesh; Byrd; Abelard

REVISION: Thoreau. See also Camus; and compare Kerouac

RIGHT USE OF LANGUAGE (Literary Matters): Rilke; Chesterfield. See also Kerouac; Agee; D. H. Lawrence (to Lady. . .)

SELF-ANALYSIS OR INTROSPECTION: Baez; Castaneda; Thomas; Frank; Agee; de Beauvoir; Nabokov; Thoreau; Mill; Boswell; Edwards; Cardano; Abelard; St. Augustine. See also McCarthy; Stein; St. Teresa

SELF-CHARACTERIZATION (cumulative or forthright disclosure of the author's nature): Baez; Castaneda; de Jesus; Dinesen; Thomas; Blake; Cress; Frank; Senesh; Agee; Nin; Nabokov; Stein; Mill; Boswell; Byrd; Cardano; Abelard; St. Augustine. See also Kerouac; Parks; de Beauvoir; D. H. Lawrence; Adams; Chesterfield; Edwards; St. Teresa

SEXUALITY: Thomas; Frank; de Beauvoir; F. Lawrence (We Meet); D. H. Lawrence (Waldbröl, to Lady. . .); Rilke (2nd letter); Boswell; Abelard

SIN (compare Religion): Edwards; St. Teresa; St. Augustine. See also de Beauvoir; Orwell; Abelard

SPECTATOR VIEWPOINT (non-participating observer): Kerouac (Paris); Adams. See also McCarthy

SPONTANEOUS WRITING (Literary Matters): Kerouac (Belief & Technique). Compare Stein

STRANGERS IN STRANGE PLACES: Kerouac (Paris); Parks; Adams. See also Castaneda; Senesh; McCarthy

TEACHER-STUDENT: Chau; Castaneda; Orwell; Stein; Steffens. See also McCarthy; Rilke; Chesterfield; Abelard; St. Augustine

TURNING POINT OR CONVERSION: Castaneda; Thomas; Senesh; Agee; Merton; F. Lawrence; Mill; St. Teresa; St. Augustine. See also Edwards; Abelard

UNCONVENTIONAL SYNTAX: Kerouac; Camus; Stein. See also Blake; D. Wordsworth

VIOLENCE & WAR (see also Military Training, Pacifism): Parks; Chau; Rowe; Abelard. See also de Jesus; Thomas; Jackson (April 11, 1968); Orwell

VISIONARY EXPERIENCE: Castaneda; St. Teresa; St. Augustine

WOMAN'S ROLE: de Jesus; Jackson (May 28, 1970); Cress; Senesh; de Beauvoir; Abelard. See also Stein; St. Teresa; and compare Adams; Boswell

WRITING & BEING A WRITER (Literary Matters): Kerouac (Belief & Technique); Cress; Senesh (November 2); Agee; Camus; Nin; de Beauvoir; D. H. Lawrence (to Linati); Stein; Rilke. See also Frank

Counter Index

The rhetorical entries are printed in boldface; the topical entries in roman.

PETER ABELARD, from The Story of My Calamities, 315
Date of Events, about 1117, at age 38 (age when written, 53)
Analytic Generalization, Argumentation, Autobiography, Narrative Structure, Self-Characterization; see also Catalogues. Heterosexual Love, Self-Analysis, Sexuality, Violence, Woman's Role; see also Religion, Sin, Teacher-Student, Turning Point

ABIGAIL ADAMS, Three Letters from France, 263
Date of Events, 1784–1785, at age 40-41
Character Portrayal, Descriptive Detail, Distinctive Voice, Letters, Spectator Viewpoint; see also Self-Characterization. City Life, Strangers in Strange Places; see also Anger, Art, Changes in Attitude, Poverty, Woman's Role

JAMES AGEE, A Letter to Father Flye, 111
Date of Events, 1930, at age 20
Analytic Generalization, Figurative Language, Letters, Self-Characterization. Despondency, Self-Analysis, Turning Point, Writing & Being a Writer; see also Father-Son, Right Use

MAYA ANGELOU, Stamps, Arkansas, from I Know Why the Caged Bird Sings, 103
Date of Events, about 1938, at age 5 (age when written, 36)
Autobiography, Character Portrayal, Descriptive Detail, Dialogue, Figurative Language, Humor. Black Culture, Brother-Sister, Childhood, Family Life

JOAN BAEZ, My Father, Morning Devils, 7
Date of Events, 1950–1967, from ages 9 to 26 (age when written, 27)
Autobiography, Plain Style, Self-Characterization; see also Figurative Language, Narrative Structure. Childhood, Family Life, Father-Daughter, Inward Experience, Pacifism, Self-Analysis; see also Despondency, Education, Loneliness, Puberty

JAMES BLAKE, Letters, 65
Date of Events, June–August 1956, at age 34
Character Portrayal, Colloquial, Descriptive Detail, Distinctive Voice, Figurative Language, Letters, Self-Characterization; see also Big Words, Narrative Structure, Unconventional Syntax. Drugs, Homosexuality, Prisons; see also Black Culture, Poverty, Sexuality

JAMES BOSWELL, The Courtship of Louisa, 271
Date of Events, 1762–1763, at age 22
Descriptive Detail, Dialogue, Diary, Distinctive Voice, Humor, Narrative Structure, Self-Characterization; see also Character Portrayal. Despondency, Heterosexual Love, Self-Analysis, Sexuality, see also Centrality of Self, Woman's Role

WILLIAM BYRD, from The Secret Diary, 295
Date of Events, 1711–1712, at age 37
Diary, Self-Characterization; see also Humor, Narrative Structure, Plain Style. Family Life; see also Black Culture, Heterosexual Love, Poverty, Religion

ALBERT CAMUS, from The Notebooks, 125
Date of Events, 1936–1937, from age 23 to 24
Character Portrayal, Descriptive Detail, Figurative Language, Notebook, Unconventional Syntax; see also Diary, Revision. Changes in Attitude, Inward Experience, Loneliness, Nature, Writing

GIROLAMO CARDANO, from The Book of My Life, 301
Written in 1575, at age 74
Analytic Generalization, Autobiography, Catalogues, Descriptive Detail, Plain Style, Self-Characterization; see also Character Portrayal. Centrality of Self, Self-Analysis

CARLOS CASTANEDA, Finding the Spot, 35
Date of Events, June, 1961, at age 30 (age when written, 37)
Descriptive Detail, Dialogue, Narrative Structure, Self-Characterization. Education, Self-Analysis, Teacher-Student, Turning Point, Visionary Experience; see also Drugs, Métier

HOANG CHAU, The Refugee Hamlet, 27
Date of Events, late 1960s, at age 42
Descriptive Detail, Dialogue, Figurative Language, Narrative Structure. Teacher-Student, Violence; see also Family Life, Nature

MISS CRESS, A Letter to William Carlos Williams, 75
Written sometime before 1948
Analytic Generalization, Argumentation, Distinctive Voice, Figurative Language, Letters, Self-Characterization. Anger, Art, Changes in Attitude, Friendship, Loneliness, Poverty, Prisons, Woman's Role, Writing

SIMONE DE BEAUVOIR, from The Prime of Life, 139
Date of Events, 1929–1930, from age 21 to 22 (age when written, 52)
Autobiography, Figurative Language; see also Analytic Generalization, Narrative Structure, Self-Characterization. Changes in Attitude, Despondency, Heterosexual Love, Inward Experience, Self-Analysis, Sexuality, Woman's Role, Writing; see also Centrality of Self

CAROLINA MARIA DE JESUS, from The Diary, 43
Date of Events, 1955, at age 42
Diary, Distinctive Voice, Self-Characterization; see also Descriptive Detail. City Life, Family Life, Poverty, Woman's Role; see also Despondency, Friendship, Violence

ISAK DINESEN, from Out of Africa, 155
Date of Events, sometime in 1920s, age about 40 (age when written, 52)
Autobiography, Character Portrayal, Descriptive Detail, Dialogue, Figurative Language, Narrative Structure, Self-Characterization. Friendship, Loneliness

JONATHAN EDWARDS, from The Diary, 287
Date of Events, 1722–1723, at age 19
Analytic Generalization, Diary; see also Self-Characterization. Changes in Attitude, Despondency, Inward Experience, Religion, Self-Analysis, Sin; see also Centrality of Self, Loneliness, Turning Point

ANNE FRANK, from The Diary of a Young Girl, 83
Date of Events, 1944, at age 14
Diary, Self-Characterization; see also Descriptive Detail. Changes in Attitude, Childhood, Dreams, Friendship, Heterosexual Love, Inward Experience, Mother-Daughter, Prisons, Puberty, Self-Analysis, Sexuality; see also Family Life, Father-Daughter, Jewry, Loneliness, Writing

GEORGE ORWELL, from "Such, Such Were the Joys," 175
Date of Events, 1911, at age 8 (age when written 43)
Analytic Generalization, Character Portrayal, Descriptive Detail, Dialogue, Essay, Figurative Language, Humor, Narrative Structure. Anger, Childhood, Education, Prisons, Teacher-Student; see also Friendship, Military Training, Sin, Violence

DAVID PARKS, from G I Diary, 18
Date of Events, 1965–1967, at age 21 to 23
Diary, Narrative Structure, Plain Style; see also Self-Characterization. Black Culture, Changes in Attitude, Military Training, Strangers, Violence

RAINER MARIA RILKE, Two Letters to a Young Poet, 211
Date of Events, 1903, at age 27
Analytic Generalization, Argumentation, Letters. Art, Centrality of Self, Heterosexual Love, Loneliness, Right Use, Sexuality, Writing; see also Inward Experience, Teacher-Student

KATIE ROWE, Slavery Days, 231
Date of Events, 1861–1938, from age 15 on (age when told, about 92)
Colloquial Language; see also Big Words, Narrative Structure. Anger, Black Culture, Poverty, Prisons, Violence; see also Childhood, Family Life

ST. AUGUSTINE, Conversion, from The Confessions, 325
Date of Events, 386 A.D., at age 32 (age when written, 43 to 46)
Autobiography, Figurative Language, Narrative Structure, Self-Characterization. Despondency, Inward Experience, Religion, Self-Analysis, Sin, Turning Point, Visionary Experience; see also Mother-Son, Teacher-Student

ST. TERESA, Visions, from The Life Written by Herself, 309
Date of Events, 1558–1559, at age 43
Autobiography; see also Analytic Generalization, Descriptive Detail, Figurative Language, Self-Characterization. Despondency, Religion, Sin, Turning Point, Visionary Experience; see also Inward Experience, Self-Analysis, Woman's Role

HANNAH SENESH, Aged Nineteen, from The Diary, 93
Date of Events, 1940–1941, at age 19
Diary, Self-Characterization. Heterosexual Love, Inward Experience, Jewry, Loneliness, Métier, Turning Point, Woman's Role, Writing; see also Nature, Religion, Strangers

PHILIP DORMER STANHOPE, 4th EARL OF CHESTERFIELD, Three Letters to His Son, 279
Date of Events, 1746–1749, from age 52 to 55
Analytic Generalization, Argumentation, Letters; see also Big Words, Figurative Language, Self-Characterization. Changes in Attitude, Education, Father-Son, Oratory, Right Use; see also Art, Teacher-Student

LINCOLN STEFFENS, I Go to College, and I Become a Student, 223
Date of Events, 1885, at age 19 (age when written, 65)
Analytic Generalization, Autobiography, Narrative Structure. Changes in Attitude, Education, Teacher-Student; see also Centrality of Self

GERTRUDE STEIN, from The Autobiography of Alice B. Toklas, 201
Date of events, 1891–1904, from age 17 to 26 (age when written, 58)
Autobiography, Distinctive Voice, Humor, Narrative Structure, Plain Style, Self-Characterization; Unconventional Syntax; see also Analytic Generalization, Descriptive Detail. Art, Education, Teacher-Student, Writing; see also Brother-Sister, Self-Analysis, Spontaneous Writing, Woman's Role

ABOUT THE AUTHORS

CHARLES MUSCATINE is Professor of English at the University of California at Berkeley where he has taught since 1948. He received the Ph.D. from Yale University and has served as a Visiting Professor at Wesleyan University and the University of Washington. A distinguished medievalist, Professor Muscatine has received Fulbright and Guggenheim research fellowships, is the author of *Chaucer and the French Tradition* and *The Book of Geoffrey Chaucer,* and has published widely in professional journals. At Berkeley he has been chairman of the Committee on Freshman English, and of the Select Committee on Education.

MARLENE GRIFFITH is on the faculty of Laney College in Oakland, California, where she is a member and former chairman of the Department of English. She has also taught at Western College for Women, San Francisco State College, and the University of California at Berkeley. She received her B.A. from American International College in Springfield, Mass., and her M.A. from Berkeley. Since 1959 she has taught literature, expository and creative writing, and basic reading and writing courses. She has been a contributor to *College Composition and Communication, Twentieth Century Literature,* and *Modern Fiction Studies.*

Professors Charles Muscatine and Marlene Griffith are editors of *The Borzoi College Reader,* Second Edition.

A NOTE ON THE TYPE

The text of this book was set on the APS-3 computer in Century Schoolbook, one of the most serviceable type faces through the years. It is commonly used in both display and text sizes. L. B. Benton is credited with the design which has almost even set proportion and color. Designed especially for periodicals, its practical nature has enlarged its application and use.

Composition by Volt Information Sciences, Inc., New York, New York.

Printed and bound by Halliday Lithograph, West Hanover, Mass.

Cover Design by Batten, Freedman and Kreloff

Typography by James McGuire